Praise for

THE LINCOLN CONSPIRACY

"Relentlessly fun to read." —NPR

"You won't be getting any sleep tonight. This book is dynamite. Meltzer does it again. History at its very best." —Brian Kilmeade, bestselling author of *Sam Houston and the Alamo Avengers*

"A brilliant combination of edge-of-your-seat history and superb storytelling." —James L. Swanson, bestselling author of *Manhunt: The 12-Day Chase for Lincoln's Killer*

"Think you know everything about Abraham Lincoln? Well, think again." —Les Standiford, bestselling author of *Last Train to Paradise* and *Meet You in Hell*

"Every page is mesmerizing and eye-opening. A must-read!" —Douglas Brinkley, Katherine Tsanoff Brown Chair in Humanities and professor of history at Rice University and author of *American Moonshot*

"Meltzer and Mensch maintain suspense despite the known outcome of the story and convincingly counter claims that Pinkerton made the whole thing up for publicity purposes." —*Publishers Weekly*

"Energetic . . . A brisk political thriller centered on a nefarious plot to murder Lincoln before his inauguration . . . A sharply drawn episode." —*Kirkus Reviews*

"A delightful addition to popular literature on the Civil War era." —*Booklist*

Also by Brad Meltzer

THE LINCOLN
CONSPIRACY

The Secret Plot to Kill America's
16th President—and Why It Failed

Brad Meltzer
and Josh Mensch

FLATIRON
BOOKS
NEW YORK

For Steven, Mitchel, and Jay Katz,
who saved me when I needed them most.
—B.M.

For Maxine, with all my love.
—J.M.

www.flatironbooks.com

An extension of this copyright page appears on pages 373–74.

Map of Northern Train Routes to Washington, D.C., circa 1861, found on
page 163 © 2020 Jeffrey L. Ward

Designed by Donna Sinisgalli Noetzel

The Library of Congress has cataloged the hardcover edition as follows:

Names: Meltzer, Brad, author. | Mensch, Josh, author.
Title: The Lincoln conspiracy : the secret plot to kill America's 16th president—
and why it failed / Brad Meltzer and Josh Mensch.
Description: First edition. | New York : Flatiron Books, 2020. | Includes
bibliographical references and index
Identifiers: LCCN 2020006774 | ISBN 9781250317476 (hardcover) |
ISBN 9781250317483 (ebook)
Subjects: LCSH: Lincoln, Abraham, 1809–1865—Assassination attempt,
1861. | Presidents—Assassination attempts—United States. | Baltimore (Md.)—
History—Civil War, 1861–1865.
Classification: LCC E457.4 .M45 2020 | DDC 973.7092—dc23
LC record available at https://lccn.loc.gov/2020006774

ISBN 978-1-250-80589-8 (trade paperback)

Our books may be purchased in bulk for promotional, educational, or
business use. Please contact your local bookseller or the Macmillan Corporate
and Premium Sales Department at 1-800-221-7945, extension 5442,
or by email at MacmillanSpecialMarkets@macmillan.com.

First Flatiron Books Paperback Edition: 2021

10 9 8 7 6 5 4 3 2 1

Contents

A Note on the Text

When quoting directly from nineteenth-century sources, we've sometimes updated the original spelling, capitalization, or punctuation to make the language accessible to modern readers. The wording itself is not changed, unless otherwise indicated in the text or endnotes.

If they kill me, I shall never die another death.

—ABRAHAM LINCOLN,

FEBRUARY 1861

Prologue

---·---

Cecil County, Maryland

February 23, 1861

There's a secret on this train.

In the northeastern corner of Maryland, roughly ten miles south of the Pennsylvania state line and five miles west of Delaware, it travels through the darkness.

The land here is mostly rural, a mix of flat farmland and rolling hills. It's after midnight, and the cold night air is silent except for the sound of the engine and wheels.

By outward appearance, there's nothing unusual about this train: a steam engine, tender, cargo car, and several passenger cars moving swiftly along the rails. Inside, there's also nothing out of the ordinary. The passenger cars are dotted with travelers, most with closed eyes. In the rear sleeper car, a handful of passengers occupy the berths on either side of the aisle. By appearances, they're also relatively typical: two middle-aged businessmen, a young woman, and her invalid brother.

Yet much about this seemingly ordinary train is not as it seems.

Before its departure from Philadelphia a few hours earlier, the railroad's staff received special instructions to delay the train's journey until a mysterious package could be delivered to it, transported aboard under strict secrecy. The package remains tightly sealed, supposedly containing government documents of urgent importance. In fact, the box contains something else entirely. None of the train's staff knows this. Only one passenger on the train is aware of the package's true contents.

In the sleeper car, the two middle-aged businessmen, sitting on different berths, are not who they'd claimed to be when they handed tickets to the conductor. The names written on their tickets are not real. One of the men, with wide girth and thick whiskers, carries hidden underneath his coat two loaded pistols, a loaded revolver, and two sharpened bowie knives. The other businessman, who is short and well built with a close-shaven beard and piercing eyes, silently gazes around the interior of the car, studying every person and movement carefully. Every several minutes, he stands up and walks to the rear platform, where he stares intently into the passing darkness as if he's searching for a secret signal.

Across the aisle in the sleeper car from the businessmen, the young woman is also not who she seems. The name on her ticket is actually her code name; she must conceal her true identity under all circumstances, for she's an undercover agent, aboard this train as part of a secret mission.

Yet the most unusual passenger is the young woman's invalid "brother," with whom she boarded in Philadelphia. When he first entered the passenger car and she guided him to his seat, he pulled the brim of his low felt hat down over his face so that no one could see it. He wore a loose overcoat over his shoulders, concealing his clothes and torso. Now, he lies behind a curtain in one of the sleeper berths, hidden from view. Because of his unusual height, he cannot stretch out his legs, so he keeps them bent.

This man is not, in fact, an invalid. Nor is he the young woman's brother. His low felt hat and overcoat are simply a disguise so that no one on the train will recognize him.

The engineer, conductor, staff, and other passengers have no idea he's aboard. But there he is—hiding in their midst.

His real name? Abraham Lincoln. President-elect of the United States.

In only nine days, a crowd of tens of thousands will gather in the nation's capital, preparing to witness Lincoln's first inauguration as President. When he's up on that platform, his every word and gesture will be observed and recorded by reporters for newspapers from every city in the country. He enters the office at a time of great peril, with a growing threat of war that could destroy the nation. Not since the founding of these United States has an incoming President been so deeply scrutinized or faced with such momentous pressure. The world is tracking his every move.

Tonight, however, he is vulnerable and nearly alone.

Tonight, his life is in danger.

And tonight, the President-elect is the target of a sinister plot calling for his murder.

This scheme, hatched by conspirators in secret rooms and underground saloons in the city of Baltimore, aims to achieve something never before attempted in the history of the country at the time: the assassination of the man elected President of the United States. If successful, they will accomplish something never accomplished since: the murder of an incoming President before taking office.

This is the story of an early conspiracy to kill Abraham Lincoln—before he served a single day as President, and on the eve of the terrible war that would define his place in history. It is a story that is not well-known by most people today. Even now, some aspects of the scheme remain mysterious. Yet this story and its strange plot, in its motives and conception, provides a gripping window into the most seismic events of the day, at a moment of great national turmoil. It's the story of a new leader, thrust from near obscurity into a position that will bring the most crushing responsibilities in our history. It's the story of a moral crisis in America so profound that our nation was almost destroyed by it—and its aftermath is still being grappled with today.

On this dark night, on this dark train, more than just the life and future of a President is at risk. This is about the destiny of a country. Forget the fate of Abraham Lincoln—this is about the fates of four million enslaved men, women, and children held in bondage, and whose best hope for liberty may be aboard this train.

From this moment, just after midnight, as the steam engine and passenger cars move through the darkness, the plot to kill President-elect Abraham Lincoln is set to be triggered within a matter of hours.

The nation's future is at stake.

PART I

The Rail Splitter

1

————— · —————

Spencer County, Indiana

January 20, 1828

Young Abraham Lincoln is freezing.

In an isolated rural region near Little Pigeon Creek in Spencer County, Indiana, he's outside, laboring in the cold.

Although only eighteen years old, he's already over six foot two—and despite this unusual height, he weighs only about 160 pounds, stretched thin and wiry on a tall frame. His long arms are skinny but strong; his calloused hands wield tools with assurance, including a long swinging ax. On this winter day, he probably wears a rough buckskin coat over his threadbare clothes, and a hat of raccoon fur over his coarse black hair. The trees surrounding this clearing are mostly without leaves, and the ground is hard from frost.

Today, he works near a smokehouse—a small, windowless wooden structure, typically about eight feet square, with a conical roof and fire pit inside. Given the season, he's probably chopping wood from nearby trees and pulling the logs inside to tend the fire. Perhaps he's also hauling salt-cured slabs of meat into the smokehouse, hanging them on hooks or rafters inside, where dry heat from the fire will preserve them during the winter months.

As he works, a small group approaches, bearing solemn expressions. When they near the smokehouse, one of them calls out his name.

"Abe."

Young Abe opens the smokehouse door to see the group. This morning, Abe's sister, Sarah, two years older than he, has been in labor with her first child. The group approaching are members of her husband's family. Perhaps they're here to bring him good news about her labor—was his first niece or nephew just born?

Instead, the group brings something far more somber. The labor went awry. The nearest doctor was many miles away, not arriving in time to help. The baby was stillborn.

Not only that. The young mother—Abe's sister—is dead.

Nine years earlier, when Abe was nine, his mother had died suddenly after contracting a disease. Since then, Sarah, his only sibling, has helped raise him.

Not long after the death of Abe and Sarah's mother, their father traveled alone from their home in Indiana to his original home state of Kentucky to find a new wife. To make this trip, he left Abe and his sister—then roughly ten and twelve—alone in their isolated frontier cabin for many weeks to feed, clothe, and otherwise fend for themselves. When their father finally returned with a woman by his side, the new wife was alarmed to see two lice-filled and nearly starving children who were "wild—ragged & dirty." It was only after she bathed and cleaned them that they "looked more human."

The hardships that Abraham and his sister endured together created a deep bond between them. A relative would later recall that Abe "dearly loved his sister, she having been his only companion after the death of his mother." Together, as brother and sister, they had navigated an often brutal childhood living in near poverty. "They were close companions and were a great deal alike," a family friend described, and Sarah was a "kind, tender, and good natured" young woman.

Now, she is gone too. For the second time in his life, he has lost the person he loves most.

His brother-in-law, one of those in the group who delivered the news, remembered the moment: Abraham "sat down on a log and hid his face in his hands while the tears rolled down through his long bony fingers." Another relative described the loss as a "great grief, which affected Abe throughout his life," and also added, "from then on he was alone in the world you might say."

The relatives who just shared the news don't know how to respond to the young man sobbing before them. After a moment, "those present turned away in pity and left him to his grief."

Few who witnessed the mournful scene that day would likely imagine that this tall, gawky, grief-stricken country boy, wearing tattered clothes and laboring outside in an obscure corner of the Indiana frontier near Kentucky, would ever rise above his humble station in life. Certainly, none could envision that this young man possessed qualities of mind and spirit that would one day lift him to the most exalted positions of leadership and responsibility in the land—and that would link his personal destiny to the fate of the nation.

Yet however exceptional Lincoln's rise will be, and whatever joys and triumphs he'll experience, he'll never be free from the pattern of tragedy and grief that shaped his boyhood. Indeed, his adult life will be characterized by shocks of violence and suffering even greater than those of his youth—including the loss of his own children. It's as if he's haunted by tragedy upon tragedy, from which he'll never truly escape.

For Abraham Lincoln, the specter of death is always near.

2

Washington, D.C.

May 22, 1856

This is an incident that illustrates the times—over four years before the Civil War, and before most Americans had ever heard of Abraham Lincoln.

It takes place on a hot summer day on May 22, 1856, in Washington, D.C.

Early on this Thursday afternoon, Senator Charles Sumner of Massachusetts sits at his desk in the main chamber of the United States Senate. Other Senators work or mill about elsewhere on the chamber floor, hurrying to finish their work for the day. Some onlookers still sit in the upper balcony, where spectators can watch debates on the floor.

Sumner, forty-six, is a five-year veteran of the Senate. On this particular afternoon, he is franking copies of a speech he wrote and delivered to the body a few days earlier. The speech, five hours long and delivered over the course of two days, was about the most debated issue of the day—the institution of slavery—and Sumner is now sending the speech to friends and newspaper editors for public distribution.

During his time in the Senate, Sumner has gained a reputation as one of the strongest and most articulate antislavery advocates in either chamber of Congress. He intended his speech—delivered on May 19 and May 20 and soon known as "The Crime Against Kansas" speech—to be a definitive treatise against an institution that he considers immoral and that he has spent much of his public life opposing.

Sumner probably doesn't much notice when a young Congressman enters the Senate chamber flanked by two companions. There's no reason why the Senator would notice these visitors; while members of the House of Representatives do not conduct their official business on the Senate floor, they frequently visit the upper chamber to meet with Senators or staffers, or to attend debates.

The Congressman is Preston Brooks, thirty-six, of South Carolina's Fourth District. He carries a walking cane in one hand, although he is perfectly healthy. Accompanying him are two other House members, one a fellow Representative of South Carolina, the other of Virginia.

At Brooks's instruction, the three Southern Congressmen wait near the entrance to the floor for some of the aides to depart the room. Brooks pays special attention to make sure no women are anywhere in the chamber. When he sees a young woman still in the room, he asks the chamber secretary, "Can't you manage to get her out?"

Once satisfied that no women remain, Brooks and his companions walk across the Senate floor toward the desk where Senator Sumner works.

In his speech three days earlier, Sumner had leveled verbal attacks against several of his Southern proslavery Senate colleagues. One of those he insulted with particular derision was the aging Senator Andrew Butler of South Carolina—who happens to be the cousin of Preston Brooks, the young Congressman now walking toward Sumner's desk carrying a cane. Brooks was not present for the delivery of Sumner's speech, but he soon learned of the insults directed at his relative and read descriptions and reports of the speech in newspapers.

Brooks, still flanked by his two companions, stops in front of

Sumner's desk. He takes a breath, then says, "Mr. Sumner, I read your speech with care and as much impartiality as was possible and I feel it is my duty to tell you that you have libeled my state and slandered a relative who is aged and absent and I am come to punish you for it."

Before Sumner can respond, Brooks raises the straight cane high above his head. The cane is solid gutta-percha, with a metal head on one end of it. The Congressman brings the cane down full force, smashing it into Sumner's skull. Brooks raises the cane again, and again brings it down on the Senator. Sumner is immediately dazed, almost unconscious, with blood pouring from his head and face. Once again, Brooks raises the cane over his head and strikes the Senator.

Startled onlookers rush to try to stop the attack. But Brooks's two companions hold them back so Brooks can continue the beating. One of them, Congressman Laurence Keitt of South Carolina, takes out a pistol to warn off any who would interfere. Sumner is now knocked out of his seat to the floor, his head and face badly wounded. Brooks smashes the cane down on him repeatedly as blood soaks the chamber rug. Sumner tries to crawl away but gets stuck in the desk legs that are affixed to the floor. He's barely conscious and totally unable to defend himself as the vicious blows continue. Even when the cane breaks in two, Brooks keeps beating Sumner with the half still in his hand.

"Don't kill him!" an older Senator, John Crittenden of Kentucky, yells out, trying to break past Brooks's companions to save his colleague.

Finally, after Brooks has delivered twenty or thirty blows, his cane shatters for good. He throws the remaining pieces on the blood-soaked floor, turns around, and walks toward the same door from which he'd entered. His two companions quickly follow him.

As the three Congressmen exit the building, Senators and aides rush to their fallen colleague. They drag the unconscious Senator out of the chamber, desperately seeking medical attention—hoping it's not already too late.

3

The country is splitting apart.

The 1856 caning of Charles Sumner by Preston Brooks is not the first act of violence on the floor of the United States Congress. In fact, it is the culmination of a two-decade-long trend of physical altercations between Senators or Congressmen, including some that involved knives or guns. The vast majority of these incidents stemmed from grievances between Southern and Northern members. The Brooks-Sumner caning—only the latest and most dramatic example of such violence—serves to illustrate an undeniable fact: The United States is a deeply divided nation, and the issue that fuels the division above all others is the institution of slavery. The fierce debate over the existence and spread of slavery is the defining debate for the soul and future of the country, and both sides know it.

In 1776, when the Declaration of Independence first introduced Thomas Jefferson's famous phrase "All men are created equal," slavery existed in each of the thirteen states whose delegates signed the document. There were close to five hundred thousand enslaved people in the states at that time, comprising about 20 percent of the population. In the decades following, the Northern states began abolishing slavery one by one; some states directly referenced Jefferson's language in the wording of their abolition.

At the same time, in the South the practice of slavery flourished and expanded. By the mid-1850s, there were some 3.5 million men, women, and children in bondage in the United States—a seven-fold increase from seventy-five years earlier—all within the Southern states and a few border states. As new western territories became states and joined the Union, the split between North and South regarding slavery remained largely fixed. By this point, slavery had existed in the American South for over two centuries and was deeply entrenched in Southern law, politics, and custom.

Of course, a key motivation was economics. The Southern states' plantation-based agricultural system, focusing on the production of tobacco, rice, sugarcane, and above all, cotton, was built from the start upon a system of brutal forced slave labor. From an economic standpoint, the white slaveholding class viewed the men, women, and children in bondage not as humans but as property, each with a dollar value. When confronted by arguments that the Southern states should free their slaves on moral grounds, the South Carolina Senator James Henry Hammond responded with a rhetorical question: Was any society in history ever "persuaded by arguments, human or divine, to surrender, voluntarily, two billion dollars?"

The explosion of cotton production in the early nineteenth century had created enormous wealth within the southern United States, but to support this production, the landowners subjected enslaved laborers to unspeakably barbaric working conditions.

To meet quotas, overseers forced field hands to toil in the hot Southern sun for fourteen hours a day, six days a week. When laborers passed out or fainted from exhaustion, they were brutally whipped and beaten, right there in the fields, until they resumed working; if after more work they passed out again, the overseers would rub salt-and-vinegar solutions onto the bloody wounds until the excruciating pain revived them. Enslaved men and women of all ages endured this treatment, as did children still in their early teens.

"Cotton Is King" was a motto pronounced throughout the

South—and the explosive success of this industry generated a flood of wealth for the white landowning class.

Yet after two centuries of existence, the institution of slavery impacted not just economics but every sphere of Southern life. As Senator Clement C. Clay Jr. of Alabama put it, slavery was "that domestic institution of the South, which is not only the chief source of her prosperity, but the very basis of her social order and State policy."

In Christian churches throughout the South, ministers taught a gospel of white racial superiority, using scripture to validate the practice of one group of humans owning another. Southern clergy wrote essays and books arguing for the divine rights of slaveholders, with titles like *Southern Slavery and the Bible: A Vindication of Southern Slavery from the Old and New Testaments* by Rev. Ebenezer W. Warren, and *Slavery Ordained by God* by Frederick A. Ross.

But for them, scriptural arguments weren't even enough. The slaveholding class based its way of life on the firm belief that one race of people was intrinsically superior to the other—that therefore slavery was not only justified but reflected the natural order and was benevolent to both parties. As one Southern essayist claimed to prove:

> The negro . . . is physiologically and psychologically degraded . . . he is of an inferior species of the human race, wholly dependent upon the Caucasian for progress, enlightenment, and well-being— and that, servitude and subjection being his natural state, the relation which he bears to superior mastership . . . is merciful to him and the cause of religion and civilization.

Indeed, the idea that slavery is *beneficial to the enslaved* was a recurring theme in the many written moral and political treatises from the South. As South Carolina Senator John C. Calhoun put it in his defense of slavery, "Never before has the black race of Central Africa, from the dawn of history to the present day, attained a condition so civilized and so improved, not only physically, but morally and intellectually."

This foundational belief in the superiority of whites over blacks was used to justify a system in which every institution of society—the justice system, law enforcement, politics, schools, churches, and social norms—was organized to ensure that blacks had no rights, no opportunities, no resources, no protections, and no hope for improvement. Enslaved people were forbidden to learn to read or write, and if caught trying were brutally punished; slaveholders then argued that the lack of education among blacks was proof of racial inferiority—thereby justifying the slave system.

As white supremacy became ever more entrenched in the South, sentiment in the Northern states moved in the opposite direction. Antislavery societies, led and supported by both blacks and whites, existed in every major city. Escaped former slaves, now living in the free North, wrote and published accounts of their former enslavement, shining a light on the horrors of the institution: rampant violence, torture, rape, and the separation of small children from their parents for sale or auction. Just as important, these accounts communicated in human terms the unspeakable suffering and despair experienced by slavery's victims.

To be clear, Northern views on slavery varied. True abolitionists were still a small minority and were often viewed as dangerous agitators. Some Northern whites outright supported slavery, especially merchant classes who benefited from the trade of Southern goods. Others were indifferent to it, or disliked the practice but did not object to its existence in the South. And some who opposed the institution did so not out of concern for black slaves, but because they feared the spread of slavery could take jobs away from poor whites.

Still, the momentum of Northern opinion was moving steadily against slavery, and some of the most influential political and religious leaders took strong positions opposing the institution on moral, religious, or political grounds. Representative Edward Wade of Ohio asserted that "there is not a more morbidly suspicious, cruel, revengeful, or lawless despotism, on the face of the earth, than this nightmare of slavery." Massachusetts clergyman Theodore Parker declared American slavery a "monstrous wrong" and a "great evil." And Senator William H. Seward of New York—one of the best-known politicians in the country—proclaimed in one of his most famous speeches that the conflict between slavery and freedom was "an irrepressible conflict between opposing and enduring forces; and it means that the United States must and will, sooner or later, become either entirely a slave-holding nation, or entirely a free-labor nation."

The battle lines were drawn—and the "irrepressible conflict" was drawing steadily nearer.

It was apt that in the late 1850s, as tensions increased between North and South, the dispute over slavery was particularly ferocious in the halls of Congress, where the battle over the status of slavery was often waged.

In 1856 there were thirty-one states in the nation; sixteen of the states were free, and fifteen were slave. Legislatively, in the Senate, this created two nearly even sides on the issue, with thirty-two Senators representing free states and thirty Senators representing slave states. In the House of Representatives, the larger populations of the Northern states gave them a greater advantage in terms of numbers of Congressmen, but they still fell short of a majority that would make their advantage decisive. The passage of legislation related to slavery often led to a closely fought struggle, with both sides galvanized and motivated to prevail. Usually, the success or failure of such legislation came down to a few votes in the "border states"—like Missouri and Kentucky—where sentiment was mixed.

With margins so thin in Congress, one of the most momentous issues of the day was the status of slavery in western territories soon to join the Union. Every new state represented either the extension of slavery or the containment of it. Just as important, each new state brought with it two new Senators and at least one new Representative. Depending on whether a new state was slave or free, the balance in Congress could tip one way or the other.

The spread of slavery into one new territory, Kansas, was precisely the subject of Massachusetts Senator Charles Sumner's "The Crime Against Kansas" speech delivered on May 19 and 20 of 1856, in which he insulted his Southern colleague. For this reason, Congressman Preston Brooks's attack on Sumner three days later occurred against the backdrop of the explosive battle between North and South over the future of the institution.

Senator Sumner did not die from the caning, but was incapacitated and would not regain his faculties for two years. Meanwhile, the sensational story of a Southern Congressman savagely beating a Northern Senator nearly to death on the floor of the United States Senate made headlines everywhere, becoming an instant symbol of the larger battle.

In Northern states, the act was condemned. Many argued that the attack was "barbarous" and "an outrage," and proved the slave states' propensity to violence. As the prominent abolitionist Wendell Phillips put it, the violence of the caning exposed "the hellish malignity of the spirit which sustains slavery."

In the South, however, the assault was widely praised. *The Richmond Whig* of Virginia declared:

> A glorious deed! A most glorious deed! Mr. Brooks, of South Carolina, administered to Senator Sumner, a notorious abolitionist from Massachusetts, an effectual and classic caning. We are rejoiced. The only regret we feel is that Mr. Brooks did not employ a slave whip instead of a stick.

Congressman Brooks became a folk hero. From all around the South, he received canes as gifts, to replace the one he destroyed in the attack. The shards of the cane he shattered on Sumner's skull became prized collector's items. As Brooks later described it, the little wooden pieces "are begged for as sacred relics." Nor did Brooks suffer any real political consequence for his act.

A House committee investigated the incident and issued a report that found Brooks guilty of the assault, but Brooks voluntarily resigned before he could be censured. A few months later, he ran in a special election for his own vacant seat and won easily. Soon he was back in the House, casting votes while Senator Sumner remained incapacitated.

In the aftermath of the attack, a palpable fear of violence pervaded the halls of Congress. Northern members who didn't want to suffer Sumner's fate began arming themselves to protect against their Southern colleagues. In response, Southerners also carried more weapons.

As Senator James Henry Hammond of South Carolina would write to a friend, "So far as I know, and as I believe, every man in both Houses is armed with a revolver—some with two—and a bowie knife."

In the next few years of the late 1850s, the battle over the future of slavery would only intensify. It was a moral issue of overwhelming magnitude. No one knew which side in the conflict would prevail—or whether a leader would emerge who could guide America through the struggle.

4

---·---

TWO YEARS LATER . . .

Ottawa, Illinois

August 21, 1858

The place is packed.

By noon, the small rural town of Ottawa, Illinois, is jammed with more than twice its usual population.

For the past twenty-four hours, thousands of visitors have been streaming into this quiet village 140 miles northeast of Springfield, traveling by train, riverboat, cart, horse, or on foot. Now, at midday, a marching band plays, vendors sell snacks and knickknacks from stands on every corner, banners wave in the air, and throngs of people surge through the town square. The mood is festive, like a county fair or a holiday parade, but the crowd today is gathered for something rather different: a three-hour-long policy debate under the hot sun between two Senate candidates.

In the nineteenth century, countywide and statewide political races are huge affairs, generating enormous local interest, turning out big crowds, and dominating newspaper coverage. Also, this is no ordinary race.

In the two years since the Brooks-Sumner caning, the division in the country on the issue of slavery has only deepened, giving every political battle what seems like colossal significance. And while states in the Northeast and in the South have taken predictably opposed positions in the fight, the state of Illinois, although not a slave state, has mixed sympathies. In modern parlance, Illinois is a "swing state," and its Senate seat is highly coveted in this midterm election.

This particular Senate race is also a critical test for the brand-new Republican Party, an entity barely four years old trying to challenge the well-established Democrats.

For all these reasons, *The New York Times* described Illinois as "the most interesting political battleground in the Union." Close to ten thousand out-of-town visitors were inspired to travel to Ottawa, Illinois, to stand in the hot August sun for three hours listening to the first of what will eventually be seven debates between two local politicians: incumbent Democratic Senator and former judge Stephen Douglas, and a little-known lawyer and former Congressman named Abraham Lincoln.

To be sure, the Democratic Party and the Republican Party of 1858 bear little resemblance to the two political parties we know today. Indeed, in a demographic sense, the two parties had almost opposite identities from those they have now. The Democrats were a national party but especially strong in the South, with a platform of state's rights to protect the slaveholding states against the federal government; the Republicans were almost entirely Northern, with strong support throughout New England and cosmopolitan northeastern urban centers like Boston and Philadelphia. The party arose as a fusion of Northern political factions that had united against the Southern effort to extend slavery to the western and northwestern territories.

For their debate, the two candidates arrived in Ottawa in very different fashion. The incumbent Douglas had traveled in a luxurious private train colorfully decorated for the campaign; he then rode from the train depot into Ottawa on a fine carriage drawn by four white horses, accompanied by a martial marching band and carefully timed blasts of cannon fire.

The challenger, Lincoln, had traveled to town as a coach passenger on a public train, accompanied by a few friends and advisors. After a brief lunch with the town Mayor, he and his group walk on foot to the town square.

Now, just before 1:00 p.m., the two candidates arrive to a chaotic scene. The morning's stampede of people on dry dirt roads had created a massive plume of dust so that, as one reporter put it, "the town resembled a vast smokehouse."

In the public square, the larger-than-expected crowd is squeezed shoulder to shoulder in front of the debate platform, thereby blocking the candidates' approach. The two teams must fight their way through the throng in a "rough and tumble skirmish" amid much shouting, itself drowned out by the blaring martial bands, cannon booms, and the "constant roar" of the gathered throngs.

When the candidates' entourages do eventually make it through the crowd and onto the platform, part of the makeshift structure immediately collapses. After several confusing minutes, the party officials finally take their seats at the rear of the platform, and—amid a chorus of cheers and jeers from the rowdy crowd—the candidates step forward.

The two men are a study in contrasts. Douglas is barely five foot four, with a stocky build and famously large head. In Congress, he's nicknamed "the Little Giant" for his short stature mixed with a supremely aggressive personality. Although born in Vermont and a longtime Illinoisan, Douglas had married into a wealthy Southern family—from which he inherited a Mississippi plantation with slaves—and as a two-term Senator and former Congressman, he had spent much of the past fifteen years in Washington, D.C., as a powerful insider allied with Southern lawmakers. Today, he wears a finely tailored dark blue suit, a fashionable white collar and tie, and expensive leather shoes.

And then there's Abe Lincoln.

At six foot four, he's probably the tallest person most attendees have ever laid eyes on, and possibly the skinniest. Many of the national reporters covering the debate have never seen him before and are amazed by his appearance. "He had a lean, lank, indescribably gawky figure," one writes. Another onlooker describes his "ungainly body." Lincoln's disheveled shock of black hair sits atop what a reporter later describes as an "odd-featured, wrinkled, inexpressive, and altogether uncomely face."

In contrast to Douglas's fancy wardrobe, Lincoln wears "a rusty black coat with sleeves that should have been longer" and similarly ill-fitting trousers that "permitted a very full view of his large feet," which are clad in dusty work boots.

In summary, one onlooker remarks that he's met "several public men of rough appearance; but none whose looks seemed quite so uncouth, not to say grotesque, as Lincoln's."

The format of the debate is grueling. The first candidate will speak for one hour; the second will have ninety minutes to respond; then the first gets thirty minutes for closing remarks. There is no moderator. The debaters have to take careful notes during their opponent's speeches and fill the large blocks of time with extemporaneous rebuttals of each point. All the while, they must project their unamplified voices through the outdoor air so that the crowds of thousands can hear.

Douglas goes first. He has a reputation as a skilled, fierce debater, perhaps one of the best in the Senate. He begins by misrepresenting aspects of his opponent's past, including a suggestion that Lincoln was once an excessive drinker who could hold "more liquor than all the boys of the town together." Although false—Lincoln never drank alcohol as an adult—these accusations are part of what one writer later describes as Douglas's "sledge-hammer style" of relentless attack.

Douglas's words are accompanied by a dramatic physical performance, pacing the stage, waving his hands, and sometimes raising clenched fists. One viewer describes him as a "springing panther"; another says he "raved like a mad bull."

As his opening speech continues, the *Chicago Tribune* reports that "he ranted, he bellowed, he pawed dirt, he shook his head, he turned livid in the face, he struck his right hand into his left, he foamed at the mouth . . . he exulted, he domineered."

In addition to this showmanship, Douglas also establishes his position on the most important topic of the day: slavery. He explains why he crafted the Kansas-Nebraska Act to allow citizens of the new Northern territories to extend slavery there if they so chose, with no regard to the rights of the enslaved: "I believe this government was

Combined photographs of Illinois Senator Stephen Douglas *(left)* and former Illinois Congressman Abraham Lincoln *(right)*, each taken near the time of their famous debates during the 1858 midterm election campaign. On the debate stage Douglas stands a full foot shorter than the six-foot-four Lincoln.

made on the white basis. I believe it was made by white men, for the benefit of white men and their posterity forever, and I am in favor of confining citizenship to white men . . . instead of conferring it upon negroes, Indians, and other inferior races."

These lines get big cheers. He points at Lincoln and says in a derisive, sarcastic tone:

I do not question Mr. Lincoln's conscientious belief that the negro was made his equal, and hence his brother [laughter], but for my own part, I do not regard the negro as my equal, and positively deny that he is my brother or any kin to me whatsoever [laughter] . . . He belongs to an inferior race, and must always occupy an inferior position. [cheers]

Douglas has veered from the specific issue at stake—the legal status of slavery in the new territories—and has focused on rousing the crowd into a frenzy with racist language. As one onlooker recalls, the Senator "roused the existing strong prejudices against the negro race to the highest pitch." Douglas continues:

"If you desire negro citizenship—if you desire to allow them to come into the State and settle with white man—if you desire them to vote on an equality with yourselves—and to make them eligible to office—to serve on juries and adjudge your rights—then go with Mr. Lincoln and the Black Republicans!"

Douglas uses this term *black Republican* repeatedly, a supposed slur often used by Southerners and Democratic politicians to refer to their rival party.

Douglas finishes his opening speech to great applause. Now, it's the challenger's turn.

When Lincoln stands up and addresses the crowd, the out-of-town reporters and onlookers again note his unusual physical presence—even more exaggerated because of his bizarre movements. "His gestures were awkward. He swung his long arms sometimes in a very ungraceful manner," one spectator observes.

Another writes, "He used singularly awkward, almost absurd, up-and-down and side-wise movements of his body to give emphasis to his arguments." But the reporters also note his strangely effective speaking voice: Unlike Douglas's guttural bellow, Lincoln has a high-pitched but expressive tenor that projects from the stage.

As one listener describes it, Lincoln's voice is "so clear and distinct that every word was heard to the farthest extreme of the assembly—a voice natural, not strained, various in its modulations, and pleasant to listen to."

Whereas Douglas was combative, Lincoln projects sincerity and warmth. He maintains a respectful tone—he refers to his opponent as "Judge Douglas" as a show of courtesy—and sometimes uses wry humor. He gently dismisses the spurious personal attacks leveled against him: "When a man hears himself misrepresented, it provokes him . . . But when the misrepresentation becomes very gross and palpable, it is more apt to amuse him."

He sometimes uses colloquial expressions, describing one of Douglas's accusations as "a specious and fantastic arrangement of words, by which a man can prove a horse chestnut to be a chestnut horse."

But it's when Lincoln gets to the key issue of slavery that his delivery becomes animated. Regarding Douglas's position allowing the extension of slavery into the Northern territories, he declares: "This . . . zeal for the spread of slavery, I cannot but hate. I hate it because of the monstrous injustice of slavery itself."

As his supporters cheer, he continues: "I hate it because it deprives our republican example of its just influence in the world . . . because it forces so many really good men amongst ourselves into an open war with the very fundamental principles of civil liberty."

As Lincoln continues to speak, his voice "rang out in clearness and rose in strength. His tall form towered to its full height, and there came an outburst of inspiring eloquence and argument."

He continues: "I hold that . . . there is no reason in the world why the negro is not entitled to all the natural rights enumerated in the Declaration of Independence—the right to life, liberty, and the pursuit of happiness. [loud cheers] I hold that he is as much entitled to these as the white man." And then, "in the right to eat the bread . . . which his own hand earns, he is my equal and the equal of Judge Douglas, and the equal of every living man."

In his arguments against slavery, Lincoln frequently evokes the Declaration of Independence and the language of the Founding Fathers. Those that would spread slavery, he says, "go back to the era of our Independence, and muzzle the cannon which thunders its annual joyous return." They "blow out the moral lights around us; they must penetrate the human soul, and eradicate there the love of liberty; and then and not till then could they perpetuate slavery in this country!"

After three hours of back-and-forth in the hot sun, the debate concludes to a mix of loud applause, cheers, jeers, and flag-waving from the boisterous crowd. As onlookers depart to find shade and refreshments, the two candidates descend the platform.

Douglas makes a regal exit, escorted by an entourage back to his four-horse-drawn carriage. Lincoln's departure is not so graceful. To his surprise, local party supporters suddenly lift him up and try to carry him off the grounds in triumph. Unfortunately, he's so much taller than they are, his feet drag on the ground, kicking up a cloud of dust that covers all of them.

According to an onlooker, Lincoln yells out, "Don't, boys! Let me down!" but they continue to carry him. When the spectacle finally ends, Lincoln good-naturedly shakes a finger at the group's leader and says, "I'll get even with you, you rascal!"

From there, party officials, reporters, and spectators immediately began assessing the contest. Onlookers knew that both candidates were effective in the debate, but the contrast in their style and politics was clear. As one reporter later recalled, Douglas "magnetized the big crowd by his audacity and supreme self-confidence," while Lincoln "impressed his audiences by . . . his always pure and elevated language, and his appeals to their higher nature."

Interestingly, while some partisan publications mocked Lincoln's performance, the general view of those who saw him for the first time was captured by a reporter from the *New York Evening Post:* "I must confess that long Abe's appearance is not comely. But stir him up and the fire of his genius plays on every feature . . . you have before you a man of rare power and magnetic influence."

The crowd has its own reactions. Six days later, giant banners are made for the second Lincoln-Douglas debate. The Lincoln supporters' largest banner reads, "All Men Are Created Equal." The pro-Douglas crowd's largest banner reads, "No Nigger Equality."

The campaign is long and brutal. In addition to the seven debates in seven counties over the course of two months, the candidates make hundreds of campaign stops and give dozens of speeches in cities, towns, and tiny villages all over the state.

Before the campaign ends, both men will log over four thousand miles crisscrossing Illinois, traveling by train, boat, and carriage. In the final stretch, Douglas loses his voice, his tongue so badly swollen that in the last debate, spectators can hardly hear him.

To pull out a win, the state Republican Party puts every resource into Lincoln's campaign, as does Lincoln himself.

In the end, however, it's not enough.

As a challenger, Lincoln can't overcome Douglas's well-funded political operation, nor can he generate enough support in the lower part of the state, where proslavery sympathies prevail. When all votes are counted after the election, the Democrats achieve a narrow win and Stephen Douglas retains his seat.

Nonetheless, Abraham Lincoln, a little-known lawyer whose political résumé was confined to the state legislature and one brief term in Congress, has made a mark and made his name. The Lincoln-Douglas debates were followed around the country, and in them Lincoln articulated opposition to slavery as memorably as any politician, while also appealing to rural voters not naturally sympathetic to the position. Most critically, his underdog campaign nearly dethroned one of the most powerful Senators in the chamber.

For Illinois Republicans, the defeat is a disappointment. But nationally, the party has success in other midterm races. And now, Republican leaders begin to focus their collective energy on one thing: the upcoming Presidential election of 1860—an election shaping up to be the most consequential of the century.

5

TWO YEARS EARLIER . . .

Chicago, Illinois

Summer 1856

Roughly eighty-five miles northeast of Ottawa, Illinois, where Stephen Douglas and Abraham Lincoln will share the debate stage, a man walks down a bustling daytime street in a very different place: the city of Chicago. The man is of medium height and barrel-chested, with muscular shoulders and arms. He wears a simple, no-frills suit. His face is wide with a close-trimmed beard.

This man, an avid newspaper reader interested in politics, is no doubt following much of the political news of the day. But today, his mind is on other matters.

The man is walking toward his office on the corner of Dearborn and Washington Streets in a busy commercial district of Chicago. He walks quickly and purposefully—this is how he almost always walks—and his bright, piercing eyes dart around watchfully. He knows that some pedestrians and onlookers may recognize him as he walks past; he also knows that of those who recognize him, some view him as a friend, and others as an enemy. He is, in fact, a person both praised and sometimes cursed in the city of Chicago, and increasingly outside of it.

His name is Allan Pinkerton. For the past few years, he's had an unusual distinction: America's first private detective. Today, he's

Allan Pinkerton is widely credited as the first private detective in America. His Chicago-based firm, Pinkerton's National Detective Agency, gained national attention starting in the 1850s and was responsible for many innovations in American law enforcement.

heading to his office for a typical day running Pinkerton's National Detective Agency.

Although Pinkerton's name has recently gained national attention, most of his work in law enforcement is connected to Chicago. Here he's taken on organized crime, white-collar crime, violent crime, and all manner of thieves and con artists. In a city such as this, where corruption rises to the highest levels of politics and business, Pinkerton has pitted himself against some very powerful people, while winning public fame for his crime-fighting exploits. That's where both his friends and enemies come from.

Pinkerton is famously organized and runs a tightly controlled office. He holds his small team of agents and assistants to the highest possible standards and demands they be as organized as he.

As part of his regimented work style, Pinkerton keeps meticulous, detailed daily records of each case he investigates. Today, once he arrives, he is likely reading over or supplementing a case file. In fact, recently he's been working one of his biggest cases of the year—an undercover operation to track down a professional forger who had defrauded multiple banks of tens of thousands of dollars (close to $1 million in today's money) and is now on the run. In a few months, this case—like many others of Pinkerton's—will make news when the agency secures the forger's arrest.

On this day, though, he's interrupted by a visitor, a walk-in at the office seeking employment. Pinkerton looks up from his files and is surprised by what he sees.

The visitor is a young woman.

At first, Pinkerton is confused. The firm had not put out any recent notices looking for a secretary. "I'm afraid there are no openings at present," he tells her.

"No," she says, "I'm afraid you have misunderstood me."

"Have I?"

She explains she's not here to be a secretary. She wants a job as a detective. She saw a job posting and would like to apply.

He looks at her in disbelief. A *woman* detective? As Pinkerton later described, "It was not the custom to employ women detectives . . . Indeed, I'd never heard of a woman detective."

It's a bit of an understatement. At this moment in history, not only were there no women detectives anywhere in the country, but none had ever been hired in *any* capacity by *any* police department or sheriff's office. It will be another thirty-five years—in 1891—before any public law enforcement agency hires a woman investigator or police officer. So here in 1856, the concept is totally foreign.

But . . . since she's here, Pinkerton asks her for more information.

She says her name is Kate Warne. Twenty-six years old. A widow with no children. She needs to work to support her parents. She saw a listing for detective work and decided to learn more about Pinkerton's agency and the work of a detective. Now she's convinced she's the perfect candidate for the job.

Why, Pinkerton asks, would a woman be suitable for the position?

"Women," she explains, "could be most useful in worming out secrets in many places which would be impossible for male detectives to gain access." A woman would also be able to befriend the wives and girlfriends of suspected criminals and gain their confidence. Furthermore, "men become braggarts when they are around women who encourage them to boast," and "women have an eye for detail and are excellent observers."

Pinkerton studies this woman. As a detective, he's often required to quickly take the measure of people just by observing and listening to them. Warne is, as he later describes, "graceful in movement and self-possessed. Her features, although not what could be called handsome, were decidedly of an intellectual cast. Her face was honest, which would cause one in distress instinctively to select her as a confidante."

More important, she came prepared for the interview and had intelligent answers for every question. Pinkerton could see that "she had evidently given the matter much study" when it came to her rationale for wanting to join his force, and she "gave many excellent reasons why she could be of service."

Still, detective work is dangerous—many of Pinkerton's cases involve agents going undercover to infiltrate criminal organizations, thereby putting their lives at risk—and the accepted practice is that only men should do it. He tells her he'll consider her application, but he still wants twenty-four hours to make the decision. She agrees, saying she'll return the next day to hear his answer.

That night, Pinkerton mulls over the decision. Hiring a woman as a detective carries enormous risks. Pinkerton knows that should any harm come to a woman under his employ, he would be censured. At the very least, to hire a woman would be seen as highly unconventional.

Then again, this particular detective has never been afraid to break from convention—in his work or in his life.

6

---·---

Baltimore, Maryland

February 1861

The night is full of mystery.

Today, over a century and a half later, it's still difficult to tell what exactly transpired and the precise date on which the events of this night might have occurred. But according to the only known account, the evening went something like this.

Roughly twenty men are gathered in a dark, candlelit room. It's a drawing room, the parlor floor of a wealthy home. Tonight, heavy curtains are drawn across all the windows, blocking the moonlight. More important, they prevent anyone from seeing inside.

Each man is there by invitation only. Each had to prove he was worthy to be invited into this group—and had to speak a vow of secrecy before entering. Earlier in the night, one of the men was sworn in during a special ceremony, bestowing upon him the trust of the others.

When the men speak, they speak in hushed tones. And Southern accents. But mostly, they are silent.

One of the men, clearly a leader, stands up in front of the rest. He has gleaming eyes, a carefully manicured mustache, and a melodious voice. For this occasion, he's dressed head to toe in funereal black. In soft but impassioned tones, he addresses the gathered group. He speaks of the fight to preserve "Southern ideals," and the need to punish the "enemies of the South" that now threaten them.

It's a cause, he says, for which each of them must be prepared to make the ultimate sacrifice. In fact, he explains, they need to choose someone in this room to make this sacrifice. He goes on to describe "the glory that awaited the man who proved himself the hero upon this great occasion."

When he finishes, the leader and an associate place a large wooden box on the table before the group. Inside the box are several ballots, one for each person in the room.

He quickly explains that one of the ballots in the box is red. The rest are blank. Each person will take a ballot from the box, then look at it in private. One of them, by chance, will draw the red ballot, bestowing upon that person a special duty. The rest of the men, however, won't know. "Everyone was pledged to secrecy as to the color of the ballot he drew."

These ballots will determine who among them will do the deed—the sacred deed—to which they are all devoted.

Several candles are snuffed out to make the room even darker. In this near darkness, the men silently form a line in front of the table.

In two days, the new President-elect of the United States will pass through this city. But the men in this room believe that he is not *their* President. He does not represent them. He is a President of the North—an abolitionist, they believe—who will destroy their way of life. On their honor, they cannot allow this man to degrade the South and take away what belongs to them.

When the leader says so, the first man in line approaches the box, reaches in, withdraws one of the ballots, and steps aside. The next man follows suit, then the next. The leader, watching carefully, nods his approval as each man follows the instructions.

After every man has taken a ballot, the leader himself reaches into the box, grabbing the last one. Without looking at it, he clasps it in a closed fist and then holds it above his head.

One of these men will be a martyr for the Southern cause.

Their plan will commence in three days, in a crowded place, in full public view.

They will all go together, as a group. Each of them will carry a firearm, but only one of them—the one who drew the red ballot—will have the honor of pulling the trigger. Their plan is set—an act of political violence designed to shock the country, create chaos and disorder, and single-handedly change the direction of the nation.

It will all happen not far from where this dark ceremony takes place. It will happen here—in the city of Baltimore.

7

---·---

Allan Pinkerton was born in Glasgow, Scotland, on July 21, 1819. He grew up poor in a poor country and spent his childhood in one of Glasgow's most notorious slums.

For the vast majority of children growing up in this environment, the deprivation, crime, and lack of opportunity were almost a guarantee of a life in poverty. But young Allan was not an ordinary child. From a young age, he showed unusual intelligence and determination. Although his schooling ended at age ten, he was already working odd jobs. At age twelve, he talked his way into an apprenticeship with a local barrel-maker, commonly called a cooper.

While still in his early teens, Allan was working thirteen-hour days hauling materials and operating heavy tools in front of a hot forge. Naturally stocky of build, he developed powerful shoulders and thick arms. Also distinctive were his piercing eyes and focused personality. One Glasgow friend always remembered Pinkerton's "searching, cool blue-gray eyes that never left your face when he spoke to you, and the intense drive that animated him."

At the age of eighteen, Pinkerton joined the coopers' union, fighting for the poor tradespersons and laborers who suffered brutal working conditions in the early Industrial Revolution. Inspired by

the union, he also joined a growing political movement at the time
known as the Chartists, devoted to securing suffrage and basic rights
for the poor and working class. Over time, the brawny working-class
kid developed a strong moral code based on simple principles: fighting against injustice and standing up for the powerless.

But when Allan and his fellow Chartists had a violent clash with
police—a clash that left a few of Allan's colleagues dead—he had to
go into hiding to avoid imprisonment. As he later described it, "I had
become an outlaw with a price on my head." So in early 1842, at age
twenty-two, he made a life-changing decision and secured a place on
a ship bound for North America. Time to start anew.

Accompanying him was his young wife, Joan, and together they
eventually made their way to the United States. They settled in a
small town in western Illinois called Dundee—a town founded by
fellow Scottish immigrants—where Pinkerton opened his own barrel-
making shop. In truth, Pinkerton's career may very well have ended
there. But soon, a strange encounter would start him on an unexpected new path.

One day in June 1846—roughly four years after his arrival in
Illinois—twenty-six-year-old Pinkerton was searching by raft for
wood alongside the Fox River just outside town. While scanning the
banks of a small island in the middle of the water, he spotted evidence
of a strange campsite, with recent signs of activity. He returned on
subsequent days and found the campsite still active, but unattended
during the day.

Suspecting something unusual and perhaps nefarious, he waited
until after nightfall to return the next time. Under cover of darkness,
he hid his raft around a bend and positioned himself in some tall
grass so that he could observe the site undetected. Soon, a handful
of men appeared, speaking in low tones. These strangers were clearly
plotting something secret, just outside the peaceful town of Dundee.

The next day, Pinkerton went to the sheriff's office of Kane County
and shared what he'd learned. The sheriff was impressed with Pinkerton's report and asked the cooper to lead him to the site on a subsequent night so that he could investigate. Pinkerton did exactly that.

A few nights later, Pinkerton was on hand when the sheriff and a few deputies raided the campsite and arrested the strangers, who, it turns out, were part of a criminal counterfeiting ring. They were planning to infiltrate Dundee and other nearby towns with forged bills.

Word of the arrests—and Pinkerton's role in aiding them—traveled through the county. Soon, every customer who passed through his shop wanted him to recount the details. His renown had an altogether unexpected consequence when, a few months later, the proprietors of the local general store approached Pinkerton and asked his help in another counterfeiting-related matter.

The proprietors believed they had identified a stranger in a neighboring town who was spreading fake bills in the area; they wondered if Pinkerton would track the man down and gather evidence that could lead to the man's arrest. Pinkerton responded that he had no qualifications whatsoever for this sort of work, but after repeated entreaties from the two men, he agreed. He tracked down the mysterious stranger, pretended to be interested in joining the man's criminal operation, and eventually set up a later meeting for a handoff of bogus bills. After tipping off local law enforcement in advance, Pinkerton secured the man's arrest at the meeting.

As the story spread, he became as well known for his crime fighting as for his barrel-making. He believed the attention was unwarranted, but couldn't prevent talk of his exploits from spreading around the region. As he later wrote, "The country being new, and great sensations scarce, the affair was in everyone's mouth. I suddenly found myself called upon, from every quarter, to undertake matters requiring detective skill."

Soon, the Kane County sheriff offered Pinkerton a part-time job as his deputy, and from there, he made his way to Chicago, eventually becoming the city's first full-time police detective. But after seeing all the corruption, graft, and organized crime that Chicago had to offer, Pinkerton had a new idea.

Together with a lawyer named Edward Rucker, Pinkerton set up a new firm—a detective agency—that would be entirely private. They'd investigate misdeeds that the police wouldn't or couldn't. More im-

The catchphrase of Pinkerton's National Detective Agency, "We Never Sleep," becomes forever associated with the firm. The company's logo—an open, watchful eye—will inspire the phrase *private eye*.

portant, they'd operate free from the bureaucracy, politics, and financial restraints that hampered the official force.

Their new name? The North-Western Police Agency.

Right away, clients came calling.

Within the first year, Rucker faded from the company, and Pinkerton changed the firm's name to something catchier: Pinkerton's National Detective Agency. With this new name came a motto—"We Never Sleep"—and a logo of a single eye, wide open. In fact, this memorable image is the origin of the phrase *private eye*.

America's first private detective was born.

Freed from constraints imposed by city hall, Pinkerton could go after any criminal, serve any client, and conduct investigations without fear or favor. Unsurprisingly, his role investigating powerful people brought him enemies. One night in 1853, while Pinkerton was taking an evening stroll, a man sneaked up behind him, pulled out a gun, and shot him twice in the back at point-blank range. Pinkerton's life was saved only by his particular habit of walking with one arm crossed behind his back; his own forearm shielded his torso from the bullets. He recovered from the injury but never determined the identity of the shooter—with so many in the city who wished he would disappear, it was hard to narrow down the possibilities.

By the summer of 1856, when Kate Warne entered the offices of Pinkerton's National Detective Agency, this man, Pinkerton, had overcome many challenges. He had endured childhood poverty, years of hard labor, a journey across the ocean; he had faced many dangerous criminals, revolutionized the field of law enforcement, and survived an attempt on his life. He achieved all of this by taking risks.

In his interview with Warne, Pinkerton had been impressed by her intelligence and confidence. Her arguments for why a woman detective could excel in the field were persuasive. If hiring a woman opens him up to derision, then so be it.

That night, after mulling it over, Pinkerton makes his decision. He'll hire her. Train her. The next day, when she returns to his office as promised, he gives her the news.

Just like that, Kate Warne becomes America's first woman detective.

At this moment, what Pinkerton can't know is that he and his new employee will soon embark together on the most momentous case of his career—a case where the life of a President is at stake.

8

---·---

Decatur, Illinois

May 9, 1860

The smell can't be good.

They're all packed inside a tent—one that's clearly too small to hold the several hundred state Republican Party officials, delegates, political reporters, and assorted onlookers who are stuffed together, shoulder to shoulder.

The occasion is the Illinois State Republican Convention, where the party will officially nominate its candidates for Governor and other statewide elected positions in the upcoming November elections.

In addition to statewide offices, the convention has another very important task: announcing whom the state party delegates will support as the Republican nominee for President of the United States, to be voted upon in two weeks at the Republican National Convention. While this selection for the party's nominee for President is not binding, it represents a unified pledge of support by the state's twenty-two delegates for at least the first round of voting at the national convention.

In the frontier states, these party conventions are rowdy affairs where liquor often flows. Indeed, today's packed crowd is in festive spirits as the Illinois sun shines through the open sides of the make-shift tent. Loud cheers arise as county and state officials walk on a modest wooden stage, accepting their nominations, giving speeches, and thanking supporters in the crowd.

Midway through the day, the chairman of the convention, Richard J. Oglesby, takes the stage for a special announcement. Oglesby has been planning this event for some time and has made every effort to deliver as much excitement as possible to the assembled crowd. The coming elections are some of the first where the Republican Party will be considered a major player—and the chairman is determined to put the Illinois state party on the map.

Standing on the speaker's platform, Oglesby pauses, hoping to build suspense. He knows what the crowd wants—the announcement of who the state party will support as a Presidential nominee. Finally, he begins: "I am informed that a distinguished citizen of Illinois, and one whom Illinois will ever delight to honor, is present, and I wish to move that this body invite him to a seat on the stand."

The chairman once again pauses for dramatic effect. Then, finally, he makes the introduction: "Abraham Lincoln!"

The crowd erupts in cheers. Although Lincoln was not born in Illinois, his entire career has been spent in the state. The party electors and delegates are delighted to be sending one of their adopted sons to compete on the national stage for the party's Presidential nomination.

Timed with the chairman's dramatic announcement, the rear entrance of the tent opens, and the candidate himself enters the venue. The applause rises as the crowd sees him.

Lincoln has earned his place in this particular spotlight. After his loss to the Democrat Stephen Douglas in the Senate race two years ago, Lincoln used the notoriety he had gained to support Republican candidates in every nearby state and local race. In the last two years, the issue of slavery has only grown more divisive in the country and, deeply motivated by this issue, he worked to help the party, while giving some of the most notable speeches of his career.

Once Lincoln was in the tent, the plan was for him to walk through the crowd to join other politicians and party officials seated on the stage. Unfortunately, no one thought about what to do if the tent is so crowded that it's impossible for anyone to walk through the packed onlookers.

To the candidate's surprise, some members of the excited crowd lift him over their heads—Lincoln seems to go through this a lot, getting lifted up against his will—and they pass him up along the cheering spectators. As one onlooker describes the scene, the long-limbed candidate is passed "kicking, scrambling—crawling—upon the sea of heads" until the crowd drops him on the stage.

He stands to his full height and looks at the gathered assembly. Fifty-one years old, tall as ever, still clean shaven, with his unruly black hair underneath what has become a trademark top hat. Once on the stage, he stands "bowing and blushing" and waves his thank-you to the crowd.

The chairman, Oglesby, is not done with his planned theater. Local party officials know that Abraham Lincoln is not well known outside the state—not compared to several other candidates who will also fight for the Presidential nomination, certainly—and they've wondered how to brand his candidacy as something memorable. Today, they're ready to unveil their vision.

Before the convention, Oglesby had looked up a cousin of Lincoln's, a local farmer named John Hanks, with whom Lincoln had once labored "splitting rails"—that is, chopping raw wood by ax into horizontal rails suitable for building fences—three decades earlier, before he got into politics. In the weeks prior to the convention, Oglesby and Hanks had retrieved some old walnut and locust rails that Lincoln and Hanks had supposedly split together.

Now, from a side entrance, John Hanks and a farmer friend enter the tent carrying two of these tall wooden rails with a big banner affixed to them. In big printed letters, the banner reads:

ABRAHAM LINCOLN

The Rail Candidate

FOR PRESIDENT IN 1860

Two Rails from a Lot of 3,000
Made in 1830 by Thos. Hanks and Abe Lincoln—
Whose Father was the First Pioneer in Macon County

In the politics of the day, nicknames are a common tool to brand candidates to the public: "Old Hickory" for Andrew Jackson in 1828, then "Tippecanoe and Tyler Too" for William Harrison and John Tyler in 1840. Earlier, as a Congressman, Abraham Lincoln was sometimes known as "Old Abe," but this isn't catchy enough for a Presidential candidate. Now, with this banner, he has a new nickname: "the Rail Candidate," or "the Rail Splitter" as he'll soon be known.

Even back then, branding mattered—and this branding is clear to the public: Other candidates may be more experienced or come from fancier places, but Lincoln is a self-made man of the people who has worked with his hands his whole life. He personally swung an ax that split the rails that made some of the early fences and turned the massive Midwestern landscape into a place where Americans can settle.

Still, the banner is technically inaccurate—Hanks's first name is conflated with Lincoln's father's first name, Thomas—and it's not really true that Thomas Lincoln was "the first pioneer in Macon County." The crowd doesn't care, though. They love the political theater as the banner makes its way around the tent.

The chairman still isn't done with the show. Onstage, he tells Abraham Lincoln to stand up and positively answer the question: Did he really split these two rails as a young man?

"Identify your work!" the watching crowd yells.

The problem is, as much as the crowd wants Lincoln to play along, he's reluctant. It seems dishonest to take credit for any work that he himself can't verify. So he leans down to inspect them.

"I cannot say that I split these rails," he admits. He then turns to his cousin and old coworker John Hanks and asks in front of everyone, "Where did you get the rails?"

"At the farm you improved down in Sangamon," John Hanks answers.

With the crowd waiting, Lincoln thinks on this a bit. "What kind of timber are they?" he asks, still looking quizzical.

"Honey locust and black walnut," Hanks says.

Can't Lincoln just go along with the show and say he split the rails to please the crowd? Of course he can. Instead, though, he inspects the two rails with a furrowed brow, as if to critique their handiwork. "I cannot say that I split these rails," he says again, but this time, a small smile grows across his face.

Looking dismissively at the two rails, he loudly admits, "I can only say I have split a great many better-looking ones."

The crowd likes the joke and responds with a "storm of approval." Three cheers erupt from the audience, and then as one onlooker described, they give "three more for 'Honest Abraham Lincoln, the rail candidate, our next President.'"

Lincoln takes a seat and says nothing further. But as the convention continues, he and the two rails remain the stars of the show. When the event adjourns later that afternoon, an attendee reports that "in a moment there was a rush of delegates to the platform. The rails were seized upon and pieces of some of them were sawed off for souvenirs."

Whatever excitement local supporters felt in that tent in Decatur, Illinois, the party officials and the candidate himself know that his chances of being the nominee of the national party are slim at best. Winning over the home state is one thing. But outside of Illinois, this candidate—a lawyer who has lost two Senate races, and who hasn't held elected office for a decade—has little support.

As Lincoln himself writes to a friend at the time, "I think the Illinois delegation will be unanimous for me at the start; and no other delegation will . . . Everywhere, except in Illinois, and possibly Indiana, one or another is preferred to me."

Although the Lincoln-Douglas debates garnered some attention, and Lincoln has since given some notable speeches, he has nothing like the name recognition of other aspiring Republican Presidential candidates—like Senator William Seward of New York and Governor Salmon Chase of Ohio—who have been nationally known for years or decades. Outside his home turf, Lincoln is mostly a nonentity.

Indeed, the next day, a reporter for *The New York Times* who was at the state convention files a story with this summary: "Resolutions were unanimously adopted declaring ABRAM LINCOLN the choice of the Republican Party of Illinois for the Presidency."

Abram.

His name recognition is so low nationally, the reporter can't even get his name right. And this won't be the last time it happens.

In less than two weeks, the Republican Party will choose its Presidential nominee at the national convention in Chicago, in preparation for the general elections in November. With the country in a state of deep discord, the upcoming election of 1860 is seen as the most momentous in anyone's lifetime. Some dozen names are being considered, and Lincoln, even at his best, is closer to the middle of the pack than he is to the top of it.

Still, on this day in Decatur, Abraham Lincoln, a tall, skinny frontier lawyer, now has a nickname that sticks: the Rail Splitter. The name will give color to his campaign and provide him a political identity on the national stage.

Most important, it will get people around the country to ask this question: Who is this strange-looking but eloquent man from Illinois? Who *is* the Rail Splitter, really?

9

———— • ————

Sometimes legends are true.

Abraham Lincoln was born on February 12, 1809, in a small, one-room, dirt-floored log cabin in Hardin County, Kentucky, near the southern border of Indiana. He spent his first few years of life there, with his parents and older sister.

Later, as a politician, Lincoln would generally refuse to romanticize or wax poetic about his frontier upbringing. Instead, he'd refer to his family's tough struggle for survival as the "short and simple annals of the poor." The fact is, his young life was mostly bleak and full of suffering.

Abraham's father, Thomas Lincoln, was known as a tough frontiersman whose guiding motivation was the family's raw survival. He himself was orphaned as a young boy after he watched his own father be killed and scalped in a skirmish with Native Americans.

He passed on to his children his skills as a carpenter and subsistence farmer, mostly of corn and beans. He worked his only son, Abe, hard, and by some accounts would strike the boy to the floor if he didn't obey.

Thomas was also functionally illiterate. As Abraham later described, "He never did more in the way of writing than to bunglingly sign his own name." Lincoln also wrote, "Owing to my father being left an orphan at the age of six years, in poverty, and in a new country, he became a wholly uneducated man, which I suppose is why I know so little of our family history."

Abe's mother, Nancy Lincoln, was also illiterate, but unlike with his father, Abe had fond memories of her from childhood, once referring to her as his "angel Mother." Not much is known about Nancy, but a few acquaintances would speak of her "kind disposition" and devotion to her children.

From the time of Abraham's birth in Kentucky, the family suffered a series of hardships. The land was not always suitable for planting, and they struggled to eat. When Abraham was three or four years old, his mother gave birth to another son, but Abe's new brother died in infancy of unknown causes.

When Abraham was seven years old and his sister was nine, his father decided to relocate, intrigued by reports of federal land for sale in the neighboring state of Indiana.

The family packed up and traveled first by boat, then by cart, and then by foot to a small plot that was about ten miles north of the Kentucky state line. There, Thomas and Abraham cleared the rough land and built another log cabin, chopping every log and crafting the door, the fireplace, and every shingle of the roof. During several weeks of clearing and building, the family slept under a makeshift lean-to, exposed to the elements every day and night.

Here, in this mostly untamed region of Indiana, the Lincoln family settled. Abraham spent most of his childhood and adolescence in the immediate vicinity of this plot of land. While this particular corner of the frontier was isolated, the Lincolns got to know some neighbors. Eventually, a few family relations settled nearby.

Mostly, however, young Abraham's life was dominated by one thing: work. Well before his teens, he was laboring twelve-hour days, wielding carpentry tools and farming equipment. There were no child labor laws at the time, so parents often hired out their children to work for others. On the days Abe wasn't working directly for his father, he was working on neighboring farms, sometimes for days or weeks at a time under harsh conditions.

For his father, one of Abe's occasional tasks was to lead a mare by himself on a five-mile walk through the woods to the nearest miller and oversee the animal as it circled around the millstone to grind wheat. At one point during this chore, the mare kicked ten-year-old Abe in the head and knocked him unconscious for several hours. He might have died had the mill operator not discovered him on the ground.

Later, the sudden and unexpected death of Abraham's mother was a calamity for the small family. He watched her fall ill, suffer horrific symptoms for one week, and then die before his eyes, the entire episode a searing trauma for the young boy. Together with the death of his sister several years later, the early familiarity with pain and loss left emotional scars that remained with him throughout adulthood. Over four decades later, as Commander in Chief during wartime, he learned of a young girl debilitated by sorrow after the death of her soldier father in battle. He wrote her this letter:

It is with deep grief that I learn of the death of your kind and brave father; and, especially, that it is affecting your young heart beyond what is common in such cases. In this sad world of ours, sorrow comes to all; and, to the young, it comes with bitterest agony, because it takes them unawares . . . You are sure to be happy again. To know this, which is certainly true, will make you some less miserable now.

So personal were these words, he scarcely needed to add one final line: "I have had experience enough to know what I say."

By his early teens, Abe's regimen of manual labor hardened him into a physically tough youth. Among the local frontier boys in southern Indiana, one-on-one wrestling was a common means of establishing a pecking order, and Lincoln's height and wiry strength made him one of the best wrestlers around.

As a backwoods boy raised in the untamed wilderness, Abe's talent with tools also impressed the locals. One nearby resident reported that young Lincoln could sink an ax deeper into a tree than anyone he had ever seen. A cousin of Lincoln's agreed, adding, "How he could chop! His ax would flash and bite into a sugar tree or sycamore, and down it would come."

These skills were fairly typical for a boy growing up in the frontier. But with Abraham Lincoln, there was also something different.

One sign of this came when Abe was eight or nine years old, out rifle hunting. He shot a wild turkey, but when he went to retrieve the game, he saw the bird writhing and bleeding on the ground and was overwhelmed with grief. That moment, he vowed to never hunt large game again. On the frontier, where hunting was a part of daily life, this position wasn't just unusual—it was totally unheard of. Yet young Lincoln stuck to his vow.

On another occasion, he encountered a group of children torturing a turtle with hot coals; he was so horrified that he rushed in to stop them by force, with tears in his eyes, ready to fight the whole group to protect the defenseless animal.

Similarly, his stepmother would recall a time when she tried to kill a snake, until Abe stopped her, crying out, "No, it enjoys living just the same as we do!"

This unusual empathy for animals remained a trait throughout Lincoln's life. As an adult lawyer, he was once dressed up in his only suit, walking near a farm on the way to a dinner party, when he saw a pig stuck deep in the mud, almost drowning. He didn't want to ruin his clothes so at first, he kept walking. That is, until he looked back over his shoulder as the pig watched him pass. As Lincoln described it, the pig's eyes seemed to say, "There now, my last hope is gone." Right there, Lincoln waded through the watery field in his suit to free the creature—and attended the dinner party covered in mud.

On another occasion as a young man, Lincoln spied two baby birds on the ground and spent an hour returning them to their nest in the tree. When the friends he was traveling with teased him for it, Lincoln responded, "Gentlemen, you may laugh, but I could not have slept well to-night, if I had not saved those birds. Their cries would have rung in my ears."

Once he had his own children, Lincoln acquired many pets for them, including horses, turkeys, rabbits, cats, pigs, goats, and a stray dog that he personally rescued.

If young Abraham's empathy for animals was atypical for a boy growing up on the frontier, another quality was even more so: a deep yearning to read and learn. In a region where literacy and education were rare, he overcame every obstacle to teach himself. Before his mother died, she had encouraged him to learn to read and write. It was a gift that would transform his life.

Although there was a one-room schoolhouse several miles from where the Lincolns lived, his father rarely allowed him to attend. At most, he would go for a few scattered days per season. Lincoln later estimated that "the aggregate of all his schooling did not amount to one year." With no teachers, no schoolbooks, no mentors, and a father who could not read or write, Lincoln was left entirely to his own devices.

Without writing materials or paper, young Abe learned "to write words and sentences wherever he found suitable material," recalled a family friend. "He scrawled them with charcoal, he scored them in the dust, in the sand, in the snow—anywhere and everywhere that lines could be drawn, there he improved his capacity for writing."

One neighbor who sometimes hired Abe to do farm labor recalled the boy's unusual method for teaching himself math during breaks: "We had a broad wooden shovel on which Abe would work out his sums—wipe off and repeat till it got too black for more: then he would scrape and wash off and repeat again and again."

As his reading and spelling skills improved, young Abe's great challenge was to acquire books. He searched far and wide in the region, begging for or borrowing any book he could get his hands on. One benefit of being hired out days at a time on neighboring farms was that he could sometimes find new reading materials. "When he worked for us he read all our books—would sit up late in the night—kindle up the fire—read by it," one farmer's wife recalled.

Once he acquired a new book, he would read it obsessively during any free moments he wasn't working. Since most of his work was out-doors, he found a favorite position to read during meal breaks—lying on the grass, with his long legs perched up on a tree stump or large rock. "While other boys were out hooking water melons and trifling away their time, he was studying his books—thinking and reflecting," one employer described. If there was a passage that he didn't understand, he would find some way to write it down—sometimes etched in the dirt—so he could memorize it, study it, and look up any words he didn't know.

To his peers and neighbors, Abe's passion for books and reading was totally baffling—a behavior that simply didn't make sense. One neighbor, after remarking that Abe was known for his "book-readin'," said that "on that account we used to think he wouldn't amount to much. You see, it warn't book-readin' then, it was work, that counted."

By the end of his teens, Lincoln had patched together, through sheer force of will, a level of literary education that is remarkable under the circumstances. He had read the Bible, some Shakespeare, *Aesop's Fables*, John Bunyan's *The Pilgrim's Progress*, even the poetry of Robert Burns.

While some books introduced him to foreign lands and peoples, others taught him about his own country—and its leaders. One of his favorites as a teenager was Mason Locke Weems's *Life of George Washington,* an early biography of the first President, which he read several times. He also studied William Grimshaw's *History of the United States*, learning about the American Revolution, the Founding Fathers, and the framing of the Constitution.

He read the Declaration of Independence—with the words "all men are created equal"—and internalized the idea that he lived in a country where a dirt-poor, uneducated frontier boy was entitled to the same rights and opportunities as any other person. This ideal of fairness and justice influenced him deeply, and he came to see its violation as a betrayal of the country.

Of course, these exalted works of literature and politics were only part of what young Lincoln's mind absorbed. He also soaked up the written and oral culture all around him: an eclectic array of tall tales, fables, country proverbs, backwoods sermons, frontier doggerel, and his favorite pastime of all: jokes.

Perhaps because his young life was often so full of suffering and pain, he found an early escape in laughter. He sought out jokes, puns, and humorous tales anywhere he could. Although he was at first a shy and awkward boy—he was self-conscious of his height and gawky appearance—he found he had an innate talent for telling funny stories and mimicking voices. As he became more confident in his middle teens, he would often hold an audience of his peers, regaling them with amusing anecdotes and a seemingly endless array of jokes.

By the end of his teens, Abraham Lincoln had endured a childhood in poverty, suffered tragic loss, and logged enough hours of brutal manual labor to fill a lifetime. But he had also filled his mind with words and ideas and a sense of higher calling. He now had a burning desire to fulfill his potential.

One of the most profound days in young Lincoln's life was when he turned twenty-one years old. By state law, his father could no longer force him to work without his consent. He was now free to forge his own path in the world.

One of Lincoln's final acts for his family was to help his father and stepmother move to the state of Illinois, pitching in with his dad to build one more log cabin. Then he said goodbye and struck out on his own.

Lincoln didn't have a coin in his pocket. Just the threadbare clothes on his back. He was in a new state, Illinois, where he knew almost no one. How would he earn some money to live?

Splitting rails, of course.

10

---•---

Charleston, South Carolina

April 23, 1860

The Year of Meteors.

That's how the poet Walt Whitman described the year 1860 in the United States of America. After more than a decade of steadily increasing sectional tension and hostility in the country, the strands begin to unravel.

It starts with the Democratic Party.

Only four years earlier, the party was in a strong position in national politics, built on a coalition between the Southern slave states and enough Northern support to hold a few states above the Mason-Dixon line. Back in the 1856 Presidential election four years ago, Democratic nominee James Buchanan won comfortably. Democrats had benefited from the collapse of the rival Whig Party, while the new Republican Party that replaced the Whigs was not yet strong enough to win the Presidency.

Just as critically for the Democrats, six of the nine Supreme Court Justices at the time were Southerners, most of them former or current slaveholders. In 1857, the Court's infamous *Dred Scott* decision was an attempt to "settle" the slavery question by essentially denying that black people had any protections under federal law. In the majority opinion, Chief Justice Roger Taney declared unequivocally that black people as a class "are not included, and were not intended to be included, under the word 'citizens' in the Constitution, and can therefore claim none of the rights and privileges which that instrument provides for and secures to citizens of the United States."

Yet the antislavery movement was also rising fast during this period, and the controversial *Dred Scott* decision—although a huge victory for slaveholders—also had the effect of galvanizing the opposition. In the 1858 midterms, the Democrats lost several races in Northern and border states, mostly to candidates in the upstart Republican Party. Responding to the changing climate, Northern Democratic officeholders began to take more modest positions on slavery. This waffling infuriated hard-line proslavery Southern Democrats, thereby creating an angry rift within the party just as the momentous 1860 Presidential election drew near.

On April 23, 1860, Democratic delegates from all over the country arrived in Charleston, South Carolina, to attend the party's national convention.

Almost from the start, the convention was acrimonious. The moderate wing of the party backed the nomination of Illinois Senator Stephen Douglas (Abraham Lincoln's debate opponent two years earlier), who was long thought to be the presumptive favorite. But in the past few years, a more extremist proslavery wing of the party had taken hold in the Deep South, and it distrusted the Northerner Douglas's fidelity to the cause.

These Southern activists—sometimes called "the Fire-Eaters"—refused to compromise in any way on the matter of slavery. They wouldn't make any concessions whatsoever in the party platform, and they refused to support any nominee who did. "The Democratic party is a proslavery party," as *The Charleston Herald* printed, and can have "no alliance with those who are polluted with the leprosy of Abolitionism."

Starting on the first few days of the convention, debate on the floor devolved into belligerent shouting matches between the party's different factions. The hostility extended beyond the floor of the convention; in a large, crowded restaurant during the lunch hour, two delegates got in a fistfight that culminated in the men hurling plates at each other across the room. This altercation had barely ended when another fistfight broke out elsewhere in the restaurant, this one between a delegate and a reporter. The second fight could be stopped only after the combatants set a later date for a duel.

On the third night of the convention, police had to intervene to stop a potential midnight brawl as a group of drunk Fire-Eaters tried to storm a hotel to assault some Northern delegates who were lodged inside.

By the fifth day, the two factions in the party were at loggerheads. They couldn't agree on a party platform or a nominee. When the moderates won a floor vote on their platform, the Fire-Eaters organized a revolt.

On the morning of April 30, the leader of the Alabama delegation stood up and declared that they were walking out of the convention in protest. As the Alabamans walked out of the hall, the delegation from Mississippi joined them. Soon, most of the delegates from Louisiana, South Carolina, Virginia, Florida, Texas, Georgia, and Arkansas also joined the walkout.

By the afternoon, the Southern exiles assembled at another space a few blocks away and declared themselves the *real* Democratic Party and began to draw up a competing platform. The two conventions happened in parallel for a few days, with emissaries running back and forth to try to broker a peace. But compromise proved impossible, and after an extended schedule of ten days, hundreds of exhausted Democratic delegates left Charleston in frustration with no platform and no agreed-upon nominee.

The two split factions each planned new conventions later in the summer while party leaders scrambled to try and bridge the divide. No one knew what would happen, but with an election on the horizon, the party appeared to be a mess—thereby setting a favorable stage for the Republicans up north.

But just like the Democrats, the Republican Party was about to get a surprise of its own.

11

———— · ————

Chicago, Illinois

May 1860

On the week of May 11, 1860, trainloads of political operatives, campaign teams, volunteers, and journalists arrive from all over the country in the city of Chicago.

After months of buildup and anticipation, they're here for one of the most hotly anticipated political events of recent years: the Republican National Convention. Here, party delegates from every registered state will meet to determine the Republican nominee for the coming Presidential election in November.

For many making the trip, the journey itself is a highly energized occasion. Traveling on a train with hundreds of delegates and campaign staffers from the Northeast, a *New York Times* reporter wrote that "time and space would fail me to describe the smoking car, the boxes of cigars, the gin cocktail jugs, the brandy flasks and the whiskey slings which were freely circulated through the cars."

In the city, massive crowds surround the convention venue—a huge meeting hall commonly known as the Wigwam—and after the venue's ten-thousand-person capacity is reached, the crowds pack into the bars, restaurants, hotels, and cafés nearby. Banners wave everywhere, cannons fire at regular intervals, and marching bands wind their way through the crowded city streets.

With the country so deeply split, the November election feels absolutely momentous. The Republican Party—the rising party of the North—is desperate to take the White House.

The question is: Who will they nominate to be their Presidential candidate?

Unlike the modern system where the general public votes in primaries and caucuses to determine a party's nominee, in the nineteenth century the decision was made entirely at the party convention, where delegates from each state converged to vote in person, more or less free to choose whomever they liked.

Leading up to the convention, the widely shared consensus is that one candidate is the front-runner: William Henry Seward, Senator and former Governor of New York. Seward is a revered figure in Northern politics, a regular fixture in Washington, D.C., social circles who boasts a lifetime of public service and recognition. He also has solid antislavery credentials and has been a leader on the issue.

After Seward, another top contender is Salmon Chase, the former Governor of Ohio. He is even more outspoken against slavery than Seward—making him harder to elect in some places—but holds the promise of delivering his coveted home state to the Republicans. By most estimates, the third position is held by Judge Edward Bates of Missouri, a moderate whose less confrontational position on slavery could appeal to border states.

Somewhere behind those three is Abraham Lincoln, the lawyer, former one-term member of Congress, and "Rail Splitter" from Illinois who is known mostly for some recent speeches and his debates with Stephen Douglas two years earlier.

According to the custom of the time, the candidates themselves do not attend the convention. Instead, their campaign operatives and surrogates come and do all the work. In fact, one indication of Lincoln's dim view of his own chances is that he actually considered making the trip to Chicago from his home in Springfield to attend the convention. He waffled on the matter, telling a friend that "he was almost too much of a candidate to go, and not quite enough to stay home." Just in case, he chose to stay in Springfield.

The 1860 Republican Convention in Chicago, Illinois, was held in this "Wigwam" packed with roughly ten thousand attendees. Many thousands more gathered in the surrounding streets and buildings during the raucous weeklong event.

Even if Lincoln himself is doubtful of his chances, his aides are not. His colorful campaign manager, a three-hundred-pound former judge named David Davis, is convinced Lincoln has an outside shot at the nomination and has arrived with a team in Chicago ready to give it their all.

In fact, heading into the convention, the Lincoln camp has a few advantages that not everyone recognizes. For one, the location of the convention in Chicago gives Lincoln an inherent home-state advantage. Seizing an opportunity, Lincoln's campaign team printed piles of duplicate tickets to the event and organized a mass of up-state Illinois supporters to travel to Chicago, flood the venue and surrounding streets, and cheer as loudly as possible for their favorite son. Although the volume of cheers plays no formal role in the proceedings, the enthusiasm for Lincoln could help build momentum.

Indeed, those delegates from Eastern states who did not initially know Lincoln's name soon knew it very well—because every time it was mentioned, it was accompanied by the ear-splitting cheers of a throng of drunken Illinoisans.

Secondly, the Republicans' rival party, the Democrats, still appear to be in a state of disarray. The rift that had developed at their convention in Charleston had thus far not been repaired, and the party remains at war with itself. Both factions—the more moderate Democrats and the Southern proslavery extremists—still plan separate conventions later in the summer, each claiming to be the "real" Democratic Party. While the outcome is not certain, some predict that the two factions would each nominate its own candidate, effectively splitting the vote.

Why is this Democratic disarray an advantage for Lincoln?

The Republicans can now sense that the Presidency is within their party's grasp. To prevail, they simply need to field a candidate who doesn't have any major flaw that could divide or alienate voters in winnable states. William Seward may have the biggest name, the most experience, and the most money, but he has a key negative: He's a Northeasterner through and through, an embodiment of the Northeastern political class, and many in the party secretly or not-so-secretly worry that his support outside New England and New York is limited. To win a general election, the Republicans need to carry western states like Ohio, Indiana, and Illinois. Meanwhile, Seward's many decades operating in the New York political establishment carry the baggage of that state's reputation for corruption and graft. As one New England Senator put it, a potential Seward administration "would be the most corrupt the country has ever witnessed."

For these reasons, an anti-Seward sentiment is spreading among some delegates and party operatives leading up to the convention.

However, the other top contenders, Governor Chase of Ohio and Edward Bates of Missouri, are also flawed. Chase's antislavery views are thought too radical to win moderate voters in border states, and some in the party also dislike him personally. Bates is well liked as a person but considered too weak on the slavery issue to galvanize the abolitionist wing of the party.

Abraham Lincoln does not have any debilitating flaws. He has strong antislavery credentials, but his name is not associated with "radical" antislavery, as Chase's is. Unlike the front-runner Seward, he is not a Northeasterner and is free of rumors of corruption. He has a base of support in the key states of Illinois and Indiana, and as one Republican newspaper said of him, there is "something in his nature . . . in his personal appearance and manners [that] commend[ed] itself to the plain simplicity of the rural populations." In other words, he could appeal to nonurban voters in every state. On top of these electoral advantages, he has a reputation for personal integrity and has few if any enemies within the party.

Lincoln and his campaign manager, David Davis, understand Lincoln's standing in relation to the others and devise a perfect strategy for it. In short, they will position Lincoln as the best *second* option for everyone. "I suppose I am not the first choice of a very great many," Lincoln explained in a letter to a friend. "Our policy, then, is to give no offence to others—leave them in a mood to come to us, if they shall be compelled to give up their first love."

According to the rules established by the party, the 466 Republican delegates will start by voting for any of the candidates in the field. To win the nomination, a candidate must receive at least 233 votes. If there is no winner after the first ballot—as is usually the case—some candidates drop out, there is a period for horse-trading, and then a second round of voting commences. The voting rounds continue for as long as it takes until someone hits the coveted number 233.

At 10:00 a.m. on Friday, May 18, the first round of voting is set to commence in the Wigwam. First, the names of every viable candidate are read aloud and formally entered on the ballot.

Here is where Lincoln's hometown advantage comes into play. When Lincoln's name is read, the packed crowd goes berserk, surpassing every other candidate in sheer noise. A journalist covering the event reports that while Seward, Chase, and others received healthy applause, when Lincoln's name was spoken, his crowd of supporters "like a wild colt with [the] bit between his teeth, rose above all cry of order, and again and again the irrepressible applause broke forth and resounded far and wide."

That's a pretty good start for the Rail Splitter.

Still, Seward is the favorite. Despite the rising enthusiasm in the room for Lincoln, Seward's team are sure that their more sophisticated political operation and greater name recognition will seal his victory.

As they'll see in the next few hours, they couldn't be more wrong.

12

———— · ————

Springfield, Illinois

May 18, 1860

There's a strange noise coming from behind the building.

The small brick building houses the offices of the *Illinois State Journal* newspaper in Springfield, Illinois, and this is the morning of May 18—the very morning when voting is to commence at the Republican National Convention in Chicago, some two hundred miles away.

The sound behind the building is of shuffling feet on the hard dirt ground, and of a hard rubber ball bouncing on the building's brick wall.

The noise emanates from a square-shaped alleyway situated behind the newspaper's offices and adjacent to the neighboring county courthouse building.

In this alley, five grown men are playing a game known as Fives, a fast-paced sport similar to modern-day handball.

One of the men is much taller than the rest, his long arms and legs flailing as he races toward the ball to hit it. This player, a regular, had stopped by on his way to the small office where he worked a few blocks away, the law firm Lincoln & Herndon.

Yes, on the morning he's in a tightly contested race to win the Republican Presidential nomination, Abraham Lincoln is playing handball.

Lincoln has always loved games and sports, and he is a regular in this alley, along with a few copy editors from the newspaper and clerks from the courthouse. The group sometimes meets to play in the morning, or during lunch breaks. Whether the unusually tall and skinny middle-aged lawyer was any good at the game was a matter of dispute. One of the players said of Lincoln, "His long arms and long legs served a good purpose in reaching and returning the ball from every angle."

Another player, one of the county clerks, was a little less generous: "Mr. Lincoln was not a good player. He learned the game when he was too old." And another said that the lanky lawyer's "leaps, and strides to strike the ball were comical in the extreme." But the players all agreed on Lincoln's enthusiasm for the game: He was "as vigorously engaged in the sport as though life depended upon it." One of them remembered that "he would play until nearly exhausted."

On this particular morning, Lincoln finishes the game at around 10:00 a.m. and says a goodbye to his fellow players.

Of course, Lincoln knows full well that today is the day Republican delegates in Chicago will choose the party nominee. For the past few days, he's been receiving regular updates from his team on the ground. Earlier in the morning, he had stopped by the *Journal*'s offices to see if there were any early updates, but the paper had not yet received telegrams from Chicago. So, a quick game of Fives was as good a way to pass the time as any.

In the warm spring air, Lincoln walks the short distance to his small law offices on the corner of Sixth and Adams Streets in downtown Springfield.

He has become a beloved fixture of the city, this tall, gangly, sometimes odd, but always affable man who was a U.S. Congressman and is now a successful lawyer, but who still milks his own cow and chops his own wood.

Lincoln first moved to Springfield over two decades earlier, in 1837, during his first term as a state legislator. At the time, it was the brand-new state capital, a picturesque, medium-sized city dominated by state politics—the perfect city for Lincoln to call his home.

As a teenager and young man, Lincoln had always been awkward and shy when it came to women and romance. Insecure because of his gawky appearance and consistently unfashionable wardrobe, he was for a time convinced no woman would ever be attracted to him. When he first came to Springfield, his losing streak continued. "I have been spoken to by but one woman since I've been here, and should not have been by her, if she could have avoided it," he glumly wrote to one of his friends.

But it was here, in this city, that he eventually met and courted his future wife, Mary Todd Lincoln. They were married in November 1842 and soon after started a family. They were an odd couple, to be sure. She was from a wealthy Kentucky family, raised with social graces and a fashionable wardrobe. She was attractive, if unusually short. In other words, she seemed to be Lincoln's opposite in every possible way. Yet they were deeply devoted to each other.

Eight years later, tragedy struck the young family when their second son, Eddie, died less than a month before his fourth birthday. Both parents were devastated—and for Abraham Lincoln, this was now the fourth sudden death of an immediate family member. Eventually, the Lincolns had two more boys, Willie and Tad, who joined the eldest, Robert Todd, to complete the family.

By the late 1840s, after serving three terms in the state legislature and one in Congress, Lincoln determined he would retire from politics and devote all his time to practicing law and raising his family in Springfield. During this time, he could often be seen walking the streets near his home, pulling a red wagon behind him with the two youngest boys in it with one hand, and reading a law book with the other.

On weekends, he often let the boys play in his office, much to the annoyance of his longtime law partner, William Herndon, who found the boys to be a menace to their workplace. "These children would take down the books, . . . inkstands, papers, gold pens, letters, etc., in a pile and then dance on the pile. Lincoln would say nothing," he groused. Herndon admitted that he "wanted to wring their little necks," but Lincoln was too fond of them to stop the mischief. Perhaps because he himself grew up in such tough conditions and with so stern a father, he showered his sons with affection at a time when the norm was to raise children with harsh discipline. "It is my pleasure that my children are free and happy, and unrestrained by parental tyranny," Lincoln once said. "Love is the chain whereby to bind a child to its parents."

Now, at 10:30 a.m. on the morning of the momentous Republican National Convention in Chicago, Lincoln is in that same small law office in Springfield passing the time with the same partner, Herndon. At the moment, both are deeply invested in what's happening upstate and have trouble focusing. For the next hour or so, they both only pretend to work.

Then, just before noon, the editor of the *Illinois State Journal,* Edward Baker, bursts through the front door of the office with a fresh telegram from Chicago. The results of the first ballot are in. The group huddles and reads the numbers on the leading contenders:

Seward: 173.5 votes*
Lincoln: 102 votes
Chase: 49 votes
Bates: 48 votes

Seward is ahead, but well short of the 233 required. Lincoln is in a strong second place. This is better than expected. The poor showing from Chase and Bates also opens the door for Lincoln's "second favorite" strategy to work: If delegates who voted for Chase, Bates, and others in the first round will switch to Lincoln rather than Seward, he can close the gap.

Lincoln remains somewhat skeptical, but is now excited enough to join Baker on a walk to the local telegraph office to see if any other messages have arrived. After waiting for a while at the telegraph office with no further news, the group impatiently heads to the *Journal* offices to wait. Soon, more of Lincoln's friends and advisors join them.

The answer comes within an hour.

---

* Based on the party's arcane mathematical system for apportioning delegates at the time, some states were afforded half delegates for balloting purposes.

13

Springfield, Illinois

An audible gasp rises from the offices of the *Illinois State Journal*. A messenger from the telegraph office has just arrived. The results of the second ballot are in:

Seward: 184.5
Lincoln: 181
Chase: 24.5
Bates: 35

Lincoln is now only a few votes behind Seward. The other main contenders, Chase and Bates, have drifted further behind. The strategy in Chicago is working exactly as planned. Lincoln picked up delegates not just from Bates and Chase but from several other minor candidates who dropped out after the first round.

Most important, Seward seems to have hit a ceiling—and Lincoln now has the momentum.

Excitement mounts. After another tense hour of waiting, the courier returns with a new telegram. The third ballot results are in, and it's now all but a two-person race:

Lincoln has 231.5 votes; Seward has 180.

Seward has actually *lost* delegates, and Lincoln has surged ahead. He's now 1.5 votes away from the nomination. It doesn't seem real, but a few minutes later, another telegram arrives with a quick update: A handful of delegates have just moved to have their third ballot votes for Seward transferred to Lincoln, therefore pushing him over the threshold. Right after that, another telegram arrives, this one directly from one of Lincoln's supporters in Chicago.

It says, simply: "We did it—Glory to God."

The newsroom erupts.

Abraham Lincoln is the Republican nominee for President of the United States. It's an incredible upset.

Up in Chicago, of course, the Midwestern Lincoln supporters in attendance at the Wigwam let loose. "Illinois, Indiana, and Ohio delegates seemed wild. They acted like madmen," a journalist writes. Another attendee, perhaps prone to a bit of overstatement, writes that after Lincoln's victory, he heard in the Wigwam "a peal of human voices, a grand chorus of exultation, the like[s] of which has not been heard on earth since the morning stars first sang together, and the sons of God shouted for joy."

Back in Springfield, the grand chorus of exultation is at first limited to those in the office of the *Illinois State Journal.* When Lincoln and his friends walk outside, Lincoln's first stop—naturally—is the alley behind the building so he can share the news with his fellow handball players. By the time he and his companions walk back out to the streets, word has spread, and soon the tall, skinny nominee is surrounded by a growing crowd of cheering well-wishers.

Lincoln doesn't stay long in the streets, however, for there is somewhere else he must be. "Well, gentlemen, there is a little woman at our house who is probably more interested in this dispatch than I am," he tells his friends. He heads straight home, in time for dinner.

Too bad the people of Springfield aren't ready to go home. As the sky grows dark, an exuberant rally assembles in front of the downtown statehouse to celebrate the city's hometown hero. "The hearty western populace burst forth in the wildest manifestations of joy . . . Lincoln banners, decked in every style of rude splendor, fluttered in the high west wind." Borrowing from the symbolism of the campaign, over a hundred revelers had brought along wooden fence rails and leaned them in rows along the statehouse walls.

Eventually, as the evening wears on, the rally forms a parade and marches through the Springfield streets to Lincoln's modest home. The crowd calls for him to make an appearance.

The tall candidate finally emerges, acknowledging everyone's excitement. When he speaks a few words, he deflects the glory away from himself, saying he "did not suppose the honor of such a visit was intended particularly for himself . . . but rather the representation of a great party."

At that, he throws open his front door, and the revelers stream into his house for a celebration.

While Springfield and Illinois celebrate, the surprise results of the convention spread through the rest of the country. That night, a *New York Times* reporter in Chicago covering the event sends back a special dispatch that characterizes the former frontiersman's unlikely victory this way:

"The youngster who, with ragged trousers, used barefoot to drive his father's oxen and spend his day splitting rails, has risen to high eminence . . . ABRAM LINCOLN, of Illinois, is declared its candidate for President by the National Republican Party."

Lincoln just won the nomination to be President of the United States—and they're still getting his name wrong.

14

Baltimore, Maryland

May 1860

There is a single, distinct knock on the door of the "castle." This is called an *11*.

The knock comes at a carefully designated time. A meeting, or ceremony, is set to begin.

The door opens, and the person who knocked steps in. He's a white man, since only white men are allowed. The one who opens the door to receive him does not greet the knocker but instead makes a gesture, running his forefinger along his upper lip. This is a *9*.

The man at the door also doesn't speak, but seeing the gesture, makes one of his own: one hand raised up, palm forward. This is a *15*.

The hand symbol indicates that the one now arriving is a *Knight*, and as such may now enter the castle.

The castle is not a literal castle; it's a clubhouse or lodge of sufficient size to serve as secret headquarters where meetings and ceremonies occur. Only Knights know the exact location of a castle and have sworn oaths not to share the location with any outsider. Similarly, Knights must never divulge their signals and numerical codes.

Why all the mystery? Why the secret locations?

These are members of a secret society: the Knights of the Golden Circle.

The designated "castles" are where local chapters meet. Castles exist in cities and towns throughout the South, and a few in Northern states too. In Texas alone, there are reputed to be more than thirty castles, with at least one in every major city.

Here in Maryland, membership is not as large as it is in states farther south, but the Baltimore chapter is something of a hub and enjoys fervent support. A city newspaper recently reported that more than one thousand members of the mysterious organization gathered in the city, many of them local residents from "respectable families."

One writer claiming to have been a member describes a local castle as a private mansion on Monument Avenue—in one of the city's wealthier neighborhoods—but this claim has not been verified. At least one castle is known to exist in the south central neighborhood near St. Vincent's Church.

The initiation ceremonies are notoriously complex. Once an initiate becomes a Knight, he is placed in one of three "Orders," which are further divided into a hierarchy of "Degrees." As members climb the hierarchy, they acquire elaborate titles known only to members above themselves.

Behind the ceremonies and symbols, the group is united by a shared purpose: upholding Southern pride and supporting Southern rights. Or to put it more bluntly, supporting *white* Southern pride and *white* Southern rights. Knights who are slaveholders gain extra respect in the group, and a special hand signal is used to indicate this status. The supremacy of the white race is an essential creed of the organization and is tied to the group's mission.

Recently, membership in the group has surged. Never before in America's history has the Southern "way of life"—in other words, slavery—been so threatened, and the Knights of the Golden Circle stand ready to defend it. The coming Presidential election, with a Northern antislavery candidate from Illinois now officially on the Republican ballot, has further intensified the group's mission.

Behind their veil of secrecy, the Knights of the Golden Circle has grand visions for how to strengthen the institutions and culture of the South. To do so, these member Knights must be organized, they must be loyal, and they must be trained.

In addition to memorizing the group's complex web of hand signals and codes, Knights must also adhere to an important rule: When in public, they should carry somewhere on their persons a loaded revolver and a sharpened bowie knife.

Sometimes, upholding Southern values means being ready for the coming fight.

15

Late May 1860

A man in his late forties sits at a desk in western New York. He has piercing brown eyes, dark skin, and abundant hair. At the top of a blank page, he writes these words: "The nomination of Mr. Lincoln has taken the people of this part of the Country by surprise."

He continues writing. In a few days, his words will appear in print, in a newspaper he himself publishes.

His name is Frederick Douglass. For the past decade and a half, he's been one of the most influential and well-known American abolitionists—and one of the most influential and well-known Americans, period.

Douglass's life story was first chronicled in his bestselling 1845 memoir, *Narrative of the Life of Frederick Douglass, an American Slave.* It became one of the iconic narratives of the day, reaching readers all over the United States and Europe.

Douglass was born into slavery on a small plantation in Talbot County, Maryland, a few miles east of the Chesapeake Bay. He was immediately separated from his mother and never knew his birth date, his birth year, or the identity of his father. From fellow slaves, he learned that his father was white, but he could never verify if it was his own enslaver or another white slaveholder who raped his mother.

Frederick Douglass, circa 1860, more than twenty years after his escape from slavery. A leader in the abolitionist movement, Douglass was one of the most influential writers and speakers of his day.

In the first few years of his life, he was aware that his mother was enslaved as a field hand on a plantation twelve miles away. On a few occasions, she traveled those miles by foot in the middle of the night to see her child for a few hours—then would make the return trip before sunrise to avoid the brutal whipping she would receive if the trip were discovered.

She died when he was seven, and he knew nothing of her illness, death, or burial.

Douglass spent his entire youth and teenage years in bondage. He was moved frequently on the whim of the extended family that enslaved him, shuttling between rural plantations and farms, as well as to homes in Baltimore. Unlike many who grow up in bondage, Douglass experienced slavery in several different forms, and bore witness to a wide range of its horrors.

As a young boy, one of his earliest memories is of an overseer regularly and repeatedly whipping his own young aunt.

> I have often been awakened at the dawn of day by the most heart-rending shrieks of an own aunt of mine, whom he used to tie up to a joist, and whip upon her naked back 'til she was literally covered with blood. No words, no tears, no prayers, from his gory victim, seemed to move his iron heart from its bloody purpose. The louder she screamed, the harder he whipped; and where the blood ran fastest, there he whipped longest . . . not until overcome by fatigue, would he cease to swing the blood-clotted cowskin.

As Douglass later described, bearing witness to such atrocities as a child, and being helpless to prevent them, was his first initiation into a life of bondage. It was, he wrote, "the blood-stained gate, the entrance to the hell of slavery, through which I was about to pass."

As a boy and teenager, Douglass himself endured periods of unspeakable suffering, and yet through sheer acts of will found moments to improve his mind. During a period when he was transferred to Baltimore to work as a "house slave" in a well-to-do home, he embarked on a forbidden mission: to learn how to read and write.

He did so at enormous personal risk. Such an act was grounds for harsh punishment. Douglass's enslaver said to him at the time: "A nigger should know nothing but to obey his master—to do as he is told to do. Learning would spoil the best nigger in the world."

But for a naturally gifted and curious child, learning to read and write gave him an understanding of his own condition—and a fierce desire to overcome it. "I distinctly remember being, even then, most strongly impressed with the idea of being a free man some day," he later wrote. "It was an inborn dream of my human nature . . . and one which all the powers of slavery were unable to silence or extinguish."

In his midteens, when he was transferred back to the rural plantations, Douglass's newfound restlessness made him defiant in the eyes of his enslavers. His overseer sent him to spend time with a local "slave-breaker," whose job was to beat and whip slaves into submission.

During this period of hellish torture, it was the desperate longing for freedom that provided a sliver of hope. "I often found myself regretting my own existence, and wishing myself dead," Douglass wrote, "and but for the hope of being free, I have no doubt but that I should have killed myself, or done something for which I should have been killed."

In 1838, at roughly the age of twenty, Douglass fled from bondage. It was a daring escape, by foot and train, planned over many months, involving forged documents. The plan easily could have failed, as it did for countless others.

Eventually, Douglass settled as a fugitive in New Bedford, Massachusetts, with his wife, a free black woman who helped him escape, and their growing family.

Here, Douglass became involved with local antislavery groups. The white abolitionist leader William Lloyd Garrison, publisher of the abolitionist journal *The Liberator,* saw something special in Douglass, and in 1841 invited him to speak at a public event about his years in bondage.

The response set the course for the rest of his life.

Douglass had a gift for language, and a powerful speaking voice that captivated the crowd. As Garrison's newspaper reported afterward, "Many persons in the audience . . . could not believe that he was actually a slave. How a man, only six years out of bondage, and who had never gone to school a day in his life, could speak with such eloquence—with such precision of language and power of thought—they were utterly at a loss to devise."

Still in his twenties, he threw himself into the antislavery cause. He would fight for a world where no child would have to enter that "blood-stained gate" into slavery that he himself had endured.

From there, he became a sought-after speaker, wrote and published his first memoir at the age of twenty-seven, and put out his own abolitionist newspaper, *The North Star,* the first of four he would edit and publish. He wrote countless articles, essays, and speeches to critique and comment upon the politics of the day, always with a focus on the great cause of his life: ending slavery.

Now, in the late spring of 1860, after a long stay in Europe, Douglass has just returned to his home in Rochester, New York. The timing of his return is fortunate, because, as he later recalls, "it enabled me to participate in the most important and memorable presidential canvass ever witnessed in the United States."

In the wake of the Chicago convention, many wonder what Douglass thinks of the Republican Party's unexpected nominee, Abraham Lincoln.

That's why he now sits, quill in hand, putting his thoughts into writing.

After remarking on Lincoln's surprise win, Douglass tells his readers what he knows of the dark horse candidate: "Mr. Lincoln is a man of unblemished private character; a lawyer, standing near the front rank at the bar of his own State; has a cool, well balanced head; great firmness of will; is perseveringly industrious; and one of the most frank, honest men in political life."

Nonetheless, Douglass has reservations.

Lincoln, like the Republican Party in general, claims to be against slavery, but is not a true abolitionist. Although Lincoln speaks often about the moral wrong of slavery—and bases his candidacy upon preventing the spread of slavery into new territories—his official position is that the federal government doesn't have the power to end slavery in states where it already exists. To do so, according to Lincoln, is unconstitutional because it violates the states' rights to enforce their own property laws. And slaves, as defined by the laws of Southern states, are property.

For Douglass, this position is infuriating. In one of his earlier speeches about the Constitution, Douglass declared:

The language is, "We the People"; not we the white people, not even we the citizens, not we the privileged class, not we the high, not we the low, but we the people; not we the horses, sheep, and swine, and wheelbarrows, but we the people, we the human inhabitants; and if Negroes are people, they are included in the benefits for which the Constitution of America was ordained and established.

In Douglass's view, Lincoln and other Republicans fail to honor this basic truth.

What's more, even in Lincoln's many antislavery speeches, he never advocates for full equality for blacks and whites. Depending on the audience, he sometimes argues the opposite: that differences between whites and blacks will "forever forbid the two races living together in terms of social and political equality." Lincoln, at this point, does not voice support for black suffrage, black service in the military, or other key rights of citizenship.

So when it comes to Lincoln and the Republicans, Douglass laments that their approach to fighting slavery resembles the "slow process of a cautious siege" rather than "the more brave and inspiring march of a storming party." Most important, "it is to be regretted that they will not come up to the glorious work of striking the shackles from four million slaves at a single blow."

Still, in the battle against slavery, every step forward matters. Abraham Lincoln has a good chance to be President, and he's stated clearly that slavery is *wrong*. No recent American President has made this declaration. That alone is grounds for hope. But it doesn't guarantee success.

For Douglass and other abolitionists, the Republican Party's nominee is an unknown. Will Abraham Lincoln be a genuine ally—or just another politician who'll turn his back on the cause?

16

———•———

Springfield, Illinois

May 19, 1860

Frederick Douglass isn't the only one carefully watching Lincoln's unexpected nomination. The rest of the country is watching too.

In the press, the Democratic Party quickly goes on the offensive and ridicules the little-known Illinoisan who is now their rival for the Presidency. The insults are personal: "Lincoln is the leanest, lankest, most ungainly mass of legs, arms, and hatchet-face ever strung upon a single frame. He has most unwarrantably abused the privilege which all politicians have of being ugly," one Democratic paper writes.

The wealthy Southern planter class finds easy fodder in Lincoln's rough-hewn manners and lack of formal schooling. He is, as one Southern writer soon puts it, "without a respectable education, or that civil and social culture, which frequently imparts refinement to the conduct of a gentleman." One Democratic newspaper describes him as a "third-rate Western lawyer"; another calls him a "fourth-rate lecturer."

While the Democrats debate where Lincoln falls in the range between third-rate and fourth-rate, many Republicans across the country also express concern regarding their party's choice of nominee. New York Republicans were said to "shed bitter tears" after Lincoln's victory, and even a member of Lincoln's team would later admit that "a great portion of the East were known to be dissatisfied at his nomination."

The day after the nomination, May 19, a delegation of top party officials come directly from the Chicago convention to meet Lincoln before traveling home to their respective states. Most of them have never met Lincoln, or even seen him in person.

At roughly 8:00 p.m., the delegation arrives in quiet Springfield, and the group finds its way to the Lincoln home. These are mostly finely dressed Easterners, well-heeled party higher-ups who are used to mingling with the wealthy and powerful in the nation's capital. Now, here they are in the middle of Illinois—farther west than most of them had ever been—knocking on the small front door of a modest wooden home.

When the door opens, the men are further irritated to be met not by their chosen nominee but by two scruffy "ragamuffins," the young boys Willie and Tad Lincoln, who pull the men into their home.

"Mr. Lincoln received us in the parlor of his modest frame house," one committee member named Carl Schurz later recalls, into "a rather bare-looking room." If the modesty of Lincoln's home and furnishing are a surprise to the visitors, they are more surprised by the look of Lincoln himself: "There he stood," in Schurz's words, "tall and ungainly in his black suit of apparently new but ill-fitting clothes, his long tawny neck emerging gauntly from his turn-down collar, his melancholy eyes sunk deep in his haggard face."

For a moment, the men stand around awkwardly. Then the leader of the committee, George Ashmun, clears his throat and gives an obligatory "dignified little speech" in which he formally offers the committee's support for their new nominee. Lincoln responds with a few "earnest, and well-shaped sentences" in which he thanks the party members and modestly conveys the "doubts of his own abilities."

The awkwardness continues, the men pretending not to stare. "Most of the members of the Committee had never seen him before, and gazed at him with surprised curiosity," Schurz recalled. "He certainly did not present the appearance of a statesman, as people usually picture it in their imagination."

Lincoln, however, is quite familiar with the reaction many people have when they first meet him in person. As the men stand in silence, he decides to use one of his favorite tricks to change the mood. Tell a joke.

He looks around to determine the second-tallest person in the room—he himself is *always* the tallest—who in this case is William D. Kelley, the head of the Pennsylvania delegation. Seemingly out of nowhere, Lincoln bluntly asks Kelley in front of everyone how tall he is.

Kelley is taken aback, but answers that he is nearly six foot three.

Lincoln smiles broadly and says with great enthusiasm, "I beat you. I am six feet four without my high-heeled boots."

This lighthearted reference to his height breaks the tension of the room. Kelley has the perfect response: "I am glad that we have found a candidate for the Presidency whom we can look up to."

The group laughs and relaxes. As one of them puts it, "Then followed some informal talk, partly of a jovial kind, in which the hearty simplicity of Lincoln's nature shone out."

The host invites the group to the dining room to sit for food and refreshments. Whatever awkwardness remains is alleviated by the appearance of Mary Todd, whose Southern manners and witty banter quickly charm the room.

By the time dinner is over, the committee has a generally favorable impression.

Still, as the group leaves the Lincoln home, there remains among them an uneasy feeling about their choice of nominee. As Schurz later describes, "An undertone of resignation and of suppressed doubt was perceptible. Some of them, who . . . saw Mr. Lincoln for the first time, could not quite conceal their misgivings as to how this single-minded man, this child of nature, would bear himself in the contact with the great world."

Some version of this misgiving is shared not just by the Republican Party leadership but by many other Americans of all political persuasions. The stakes of the coming election could not be higher. The country is divided as never before. The great moral question of slavery hangs over the land. Does this Illinoisan, Abraham Lincoln, possess the qualities of leadership this moment in history demands?

This concern is perhaps captured best by a Republican Party member who, upon learning the results of the convention, reportedly berated one of the delegates who attended: "You fellows knew at Chicago what this country was facing . . . You knew that above everything else, these times demanded a statesman and you have gone and given us a *rail splitter.*"

17

⸺ • ⸺

Baltimore, Maryland

July 1860

In Barnum's City Hotel in Baltimore, many prosperous gentlemen frequent a small business that operates on the hotel's basement floor.

It's a barbershop.

Here, well-heeled men of all ages converge to fraternize and gossip while receiving the careful hairdressing and beard-grooming seen on the heads and faces of the wealthier classes.

Because this is 1860, wherever men gather to talk, they talk politics.

At the time, Baltimore is a complicated city. With a population of more than two hundred thousand, it's the fourth-largest city in the United States, and the largest south of Pennsylvania. Its crowded streets, manufacturing base, and busy commercial ports bear resemblance to industrial northern coastal cities like New York and Boston. Geographically, Baltimore is only one hundred miles southwest of the northern city of Philadelphia and is less than forty miles from the nation's capital.

But Maryland is a slave state. And culturally, Baltimore is very much a city of the South.

In fact, Baltimore's port is a key hub in the nation's domestic slave trade. A city directory from the era lists "Slave Dealers" alphabetically between "Silversmiths" and "soap." Several large "slave pens," jail-like structures where enslaved persons are held in brutal conditions before being shipped or traded, line the waterfront district.

On bustling Pratt Street, a common sight throughout the day is the procession of groups of shackled black men, women, and children being led by traders to the slave ships in the port. From here, many of the ships will travel to New Orleans, where the enslaved are put on auction blocks to be sold to slaveholders throughout the cotton states.

So politically, Baltimore is adamantly proslavery. The young white men of the city—some of them scions of wealthy families who profit directly from the slave trade—usually adopt the dress, manners, and values of Southern gentlemen.

These are the sorts of men who visit the barbershop in Barnum's Hotel.*

When the discussion is about politics, there is, no doubt, much talk about the Southern cause, the need to preserve Southern institutions, and a visceral hatred of Northerners, abolitionists, and their loathsome new "Black Republican" Presidential candidate Abraham Lincoln.

Interestingly, one of the most outspoken voices in the barbershop is not one of these customers but the barber himself. On political matters, his eloquence is striking. His Southern accent is clear and melodious, and his words rise and fall with passion.

This barber, in his late thirties, has a name not typical for a man of the South: Cypriano Ferrandini.

He was born in Corsica, a Mediterranean island with a complicated history under both French and Italian rule. After immigrating to the United States in his youth, he has lived the better part of two decades in Maryland, vigorously embracing the values and codes of the American South. He has been the barber at Barnum's for at least a dozen years. Despite his relatively working-class job, he socializes in

---

* The official name of the establishment is Barnum's City Hotel, but in common parlance it is often referred to as "Barnum's Hotel," "the Barnum Hotel," or simply "Barnum's."

wealthy circles. He has natural charisma and charm. He is a regular at the hotel's posh lounge and belongs to at least one of the social clubs in the city.

Ferrandini also belongs to another club, but one he cannot speak of with customers—unless they happen to be fellow members.

He's a member of the Knights of the Golden Circle.

Lately, this mysterious group has been getting more and more attention, and more details about their organization have become known to the public.

The Knights of the Golden Circle was founded in the mid-1850s by a Virginia-born doctor and white supremacist named George Bickley. The organization—often abbreviated as the KGC—was devoted from the outset to the objective of maintaining "southern values," which really meant the institution of slavery, at all costs.

A decorative seal of the Knights of the Golden Circle, the white supremacist secret society formed in the 1850s. The group's goal was to create a slave empire that began in the American South and extended south through Mexico and east through the Caribbean Islands.

The group was formed with a vision that stands out from the standard proslavery agenda. Drawing inspiration from earlier movements based in Texas, Bickley believed that the American South should expand militarily below the Texas border and spread slavery to Mexico and into other southern territories. The ultimate goal was to form a small slave empire that would encompass the Southern states but also extend to Cuba and the West Indies to the Southeast, as well as through Mexico to Central America.

This Southern empire—a slave empire—would form the hallowed "Golden Circle" of the group's name.

According to newspaper estimates as well as the group's own proclamations, in 1860, the KGC boasts tens of thousands of dues-paying members, possibly as many as forty thousand. Members carry special badges and seals. Much like the Ku Klux Klan years later, the group's membership is reputed to include Southern and Midwestern politicians, business leaders, and other prominent citizens.

Ferrandini joined the KGC in the summer of 1859. Based on the known dates on record, his initiation probably occurred during a convention that the group held in Montgomery, Alabama. Not much is known about his specific role in the organization, but he took a trip to Mexico several months after joining that was probably connected to the group's grand plans of southern expansion into that country.

Why a Corsican immigrant would be so drawn to the cause of Southern white supremacy in the United States is, to this day, something of a mystery. For reasons that may never be entirely known, he threw himself into the pro-Southern politics of the day with passion and fury.

In the fall of 1860, this fury—and the fury of most Baltimoreans—is directed at the coming election. They can see that the Northern Republicans, with their antislavery candidate from Illinois, are in a position to win the Presidency. If so, Southern honor and Southern values are at risk. The institution of slavery is at risk. Ferrandini and his customers surely agree on one thing: Whatever happens, the South cannot submit. If Abraham Lincoln wins the election, they must find a way to stop him.

In the barbershop of Barnum's City Hotel, the white gentlemen of Baltimore talk about all of this, their voices rising with emotion. The patrons leave the shop flush with passion and full of Southern pride.

They also leave with stylish haircuts—for Cypriano Ferrandini is an accomplished barber.

But the number one thing they leave with? An idea.

18

—·—

Chicago, Illinois

August 1860

Election fever has swept the nation—and it's no different for Allan Pinkerton.

Nearly every city, every town, and every county across the states hold political rallies, picnics, speeches, parades, and other events in anticipation of the coming Presidential contest, each with different regional interests and attitudes.

But Chicago detective Allan Pinkerton? His view of the contest is simple and clear:

He absolutely abhors slavery.

Having grown up in near poverty in Scotland, where poor laborers at the time were exploited and treated as expendable—and having been one of those exploited laborers himself—Pinkerton had an instant and powerful hatred of the institution of slavery in America.

He is a man who lives by a strict moral code, and slavery violates that code in every way. "The institution of human bondage always received my most earnest opposition," he would later write. "Believing it to be a curse to the American nation, and as evidence of barbarism, no efforts of mine were ever spared in behalf of the slave."

His devotion to ending this barbarism was unyielding, and he never wavered from it. And unlike many others who opposed slavery in the abstract, Pinkerton threw himself into the cause at great personal risk.

Almost as soon as he and his wife had first arrived in small-town Illinois and set up his cooper shop, he searched for ways to aid the antislavery cause. In no time, his small home became a stopping place on the legendary Underground Railroad, which helped the enslaved escape, hide, and find freedom.

On regular occasions, he and his wife housed and fed runaway slaves traveling north toward the Canadian border. "I have assisted in security and freedom for the fugitive slave, no matter at what hour, under what circumstances, or at what cost, the act was to be performed," he wrote.

Since the passage of the Fugitive Slave Act in 1850, aiding escaped slaves was a federal crime and Pinkerton risked arrest each time he did so.

Remarkably, after becoming a law enforcement officer and eventually a sheriff, Pinkerton continued to play a role in the Underground Railroad, and in fact became instrumental.

Once he and his family moved to Chicago, his modest clapboard two-story home on Adams Street—already crowded with the Pinkertons' six children—often housed several escaped men, women, and children at once. Sometimes, they slept under floorboards and in closets. He became personal friends with prominent black and white abolitionist leaders in Chicago, who reliably turned to him for money, shelter, and organizational assistance.

On one particular night in March of 1859, Pinkerton heard a knock at his door at 4:30 a.m. He opened it to find the legendary radical white abolitionist John Brown standing there, with nine escaped slaves behind him whom he had personally escorted to freedom through three states. The fugitives included a tiny infant, carried by the mother, who had given birth along the journey.

Without hesitation, Pinkerton took in the entire group, set them up to sleep, and he and his wife prepared a hot meal for them. They helped care for the infant and the mother. That morning, Pinkerton went out and personally raised money for their travels. With the help of his teenage son, he arranged with a local railroad depot to hide the group and ferry them aboard a cargo train heading farther north.

At the time, John Brown was a wanted criminal in multiple states, with rewards out for his capture. Any public association with him could have gotten Pinkerton arrested, ending his career. Yet Pinkerton considered Brown a personal idol, never failing to work with him.

As Pinkerton himself described it, John Brown "was my bosom friend, and more than one dark night has found us working earnestly together in behalf of the fleeing bondsman who was striving for his liberty." Even after Brown was sentenced to death in late 1859 for leading his notorious attempted slave insurrection in Harpers Ferry, Virginia (present-day West Virginia), that shocked the nation, Pinkerton praised him and considered him a national hero.

In a sense, the detective was living a paradox. As one admirer put it, "While Pinkerton's right hand caught lawbreakers, his left hand broke the law." But Pinkerton didn't see it as a contradiction. He believed without question he was doing the right thing—the "lawful" thing in a higher sense—and that's all that mattered. As he later stated regarding his illegal work for the Underground Railroad, "I have not a single regret for the course I then pursued."

As someone active in the antislavery cause, Pinkerton must have placed hope in the coming election. He was not publicly involved in Republican politics, but his adamant opposition to slavery made clear which side he was on.

Like many others in abolitionist circles, he wondered: Would America finally elect a President who could end this "curse" that caused such immeasurable suffering?

Still, in the summer and early fall of 1860, while Pinkerton was no doubt pondering the great moral questions raised by the election, he was almost impossibly busy.

In the past few years, Pinkerton's private detective firm has expanded and thrived, with field offices now in several states. He has a larger staff and greater resources. His Chicago-based company is now truly a national entity, and Pinkerton's personal reputation and notoriety have grown with it.

A year earlier, in 1859, his team had won widespread attention for solving a headline-grabbing crime involving the mysterious theft of $40,000 from Adams Express, a popular railroad-based delivery service. After studying the circumstances, Pinkerton deduced that the theft was an inside job—the guilty party was a stationmaster named Nathan Maroney who worked in the company's Montgomery, Alabama, field office. The fact that Maroney was the scion of a wealthy Southern family made the case extra sensitive. To establish sufficient evidence for a prosecution, Pinkerton had to set up an elaborate months-long sting operation that involved several agents going undercover in multiple cities.

The hero of the investigation, however, was Pinkerton's newly hired detective Kate Warne. To investigate the case, Warne went undercover as the wife of a wealthy businessman, moving to Jenkintown, Pennsylvania, where Maroney's wife, a society woman, was staying at a boardinghouse. Pinkerton's team suspected that Maroney's wife had secret access to the stolen $40,000, and Warne's job was to befriend the woman and locate it.

Checking in at the same boardinghouse, Warne posed as a fellow socialite—complete with elegant wardrobe and aristocratic Southern accent—gaining an introduction to her. Over the course of several weeks, Warne became her close friend and confidante, and the normally tight-lipped woman began sharing information with Warne about her husband, which Warne steadily passed along to her colleagues.

Warne and her Pinkerton coworkers eventually set up a complicated scheme in which Warne convinced the wife to provide a cash payment to a legal fixer who promised to procure her husband's innocence—but who was in reality another undercover Pinkerton agent.

Sure enough, the wife accessed bills from the stolen stash to pay the fixer. These bills would prove to be the key physical evidence in her husband's trial. Eventually, he was found guilty, and the money was returned.

Warne proved two things during the operation. First, as she'd said in her initial job interview with Pinkerton, she showed that women detectives could indeed "be most useful worming out secrets in many places which would be impossible for male detectives to gain access." Second, she proved that she herself was a superb agent who could handle a high-pressure, complicated case. As Pinkerton put it, Warne "succeeded far beyond my utmost expectations."

From there, Pinkerton quickly hired more women detectives, and even created a unit within his agency called the Female Detective Bureau. Naturally, he put Kate Warne in charge of it.

Now, by the fall of 1860, Allan Pinkerton's firm is at the height of its powers.

As he's about to find out, he'll need them. The future of the country hangs in the balance.

19

Springfield, Illinois

September 1860

Abraham Lincoln is frustrated.

In the nineteenth century, unlike today, Presidential candidates in the major parties were expected to refrain from making public statements or appearances. Instead, party surrogates campaigned and gave speeches, while the actual candidates remained aloof and worked only behind the scenes.

This was highly unnatural for Lincoln, whose own brand of politics was of the retail variety, giving speeches on soapboxes, shaking every hand, and often inviting constituents into his home. Running for President, he is almost totally removed from the people voting for him.

Also unlike in modern elections, Lincoln doesn't choose his own running mate. This decision was already made for him back at the Chicago convention, where the delegates chose Senator Hannibal Hamlin of Maine for Vice President.

Before the convention Lincoln had never before met Hamlin, never corresponded with him, and knew little about him. Aside from one meeting that took place shortly after the convention, there are no plans for them to meet or talk before the general election.

Oh, and there's one other thing utterly frustrating to Lincoln:

People are still spelling his name wrong. He's the likely front-runner to be President of the United States, but some campaign flags look like this:

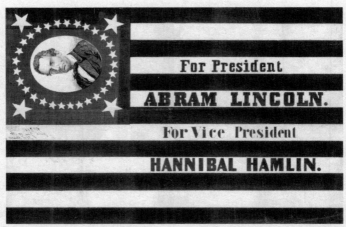

One of many campaign flags for Lincoln's 1860 Presidential race. Some members of the press, as well as some officials in his own party, continue to misspell his first name even in the heat of the campaign.

Despite these setbacks, Lincoln never stops working.

His small law office is immediately overwhelmed by visitors and, lacking anywhere else to meet the many people now coming to Springfield to visit him, he accepts an offer from Illinois Governor John Wood to set up his headquarters in a second-floor suite in the statehouse a few blocks away.

Lincoln will remain in this new office for the duration of the summer and early fall leading up to the November election, and here, surrounded by a small but growing team of loyal advisors, he conducts the around-the-clock business of being a Presidential candidate.

As a candidate, Lincoln dutifully fulfills all the obligatory rituals. Images of him are suddenly in demand all over the country, so he sits for several portraits and photographs. Because his homely looks have become something of a national punch line, one high-level Republican official commissions the renowned artist John Henry Brown to paint a portrait of Lincoln with the instruction for it to be "good-looking whether the original would justify it or not."

Lincoln handles all of this with typical self-deprecation. After he sits for a Chicago photographer, he remarks lightheartedly that the image is "a very fair representation of my homely face."

In the weeks and months following the convention, the Republican Party's East Coast leaders continue to visit, trying to get a handle on the man who is now their standard-bearer. What they find is that behind the rough exterior, the candidate is deeply versed in all aspects of policy and politics. When shortly after the convention legendary Republican Party strategist and political operative Thurlow Weed—former campaign manager of William Seward—travels to Springfield to meet Lincoln for the first time, he concludes after a long conversation that the candidate possesses "so much good sense, such intuitive knowledge of human nature, and such familiarity with the virtues and infirmities of politicians, that I became impressed very favorably with his fitness."

Another Republican official visiting from New York is astounded by Lincoln's deep understanding of local-level politics all over the country, including in regions far from Illinois. As the official describes it, Lincoln "commenced talking about political affairs in my own State with a knowledge of details which surprised me. I found he was more conversant with some of our party performances in Oneida County than I [was]."

Among many of his fellow Illinoisans, Lincoln has become something of a folk hero. As the summer turns to fall and the election draws nearer, local enthusiasm reaches a near fever pitch. When the candidate makes a rare public appearance at a rally outside Springfield to publicly thank some top supporters, the dazzled crowd afterward swarms around his carriage, preventing him from leaving until his aides are able to lift him out and get him on a horse to make his escape.

Throughout the Northern states, the enthusiasm for Lincoln grows. The fact is, the Republicans are lucky. The Democrats never were able to repair their party after the rift that split them in two at the Charleston convention. The northern wing of the party moves forward and nominates their favored candidate, Stephen Douglas. The Southern extremists nominate their own candidate, current Vice President John C. Breckinridge of Kentucky, who is staunchly pro-slavery. And to further complicate matters, a fourth-party candidate also enters the race, John Bell of Tennessee, a moderate who scarcely mentions slavery and hopes to win middle-of-the-road voters in the border states.

All of this division favors Lincoln and the Republicans, who maintain a strong hold on the North while the others seem likely to divide the vote everywhere else. As summer turns to fall, Lincoln supporters have good reason for optimism.

And yet, outside of electoral politics, there are ominous signs ahead.

The attacks on Lincoln—especially from his opponents in the South—are exceedingly vicious and ugly. Some of it is just the usual knocks about his inexperience and lack of education. He is "coarse, vulgar, and uneducated," and a "weak and unfit man for so high a place."

Beyond these minor insults, though, there is a deeper current to the animus that's rising. Lincoln is, according to Democratic and Southern newspapers, "an illiterate partisan . . . possessed only of his inveterate hatred of slavery and his openly avowed predilections for negro equality." He is an "extreme abolitionist of the revolutionary type," whose goal is "to sink the proud Anglo-Saxon and other European races into one common level with the lowest races of mankind."

If Lincoln is elected, according to one newspaper, "we shall have the nigger at the polls, the nigger on our juries, the nigger in the legislature." In a public speech before a cheering crowd, a Democratic Congressman says that by selecting Lincoln as the nominee, the Republican Party "ate nigger—they drank nigger—they slept nigger. . . . When nominating a rail splitter for the Presidency they were really resolved that they saw a nigger in the fence."

As Election Day nears, Southern fury continues to rise. For the first time in its history, America may have a President who could threaten the institution of slavery.

Until this point, Abraham Lincoln's career in politics has been based around the values of empathy, compromise, and forging bonds of common ground between people. But on the issue of slavery, there is no compromise. He is on one side of a great divide.

More and more, the rhetoric about the election is framed in violent, almost apocalyptic terms.

"As soon as Lincoln is installed into office . . . he will wave his black plume Southward," one Texas newspaper writes. "With the army and navy, and the fanatical North, he will invade us." He will "enfranchis[e] the negroes, and arm them . . . and commend us to the mercy of torch and steel."

In Alabama, two weeks before the election, the *Montgomery Weekly Mail* declares: "Let the North . . . be the home of the mixed race; and let the South be the home of the white man, proud of his race, and proud of his race's superiority! . . . If Lincoln and his free nigger outrider are elected, we must not submit."

This isn't just the language of political disagreement; this is the language of outright revolt.

The country is heading toward a storm—and Abraham Lincoln is at the center of it.

20

---·---

Springfield, Illinois

November 6, 1860

Election Day in Springfield is a whirlwind, full of intense energy and anticipation. The day begins with a cannonade and a marching band, intended to wake "whatever sluggish spirits there might be among the populace." As citizens throng to the polls, excitement surges through the streets.

Under the circumstances, Abraham Lincoln tries to maintain a relatively low profile, at least in the early part of the day. He spends the morning at his office in the statehouse, accompanied by his usual small group of allies, receiving visitors as time allows. A *New York Times* reporter stationed in the city was surprised at the candidate's low-key demeanor on the biggest day of his life, remarking that Lincoln "was chatting with three or four friends as calmly and as amiably as if he had started on a picnic."

Tradition at the time says that it is unseemly for a Presidential candidate to cast a vote for himself, and Lincoln has no intention of breaking the tradition. He is, however, determined to vote in the various local and state races also on the ballot, many of which include candidates he knows personally or had endorsed. So at approximately 3:00 p.m., Lincoln departs his makeshift office and, surrounded by allies, makes his way to the nearby county courthouse that houses the voting booth.

The sight of the candidate's entourage approaching the courthouse—Lincoln's top hat usually towers a foot above everyone near him—draws a wave of applause from the large group of voters already gathered outside the polling station. The crowd "welcomed him with immense cheering," and "followed him in dense numbers along the hall and up stairs into the Court room," where he is also met by a wild "burst of enthusiasm."

When it's Lincoln's turn, as his allies shield him from the pushing crowds, he calmly takes the Republican ballot and proceeds to the designated station. Carefully, he tears his own name from the top of the ballot so everyone can see he's not voting for himself. Then he marks the ballot straight Republican for the various local and state races.

After casting his vote, Lincoln and his team walk back to his office in the statehouse, now surrounded by crowds of well-wishers and journalists. Once settled, Lincoln and his team start receiving regular telegraphs containing early returns from around the country. Lincoln, who always relished the complicated math of election returns, begins calculating probabilities of every race in the region based on returns coming in and comparisons to previous elections.

He shows little emotion about the early returns from his own race, but he throws himself passionately into the minutiae of state and local races, so much so that, as a *New York Times* reporter put it, "one would have concluded that the District Attorneyship of a county in Illinois was of far more importance than the Presidency."

But the fact is, the early Presidential returns are mostly pointing in one direction: victory.

In almost every state in the North, the votes for Lincoln are meeting or exceeding expectations. As long as he can sweep the Northwest and carry every large state in the Northeast, the electoral map is in his favor. In the border states, where he would like to perform well but does not necessarily need the electoral votes to win, he is mostly in a three-way battle against Bell and Douglas.

Throughout the late afternoon and evening, Lincoln remains

surrounded by friends and colleagues. Telegrams come almost by the minute, bearing updated numbers and generally optimistic reports.

At roughly 9:00 p.m., when early returns arrive from New York—an essential state for Lincoln—the math becomes clear. As the numbers are posted, Lincoln's friend and fellow Republican Lyman Trumbull bursts into the room and declares:

"Uncle Abe, you're the next President, and I know it."

It's true. Abraham Lincoln will be the next President of the United States. The rest of the night is a mad blur of celebration, with Lincoln trying to thank everyone in Springfield who helped him along the way.

But by 3:00 a.m., in Lincoln's home, the wild whirlwind of a day is over.

Now, Abraham Lincoln is alone. His wife and children are quiet in bed in separate rooms. He's in his bedchamber, exhausted, but unable to sleep.

As he later described the moment, "The excitement which had kept [me] up through the campaign had passed away." Now "[I] was oppressed with the load of responsibility that was upon me."

The nation is divided, more divided than at any time since the founding. Thus far, Lincoln's only national political experience has been one term in Congress, over a decade ago. He knows there are many who believe he's unfit to lead the country.

Does he believe in himself?

Reclining in a lounge chair, alone in his dimly lit chamber, deliriously tired, Lincoln is overcome by a feeling of foreboding.

At this moment, he happens to glance at a mirror affixed to a bureau across the room. In this mirror, he sees something that disturbs him. "Looking in that glass," he'd later describe it, "I saw myself reflected nearly at full length; but my face, I noticed, had two separate and distinct images, the tip of the nose of one being about three inches from the tip of the other."

It's a double image of his face, and "one of the faces was a little paler—say five shades—than the other." When he stands up to look closer, "the illusion vanished," but when he lies on the lounge again, the double image reappears: the "ghostly face in the mirror, mocking its healthy and hopeful fellow."

Lincoln prides himself on being a man of science, a believer in rationality and progress. But sometimes, especially in his darker hours, his mind would return to the backwoods superstitions of his youth. He sometimes surprised colleagues and friends by occasionally professing belief in dark spirits and supernatural omens.

Here, tonight, this strange, pale double image of his face in the mirror seems to him to be a "portentous horror" and "a premonition of impending doom."

Though others may scoff, there is one person who encourages Lincoln's belief in the spirit world. His wife.

Mary Todd was what was then called a "spiritualist"—a believer in ghosts and the supernatural—and she sometimes enlisted mediums or conducted séances to communicate with the dead.

Together with his wife, Lincoln would brood over the significance of the double image in that mirror. Within a few days, as Lincoln later told a friend, he and his wife determined that "the mystery had its meaning," and that "the illusion was a sign—the life-like image betokening a safe passage through his first term as President; the ghostly one, that death would overtake him before the close of the second."

There, in the mirror, he believes is a premonition of his own death—and not by natural causes. The ghostly image signifies that he "would surely hear the fatal summons from the silent shore," and that from now on he will await "the inevitable hour of his fall by a murderous hand."

From the beginning, Abraham Lincoln's journey in the world has been marked by the nearness of death. When he was three or four, his infant brother died; when he was nine, his mother died; when he was eighteen, his sister died; when he became an adult and a father, his second child died.

Now, sitting alone in his chamber, only hours after being elected President of the United States, he is convinced of one thing: Death may soon claim him as well.

PART II

The President-Elect

21

---·---

Springfield, Illinois

November 7, 1860

It starts with the mail.

Abraham Lincoln has been elected President of the United States, and his life will never be the same. He knows this, his family knows this, and his longtime friends and colleagues know this.

Starting the morning after his election, he is surrounded on an hourly basis by well-wishers, aides, volunteers, reporters, and party officials. There is an intense schedule of meetings to attend, decisions to make, telegrams to write, hands to shake, favors to return.

Quickly, Lincoln and his small group of supporters are overwhelmed by the multitude of visitors who swarm into Springfield from all over the country, hoping to see him, meet him, advise him, or be hired by him.

For the most part, this round-the-clock chaos was to be expected.

What's surprising, however, is the mail. It gives Lincoln his first glimpse of the true nature of his coming Presidency—at least, the dark side of it.

In the first few days after his election, his office receives some fifty letters from around the country. In subsequent days, the number will grow to about seventy per day.

By today's standards that's a trifle for an incoming President. But by the standards of 1860 it's a deluge, especially since Lincoln does not have a staff in place to read, organize, and help him respond to all of it. While many of the letters are trivial, some are from high-level party officials and potential cabinet members—there are no telephones, of course, and there's only so much one can say in a telegram—and he worries that genuinely important letters could go unread due to the incoming volume.

To address the tedious task of sifting through all these letters, Lincoln enlists his first important full-time staff appointment: John G. Nicolay.

Nicolay is a pale-faced, bookish twenty-eight-year-old of German descent who had once served as a clerk to the Illinois Secretary of State and was trying to make a living as a journalist focusing on the Republican Party. He had become smitten with Lincoln after seeing him speak on a few occasions—a contemporary described Nicolay as Lincoln's "ardent personal follower"—and after the Chicago convention, Nicolay appeared unannounced in Springfield, making the somewhat odd pitch to be Lincoln's official biographer.

Lincoln didn't need an official biographer, but he took a liking to Nicolay and offered him the position of personal secretary, which Nicolay accepted. Now that Lincoln is President-elect, Nicolay's job is to deal with his boss's complicated schedule and growing mountains of paperwork—including all the incoming letters.

Nicolay can help manage the sheer volume of mail, but it's not the quantity of letters that's so surprising. It's the contents.

The majority of the letters are from the general public, and of these, many are inconsequential or amusing. One of the very first letters written to Lincoln after his victory was from William F. Smith, an insurance salesman in Germantown, Pennsylvania. Smith wanted to share that his son was born at 2:00 a.m. the morning after the election, only moments after the final returns were announced, and therefore he and his wife have named the child after the new President—making the boy the first "Young Abe." Along with this flattery, Smith attached with his letter a sales brochure entitled *Some among the many reasons you should Insure your Life,* including a list of

22

—— · ——

Springfield, Illinois

November 9, 1860

Three days. That's how long it takes.

Many Northerners predicted that the South would react swiftly and negatively to the election of Abraham Lincoln. But most Northern Republicans, including the new President-elect himself, did not predict how extreme the reaction would be.

True, there were signs; in the weeks leading up to the election, Southern rhetoric was heated and as dire as it had ever been.

"The existence of slavery is at stake," *The Charleston Mercury* had written only days before Election Day, and if "the Abolitionist White Man" Lincoln should win, then "each and all the Southern states" should initiate proceedings to secede from the Union.

In Louisiana, a broadside entitled *The Indications of the Coming Storm* circulated a week before Election Day, declaring, "We can never submit to Lincoln's inauguration," and if he should win, "let us drop all discussion and form a Union of the South."

Even so, it was possible to interpret these and other similar statements as exaggerations born from the high passions of a tumultuous campaign season. Surely, most Northern Republicans now imagine, once the dust settles in the wake of the election, the temperature in the South will cool. Lincoln's inauguration is not scheduled until

March 4, 1861—a full four months away—and Republicans mostly assume that Lincoln will be given a proper chance to take office and establish his policies before the South takes any drastic action.

Plus, Lincoln's previously stated policy positions didn't call for any immediate change. In debates and public statements, he had vigorously opposed the expansion of slavery into new territories, but had also clearly stated that he would not attempt to use the federal government to abolish slavery where it already existed.

But Southerners do not see it that way.

They've read Lincoln's speeches—his lofty rhetoric adamantly denouncing slavery, and his belief that the institution violated the most sacred American ideals set forth in the Declaration of Independence. He believes that slavery is *immoral,* and this stated conviction combined with a Northern-weighted Congress is enough for many Southerners to view his election in apocalyptic terms.

Underlying this sentiment is the fact that Lincoln's victory was the most bitterly sectional in the nation's history.

Lincoln did not carry a single slaveholding state, and throughout most of the South his candidacy was so unpopular the Republican Party did not even distribute ballots for him. As a result, not a single person voted for Abraham Lincoln in Alabama, Arkansas, Georgia, Mississippi, Louisiana, North Carolina, Florida, Tennessee, or Texas.

In an atypically large field of four major candidates, Lincoln won a solid majority of the Electoral College—the final tally was Lincoln, 180; Breckinridge, 72; Bell, 39; and Stephen Douglas, 12. But in the popular vote, he won only a plurality: Against a divided field, he received less than 40 percent of the total vote, and his portion of the vote was almost entirely concentrated in the Northeastern and Northwestern states.

Lincoln was, in the Southern mind, the President of the North. He was not *their* President. Most important, he and the "Black Republicans" were an enemy to the institution that was at the core of Southern pride and prosperity.

Shortly after the election, the *Richmond Enquirer* declares, "A party founded on the single sentiment . . . of hatred of African slavery, is now the controlling power." A New Orleans paper summarizes the sentiment of Southerners perhaps most succinctly: "The Northern people in electing Mr. Lincoln, have perpetuated a deliberate, cold-blooded insult and outrage upon the people of the slaveholding states." And using language that captures the deep hysteria in Southern states, an Arkansan writes: "Lincoln intends to use every means to instigate revolt among the slaves; . . . the Republicans are organized into military companies, and intend to march against the South . . . to cut the throat of every white man, [and] distribute the white females among the negroes."

Now, on November 9—three days after Election Day, and barely sixty hours after Lincoln's victory was declared—the members of the South Carolina General Assembly convene. They'll vote on a hastily crafted resolution entitled "Resolution to Call the Election of Abraham Lincoln as U.S. President a Hostile Act."

The resolution states that "said election has been based upon principles of open and avowed hostility to the social organization and peculiar interests of the slaveholding states."

The document further declares that "South Carolina is now ready to dissolve her connection with the government of the United States," and calls for the creation of a special state convention before the end of the year to debate and vote on this measure.

This is just a resolution and not binding. At this point, it's only words. The next day, November 10, the Assembly convenes again and sets a date of December 17 for the special convention of state delegates. In other words, in less than five weeks, delegates will vote on whether South Carolina will officially secede from the United States of America.

Lincoln has been President-elect for three days, and the Union is in peril.

23

Springfield, Illinois

November 1860

How can Abraham Lincoln, the new President-elect, respond to the news of South Carolina's new resolution?

He can't do much. For one thing, at that time, newly elected Presidents were expected to remain largely silent and out of the public eye until assuming office. To follow this accepted practice, he must wait for his inauguration on March 4—nearly four months away—before making any meaningful statements about matters of national interest.

What's more, at this point, the South Carolina resolution may be a merely symbolic gesture. Until the state actually votes to take concrete action, the rhetoric in the resolution is regarded with some skepticism. Southern states had threatened to secede before and never went through with it. Perhaps this was more of what the Mayor of Chicago once called "the old game of scaring and bullying the North into submission to Southern demands." And Lincoln, surrounded by Northerners and mostly fellow Republicans, shares the opinion of many that Southern threats to rebel or secede are mostly bluster.

So at least for now, the President-elect busies himself with the more tangible tasks that lie directly before him.

First, Lincoln must manage the rapidly growing volume of visitors, meetings, and correspondence that demand constant attention.

Governors, Senators, Mayors, and state politicians all over the region want to meet with him. In the weeks after the election, his office and home are also besieged with unsolicited job-seekers who hope to land positions in the new administration. As the incoming President, Lincoln has the power and responsibility to fill several thousand positions in the federal government, and his many old friends, former associates, and recent campaign donors harass him night and day with hopes of being hired.

Also, in late November, Lincoln makes a seemingly small decision that will ripple through the ages.

About a month earlier—a few weeks before the election—he had received a letter from an unusual supporter. The author was an eleven-year-old girl named Grace Bedell from the small town of Westfield, New York. She had taken an interest in the coming election and had determined that Lincoln was her favorite candidate. Her note contained a specific piece of advice:

Hon. A. B. Lincoln,

Dear Sir:

I am a little girl only eleven years old, but want you should be President of the United States very much so I hope you won't think me very bold to write to such a great man as you are. Have you any little girls about as large as I am? If so give them my love and tell her to write to me if you cannot answer this letter.

I have got 4 brothers and a part of them will vote for you . . . and if you will let your whiskers grow I will try and get the rest of them to vote for you; you would look a great deal better for your face is so thin. All the ladies like whiskers and they would tease their husbands to vote for you and then you would be President.

Good bye.

Grace Bedell

A beard. She tells Abraham Lincoln to grow a beard.

So what does Lincoln think?

He was used to getting comments on his appearance, almost all of them negative, and had long stopped placing much importance on it. He wasn't inclined to make any particular change in how he looked. But he almost always made time to respond to letters from children, and on the day after he received her letter, he wrote this reply:

> Miss Grace Bedell:
> My dear little Miss: Your very agreeable letter of the 15th is received. I regret the necessity of saying I have no daughter. I have three sons—one seventeen, one nine, and one seven years of age. They, with their mother, constitute my whole family.
> As to the whiskers, having never worn any, do you not think people would call it a piece of silly affectation if I were to begin it now?
>
> Your very sincere well-wisher,
> A. Lincoln.

Although he did not immediately take her suggestion, Lincoln was fond of the girl's letter and carefully saved it.

That was a month ago. Now, he's preparing to be the President of the United States. Perhaps some of the comments in the press—that his rough appearance is not sufficiently "statesmanlike"—are getting under his skin. Whatever the case, for reasons he never shares, Lincoln changes his mind and follows Grace Bedell's advice. Silly affectation or not, he starts to grow whiskers.

A week or so later on November 25, when the President-elect briefly visits Chicago, he sits for a portrait—the first photograph ever to capture Abraham Lincoln with a beard (see page 115).

Once the change in Lincoln's face is visible to onlookers in the streets of Illinois, word quickly travels. The more gossipy newspapers make a story out of it, and predictably the candidate endures additional mockery.

Probably without thinking of it, Lincoln's abrupt decision causes headaches all over the country—specifically, for the many photographers and artists who had recently traveled to Illinois to create portraits of him, and for the various publications and organizations that commissioned their work.

Inspired by advice from an eleven-year-old named Grace Bedell, Lincoln begins growing a beard a few weeks after his election. This photograph by Samuel G. Alschuler, taken on November 25, 1860, in Chicago, is the first to capture Abraham Lincoln with whiskers.

Any photograph, painting, or bust that was recently completed, including many commissioned since his nomination over the summer, is now out of date. Scrambling to remain current, some publications upon learning of Lincoln's new facial hair resort to superimposing a beard on their existing photographic prints of Lincoln. These efforts are crude at best—and in most cases, they make the famously awkward-looking President look even more so.

Similarly, the portrait artist Jesse Atwood makes a bad situation worse by simply painting a beard from scratch on the clean-shaven image of Lincoln he had completed in person only a few weeks earlier—but since he had no visual reference to work from, the resulting beard is in the wrong shape.

Lincoln would never be clean-shaven again. Surely, he had no idea that when he decided to follow eleven-year-old Grace Bedell's advice, he was about to grow one of the most famous beards in American history.

24

—·—

Baltimore, Maryland

December 1860

A group of men are gathered in a large, cavernous room.

There are roughly fifteen or sixteen of them, arranged in straight lines facing forward. They stand in military-like formation, but wield mock wooden rifles rather than real firearms.

The room they stand in is on the second floor, up a staircase from a commercial street in Baltimore, Maryland. It's a wide space with high ceilings—perhaps a warehouse, former armory, or some other industrial place.

The men do not wear uniforms, not today, but some have a small ceremonial pin on their chests bearing the symbol of a palmetto tree. These pins have special significance, especially in the days and weeks since the Presidential election. The palmetto tree appears on the state flag of South Carolina, and in the wake of that state's public threat to secede from the Union, the symbol of the tree has come to stand for unified Southern resistance against Abraham Lincoln.

There is only one voice in the room, shouting commands to the rest. He is their captain and drill instructor—he teaches the men weapons handling, marching technique, and other military maneuvers. He is experienced—he has drilled men before—and his voice has a musical quality with a distinct Southern accent.

This is no ordinary drill instructor. It's Cypriano Ferrandini, the barber. The man who commands an audience of Southern gentlemen when talking politics at his popular shop in the basement of Barnum's City Hotel.

Since his early days in Baltimore, Ferrandini has been involved with local volunteer militia groups. This itself is not unusual, as the organization of armed volunteer militias is a popular practice at the time.

In 1852, he was a founding officer of a group called the Lafayette Guards, who drilled regularly around the city. Ferrandini soon became the captain of the company and led the group in parades and civic events. His name was mentioned in Baltimore newspapers at least two dozen times in the 1850s in connection with his leadership of the group.

By early 1858, Ferrandini resigned from the Lafayette Guards— still maintaining an honorary title—and that spring received his membership to the Knights of the Golden Circle. His subsequent trip to Mexico was quasi-military in nature. He will later testify that he traveled there to enlist in the "army of Juárez," the rebel army in the ongoing Mexican Civil War. A known plan of the Knights was to aid these rebels in destabilizing the country, allowing an incursion of KGC-led troops to gain a foothold in the country's eastern regions. Whether Ferrandini really served with Juárez is not known, but he claimed to have spent three months in the country.

But now, the barber is focused on urgent matters at home.

After the election in 1860, Ferrandini is hard at work drilling a new Baltimore-based militia group called the Constitutional Guards. They usually meet in the evenings, in this second-floor space.

It is unknown whether some of the men Ferrandini is now drilling are fellow members of the Knights of the Golden Circle. But certainly, the KGC would be an apt place for him to recruit militia soldiers. Much like that secret society, this new militia group is, as he himself describes it, "political in nature."

Quasi-political militia groups are common throughout the South, but in the days following Abraham Lincoln's victory, these groups have taken on a new urgency. A "Black Republican" will soon be

President, and the South believes it is under attack. If Lincoln and the Northern abolitionists try to change the Southern way of life—that is, try to end slavery—proud Southerners believe they must be ready to fight back.

Unlike the states of the cotton belt, where ballots for Lincoln were not even distributed for the election, here in Maryland the Republican Party has a presence. But it is a very small one: of the 30,000-plus votes for President cast in the city of Baltimore, just under 1,100—less than 4 percent—were cast for Abraham Lincoln. Statewide, the percentage is even smaller. In some rural Maryland counties, Lincoln received only one or two votes; in two counties, he received zero.

Ferrandini's small militia group will soon be under the umbrella of a larger regional organization called the National Volunteers. With a growing presence throughout Maryland and Washington, D.C., the Volunteers is becoming a loose-knit armed resistance to the incoming administration. The wooden rifles will gradually be replaced by real ones, and some members will wear uniforms on which to display their palmetto pins.

So what form of armed resistance do the members of groups like the Constitutional Guards actually hope to provide? In the tense early weeks after the election, they themselves don't know. They just know they need to be ready.

For that, their captain, Cypriano Ferrandini, is working on a special plan all his own.

25

Springfield, Illinois

December 1860

Lincoln is set to take office in three months. As a growing sense of tension sweeps the country, his small team in Springfield presses forward trying to prepare.

Of the tasks before the President-elect, one of the most time-consuming and complex is also the most critical: the formation of his cabinet. Each passing week brings evidence that Lincoln's Presidency will face unprecedented challenges, putting enormous pressure on the selection of his team. Lincoln is acutely aware that many in the country view him as a novice with little experience in national politics, and he knows his choice of cabinet members will be closely scrutinized.

Among many other considerations, Lincoln's selections must unite the Republican Party in the wake of the tumultuous Chicago convention. To do so, he embarks on a plan to fill his cabinet's top positions with the candidates he ran against at the convention. This group—these days often referred to as the "Team of Rivals"—will be composed of some of the most experienced politicians in the country. In addition to healing party wounds and promoting unity, the plan has regional advantages. Lincoln's appointment of Edward Bates of Missouri as Attorney General will hopefully please moderates from the border states whom the President-elect desperately hopes will not drift south, while his appointment of Governor Salmon Chase of Ohio as Secretary of the Treasury should please the antislavery wing of the Republican Party.

But when it comes to his former rivals, one is more important than the rest: Senator William H. Seward of New York, the former Governor and longtime party leader who started the year as the presumed front-runner for the Presidency. No other person would add greater credibility and experience to Lincoln's cabinet, while also bringing along a base of powerful supporters and party insiders. Lincoln decides to offer Seward the job of Secretary of State, at the time the most prestigious and powerful position in any President's cabinet.

The question remains, will Seward accept? This was supposed to be Seward's Presidency—he raised more money and had far more support. The unexpected loss to the little-known Lincoln was one of the greatest political humiliations of the century.

To his credit, Seward made no public show of anger or grievance after his loss. In fact, once Lincoln was the nominee, Seward nobly campaigned all over the country on behalf of the party he helped create and the man chosen to be its leader.

Still, Seward's pride had been deeply wounded and would take some time to recover. After an acclaimed career in politics, Seward now had every reason to finish his last term in the Senate and retire with his family to his estate in Auburn, New York—away from public view—rather than work for a less experienced person who was the source of his public humiliation.

To bring him aboard, Lincoln embarks on a long, careful courtship. The situation is delicate; Lincoln must appear neither condescending nor too desperate, yet make his offer appear firm and considered.

After almost a month of trading messages through intermediaries, Lincoln is prepared to officially offer Seward the position. His plan is almost derailed, however, when a false rumor spreads through the political press that Lincoln's planned offer to Seward is merely a formal gesture—that he really prefers someone else for the position and hopes Seward will decline. Seward could easily interpret this as an intentional leak from Lincoln's side, meant to dissuade him, and could therefore refuse the offer.

William Seward, Senator and former Governor of New York, was once the front-runner to win the Republican nomination for the Presidency in 1860. When Lincoln offers him the position of Secretary of State in his cabinet, Seward has to overcome his own wounded pride to consider the offer.

Lincoln must do damage control. On December 8, he writes two letters to Seward and asks his Vice President, Hannibal Hamlin, to deliver both in person. One is a formal letter offering Seward the position of Secretary of State. The other is a personal note, candidly addressing the rumors that the offer is insincere:

> I beg you to be assured that I have said nothing to justify these rumors. . . . I now offer you the place, in the hope that you will accept it, and with the belief that your position in the public eye, your integrity, ability, learning, and great experience, all combine to render it an appointment pre-eminently fit to be made.

Seward reads the letter carefully. His ego is apparently mollified. But he doesn't respond with a yes or no. Instead, he writes a message to Lincoln asking for "a little time to consider whether I possess the qualifications and temper of a minister," and whether he ought to "continue at all in the public service."

More than a week goes by. Still no response. Since Seward's is the key position, his answer will affect the other choices. Lincoln is growing desperate for help—but at least for now, his former rival is making him wait.

Today, it may seem like petty politics, but at the time, neither man realizes that within a matter of weeks, William Seward will play an unexpected role in uncovering the secret conspiracy that threatens Lincoln's life.

26

---·---

Columbia, South Carolina

December 17, 1860

All eyes are on South Carolina.

Despite the threats, the President-elect remains skeptical of Southern secession. "People of the South have too much good sense, and good temper, to attempt the ruin of the government," Lincoln had said to supporters shortly before his election. Like many in his party, he believed the threats from "disunionists"—a term often used to refer to those who argue for Southern secession—were "a sort of political game of bluff, gotten up by politicians, and meant solely to frighten the North."

However, Lincoln and his party were mistaken. Throughout the South, secessionist fervor did not die down once the dust settled after the election. In fact, it has only intensified. The Southern states now all look to South Carolina to make a bold statement of resistance to the incoming "Black Republican" administration.

Why is South Carolina first?

Some reasons are cultural. The Southern aristocratic tradition runs as deep or deeper in South Carolina than anywhere else in the South, and the culture of Southern pride and honor—that is, *white* Southern pride and *white* Southern honor—are especially pronounced. A corollary of these traditions is an unyielding loathing for the North.

"There is nothing in all the dark caves of human passion so cruel and deadly as the hatred the South Carolinians profess for the Yankees," as one writer put it.

After all, it was a Congressman from South Carolina, Preston Brooks, who four years prior had nearly beaten to death Massachusetts Senator Charles Sumner on the floor of the Senate—and became a local hero for committing the act.

Yet the real answer may be demographics. At the start of 1860, South Carolina contains a higher proportion of enslaved persons—402,406 out of 703,708, or 57 percent—than any other state. A threat to the institution of slavery, especially one that might encourage existing men and women in bondage to rebel or revolt, ignites panic for white South Carolinians.

Economically, the institution of slavery is so deeply entrenched in the state that the wealthy slaveholding classes can scarcely imagine their lives without it. The port of Charleston is one of the country's busiest hubs in the domestic slave trade, and one of the most lucrative. As one South Carolinian puts it, acquiescing to Lincoln and the Republicans means "the loss of liberty, property, home, country—everything that makes life worth having."

In this state, the notion of blacks having equality strikes a deep, primal, racist fear. As a South Carolinian Baptist clergyman tells his congregation: "If you are tame enough to submit [to Lincoln], Abolition preachers will be at hand to consummate the marriage of your daughters to black husbands."

Now, on December 17, 1860, six weeks after Lincoln's election, delegates appointed from around the state meet in South Carolina's capital city of Columbia for a special "secession convention." When the motion to draw up an ordinance of secession is put before the floor, the delegates vote unanimously, 169–0, in favor.

The following day, a special committee from the convention adjourns to Charleston to draft the official document, which declares "the union now subsisting between South Carolina and other States, under the name of 'The United States of America,' is hereby dissolved."

Along with the formal one-page ordinance, the committee produces a longer document called "Declaration of the Immediate Causes Which

Induce and Justify the Secession of South Carolina from the Federal Union." Modeled after the Declaration of Independence, it outlines the state's grievances and its reasons for taking this momentous step.

Above all else, the document points to "an increasing hostility on the part of the non-slaveholding states to the Institution of Slavery." Furthermore, the Northern states have "denounced as sinful the institution of slavery . . . they have encouraged and assisted thousands of our slaves to leave their homes; and those who remain, have been incited by emissaries, books and pictures to servile insurrection." According to the Declaration, the Northern states have "undermined the Constitution" by "elevating to citizenship, persons, who, by the Supreme Law of the land, are incapable of becoming citizens."

Finally, the Declaration asserts the ultimate sin of the North: They have "united in the election of a man to the high office of President of the United States, whose opinions and purposes are hostile to slavery." The Declaration asserts this new President and his government will assume power with the agenda that "war must be waged against slavery until it shall cease throughout the United States."

At approximately 1:15 p.m. on Thursday, December 20, 1860, the delegates ceremoniously sign their names to the ordinance as South Carolina officially becomes the first state since the founding to formally secede from the United States of America.

Word spreads rapidly. Within hours, Charleston's leading paper publishes a special broadside (see page 126).

Throughout the afternoon and into the evening, South Carolinians all over the state celebrate with parades, rallies, fireworks, and musical performances. The American flag that had flown above the statehouse in Columbia for some eight decades is removed, soon to be replaced by a state flag of South Carolina bearing the image of the palmetto tree.

Reporters from around the country had been in the state, anxiously following every detail, and as they file their reports, headlines begin to appear around the nation. In the South, the news is met with jubilation; at least four other Southern capitals have hundred-gun salutes.

CHARLESTON

MERCURY

EXTRA:

Passed unanimously at 1.15 o'clock, P. M., December 20th, 1860.

AN ORDINANCE

To dissolve the Union between the State of South Carolina and other States united with her under the compact entitled "The Constitution of the United States of America."

We, the People of the State of South Carolina, in Convention assembled, do declare and ordain, and it is hereby declared and ordained,

That the Ordinance adopted by us in Convention, on the twenty-third day of May, in the year of our Lord one thousand seven hundred and eighty-eight, whereby the Constitution of the United States of America was ratified, and also, all Acts and parts of Acts of the General Assembly of this State, ratifying amendments of the said Constitution, are hereby repealed; and that the union now subsisting between South Carolina and other States, under the name of "The United States of America," is hereby dissolved.

THE

UNION

IS

DISSOLVED!

In New Orleans, the word reaches backstage at a large, crowded theater in the middle of a popular play. The main actor stops mid-performance to read the news aloud from the stage—and the audience erupts into cheers.

In the North and in border states, the news has a very different effect. Although many in the political arena had begun to soberly predict the correct outcome of the vote, the magnitude of the act nonetheless sends shock waves.

The mighty dam of the United States of America is now cracked, and water starts flooding.

27

Springfield, Illinois

December 1860

Abraham Lincoln has no choice.

In the first weeks after his election, he tried to stay silent on the unfolding events. So long as another President was still in office, Lincoln had no authority and no ability to govern. As such, he believed it wrong—that it would sow confusion—if he made public declarations about what he might or might not do once he took office.

He also worried that anything he said or wrote could be misconstrued or taken out of context. He had mostly avoided, deferred, or deflected any attempts from journalists to force him to give a clear public signal of what actions he planned to take.

But pressure was steadily mounting for him to assert his position. Because the Southern states' movements toward secession were largely based on fears of what Lincoln would supposedly do once in office, many now cry out for him to clarify what he *actually* will do. One Marylander writes to him:

> Many reports are circulated . . . that you will use all the means in your hands as President to abolish Slavery in the South . . . if you could write a short letter denying this, it would have a good effect in quelling the insurrectionary tumults in the section where I live.

Do not wait for the Inaugural Address; people are in such a fever as to be almost beyond the words of reason . . . You can, I firmly believe, stop the progress of disunion by a word; I beseech you to speak it.

At first, Lincoln referred journalists and others to examine his prior speeches, as well as the published transcripts from his old debates with Stephen Douglas. As he wrote to a newspaper editor who pressed him for a comment shortly after the election, "I could say nothing which I have not already said, and which is in print, and open for the inspection of all."

Those speeches and debates, Lincoln thought, expressed his views: He believes slavery is morally wrong, but he does not believe the federal government has the right to abolish or otherwise interfere with the institution of slavery in those states where it already exists. He is, however, adamant that the federal government should prevent the spread of slavery into western territories, thus ensuring that new states admitted to the Union are free. This, he believes, is the best way to contain and isolate slavery such that it will meet its "ultimate extinction."

This key issue—the extension of slavery into new territories—is at the crux of all debates, and many believe that the future of the institution hinges on this question. Lincoln's speeches over the years make his points clearly.

But after the election, the public doesn't want to read old speeches; they want to know what Lincoln thinks *now*. South Carolina has already declared secession, and more Southern states threaten to do the same. The country's economy, dependent on trade between North and South, is already plummeting due to fears of what comes next. The current President, sixty-nine-year-old James Buchanan, is on his way out and has little or no influence. The country is in a state of panic.

What should Lincoln do?

Many urge him to make a grand statement of conciliation, words to both mollify the South and ensure that the slaveholding border states stay comfortably on the side of the Union. In short, he should show that he's willing to compromise on slavery to keep the country together.

At the same time, some of his strongest supporters in the North—those who elected him—urge the opposite. The worst thing he can do, they argue, is compromise principle in the face of Southern belligerence. "The North would despise such an act, and by it the South become more rampant in its foolish disunion threats," one Ohio Republican writes to Lincoln. "Nothing could be more humiliating to us and disastrous to our cause, than to see you, the chosen leader of a bold and noble party, crawl upon your belly before a handful of traitors in the South."

Lincoln's position is further complicated by a series of potential compromises making their way through Congress around the time of South Carolina's momentous declaration.

Desperate to preserve the Union, border state legislators and moderates from both North and South initiate a series of proposals intended to find common ground. The "Crittenden Compromise," named for its sponsor, Senator John J. Crittenden from the border state of Kentucky, is the first and most important of several. Among other components, it proposes that slavery be extended and protected in new territories south of an agreed-upon latitude. Soon, alternate proposals emerge in both the House and Senate, each containing another compromise about slavery's extension.

At this point, the pressure is so great to prevent the catastrophe of full-scale Southern secession, many Northern legislators begin to waver on antislavery principles. As one fearful New Hampshire Republican writes to Lincoln in late December, "On reaching Washington I found great numbers of our friends afflicted with the secession panic, and almost ready to concede away the entire Republican platform to pacify the secessionists."

This compromise would be devastating to abolitionists, many of whom supported Lincoln. If it happened, it could extend slavery in the country for decades.

Finally, Lincoln makes his move. Rather than deliver a formal public speech—he's determined that his coming inaugural address will be his first official statement—he writes a series of letters to party leaders clarifying his position, knowing that these words will be scrutinized and widely shared. None of the compromises can succeed without his support, and every member of Congress knows this. These behind-the-scenes letters, therefore, will determine their fate.

In writing, Lincoln repeats his position that, despite Southern fears to the contrary, the federal government will not interfere with slavery in states where it already exists. He also suggests that he's willing to compromise in some areas—for example, as part of a larger compromise, he's willing to insist that Northern states fully comply with the Fugitive Slave Law, loathed by abolitionists, that allows Southern slaveholders to reclaim enslaved persons who escape to free states.

But on the absolutely essential question of the day—the spread of slavery into new territories—Lincoln will not budge. Preventing the spread of slavery is his bedrock, the foundation on which he was elected. "Have none of it," he writes to Illinois Senator Lyman Trumbull. "Let there be no compromise on the question of extending slavery. If there be, all our labor is lost, and, ere long, must be done again . . . Stand firm."

To his antislavery colleague Illinois Representative Elihu Washburne, Lincoln further urges, "There is no possible compromise. . . . On that point hold firm, as with a chain of steel."

To clarify beyond a doubt, he writes to a Southern politician, "On the territorial question, I am inflexible. On that, there is a difference between you and us; and it is the only substantial difference. You think slavery is right and ought to be extended; we think it is wrong and ought to be restricted."

Lincoln and his allies know that this position will probably undermine any congressional compromise. Southerners will never accept a deal in which slavery remains restricted to its current state borders.

But for those on the antislavery side, Lincoln's position provides much-needed support. Missouri's Republican Congressman Francis Blair happily reports that "[Lincoln] will live up to the principles on which he was elected," and on the slavery question is "firm as the rock of ages."

Charles Sumner—the Massachusetts Senator who was nearly

beaten to death four years ago on the floor of the Senate chamber and who eventually recovered to serve another term—is gratified to know that the first-ever Republican President will not capitulate to Southern slaveholders and betray the cause that Sumner almost died for.

"Lincoln stands firm," Sumner declares. "I know it."

28

Washington, D.C.

December 1860

Plots. Conspiracies. Threats of violence.

In the wake of Lincoln's election, and even more so in the wake of South Carolina's momentous decision to secede, Washington, D.C., is thrown into a state of convulsion.

Disorder and panic quickly hit the halls of the U.S. Capitol. The institution of Congress "was in a condition of utter disorganization," as the journalist and writer Henry Adams, who covers Capitol Hill closely during this period, puts it. "There was a strange and bewildering chaos, the fragments of broken parties and a tottering Government." The threat of secession alone has brought havoc to the normal mechanisms of the federal government.

In Washington, D.C., somewhere between one-third and one-half of the few thousand government employees—from clerks and assistants, up to Congressmen and Senators—either represent Southern states or are sympathetic to them. Many of these federal employees are now openly advocating for the destruction of the very government they serve.

"The most flagrant treason was openly proclaimed," as Adams describes, and the halls of Congress are split bitterly into warring factions. It's no longer just North versus South; it's the Unionists versus the secessionists—those who wanted to preserve the country versus those who want to split it in two.

Certainly, there are moderate members of both houses working desperately to hold the body together, but these efforts are mostly drowned out by the increasing fervor of Southern members rejoicing openly at South Carolina's act of secession—and threatening the same for the states they represent. Northern members are split between those who seek reconciliation and those who refuse to compromise with secessionists.

The distrust and discord become so intense that fears of armed insurrection on the part of secessionists seize the city. "Crowds came up to the Capitol expecting to see some violent and probably bloody explosion," Adams describes. "Through the whole month . . . the panic there was terrible and always increasing." By the end of the month, the "panic had already risen to a fever heat," and "the belief was universal in Washington that there would be fighting in the city within the month."

Normally, the executive branch, with its control of the Army and Navy, would protect the city from violence. But many people believe that the unpopular lame-duck President, sixty-nine-year-old Democrat James Buchanan, is at best ineffectual, and at worst consorting with the Southerners bent on destroying the Union.

One Army insider writes to John Nicolay that there is "no doubt in my mind of the complicity of the President with the designs of the secessionists," and according to a Northern Republican stationed in Washington, "The greatest apprehensions . . . were from the treachery of the President. He is openly denounced by all the friends of the Union, as a traitor to it."

Just as worrisome are the suspected dual loyalties of those in President Buchanan's cabinet, some of whom are Southern slaveholders. "It was well known that three of the Cabinet officers were disunionists, and that the President was under their influence . . . it was said that they had placed him under a system of actual surveillance, so that he never was out of their sight," Adams reports.

Northerners in the capital are particularly alarmed to hear rumors that the Secretary of War, John Floyd, is strategizing directly with South Carolina secessionists and sending them arms, rather than preparing the federal army to protect Washington, D.C. "Secretary Floyd is a traitor and deserves death on the gallows for his behavior," a Northern Congressman writes.

By the end of December, the swirl of rumors begins to crystallize into something more definitive. Armed pro-Southern militia groups in and around the city are secretly conspiring to seize federal buildings, including the Capitol, on or before March 4. Their goal? To prevent, by force, Abraham Lincoln's inauguration.

Furthermore, according to the rumors, Secretary of War John Floyd, with or without President Buchanan's blessing, is refusing to arm the city so that the Southern militias will meet no resistance.

So bold are these plans, some Southern sympathizers don't even conceal their intentions. "Clerks in the Government Departments mounted the disunion badge and talked openly of oaths they had taken never to permit the inauguration of Abraham Lincoln," Adams writes.

Frightening signs are everywhere. Late at night, residents can see "men drilling at midnight in the environs of the city," presumably planning military maneuvers. High-ranking officials throughout the government receive anonymous or nonanonymous threats and warnings regarding "designs of violence to be used against the Capitol."

The circumstances are especially ominous given the geographic position of Washington, D.C. The capital city is entirely surrounded by two slave states, Maryland and Virginia. While neither state has yet taken official steps to follow South Carolina down the path of secession, many predict that one or both states will eventually do so—and regardless, both are strongly pro-South, proslavery, and anti-Lincoln. If Southern militias somehow seized Washington, D.C., the city would be completely surrounded by hostile territory and isolated from friendly Northern states.

Eventually, the threats get so bad, several of Lincoln's allies contact him directly warning him of a "secret organization" that poses a danger to his inauguration. On December 26, Joseph Medill, the editor and publisher of the *Chicago Tribune,* writes from Washington, "The evidences of my ears and eyes are forcing me to believe that the

secessionists are seriously contemplating resistance to your inauguration in this Capitol. There is certainly a secret organization in this city
numbering several hundred members having that purpose in view."

Medill goes on to describe "sworn armed men, and branches or
lodges affiliated with them" organizing both within the city and in
the surrounding regions of Virginia and Maryland. These groups are
engaged in a "great conspiracy to seize this capital and drive you away,
at the point of the bayonet."

Lincoln's life is in danger.

The "bodies of men drilling at midnight" and the "sworn armed
men" with "branches or lodges" almost certainly refer to the shadowy
organization called the National Volunteers. Originally formed in
support of Southern Democrat Presidential candidate John Breckinridge, this loose-knit organization has, since the election, recruited
and armed Southern sympathizers in Washington, D.C., and the surrounding regions of Virginia and Maryland.

Two days after Medill's letter, Lincoln receives a similar warning
from someone who can't be ignored: William Seward, who recently
returned to Washington to finish his final term as a New York Senator. On December 28, he writes directly to Lincoln and urges an
unusual plan:

> There is a feverish excitement here which awakens all kind of ap-
> prehensions of popular disturbance and disorders, connected with
> your assumption of the government. Habit has accustomed the
> public to anticipate the arrival of the President Elect in this city
> about the middle of February and evil minded persons could ex-
> pect to organize their demonstrations for that time. I beg leave to
> suggest whether it would not be well for you . . . to be prepared to
> drop into the City a week or ten days earlier.

In other words, if Lincoln were to secretly travel to the capital
sooner than expected, he could safely ensconce himself in the city
before any conspirators could plan to harm him.

Seward writes a follow-up letter the very next day, more urgent in
tone, reiterating the warning: "A plot is forming to seize the Capitol

on or before the 4th of March . . . I could tell you more particularly than I dare write. But you must not imagine that I am not giving you suspicions and rumors—Believe that I know what I write." He repeats his previous advice: "I therefore revive the suggestion of your coming here earlier than you otherwise would—and coming in by surprise—without announcement."

In the next three days, several other Lincoln allies stationed in Washington write him similar letters about possible plots to seize the city and prevent the inauguration.

For the U.S. government, these are uncharted waters. One state has seceded, and more threaten to do so. Plans are afoot to seize the nation's capital and prevent the inauguration of an elected President.

This is the state of the nation as the year 1860—the "Year of Meteors"—comes to a close.

No one, least of all the incoming President, can possibly imagine what else the new year is about to bring.

29

---·---

Samuel M. Felton is no fool.

He is the president of the Philadelphia, Wilmington and Balti-more Railroad. In such capacity, he controls one of the largest rail-road networks in the Northeast, and one of the busiest in the country. Felton is a wealthy man, a busy man, and—perhaps above all—an *important* man. Which is to say, he is not one to concern himself with trifles, rumors, or foolish stories. But he is about to learn something that is both outlandish and deeply worrying.

He is in his large Philadelphia office on a Saturday in early January, probably the first Saturday of the new year, conducting busi-ness as he often does on weekends. On this day, he has an appoint-ment with an unusual visitor who is not connected to his business affairs, but whom he knows and admires.

She is Dorothea Dix, a well-known reformer and educator. Dix is best known for almost single-handedly transforming the treatment and care of the mentally ill in the United States, opening hospitals and lobbying for federal and state resources to be devoted to the issue. She is a woman of serious purpose, intelligent and dedicated, and is well respected by the Governors and Senators whom she's lobbied over the years to enact her reforms.

Mr. Felton had once worked with Dix on one of her initiatives and had a high regard for her. When he heard that she had requested an appointment with him and "had an important communication to make" that must be made in person, he was more than willing to meet with her.

When Dix arrives in Felton's office, she is in a hurry. A no-nonsense woman now in her late fifties, she has no time for small talk. She insists it must be in private.

Dix explains that she has just returned from a journey throughout the Southern states related to her reform work, visiting hospitals and meeting with public officials. Her extensive travels, she says, had "brought her in contact with the prominent men [in the] South" and that after all her time spent there she had "become familiar with the structure of southern society, and the workings of its political machinery."

In recent weeks, she tells Felton, she's learned through some of these prominent people of alarming plans underway from various quarters to prevent, at any cost, the inauguration of the new President. As Felton would later describe it, she told him, "There was a deep-laid conspiracy to capture Washington, destroy all the avenues leading to it from the North, East, and West, and thus prevent the inauguration of Mr. Lincoln in the capital of the country."

Even more alarming, she says, "if this plot did not succeed, then to murder him while on his way to the capital, and thus inaugurate a revolution."

After this "extensive and organized conspiracy" was able to "seize upon Washington," those who undertook it would "declare the Southern conspirators de facto the Government of the United States." Meanwhile, the hostile parties would "cut off all modes of communication between Washington and the North, East, or West and thus prevent the transportation of troops to wrest the capital from the hands of insurgents." She repeats again the conspirators' ultimate resolve: "Mr. Lincoln's inauguration was thus to be prevented, or his life was to fall sacrifice to the attempt at inauguration."

For over an hour, Felton listens attentively to Dix's every word. Like anyone who follows current affairs, he's already heard piecemeal rumors regarding Southern plots to somehow interrupt the coming inauguration. But never had he heard something so concrete and comprehensive, and from such a serious source. As he later wrote, she presented what she had learned in a "tangible and reliable shape."

Felton is deeply alarmed. As a current Philadelphian originally from Massachusetts, he is a Northern man through and through, so the idea of a Southern conspiracy to "seize" the capital and threaten the life of the new President is abhorrent to him.

But Felton also has a very immediate stake: According to Dix's account, a key component of the Southern conspirators' plans is the destruction of transportation lines to and from the capital. If so, Felton's signature railway lines from Philadelphia to Baltimore—a key link in the larger transportation chain connecting northern cities to Washington, D.C.—is at imminent risk.

Felton thanks Dix for sharing her story, and they quickly part.

What can the president of the Philadelphia, Wilmington and Baltimore Railroad possibly do in such a situation?

First, he must try to learn more information. He immediately dispatches an emissary to Washington, D.C., to speak to high-level military officials, share what he has learned, and urge action to secure the city and the transportation lines. He also sends letters to his top officers along the railway, urging them to seek any evidence of plots afoot.

The news that comes back is bad.

After securing meetings with top officials in Washington, Felton's emissary learns that Dix had it right. Some Unionists within the War Department are also very worried about Southern plots to disrupt the inauguration, but they've largely been prevented by the current administration—in particular, Secretary of War John Floyd—from deploying armed forces to prevent any such plot.

Even more troubling, in the next few days, Felton learns more information from one of his stationmasters in Maryland. An anonymous source had recently approached the stationmaster with information about a detailed plot to prevent the inauguration that originates from a very specific place: the city of Baltimore.

According to the source, "a party . . . then organized in Baltimore" was planning to strategically burn Felton's railroad bridges that span rivers near the Chesapeake Bay to prevent either Abraham Lincoln's arrival or the deployment of federal forces to protect the capital.

The plotters "had combustible materials to pour over the bridges" and were planning to "be at the bridge just before the train in which Mr. Lincoln travelled had arrived. The bridge was then to be burned, the train attacked, and Mr. Lincoln to be put out of the way."

Felton is concerned enough about the latter threat that he sets up a meeting with George P. Kane, Baltimore's Marshal of Police. But Kane, rather than expressing alarm, casually dismisses the threat and declines to take any action to protect the bridges or railroads in or around Baltimore.

Naturally, Felton is frustrated by the lack of action. There are so many unanswered questions. Are these rumored plots all connected? Hell, are they even real? Felton desperately needs more information.

He quickly determines that politicians cannot or will not help him. He must "investigate the matter in his own way."

A week or so after the visit from Dix, Felton sits down to write a letter soliciting the services of a man who previously helped his railroad. This someone is a "celebrated detective" who "resides in the West" and is "a man of great skill and resources."

Samuel M. Felton is no fool. He wants the best person in the country—the one man who can help him on this matter of national importance.

The letter is sent.

To Allan Pinkerton.

30

***

Springfield, Illinois

January 9, 1861

"The Great Secession Winter."

That's the name soon given to the long, anxious months following South Carolina's act of defiance—when the country has no real leader.

What happens next? Will other states follow South Carolina? Will the nation's capital descend into violence? Will the new President even make it to his inauguration?

The most optimistic voices still hope that the secession movement can be contained, that reason will prevail, and that the transfer of power will be peaceful.

In the states of the Deep South, however, the fear that the new Northern President will limit, interfere with, or potentially abolish the institution of slavery—in other words, will dare to confer upon black people basic rights as human beings and citizens—has unleashed waves of hysteria and rage seemingly impossible to contain.

South Carolina's decision has galvanized the Southern extremists, many of whom have always wanted secession and whose ultimate goal was to form an independent slave-based Southern nation. Now that momentum is on their side, the slaveholding class embarks on a campaign of fear and incitement to rally the whole South to the secession cause.

Southern newspapers are full of editorials, each more furious than the last. With Lincoln in charge, *The Charleston Mercury* promises, armed abolitionists will soon stir a slave revolt. "Violence, murder, poisons and rape will fill the air with the demonic revelry of all the passions of an ignorant, semi-barbarous race, urged to madness by the licentious teachings of our Northern brethren."

Repeating the same theme, the Texas *Methodist Weekly*—a Christian newspaper—declares that the "the designs of the abolitionists are . . . poison [and] fire," and the plan to "deluge [the South] in blood and flame . . . and force their fair daughters into the embrace of buck negroes for wives."

These viewpoints are no longer on the fringe but the prominent views of Southern leaders and politicians. "Our young girls—Daughters—from 12 to 15 years of age are entreating us—their Fathers—to train them in the use of fire arms and daggers," a South Carolina Congressman writes to a friend. "We will arm them, and . . . carry them to the battle field with us. Better for them that they encounter the horrors & chances of war, than endure 'negro equality,' and 'emancipation' and its logical result 'amalgamation.'"

To sway public opinion to their rallying cry of secession, the Southern slaveholding class—a minority of wealthy families—has had to convince the poor white laboring class, who profit nothing from slavery, to join their cause.

The Governor of Georgia makes this pitch to the working-class whites in his state: "Among us the poor white laborer . . . does not belong to the menial class. The negro is in no sense his equal . . . He belongs to the only true aristocracy, the race of *white men*."

The hysteria spreading through the South is not only expressed with words. When a fire breaks out in a small Texas town—probably due to record-setting heat and poor construction materials on the buildings—word spreads through local newspapers that the fire was an act of arson by revolting slaves led by "abolitionist spies" from the North.

False rumors emerge about other fires in neighboring towns—and soon white vigilante groups are on the move. The vigilantes round up and terrify or torture enslaved people until they "confess" names of fellow slaves who are responsible for the revolt and arson. Those named are rounded up and hanged without trial or jury.

Reports of mob violence arise from elsewhere in the South. Northern visitors are beaten and run out of town, suspected of being abolitionist spies.

Some moderate Southern leaders try to calm things down. But this shrinking minority can do little to stop the wave of secessionist fervor sweeping the region. Moderates are not "able to stem the wild torrent of passion which is carrying everything before it," one Louisiana man laments. "It can no more be checked by human effort . . . than a prairie fire by a gardener's watering pot."

This wild torrent of passion reaches its culmination in a stunning series of events during the second week of January. Back in December, several Southern state legislatures had, with approval from their Governors, already voted to schedule special conventions to consider secession shortly after the new year.

Now, on Wednesday, January 9, 1861, a special convention of Mississippi's delegates meets in the state's capital building and, following South Carolina's lead, votes 84–15 to "dissolve the union between the State of Mississippi and other states united with her under the compact entitled 'The Constitution of the United States of America.'"

The very next day, January 10, Florida state delegates gather for a special convention in Tallahassee and vote, 62–7 in favor, on an ordinance declaring, "The State of Florida hereby withdraws herself from the Confederacy of States existing under the name of the United States of America."

Less than twenty-four hours later, state delegates from across Alabama convene in a special session in Montgomery and vote, 61–39, to secede from the United States of America.

In each case, slavery is described as the primary, if not the only, motivation for the decision. Mississippi's official "Declaration of the Immediate Causes" states, at the top, "Our position is thoroughly identified with the institution of slavery," and "a blow at slavery is a blow at commerce and civilization."

The Alabama declaration further states that "the election of Abraham

The Weekly Advertiser.

G. H. SHORTER & S. G. REID,
STATE PRINTERS.

MONTGOMERY:

Saturday Morning, January 12, 1861.

ALABAMA OUT OF THE UNION!

THE VOTE SIXTY-ONE TO THIRTY-NINE!!

A GLORIOUS DAY!!!

We have only time to announce, as our evening edition goes to press, that the State Convention has withdrawn Alabama immediately and unconditionally from the Union.

The vote was taken about half-past two o'clock, and resulted 61 in favor to 39 against the Ordinance.

Truly, this is glory enough for one day. Our citizens are hailing the new era with demonstrations of profoundest emotion. The Capitol grounds and streets are alive with the moving mass of the cheering throng. Cannons are booming and bells ringing.

On January 11, 1861, Alabama votes to become the fourth Southern state to formally secede from the Union. As the *Montgomery Weekly Advertiser* describes, the news is met with celebration: "The Capitol grounds and streets are alive with the moving mass of the cheering throng. Cannons are booming and bells ringing."

Lincoln . . . is a political wrong of so insulting and menacing a character as to justify the people of the State of Alabama in the adoption of prompt and decided measures for their future peace and security."

In one three-day period, three states have left the Union. In Alabama, the *Montgomery Weekly Advertiser* describes the momentous developments this way: "The Union is already dissolved, and we will at once set about the work of . . . uniting with those gallant Southern States that are determined not to live under the free negro rule of Lincoln."

It is now two months before Lincoln's planned inauguration. He has not enacted a single policy, nor given a single speech, in his capacity as the next President. And yet because of his election, four Southern states have seceded from the United States of America.

A Republican supporter of Lincoln's had recently written him, trying to be optimistic: "If Georgia can be held back, the point of serious danger will be passed. If she joins South Carolina, the future will be gloomy." The writer warns, in the case of Georgia also seceding, of "the thorny crown of horrors you will be compelled to wear."

On January 19, just one week after Alabama's vote, Georgia also votes to secede. That makes five. The "thorny crown of horrors" is now squarely on Lincoln's head.

31

Chicago, Illinois

January 19, 1861

Like most Americans at the start of 1861, Allan Pinkerton is following the national crisis through the newspapers. At the time, he didn't share his political views with the public, probably because he had high-level clients of all political persuasions. But in private, his assessment was similar to that of many Northerners. At first, in the weeks after Lincoln's election, he was optimistic about the country's future.

"I entertained no serious fears of an open rebellion," he would later write. "I believed that with the incoming of the new administration, determined or conciliatory measures would be adopted, and that secession and rebellion would be either averted or summarily crushed."

He did resent the way the Southern press continuously attacked and disparaged the country's new President-elect—a fellow Illinoisan—to incite secessionist fervor. Pinkerton wrote:

Special efforts had been made to render Mr. Lincoln personally odious and contemptible, and his election formed the pretexts of these reckless conspirators, who had long been plotting the overthrow of the Union. No falsehood was too gross, no statement too exaggerated, to be used for that purpose, and so zealously did these misguided men labor in the cause of disunion, and so systematically concerted was their action, that the mass of the people of the slave States were made to believe that this pure, patient, humane, Christian statesman was a monster whose vices and passions made him odious, and whose political beliefs made him an object of just abhorrence.

Still, even if Pinkerton is opposed to Southern secessionists and has an admiration for Abraham Lincoln, these are the opinions of a private citizen. He is not, at this point, someone directly involved in affairs of state.

All of that is about to change.

On Saturday, January 19, Pinkerton finds a letter on his desk from an address in Philadelphia. It bears the name of a prominent man he once worked for, a name that immediately grabs his attention.

As Pinkerton describes it, "At this time I received a letter from Mr. Samuel H. Felton, the president of The Philadelphia, Wilmington and Baltimore Railroad, requesting my presence in Philadelphia upon a matter of great importance."

Felton's letter describes some of the threats to his company's rail routes in Maryland, threats apparently originating in the city of Baltimore. "It appeared that rumors were afloat as to the intention of the roughs and secessionists of Maryland to injure the [rail]road of which he was the president."

The letter does not include some of the more outlandish rumors—there is no mention of an attack on the incoming President's inaugural train or on the President himself—but it includes conspirators' specific rumored plans to damage Felton's tracks and infrastructure at the line's most vulnerable points in Maryland.

As Pinkerton paraphrased, "It was feared that their designs were to prevent travel upon the [rail]road either by destroying the ferryboats that carried the trains across the Susquehanna River . . . or by demolishing the railroad bridges over the Gunpowder River."

The conspiracy, as Felton described it, was political in nature: Southern secessionists conspiring to prevent Northern access to Washington, D.C., by blocking transportation through Maryland. If secessionists managed to seize the nation's capital, the destruction of the railroad would serve to isolate the capital city from Northern States.

Felton had been one of Pinkerton's most prestigious clients in the past, and the detective knew him to be a serious man. If Felton believes these plots to be more than rumor, then they demand attention.

"This letter at once aroused me to the realization of the danger that threatened the country," Pinkerton later wrote. "I determined to render whatever assistance was in my power."

Whatever plans Pinkerton may have had for the rest of the weekend, he cancels them. At the time, traveling from Chicago to Philadelphia is no small effort. Even for an experienced traveler like Pinkerton, who has privileged access to most railroad lines, this is a major cross-country trip. But by that night, Pinkerton is already boarding a train to begin the first leg of a day-and-a-half-long journey. Within forty-eight hours after reading Felton's letter, he pulls into the rail station in downtown Philadelphia.

"Upon arriving in that city, I went directly to the office of Mr. Felton," Pinkerton wrote, "and obtained from him all the information he possessed of the movements and designs of the Maryland secessionists."

Allan Pinkerton, without question, is on the case.

32

Springfield, Illinois

January 1861

The news is getting worse. The threats are real.

So for Lincoln's team in Springfield, here's the puzzle: How and when should they transport the President-elect to Washington, D.C., for his inauguration?

Dating back to George Washington, American Presidents had established a loose tradition of making ceremonial journeys from their home states to the national capital, en route to assuming the office. Part political rally and part public service, these journeys were means for ordinary citizens to catch a glimpse in person of their President-to-be in the cities and towns along the way, and for local elected officials to meet, receive, and entertain the new Commander in Chief.

In the days before air travel, these journeys were also—for many Presidents—a real farewell to home. They were transporting their families and belongings from one city to another, often with little or no chance to return during their term.

Lincoln has extra reason to honor this tradition. Outside of Illinois, he is still largely unknown. Relatively few Americans have laid eyes on him, and few Governors or Mayors have ever met him. With the country hanging on a precipice, he needs as much support as possible.

As a resident of the westernmost state of any President before him, Lincoln's inaugural journey will be the farthest on record. The only comparable route was President Andrew Jackson's 1829 trip, mostly by steamboat, from his home in Tennessee to the nation's capital. Lincoln has the benefit of a faster mode of transportation—the railroad—but the planning of his journey won't be easy.

One of the first challenges, of course, is that the capital city itself is potentially under siege by Southern secessionists determined to prevent the inauguration. Lincoln has carefully assessed the various warnings he has received, but is determined not to let these rumors prevent his travel. Nor does he heed Seward's advice to forgo his public journey and arrive in Washington a week early.

Instead, Lincoln's friends in Washington enlist the one person they believe can protect the city from insurrection: the seventy-four-year-old ranking officer in the U.S. Army, Gen. Winfield Scott.

General Scott is a legendary hero of the Mexican-American War, has held multiple officer's commissions, and understands the federal military and the state militias as well as anyone.

Learning of the threat, the grizzled warrior immediately agrees to draw up a plan to protect the capital city. He'll use every resource he can muster, even if it means a conflict with the outgoing Secretary of War. Scott has fought on behalf of the United States of America most of his life, and he's not about to let a bunch of traitors seize the capital or harm a duly-elected President.

This leads to the next piece of the puzzle, one that has both safety and political concerns. When it comes to Lincoln's trip to D.C., which route should he take?

Lincoln's first instinct is to travel for at least part of his journey through slaveholding border states. He knows he's viewed as a Northern candidate, so this trip could be a gesture of national unity, a signal that he intends to be a President for *all* Americans, including those who didn't vote for him.

Given the barrage of death threats against Lincoln, and the recent secession of Southern states, such a route would also signal courage. "I think Mr. Lincoln's preferences are for a southernly route," writes Henry Villard, a *New York Herald* reporter stationed in Springfield throughout the winter, "doubtless to demonstrate how little fear he has for his personal safety."

Lincoln's secretary John Nicolay has a similar impression: "He knew that incitements to murder him were not uncommon in the South, but as the habit of men constitutionally brave, he considered the possibilities of danger remote, and positively refused to torment himself with precautions for his own safety."

However, as the political situation worsens, and as threats of violence continue to pour in, Lincoln's advisors and influential Republicans persuade him against exposing the inaugural train to attack in such a delicate moment. "Your life is not safe, and it is your simple duty to be very careful of exposing it," the newspaper editor Horace Greeley writes to Lincoln. "I doubt whether you ought to go to Washington via [the South] unless you go with a very strong force."

In addition, as the standard-bearer of a new party, Lincoln is under pressure to rally Republican support behind him after a tumultuous election season. A northerly inaugural route would afford that chance. "He knows that those who elected him are anxious to see how he looks and hence is willing to gratify this," Villard writes in *The Herald*.

To plan and organize the journey, Lincoln utilizes the services of a dapper but mysterious New Yorker named William Wood. Wood first appeared in Springfield in December with an offer to coordinate the trip. He'd been sent on the recommendation of Thurlow Weed—a Republican Party operative and William Seward's former campaign manager—but aside from Wood's self-description as a "railroad man" and a "hotel man," little else is known about him, even today.

Under Wood's direction, the planning of this complex trip begins. Throughout the 1840s and 1850s, railroads had been expanding rapidly all over the states and territories. By Lincoln's election, every major city has rail access, but there is still no single railroad line that connected the country. Instead it's a complicated patchwork of competing rail companies that control each regional segment.

To piece together a route from Springfield, Illinois, to the nation's capital, Lincoln's team has to coordinate with almost twenty different rail companies, each with a unique set of regulations. And since most companies operate out of separate stations, in most cases, the passengers will have to travel from one station to another within a city to catch a connecting train.

All of this has to be mapped out, taking into account an entourage of several dozen people, along with carefully timed stops every few hours for staged events in many small towns and most major cities along the route.

On top of that, complicated arrangements have to be made with local Governors, Mayors, state legislators, and various greeting committees who want to meet Lincoln, escort him, and share the stage with him for speeches, receptions, parades, and other events. Plus, his team has to book hotels, restaurants, and complicated ground transportation for all the passengers and for every day and night on what will eventually be a twelve-day journey.

At every stop—even the small towns—large and sometimes massive crowds are expected, preventing easy movement to and from the train, to and from hotels, and between train stations when transfers were necessary. The personal baggage of some thirty passengers, including the packed luggage of the President, his wife, and their children, will have to be monitored, protected, and transported every step of the way.

From the point of view of Lincoln's friends and advisors, however, the main concern is safety. At this time, the Secret Service doesn't exist yet. With so many crowds in so many towns and cities, with so many local stops, it'll be essentially impossible to protect the President-elect.

Some advisors recommend that Lincoln travel with a full company of soldiers, but he refuses. With the country already in an agitated state, the optics of an armed military procession are the last thing the President-elect wants. He'll allow for a handful of personal bodyguards to accompany him, but that's all. As Nicolay later describes it, "His life was therefore in reach of anyone, sane or mad, who was ready to murder and be hanged for it."

The team begins to sort through options, favoring the North and weighing which cities are most important for Lincoln to visit. They settle on a wide-ranging and circuitous route—a total of two thousand miles—through the Great Lakes region and the north, not crossing into New England, but otherwise traversing every big state. Among the bigger cities, they plan to pass through Indianapolis, Cincinnati, Cleveland, Pittsburgh, Buffalo, Albany, New York, Trenton, Philadelphia, and Harrisburg before descending south to the capital. In between, they'll plan to stop in dozens of smaller cities, towns, and villages.

With this route, Lincoln's advisors can at least expect that the majority of people who come to see the President-elect will be supporters rather than enemies.

Of course, all these plans mean nothing for the last leg of the trip.

No matter which route they take, there's still this problem: Washington, D.C., itself is surrounded by two slaveholding states— Virginia to the west and south, and Maryland to the north and east. Given the geography and the available railroad lines, there is simply no way to reach the nation's capital by rail without traveling straight through the slave state of Virginia or the slave state of Maryland.

Either way, the final stretch will take Abraham Lincoln deep into hostile territory.

33

———— · ————

Baltimore, Maryland

January 1861

Cypriano Ferrandini starts his mornings in his home on East Baltimore Street near Broadway, in what is now the Washington Hill district of Baltimore. He's married and has at least two children. Every day, he commutes roughly a mile due west to get to his downtown workplace, the barbershop in the basement of Barnum's City Hotel.

These are the basic and known facts of Ferrandini's life at the end of 1860. Little else is known about him or his daily life. The first-ever public mention of his name—over a decade earlier—is this newspaper ad:

> WANTED—a good white JOURNEYMAN BARBER; also, an apprentice to the hairdressing business. Apply at once to C. FERRANDINI'S Hair Dressing Saloon, 144 Baltimore street, near Calvert street.

This notice appeared in the August 5, 1848, edition of *The Baltimore Sun.* Right in the ad, he makes it clear that he'll only work with you if you're white.

Although a slave state, Maryland has a significant free black population, so black workers were available. Whether Ferrandini hired only whites to please his potential customers, or due to his own prejudice, there's no way to know for sure. But based on the city and the man, it was probably a bit of both.

Every subsequent time Cypriano Ferrandini posted a notice for a new hair assistant in the coming years—and he did so several times, from multiple shops—he always specified that prospective job candidates must be white.

Throughout the 1850s, public records and newspapers give a few more details of Ferrandini's life in Baltimore.

In July of 1852, four years after the first help wanted ad, *The Sun* posted this notice:

New infantry company.—A number of adopted citizens have resolved on the formation of a military corps. The uniform will be that of the French Light Infantry, and the title "The Baltimore Lafayette Guards." The following have been elected officers: Charles A. Leloup, Captain; _____ Ferrandini, 1st Lieut.

It is not clear why Ferrandini's first name was excluded from the notice, but this appointment as an officer of a drilling corps begins the barber's long immersion in the rituals and practices of local volunteer militia groups.

These organizations of armed and sometimes uniformed men—operating independently from the official state militias—were common across America at the time, but especially in the South. They often served a ceremonial purpose—marching in parades and appearing at public ceremonies. Still, many had political agendas and were prepared to raise their weapons in a paramilitary capacity. In small towns and rural areas where law enforcement was lacking, these groups could also serve a vigilante form of justice.

Around six months after the formation of the Baltimore Lafayette Guards, Ferrandini posted another help wanted ad in *The Sun*—for a white apprentice, of course—but now it was from the saloon in the basement of Barnum's City Hotel.

This new position in a popular gathering place for the well-to-do in the center of downtown seems to catapult Ferrandini to a new social position. That year, the Baltimore Lafayette Guards—soon just referred to as the Lafayette Guards—marched in a procession to lead then-President Franklin Pierce during a visit to the city.

Barnum's City Hotel, usually just called Barnum's, was one of Baltimore's most bustling social hubs. This illustration dates from the mid-1850s, at roughly the time Cypriano Ferrandini began working in the hotel's popular barbershop in the basement.

In 1855, Ferrandini was promoted to captain of the Lafayette Guards, and is from that time often referred to as "Captain Ferrandini." He's their organizer and drillmaster—the equivalent of a modern military drill sergeant, who teaches the group maneuvers, weapons handling, and marching technique—leading them in various parades and at social occasions, including their annual anniversary ball, of which he is listed as "executive director."

In 1856, when the Guards are enlisted to march in a citywide ceremony to celebrate George Washington's birthday, *The Sun* describes the ensuing event this way:

> The spirited corps of the LaFayette Guards made a full dress evening parade, accompanied by Capt. Buckley's martial music, and after proceeding through the western section of the city, marched

to the residence of First Lieutenant Ferciot, Holliday street, and partook of the sumptuous repast, the good things of this life being provided in abundance, and served up in admirable style. Speeches were made by Capt. Ferrandini and Lt. Ferciot, of the corps.

Unfortunately, the contents of Ferrandini's speech—presumably waxing poetic about George Washington—were not preserved.

By the mid- to late 1850s, Ferrandini is a regular at various balls and parties around the city, both connected to his own militia group and other similar organizations. At one point, he hosts a ceremony with the Lafayette Guards in which he presents to a "brother soldier"—a veteran of Maryland's Fifty-Third Regiment during the Mexican-American War—a "splendid sword and pair of epaulettes."

During this period, he remained in his regular position as the barber at Barnum's City Hotel, where many of the city's aristocratic class would come for haircuts, gossip, and, of course, heated discussions about current events.

To this day, there's no way to know precisely when or how Ferrandini became deeply engaged with politics, but his fervent passion on behalf of the South in the late 1850s makes him pretty typical for a Marylander.

One public signal of Ferrandini's sympathies occurred in the immediate aftermath of abolitionist John Brown's raid on Harpers Ferry, on October 16, 1859. Although Brown's raid failed, Virginia authorities worried that a wider slave insurrection was imminent as news of the event spread around the region. Armed white militias in nearby states prepared to travel to Virginia to help suppress any slave uprising.

On October 19, 1859, when fear of an insurrection was reaching its peak, Baltimore's *Daily Exchange* newspaper reported, "At an early hour yesterday morning, the Lafayette Guards [under] Capt. Ferrandini . . . and the Artillery companies, presented themselves at the Camden station, ready to proceed to the seat of war."

As it turned out, "it was deemed unnecessary to call their services into action," so the Lafayette Guards and their captain never left Baltimore. Still, Ferrandini demonstrated that he was prepared to drop everything and use force to protect slaveholders.

It was also during 1859 that Ferrandini joined the Knights of the Golden Circle. How exactly he was introduced to the secret society is lost to history. But the KGC had at least one prominent "castle" in Baltimore, and the group's infamous leader, George Bickley, spent some time in the city earlier in the year.

During his time there, Bickley edited and published at least one issue of a KGC-themed newspaper called *American Cavalier: A Military Journal Devoted to the Extension of American Civilization,* with articles outlining the group's grandiose vision of expanding a Southern slave empire into Mexico, Central America, and the Caribbean.

Whether Ferrandini ever interacted personally with Bickley in Baltimore is unclear, but both men probably attended the same KGC secret meetings at the local castle during this period.

Ferrandini also appears to have attended a Knights of the Golden Circle convention that summer at a resort in White Sulphur Springs, Virginia (present-day West Virginia). The convention included somewhere between eighty and one hundred "military men and noted political leaders" in attendance and close to 1,200 guests. The conference was billed as a means "to consider the steps necessary to render the political standing and material interests of the south more permanent," and Bickley gave at least one speech.

A reporter who gained entrance to the convention filed a story describing the Knights as a "secret southern military organization," and noted that in the convention speeches, "the relations of the north and south were examined, and a large amount of disunion feeling was expressed."

Even at this relatively early point, Bickley advocated Southern secession from the Union to ensure the preservation of slavery, and the reporter concluded at the time that Bickley was a "most dangerous man" who is "playing with the most dangerous passions of the Southern people."

Cypriano Ferrandini, the barber, is one of those people. And Ferrandini and the rest of the members of the Knights of the Golden Circle would soon find a new target on which to direct these passions.

In the aftermath of Lincoln's election, as rage and talk of secession reached a fever pitch, the KGC changed its focus from international expansion to the domestic emergency. The group's already existing ideology of white supremacy and its practice of recruiting and training secret "soldiers" ready to fight for the Southern cause was perfectly attuned to the political moment.

Rather than deploying members to expand slavery in Mexico, the Knights of the Golden Circle can now deploy its members to protect slavery from Abraham Lincoln and the Northern abolitionists.

As a member of the Baltimore KGC castle, Ferrandini would have met and known a fellow Baltimorean member of the KGC by the name of William Byrne. Byrne was a local businessman who, like Ferrandini, was a pro-Southern white supremacist who was deeply opposed to the new President.

In the summer of 1860, shortly before the Presidential election, Byrne founded and organized the regional militia group soon to be known as the National Volunteers. He originally created the group to march and rally for the Presidential campaign of the Southern Democratic Party candidate, John C. Breckinridge. After Breckinridge's defeat by Lincoln in November, the National Volunteers stayed together and, with a membership of several hundred men spanning the region between Baltimore and Washington, D.C., took on a more militant mission.

According to their postelection published manifesto, the group swears to "stand by and defend the South" against "abolitionist violence" and the imminent threat posed by the "Black Republican party." The incoming administration is, in their words, a "reign of terror" and "a system of tyranny which calls for the most emphatic rebuke."

Most important, according to the many rumors swirling around Washington, D.C.—and picked up by William Seward and others— one of the group's initial goals is to prevent the inauguration of Abraham Lincoln by any means necessary.

As these new plans take shape, the barber Ferrandini apparently leaves the Lafayette Guards and—near the start of 1861—forms his new militia organization, the Constitutional Guards. This group quickly falls under the umbrella of the larger National Volunteers.

No question, there are a lot of different militant groups—but a picture of Ferrandini's place in the web of Baltimore's white suprem-acist organizations begins to emerge.

He is a member of the proslavery secret society the Knights of the Golden Circle. He is also the leader of a militia group called the Constitutional Guards. The Constitutional Guards are part of a larger paramilitary group called the National Volunteers, and these National Volunteers were formed by fellow Baltimorean William Byrne, who himself is a member of the Knights of the Golden Circle and belongs to the same castle as Ferrandini.

In the early weeks of 1861, the world of Baltimore secessionists and Southern militants is an interconnected network—with Cypri-ano Ferrandini somewhere near the center.

It is from this center that Ferrandini launches his newest plan, recruiting and building a brand-new secret group in Baltimore—a group with a specific and more violent mission.

Their goal isn't just to seize the capital or disrupt the inauguration. As January arrives, they aim bigger.

Their target?

The incoming President himself.

34

Chicago, Illinois

January 24, 1861

Allan Pinkerton is watching from the window of his train. Slowly, the familiar sight of Chicago's Great Central Station comes into view.

He's returning from what turned into a forty-eight-hour stay in Philadelphia, Pennsylvania. There, he attended a series of high-level meetings in the downtown offices of Samuel Felton, president of the Philadelphia, Wilmington and Baltimore Railroad.

In the meetings, Felton shared the details of the suspected conspiracy to sabotage his railroad line—a line that runs straight from Philadelphia to Wilmington to Baltimore, where travelers can then transfer (after a short carriage ride between the two train stations) to the Baltimore & Ohio Railroad for a southbound train to Washington, D.C. The conspiracy supposedly originates from Maryland's largest city of Baltimore, which is roughly midway between Wilmington and Washington.

Hearing from Felton directly and studying various maps, Pinkerton gained a full understanding of the geographical significance of Felton's rail line. As Pinkerton put it, "This road was the great connecting link between the [northern] metropolis[es] of the country and the capital of the nation, and it was of the utmost importance that no interruption should be permitted to the free communication between Washington and the great cities of the North."

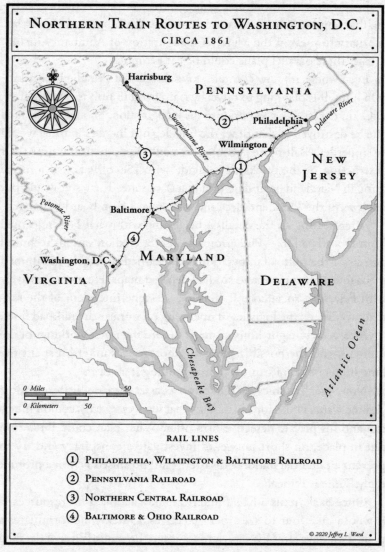

NORTHERN TRAIN ROUTES TO WASHINGTON, D.C.

CIRCA 1861

Harrisburg

PENNSYLVANIA

Susquehanna River

② Philadelphia

Delaware River

Wilmington

①

NEW
JERSEY

③

Potomac River

Baltimore

④

Washington, D.C.

MARYLAND

VIRGINIA

DELAWARE

Chesapeake Bay

Atlantic Ocean

0 Miles 50

0 Kilometers 50

RAIL LINES

① PHILADELPHIA, WILMINGTON & BALTIMORE RAILROAD

② PENNSYLVANIA RAILROAD

③ NORTHERN CENTRAL RAILROAD

④ BALTIMORE & OHIO RAILROAD

© 2020 Jeffrey L. Ward

The Philadelphia, Wilmington and Baltimore Railroad provides one of only two rail routes from the Northern states to Washington, D.C. Both of these routes converge in Baltimore, Maryland, where passengers can catch a connecting train on the Baltimore & Ohio Railroad to the nation's capital.

In addition to the railroad sabotage, there are also rumors circulating that Southern secessionists plan to seize Washington, D.C., in late February to prevent the March 4 inauguration of Abraham Lincoln. If true, these parallel plans could be catastrophic.

Even worse, it's now common knowledge that President-elect Lincoln himself is planning to travel by train from Illinois to Washington, D.C., in the week or two prior to his inauguration. Should Felton's rail line be destroyed at that time, the final leg of Lincoln's journey would be imperiled. Baltimore conspirators could hypothetically time their destruction of the tracks to coincide with Lincoln's actual journey through Maryland, stranding him in a slave state. The result would put the lives of the President-elect and everyone else on board in danger.

After hearing all the details—beginning with what Felton learned from Dorothea Dix—Pinkerton was also briefed on various technical aspects of the railroad's operations. He learned timetables, examined mechanical blueprints, and studied detailed maps. He met extensively with Felton's associate H. F. Kenney, the superintendent of the railroad, to discuss the logistics of operating on or near the railroad lines.

After a forty-eight-hour immersion into the inner workings of the railroad, and the possible plots to sabotage it, Pinkerton spent the long hours of his return trip home mulling it all over.

Now, back in Chicago, Pinkerton assesses the case. Felton made it clear he wants Pinkerton's help. But what services, exactly, could Pinkerton and his private detective firm offer? What plan could Pinkerton put in place, on short notice, to investigate a conspiracy and try to prevent a potential national disaster? He'd promised Felton a prompt reply. Time is critical.

Once back in his office, Pinkerton takes a look at his resources—it would take four to six other detectives. Quickly, he formulates a plan. Two days after his return to Chicago, he sends Felton a detailed seven-page letter that begins:

Dear Sir,
Should the suspicions of danger still exist, as was the case at our interview on the 19th, I would suggest in view of the brief time we now have to operate in—that I should myself with from four to

six operatives, immediately repair to the seat of danger and first endeavor to ascertain if any organization is in existence which might
directly or indirectly have for its object the commission of the offence you allude to.

Pinkerton and these "four to six operatives" will go straight to the
"seat of danger"—that is, to Baltimore. But this isn't a passive investigation. Their goal, he continues in the letter, will be "to become acquainted with some of the members of such body, and, if practicable,
some of my operatives should join the same."

This is what Pinkerton's agency does best: going undercover.

In his mind, this is the essence of real detective work. In Baltimore, he and his agents will try to learn which group or groups are
planning to attack and, using fake identities, befriend some of the
members and join the group themselves. Only from within can they
hope to learn about and stop this secretive organization.

In his letter, Pinkerton elaborates on his strategy. "As soon as we learn
positively who the leading spirits are . . . on the project you alluded to,
an unceasing Shadow should be kept upon them every moment." The
Shadow, of course, will be Pinkerton or one of his agents, monitoring
the "leading spirits" of the plot from an undercover position.

By taking such steps, Pinkerton writes, "I could be able to learn
their secrets and proposed plans of operations in sufficient time to be
able to communicate them to you."

Again, time is of the essence. Pinkerton explains that normally
he'd lay the groundwork over a period of several months, if not
longer. Here, there's no such luxury. Lincoln's inaugural ceremony,
planned for March 4, is now just over six weeks away. And since
Lincoln will no doubt plan his arrival in Washington at least several
days earlier, the entire plot in Baltimore—timed to Lincoln's passage
through Maryland—would most likely trigger even sooner. In other
words, Pinkerton and his agents need to get moving. Fast.

In the end, there's one final condition that Pinkerton asks for:

Secrecy is the lever of any success which may attend my operations
and as the nature of this service may prove of a character which

might . . . be dangerous to the persons of myself, or any operatives, I should expect that the fact of my operating should be known only to myself or such discreet persons connected with your Company as it might be absolutely necessary should we be entrusted with the same.

In other words, only Felton and his most trusted aides can know about the operation. Pinkerton always demands absolute secrecy for any investigation his firm undertakes, and only he himself can personally control who knows about the operation. When you're undercover against criminals, one slip of the tongue can get everyone killed.

Pinkerton sends the letter via express mail. A response comes a few days later.

Felton agrees to every term. Time to infiltrate.

Allan Pinkerton is going to Baltimore.

35

Washington, D.C.

January 29, 1861

The hearing room is private.

On Capitol Hill, five members of the U.S. House of Representatives are meeting in a closed session. It's just a few days after Allan Pinkerton sends his letter to Samuel Felton, and these five members are part of a special select congressional committee. Their mission is to conduct a series of secret examinations that—although neither party knows it—overlaps somewhat with Pinkerton's.

This special "Committee of Five" was first established almost three weeks earlier, on January 9, as rumors swirled of a secret conspiracy to seize Washington, D.C.

Technically, the committee is a "Select Committee of Five" to examine "Alleged Hostile Organization Against the Government Within the District of Columbia." But reporters soon give the group a more memorable nickname: the Treason Committee.

It's the brainchild, at least in part, of Senator William Seward. At the start of the new year, Seward finally accepted Lincoln's offer to be Secretary of State, leading the incoming cabinet.

Since accepting the position, Seward has thrown himself into the work of protecting the incoming President and trying to ensure the peaceful transfer of power.

The committee's mission is focused around a resolution that Seward supposedly drafted himself. It lays out the dangers facing the capital city on the eve of Abraham Lincoln's inauguration:

Resolved, That the select committee of five be instructed to inquire whether any secret organization hostile to the government of the United States exists in the District of Columbia; and if so whether any official or employee of the city of Washington, or any employees or officers of the federal government in the executive or judicial departments, are members thereof.

In its official report, the committee's chairman, Representative William A. Howard of Ohio, describes the specific context that motivated the committee's investigation:

The extraordinary excitement existing prior to the late presidential election led disaffected persons of high and low position, after the result of that election became known, to [contemplate] . . . various modes of resistance. Among other modes, resistance . . . to the inauguration of Mr. Lincoln, the seizure of the Capitol and the District of Columbia, were discussed informally in this city and elsewhere.

After the committee's inception on January 9, the members spent the next three weeks lining up various witnesses to testify under oath, in closed committee, regarding the rumors of violent plans to prevent Lincoln's inauguration.

To this day, it's unknown how the committee found and selected their particular witnesses, but the resulting lineup of over two dozen people—testifying over the course of two weeks—includes public officials and private citizens from Washington, D.C., and nearby Baltimore.

Now, on the morning of January 29, the hearing begins. At first, much of the testimony is frustrating and inconclusive. Some witnesses clearly have pro-Southern sympathies and are reluctant to reveal any information that may incriminate themselves or their fellows. Several witnesses feign ignorance—and, for others, the ignorance appears genuine.

At its core, it's simply hard to tell who's lying. For example, when they call James G. Berret, the Maryland-born Democratic Mayor of Washington, D.C., he insists there isn't the "slightest ground" that there's "any foray or raid upon the city of Washington." The Mayor adds, "I do not believe there is a solitary man in this city, with any claims to decency and standing, who would attempt to place the slightest impediment in the way of the peaceable inauguration of Mr. Lincoln."

This is the Mayor. He's supposed to be trustworthy. But when they ask him specifically about the National Volunteers—the shadowy militia group that has been at the center of many rumors—he replies, "I know them to be not only respectable, but they are stakeholding citizens, a great many of them, who would scorn to do anything that would bring reproach upon the city."

It's a response that's almost implausible. The formation of the National Volunteers was based almost entirely upon resistance to the incoming Lincoln administration, and one of their public manifestos includes thinly veiled threats of violence. Yet it's Mayor Berret's answer to the next round of questioning that's even more ridiculous.

The Chairman asks about "a secret organization called the 'K. G. C.' or the 'Knights of the Golden Circle,' or something of that kind; have you any information of, or do you believe that any such organization ever existed here?"

"I have never heard of any such organization here," Berret replies. "I certainly never heard that there was a meeting here. I do not think that there ever was."

Considering that one of the KGC's main headquarters is in Washington, D.C., and several Southern Senators and Congressmen are suspected supporters or even members of the group, it's nearly inconceivable that the Mayor of their same party wouldn't know of them.

Other witnesses are even more evasive. When the Congressmen question George R. Wilson, an officer of the United States Capitol Police, about the various plots, the officer says, "There was a general rumor about town that the Capitol was to be blown up, and all the Black Republicans hung up, and so on. Indeed, I was notified the other day, but I paid no attention to it."

Why would someone in law enforcement pay no attention to a rumor this serious? Perhaps for the same reason as the Mayor—they're secretly on the side of the secessionists.

By contrast, Charles P. Stone, a former career Army officer and current Inspector General of the Washington, D.C., militia, provides some helpful testimony. When questioned about potential attacks on the city, he explains, "I have had a vast number of intimations brought to me." And when it comes to the National Volunteers, he reports, "It has been stated to me that they would, . . . in case of an opportunity, oppose the inauguration of Mr. Lincoln." He further explains about the group: "I have been informed that . . . there were in this town some 1,500 men who could be depended upon to take this city."

This information is confirmed by lengthy testimony from Gen. Winfield Scott, the decorated war hero who had recently taken on the responsibility to oversee the safety and security of the city prior to and during Lincoln's inauguration. During questioning, the General reveals he's also received "innumerable letters" from informants, "three, four, up to seven a day" containing serious and sometimes specific warnings.

As the General describes it, these threats involve "seizure of the Capitol" and "other public buildings of this city" or are threats to "prevent the inauguration of the President and Vice President" by the exercise of force before or on March 4.

According to the General, the threats originate from many different states, but with a majority from Virginia and Maryland. He concedes that some of the warnings are anonymous and appear frivolous, but some are from reputable sources. One letter contains "so much precision" and detail that Scott believes the writer must be "sworn a member of the conspiracy which he alleged to exist."

The General even brings a few sample letters to share with the committee, though he's careful to excise names to protect his informants. One letter describes a plot in which "vast numbers of men, say 400 or 500, are coming, and will come from the south and north with arms concealed in their baggage." Although this plot involves pro-Southern "invaders" from outside of the capital, the writer of the letter also claims that "some men in [Washington, D.C.] are in the plot, and they are making lists of prominent men to arrest or put to death."

Another letter, addressed from Nashville, Tennessee, repeats the threat of a secessionist plot against the capital city, with this additional warning: "You can hardly be fully acquainted with the magnitude of the danger, and the extent of the preparations to prevent Mr. Lincoln's inauguration. A secret society exists throughout all the southern States, bound together by solemn obligations to prevent it at all hazards, even to the extent of causing his assassination before taking the oath of office."

If this direct warning of Lincoln's murder wasn't clear enough, the writer adds that "if the attempt be made to inaugurate Mr. Lincoln . . . the probabilities are great that someone will be willing to run the risk of immortalizing himself by propitiating the extreme southern feeling, and will make the attempt upon his life."

To drive home the point, the writer offers this ominous warning: "Treason is all around you, I fear to a far greater extent than you are aware."

It's hardly an uncrackable code. Clearly, the committee should find out more about this secret society.

In fact, the group described in the letter seems a close fit for the profile of the Knights of the Golden Circle. Indeed, the KGC has a significant presence in Tennessee. This could be a fruitful avenue of investigation.

Yet the members of the Treason Committee don't seem to make the connection. They don't pose a single question to General Scott about the Knights—and the General never even mentions the group's name.

In the end, after looking at all the evidence, the General believes that "some sort of conspiracy undoubtedly exists."

For the committee, though, without the right witness—and more important, the right questions—there's no way to stop it.

Soon enough, however, the Treason Committee will hear testimony from someone who knows far more than anyone realizes.

36

---·---

Springfield, Illinois

January 30, 1861

Abraham Lincoln has changed.

In the first weeks after his election, he had adjusted to his new position of immense responsibility with—at least outwardly—characteristic good cheer and humor.

But by the end of January 1861, his countenance is different. Weeks of dire national news, continued threats and warnings for his safety, increasingly stressful and complicated planning—all of this, combined with a brutally cold Illinois winter—had cast a dark pall on the President-elect and his team in the final weeks before his planned departure on February 11.

On January 30, twelve days before he's scheduled to leave, Lincoln surprises his friends by taking a last-minute trip to Coles County, a rural county in southeastern Illinois. He travels there not with his aides but with his cousin John Hanks—he's the one who Lincoln used to split rails with as a young man—and a few others who knew Lincoln during his earliest days in Illinois.

To get to Coles, Lincoln and his companions first take a passenger train and then a freight train to the village of Charleston, where a few locals who learned of Lincoln's visit brave the freezing cold to catch a glimpse of the soon-to-be President. Lincoln knows this village well;

it's where he first arrived in the state almost thirty years earlier with the dirt-poor family who raised him, pushing an oxcart that contained all their possessions. In this still humble place, Lincoln now spends the night.

Early the next morning, Lincoln joins up with another cousin, Dennis Hanks, and together they ride due south in a small two-horse buggy along a rugged dirt road. At one point, they have to step out in the freezing cold to wade the horses through icy Kickapoo Creek. Finally, they reach a small obscure backwoods village known as Farmington.

So why does Lincoln take this trip? First, to visit his father's grave. He and his father were never close—Thomas Lincoln was a stern, cold man who sometimes treated his son harshly—but the younger Lincoln felt compelled to see his father's small, unmarked grave one last time, to remember the man who nonetheless kept him housed and fed through two decades of poverty and struggle.

More important, Lincoln is here to say goodbye in person to his stepmother, now seventy-two years old, who still lives in a small log cabin with a few relatives outside Farmington.

Sarah Bush Lincoln was the one who laid eyes on Abraham for the first time as a filthy, near-starving, lice-covered ten-year-old boy. Back then, he'd just been left alone with his twelve-year-old sister for many weeks in a dirt-floor cabin in the remote woods of Indiana.

A woman from a poor background who could neither read nor write, Sarah Bush became a devoted stepmother, and she and Abe developed a deep, warm bond. She described him as "the best boy I ever saw." She said, "His mind and mine . . . seemed to run together—move in the same channel." Through the first two decades of his life, she may be the one person truly close to Lincoln who didn't die.

Now, when Lincoln and his cousin knock on her door, the reunion is emotional. By one account, Lincoln wraps his long arms all the way around the rocking chair where she sits, and she "embraced and cried over him."

Lincoln stays for dinner. Roughly a month before his planned inauguration to become President of the United States, he eats in this tiny backwoods cabin with his stepmother's family, many of whom never learned to read or write. During the visit, Lincoln speaks with enormous warmth of his stepmother, telling his companions that while growing up "she had been his best friend in this world and that no son could love a mother more than he loved her."

Lincoln spends another full day in Farmington and Charleston, seeing old friends and relatives from his younger days. "He seemed to enjoy it so much that his face was continually lit up with a sunny smile," one companion said. After so many stressful weeks of endless preparation, the wash of memories is a welcome break.

Whatever happiness Lincoln is able to enjoy during the visit evaporates when it's time to depart back for Springfield. Once again, he has to say goodbye to his stepmother.

"She embraced him when they parted," one onlooker remembers. But then she begins crying, almost uncontrollably. She is overcome by foreboding. She says she knows that "she would never be permitted to see him again" because if he goes to Washington "his enemies would assassinate" him.

Even in this tiny corner of rural Illinois, people are aware of the political rage coursing through the country.

"No, no, Mama," Lincoln says, trying to calm her. "They will not do that: trust in the Lord and all will be well. We will see each other—again."

But as her son says his final farewell and departs, she is inconsolable.

"I did not want Abe to run for President—did not want him elected," she later says. "Something told me that something would befall Abe and that I should see him no more."

Sarah Bush Lincoln is right; it's the last time she will ever lay eyes on her son.

37

Philadelphia, Pennsylvania

February 1861

Once again, Allan Pinkerton is on a train.

He's racing toward Philadelphia for a final meeting with executives of the Philadelphia, Wilmington and Baltimore Railroad—including the president, Samuel Felton—before traveling south to begin his investigation in and near Baltimore.

The rail trip from Chicago to Philadelphia requires many tedious line switches in different cities, sometimes transferring to different stations within a city to wait for a connecting train. Some parts of the journey involve long, continuous hours with only the flat Midwestern scenery to provide distraction as the trains pass through Indiana, Ohio, and western Pennsylvania.

On this particular journey, however, Pinkerton is not alone. Several companions are with him for the briefing in Philadelphia, and they'll accompany him to Baltimore. All are employees and agents from Pinkerton's National Detective Agency—the "four to six operatives" he'd suggested to Felton—and they're now involved in every aspect of the investigation.

Among the small group are some of his finest and most talented agents.

One of them is a bearded, athletic man in his late thirties named

Timothy Webster. "He was a man of great physical strength and endurance, skilled in all athletic sports, and a good shot," Pinkerton later described him. Originally from England, Webster served as a policeman in New York City for several years before meeting Pinkerton and joining his agency. He's now one of the firm's most seasoned agents. He is "brave, honest and intelligent," according to his boss. "No danger was too great, no trust too responsible, no mission too delicate for him to attempt."

Another member of the team is "a young man of fine personal appearance" by the name of Harry Davies. Originally educated to be a Jesuit priest, Davies is a well-dressed man in his twenties who had traveled extensively and possessed, according to Pinkerton, "the ability to speak, with great facility, several foreign languages." More important, he'd lived for a time in New Orleans and other Southern cities. He therefore "had a thorough knowledge of the South, its localities, prejudices, customs and leading men." Although Davies is one of the younger and less experienced detectives in the agency, Pinkerton sensed that his sophisticated manner and knowledge of the South would be of unique benefit in Baltimore.

Accompanying these and a few other men are two women. One of the women, Hattie Lawton, is a younger member of Pinkerton's staff and a recent addition to the "Female Detective Bureau" in the agency. Not much is known about Lawton or how she came to work with Pinkerton, but she's described by some as vivacious and friendly. Some of this friendliness was probably an act, though, to win over the trust of unwitting targets of investigation. As Pinkerton described Lawton, "She appeared careless and entirely at ease, but a close observer would have noticed a compression of the small lips, and a fixedness in the sparkling eyes that told of a purpose to be accomplished."

Some researchers today speculate that Lawton was of mixed race, although this is difficult to confirm. If so, her skin was pale enough that she regularly went undercover as white. Regardless, she was a pioneer as probably only the second female detective in the country. Pinkerton—who viewed the detective profession as a noble one—probably gave Lawton this pitch when he hired her, as it is the pitch he supposedly gave to every woman whom he hired: "In my service, you will serve your country better than on the field. I have several female operatives. If you agree to come aboard you will go in training with the head of my female detectives, Kate Warne. She has never let me down."

Kate Warne, naturally, is the other woman on the train. Now in her fifth year working for the firm, she's established herself as one of the most reliable agents on Pinkerton's staff, and sometimes seems to play a second-in-command role in the company.

"Of rather a commanding person," Pinkerton described her, "and with an ease of manner that was quite captivating at times, she was calculated to make a favorable impression." Her poise and competence make her someone he can send as an emissary to high-level clients to speak on his behalf. In the field, she's one of his best assets.

Considering the urgency of the case, Pinkerton and his team haven't had much time to prepare for the investigation. In only a few days, they've had to craft alternate personas from scratch, practice Southern accents, and gather wardrobe and other disguise elements for their coming undercover work. Each of them has a different part to play, and once they assume their false roles, they will rarely revert to their true identities. Not until the case is done.

When the team reaches Philadelphia, Pinkerton has a final briefing with Felton and the railroad's superintendent. Then, he and his group head to the West Philadelphia station and board one of the PW&B's own busy southbound trains. Their route will be direct, a line that travels southeast from Philadelphia along the Delaware River to the Delaware state line, then passes through the narrow northern section of Delaware via Wilmington, then continues due southwest over the Maryland line in the direction of Baltimore.

This route that Pinkerton and his team now travel is on the very same railroad line that Samuel Felton learned is under threat of sabotage. It is also the same railroad line that Abraham Lincoln may eventually travel en route to the nation's capital.

Now, as the train's locomotive churns over the state line to the slave state of Delaware, and then, soon after, over the line into Maryland, Pinkerton's investigation is officially under way.

38

Washington, D.C.

February 5, 1861

For two and a half weeks, the House committee continues its investigation.

Dozens of witnesses are called, hundreds of questions are asked.

But of all those whom the Treason Committee puts under oath, two seem to fly below the radar. They're both private citizens—both from Baltimore—interviewed on consecutive days on Tuesday, February 5, and Wednesday, February 6.

Their examinations are brief, their testimony almost forgettable. One of these men is Otis K. Hillard, a twenty-eight-year-old from a privileged Baltimore family. He was born and raised in the city, but has spent several years traveling around the country—"partly on business, and partly for pleasure," he says—including the last two years traversing the Southern states. He has recently returned to Baltimore and is immersed in the city's social scene, as well as its politics.

Through his social connections, Hillard seems to know something of the shadowy secret societies and secessionist paramilitary organizations now coalescing in and around Baltimore.

"Have you any knowledge of an organization existing in the United States called the KGC?" the committee asks.

"I have some knowledge of such an institution," Hillard replies.

But he denies being a member and refuses to say much else about the Knights.

When the Congressmen ask about the National Volunteers, Hillard also denies being a member. But this time, he hints that he's got a bit more information about them.

"It numbers six thousand men," he says. And that's just in Baltimore, not including D.C.

He also claims to know the names of the group's leaders. When pressed to provide these names, Hillard refuses, saying that revealing them could be a risk to his personal safety. "You know what Baltimore city is; it is a wild place," he explains. "If they were to know that I disclosed these names, I have no idea what the consequence might be."

Interestingly, when they ask Hillard about the actual mission of the National Volunteers, he denies that they want to seize the capital or interfere with the inauguration. He claims their motive is merely defensive, a response to rumors that Lincoln is bringing a large military escort with him through Baltimore en route to the capital.

As Hillard explains, the object of the National Volunteers is to prevent any "armed body of men, from coming on to Baltimore with Mr. Lincoln. Mr. Lincoln will not be interrupted as a citizen alone, but with an armed body of men he would be."

In other words, they don't object to Lincoln himself; they object to him showing up escorted by soldiers or a militia.

Regardless, after Hillard says he won't reveal any names, the committee decides not to press him on the subject.

It's a big mistake.

But not nearly as big as what happens with the other witness from the same city.

Like Otis Hillard, he's a civilian. When asked where he resides, he responds, "I reside in Baltimore. My place of business is under Barnum's Hotel."

The new witness's name?

Cypriano Ferrandini. The city's most powerful barber.

39

---·---

Springfield, Illinois

February 10, 1861

It's been a mess.

For Abraham Lincoln, the first several days of February have been a hurricane of planning and preparations for his trip to the nation's capital. He and his family have been staying in a local hotel while their belongings are packed and their home cleared.

Lincoln's younger sons, Willie and Tad, were devastated when their father determined that their family dog, Fido, would not join them on their move to Washington. Instead, the pet would remain in Springfield under the care of their longtime neighbors.

Feeling guilty, Lincoln arranged a home photography session with the dog so that Willie and Tad could bring Fido's portrait on the journey to their new home.

At the hotel, Lincoln also set up a local auction to sell most of his furniture, then rented his soon-to-be vacated home to an Illinois businessman. All that was left was the mundane: settling debts, buying some clothes to supplement a few suits that were gifted to him, and sorting through his personal papers.

At the local Springfield bank, he took out $400 for the coming trip, leaving $600—just over $17,000 in today's dollars—in his bank account. (Abraham Lincoln was at the time the least wealthy person ever to be elected President of the United States.)

For weeks now, they've been planning. Every day, he's been surrounded—constantly—by supporters, advisors, and visitors. What he needs is some time alone.

On the afternoon of February 10, the day before his planned departure, Lincoln slips out of his busy office and walks quietly toward the small, second-story law firm that still bears his name.

When he arrives, the wintry air is blowing. He walks up the familiar stairs to the tiny, one-room corner office where he and his partner, William Herndon, had practiced for almost two decades. As usual, Herndon is at his desk.

Nearby, the firm's only clerk, a young man who had been with them for the past year or so, understands the significance of the moment and quietly leaves.

For the President-elect, the past several weeks have been mostly trial and misery. The country has been pulled apart, and Lincoln has been powerless to stop it. Yet another state, Louisiana, has recently seceded, bringing the total number to six.

Colleagues and friends of Lincoln have seen a growing pain and darkness in him. By most measures, he's the least experienced President ever to take the office and is now facing what looks to be the greatest challenge in the nation's history.

Many are beginning to predict that bloodshed is coming. Even war.

But right now, in this humble law office, Lincoln sits and reclines on the room's only couch. He and Herndon make small talk and then reflect on some of their early cases. Herndon, who knows Lincoln's moods as well as anyone, can see that his former partner is in a contemplative state. After a long pause, Lincoln finally speaks.

"Billy, how long have we been together?"

"Over sixteen years," Herndon replies.

"We've never had a cross word during all that time, have we?"

"No, indeed we have not."

The two men sit in silence for a moment, then Lincoln swings his long legs off the couch, and Herndon gets up to help Lincoln pack up a few assorted books and papers. When the two men walk down the stairs, Lincoln turns and takes a final look at the LINCOLN & HERNDON signboard that still "swung on its rusty hinges at the foot of the stairway."

For a moment, Lincoln gazes at the sign. "Let it hang there undisturbed," he says softly. "The election of a President makes no change in the firm of Lincoln and Herndon. If I live, I'm coming back sometime, and then we'll go right on practicing law as if nothing ever happened."

Before he departs, he turns to Herndon one last time. "I am sick of office-holding already," he says. "And I shudder when I think of the tasks that are still ahead."

From there, he puts on his top hat and walks away.

40

Washington, D.C.

Five Days Earlier

The Treason Committee has Cypriano Ferrandini exactly where they need him. Under oath.

In a private hearing room on Capitol Hill, the Chairman himself, Representative William A. Howard of Ohio, is asking the questions.

Ferrandini—the barber from Baltimore—acknowledges that, yes, in the past he was a "drill instructor" with various independent militia organizations. "I was at one time commanding the Lafayette Guards, a company in Baltimore," he explains, as well as other "companies I was connected with in the state of Maryland."

But it's Ferrandini's current activities that the Congressmen are more interested in.

"Have you been engaged in drilling any company lately?" they ask.

"I have."

"What is the name of the company?"

"The Constitutional Guards," Ferrandini replies.

"Are you hired to drill them?"

"No, sir; I do it voluntarily."

Ferrandini goes on to explain that his new group, the Constitutional Guards, began as a small company, but they're now operating under the umbrella of a larger organization. "[We] have adjourned now to the headquarters of the National Volunteers, and drill there."

The National Volunteers. The group that, over and over, keeps coming up in numerous testimonies—and is repeatedly mentioned in newspapers around the city as being the most likely armed conspirators.

Naturally, the Chairman asks Ferrandini to describe the nature of the National Volunteers. Here, the barber gets vague, saying they used to be "a political association" but that they're now "drilling as a military volunteer corps."

The Chairman asks: What are the group's motives?

Now, Ferrandini simply lies.

He testifies that the group has no violent designs on Washington, D.C., and no designs against Abraham Lincoln's inauguration. Echoing the testimony of Otis Hillard, he explains that the group's primary purpose is simply "to prevent northern volunteer companies from passing through the State of Maryland."

If the Chairman is suspicious, he doesn't show it. Instead, he asks more generally, "Do you know of . . . any military company, or any secret society" that wants to prevent "the inauguration of Mr. Lincoln on the 4th of March?"

"No, sir."

"Or to prevent his coming through the State of Maryland?"

"No, sir; none whatever."

So it's simply "to prevent northern volunteer companies from coming through?"

"A northern invasion; that is about the whole of it," the barber says.

He then clarifies that whether it's the National Volunteers or any other group disrupting the inauguration, "there is nothing connected with the city of Baltimore that has any intention of that sort. If there was one I should know it."

Ferrandini is adamant. And quick.

In no time, his testimony is over. Like Otis Hillard, a footnote to history.

In retrospect, though, here's what's worth noting: Out of twenty-eight committee witnesses, Ferrandini is the *only* one who actually admitted to being a current member of the National Volunteers. Yet the so-called Treason Committee never really pressed him about the organization, its leadership, or its makeup. Nor did they ask Ferrandini whether he was a member of the Knights of the Golden Circle, or whether he knew anything about that group.

These are glaring errors. And potentially deadly ones.

For the rest of their investigation, the committee veers away from the threat to Abraham Lincoln and instead focuses almost entirely on rumors of a pending attack on the city of Washington itself.

Ferrandini and Otis Hillard walk away scot-free—despite all the lies they'd just told.

Despite the fact they know each other.

Despite the fact they're part of the same secret group in Baltimore.

And despite the fact that, together, they have a very specific plan to make sure that once Abraham Lincoln embarks on his journey, he'll be dead long before he gets to his new home.

41

Maryland

February 1861

The investigation has begun.

Although the conspiracy apparently has its roots in Baltimore, the targeted railway lines are northeast of the city. As a result, Allan Pinkerton and his agents start searching for clues through the upper portion of Maryland—along the very railroad tracks being threatened.

Rather than racing straight to Baltimore, the team makes short stops along the route to gain impressions of the region, engage locals in political conversation, and try to glean any rumors or loose talk that may refer to the secret plot.

In Maryland, their first stop is Perryville, in the northeastern corner of the state, ten miles from the Delaware line. Here, Pinkerton finds the same thing that's happening everywhere: heated political debate. "Men indulged in fierce arguments, in which both sides were forcibly represented," Pinkerton would later recall, "but aside from this I discovered no cause for apprehension, and no occasion for active detective work as yet."

The next stop is Havre de Grace, a few miles south from Perryville, but of greater strategic significance. Havre de Grace is a town along the southeastern bank of the Susquehanna River, at the spot where the PW&B Railroad must cross the water. Because there's currently no rail bridge built to span the mile-wide width of the river, train cars are instead detached and ferried across individually on flatboats. This creates an obvious vulnerability.

As Pinkerton observes, Havre de Grace is where "serious damage might be done to the company, should the ferries be destroyed." Pinkerton also notes that in his team's cursory assessment of the area, "the [political] lines were more clearly drawn and the popular feeling much more bitter."

For these reasons, Pinkerton determines that the town warrants further investigation. "I therefore left one man at this place, with instructions to become acquainted with such men as he might, on observation, consider suspicious, and to endeavor to obtain from them, by association, a knowledge of their intentions."

Leaving a junior member in Havre de Grace, the rest of the team continues south on the train. The next stop is a town called Perryman, where, as Pinkerton describes it, "the feeling was considerably more intense."

When it came to political sympathy, there is no longer any ambiguity about which side the public supports. Cataloguing his impressions, Pinkerton wrote: "Under the influence of bad men the secession movement had gained many supporters and sympathizers. Loud threats were uttered against the railroad company, and it was boastfully asserted that 'no d—d abolitionist should be allowed to pass through the town alive.'"

If anything, Pinkerton found that these uttered threats are almost too bold and overt to take seriously. "I have always found it a truism that 'a barking dog never bites,' . . . and although I had but little fear that these blatant talkers would perform any dangerous deeds, I considered it best to be fully posted as to their movements, in order to prevent a catastrophe, if possible."

As a result, Pinkerton instructs his agent Timothy Webster—the strapping, athletic man from England—to remain in Perryman and blend in among the local laborers and railroad workers to see what he can learn. Pinkerton tells Webster to "carefully note everything that transpired which had any relation to attempted violence or a disposition to resort to aggressive measures."

Not surprisingly, as the rest of Pinkerton's team makes their way farther south, "the opposition to the government and the sympathy with secession was manifestly more intense."

In the town of Magnolia, about ten miles northeast of Baltimore, Pinkerton recalls that "I observed a very dangerous feeling, and among men of all classes the general sentiment was in favor of resistance and force." Here he dispatches another agent, John Seaford, to embed with the locals and learn what he can.

Then, finally, Pinkerton and the remainder of his team reach the city of Baltimore. All of Felton's intelligence suggests that whatever the conspiracy may be, it's most likely based here. As a pro-Southern stronghold in the region—home to wealthy slave traders, pro-Southern militias, and an aristocratic class with secessionist sympathies—Baltimore is the natural place for an organized and well-funded conspiracy to take root.

Indeed, as Pinkerton arrives in the city, he reports that when it comes to political sentiment, "[here] I found the greatest amount of excitement that I had yet experienced." He and his team take up residence at a hotel called the Howard House.

Now, they formulate a plan. The goal is "to inquire closely and carefully into the political situation."

Almost immediately, Pinkerton senses a menacing sentiment in the city, much of it directed at one target. "The opposition to Mr. Lincoln's inauguration was most violent and bitter," he writes, "and a few days' sojourn in this city convinced me that great danger was to be apprehended."

Pinkerton is so convinced of the coming danger, he immediately sends for "an additional force of men" from Chicago to bolster his existing team and aid the investigation.

In addition to these ominous signs—even as he's formulating a plan to penetrate the inner circle of secessionist plotters in the city—Pinkerton is also acutely aware of a key fact that bears directly on his investigation.

Abraham Lincoln's team in Springfield has not yet released a formal itinerary for his inaugural trip. But leaks and rumors—as well as common sense—have continued to suggest that the President-elect will take a northerly route toward the capital. Some Midwestern newspapers have already reported that Lincoln's train will travel through Pennsylvania and then southward—by way of either Philadelphia or Harrisburg—through Maryland and then to Washington, D.C.

If Lincoln travels to Washington by way of Philadelphia, it will be on Felton's PW&B line. If by way of Harrisburg, it will be on the Northern Central line. But either way, to get to Washington, D.C., he'll have to first make a stop in one place: Baltimore. Only here can southbound passengers on either line disembark, cross the city to the B&O Railroad's station, and catch the one and only southbound train to the nation's capital.

For Abraham Lincoln, all roads lead through the hostile city of Baltimore. Pinkerton knows this. In fact *everyone* knows this—including Lincoln's enemies.

42

Springfield, Illinois

February 11, 1861

Today, they leave.

It's cold, rainy, and gray out.

At 7:30 a.m., after breakfast at his hotel, Abraham Lincoln personally ropes up the family's trunks and luggage and writes on them the simple inscription: "A. Lincoln, White House, Washington, D.C."

By 7:45 a.m., he and a few aides are in a small public carriage en route to the Great Western Depot far across town. There, they'll meet the rest of Lincoln's entourage, who will join him for the first leg of the planned twelve-day journey to Washington, D.C.

According to his secretary John Nicolay, who's on the carriage ride with him, Lincoln's mood during the trip to the station is one of "gloom and depression."

As the President-elect watches the familiar streets pass by, the stormy skies add to the feeling of "subdued anxiety, almost of solemnity." Whether Lincoln's darkness comes from sorrow at leaving his home or from the overwhelming burden of responsibility bearing on his shoulders, no one knows for sure.

Then, as the carriage nears the modest depot on the outskirts of the city, the group encounters something that none of them was expecting: a crowd of over a thousand residents who'd made the long trek to the station in the cold and rain to bid their hometown hero goodbye.

Lincoln, who rarely if ever shows raw emotion in public, is suddenly overwhelmed. The crowd cheers as he steps down from the carriage. He begins warmly embracing and shaking hands with the hundreds of friends, neighbors, relations, and colleagues, "almost all of whom I could recognize." As he says his goodbyes, one onlooker reports that "his face was pale, and quivered with emotion, so deep as to render him unable to render a single word."

Eventually, the crowd parts, allowing Lincoln and his entourage to cross through the depot and approach their waiting train. As the bell sounds to signal the pending departure, members of Lincoln's party begin climbing the ladders to enter the passenger cars. Lincoln himself climbs up the back ladder to the rear platform of the train and turns to face the crowd. He wasn't planning to give any sort of farewell speech—and he has no remarks prepared. Instead, he speaks from the heart.

My friends,
No one, not in my situation, can appreciate my feelings of sadness at this parting. To this place, and the kindness of these people, I owe everything. Here I have lived a quarter of a century, and have passed from a young to an old man. Here my children have been born, and one is buried. I now leave, not knowing when, or whether ever, I may return, with a task before me greater than that which rested upon Washington. Without the assistance of that Divine Being, who ever attended him, I cannot succeed. With that assistance I cannot fail . . . let us confidently hope that all will yet be well. To His care commending you, as I hope in your prayers you will commend me, I bid you an affectionate farewell.

In the crowd, handkerchiefs start appearing.

The brief words "left hardly a dry eye in the assemblage," as one observer put it. Another onlooker describes the same: "Many eyes were filled to overflowing as Mr. Lincoln uttered those few simple words. His own breast heaved with emotion and he could scarcely command his feelings to commence."

With a final wave, Lincoln turns from the train's rear platform and lowers his head to step into the passenger car.

"We will pray for you!" several voices shout as the door closes behind him.

The train whistle blows again, and with a loud hiss, the engine's steam fills the air. At exactly 8:00 a.m., the locomotive's large iron wheels begin to turn, and the train soon disappears through the steam into the dark morning.

Part III

The Most Fiendish Plot

43

Baltimore, Maryland

February 11, 1861

John H. Hutcheson.

That's the name on the door of a suite of offices at 44 South Street, an address centrally located near Baltimore's busy commercial district.

Hutcheson is a stockbroker from the South, visiting on business, and about a week ago he rented these offices to house his operations while in the city. He is well dressed and outgoing, with a Southern accent and close-cropped beard. Since setting himself and a few employees up in the building, he has befriended several other businessmen and employees who also work there.

There is only one sort of visitor that Hutcheson would not welcome into his office to chat or do business with, and that would be any visitor from the city of Chicago, Illinois.

Why? For one simple reason. A visitor from Chicago might recognize his true identity.

His real name is Allan Pinkerton, and everything about his persona and stockbroking business is an undercover alias. The firm's associates who sometimes dart in and out of his office are indeed his employees, but they're employees in his detective business, not the securities business, and they likewise have created assumed identities with fake names.

Pinkerton's selection of the building at 44 South Street was very deliberate. Because the location is downtown and equidistant from the city's three major train depots, it is, as he says, "in a position where I could receive prompt reports from all quarters of the metropolis."

The building also has another attractive feature. It is "so constructed that entrance could be gained to it from all four sides, through alleyways that led in from neighboring streets." This way, his undercover operatives can enter and leave discreetly at all hours, never in groups, and avoid drawing notice or being seen together.

Thus situated, Pinkerton has taken greater stock of the city and the various secessionist organizations therein. He is continually alarmed by the fervor and rage coursing through the city. "I could not fail to notice an increase in the excitement and the indications of . . . open revolt," he later writes. "Everywhere the ruling principle seemed to be opposition to the new administration and a decided inclination to aid the Confederacy."

Pinkerton quickly determines that "the state of feeling in Baltimore" is so "embittered and poisoned" that extremists are ready to resort to violence. As he describes, "Secessionists of that city were prepared to do anything which they deemed necessary in order to break up the Union."

Pinkerton's mission, technically, is to investigate the possible sabotage of Samuel Felton's railroad tracks that run northeast from the city. However, Pinkerton now senses, from all he has learned, heard, and observed thus far, that the excitement and fervor among secessionists is not directed at railroad tracks but at the President-elect himself and his pending inauguration. As Pinkerton later put it:

> The chief opposition seemed to be to the inauguration of President Lincoln, and the plan of the conspirators was to excite and exasperate the popular feeling against the President-elect to the utmost, and so successfully had this been done that a majority of the wealthier classes, with few exceptions—those in office—and

the mob element in general were in full accord in their desire to prevent the inauguration from taking place.

So while Pinkerton continues to investigate the plot to sabotage railroad tracks and bridges north of the city, he is now also increasingly convinced that there are secret plots afoot focused on Lincoln's actual passage through Baltimore—with Lincoln himself as the target.

With this in mind, Pinkerton carefully studies the logistics of train travel through Baltimore as it pertains to Lincoln's inaugural journey.

As is true in most larger cities, rail passengers who arrive in Baltimore must disembark and travel to a different station in order to catch connecting trains. In the case of travelers coming from the northern states and traveling through to Washington, D.C.—Lincoln's probable route—there are two distinct possibilities.

Those passengers traveling from Philadelphia via Felton's PW&B line arrive in Baltimore at the President Street Station on the eastern side of the city. From there, the train's passengers must cross the city by public streets to get to the Camden Street Station—a trip of just over a mile—in order to catch a B&O train to Washington.

Alternately, passengers traveling from Harrisburg via the Northern Central line arrive in Baltimore at the Calvert Street Station on the north side of the city. There, they disembark from the train and travel through the city streets southwest to the Camden Street Station—also about a mile—in order to catch the B&O train to the capital.

Either way, accounting for the expected crowds, Lincoln and his entourage will probably spend a half hour or more traversing Baltimore streets, traveling from one station to another. In other words, Lincoln will be exposed to the public.

The Southern extremists in Baltimore—so adamantly determined to prevent Lincoln's inauguration—all know this. Once Lincoln's team makes the travel itinerary public, Baltimoreans will also know the precise date and time of his planned passage through the city.

For now, however, the detective's concerns about the President-elect's safety are speculative, based largely on rumor and intuition. What Pinkerton needs is evidence—and he and his agents are now working against the clock to try to infiltrate whatever group or groups might be plotting violence against Abraham Lincoln.

In the same building as his new rented office room at 44 South Street, Pinkerton quickly identifies a person of interest to the investigation. He's a stockbroker named Thomas Luckett, who works in an office on the same floor as Pinkerton and who's an avowed secessionist who loudly curses Lincoln. Pinkerton, maintaining his alias "John Hutcheson," befriends Luckett and learns of his strong pro-Southern sympathies. Pretending to share the same extremist views, Pinkerton frequently draws Luckett into political conversations—and now suspects that his floormate may be helping to bankroll some of the secret groups in the city.

Through Luckett, Pinkerton learns of a hotel only a few blocks away from his office that serves as an informal "Head Quarters of Secessionists from all parts of the country." It's a social hub in the city, featuring a popular restaurant and bar. As Pinkerton describes it, "The visitors from all portions of the South [gathered] at this house, and in the evenings the corridors and parlors would be thronged by the tall, lank forms of the long-haired gentlemen who represented the aristocracy of the slaveholding interests."

For Pinkerton—a.k.a. John Hutcheson—it's an obvious place to embed, listen, and try to learn more about the world of white supremacist organizations in Baltimore. "There every night I mingled among them I could hear the most outrageous sentiments enunciated," Pinkerton writes. "No man's life was safe in the hands of those men."

The name of the headquarters?

Barnum's City Hotel.

44

Illinois

February 11, 1861

After so much anticipation, so much difficult planning, after being under so much pressure—and after the relentless stream of increasingly grave news—Lincoln and his team are relieved to finally be on the move.

The custom-designed train commissioned for the first leg of the trip consists of three cars: a brand-new Rogers Locomotive, a baggage car, and a long yellow passenger car to seat Lincoln's traveling entourage of over thirty people. It's a wide-ranging group, composed of both old friends and new colleagues, as well as a mix of political neophytes and seasoned advisors.

In typical Lincoln fashion, it's a colorful, eclectic group. There's Judge David Davis, the gregarious three-hundred-pound friend who was campaign manager for the Chicago convention. There's Norman Judd, the white-bearded former State Senator and Lincoln's longtime advisor on Illinois politics. There's William S. Wallace, a country doctor and the Lincolns' family physician. There's twenty-eight-year-old John Nicolay, Lincoln's pale, bookish, German-born personal secretary. There's another fresh-faced young acolyte, John Hay, who will soon join Nicolay as one of Lincoln's most trusted aides. And there's William Wood, the suave, well-dressed New Yorker who had organized most of the travel and hotel arrangements, but whose arrogant manner has sometimes been a source of irritation for the more informal Midwesterners who make up Lincoln's inner circle.

Lincoln had steadfastly refused all recommendations to travel with a military escort, but at the insistence of his advisors, who lived in fear of an assassination attempt, he had agreed to bring along a "security force." Hard-drinking, banjo-playing Ward Hill Lamon—Lincoln's old friend from the Illinois law circuit who weighs upwards of 260 pounds—is a known barroom brawler who vows to stay by the side of the President-elect and shield him from harm.

George Hazzard, a grizzled former soldier who still wears his uniform every day, promises to act as a "security advisor" and "military liaison" for the duration of the trip. Maj. David Hunter, a current officer of the Army, is also on board for protection. Another aging Army veteran, Col. "Bull Head" Sumner, is set to join the entourage farther east.

Finally, there's Elmer Ellsworth. He's a dashing, handsome twenty-three-year-old militia officer—he trains with a flashy touring drill team called the Zouave Cadets of Chicago—who in recent years befriended the Lincoln family and of whom the President-elect is particularly fond. Despite his youth, he's appointed to be Lincoln's armed personal escort for every moment of the journey.

What the members of this ad-hoc security team lack in numbers or organization they make up for in loyalty and enthusiasm, and, for better or worse, they will constitute Lincoln's personal protection during the twelve-day trip.

Mary Todd Lincoln had taken Willie and Tad to Indianapolis in advance to see family friends before their move east, so she and the younger children are not on board for the first day. They plan to join when the train catches up to them in Indianapolis. However, Lincoln's eldest son, eighteen-year-old Robert Todd Lincoln, has just come home from his freshman year at Harvard University to join his father for the inaugural journey and is on board when the train departs Springfield.

Accompanying these core team members will be a rotating cast of friends, advisors, Republican officials, local politicians, and others who will join for different legs of the journey. Finally, a handful of reporters from newspapers in different states are "embedded" on the train to observe every detail of the trip and file stories to their home cities.

As the train ride gets under way, the festive atmosphere that emerges inside the crowded passenger car—led by the more voluble members of Lincoln's circle, who immediately start passing whiskey bottles around—is a welcome respite from the gloom that had descended upon Lincoln in Springfield. Gradually, the President-elect's spirits begin to lift. He isn't a drinker, but soon he's chortling and telling jokes, talking politics with the rest of the crew.

Yet it's not the entourage inside the train that truly begin to energize the President-elect—it's the people outside of it.

Within the first hour, the gleaming inaugural train passes through a half dozen small towns along the rail line through central Illinois—and at every stop a crowd is gathered to cheer it on. "I never knew where all the people came from," the brakeman later recalled. "Not only in the towns and villages, but . . . along the tracks in the country." Banners and flags wave on the modest depots, general stores, and homes. When the train passes the tiny villages where crowds have gathered, Lincoln moves out on the passenger car's rear platform to wave or shout out a few words as the people wave back, "all enthusiastic, vociferous and fluttering with handkerchiefs and flags." In larger towns, where full stops or speeches have been prearranged, brass bands play and parades march along the streets.

The train makes its first scheduled full stop in Decatur, Illinois, at 9:24 a.m., where a throng of several thousand has swarmed around and filled the station to greet the train's arrival. Accompanied by a few aides, Lincoln steps out of the passenger car onto the platform and, according to the *Illinois State Journal,* "moves rapidly through the crowd at the depot, shaking hands left and right."

This is a part of politics that has always come naturally to Lincoln—the personal interaction with people from all walks of life, the sights and smells of farmers, working people, children, babies, dogs, and the occasional pig or sheep. Here in Decatur, Lincoln's young secretary John Hay writes of the "frank, hearty display of

GREAT WESTERN RAILROAD.

TIME CARD

For a Special Train, Monday, Feb. 11, 1861,

WITH

His Excellency, Abraham Lincoln, President Elect.

Leave SPRINGFIELD,	8.00 A. M.	
" JAMESTOWN,	8.15	"
" DAWSON,	8.24	"
" MECHANICSBURG,	8.30	"
" LANESVILLE,	8.37	"
" ILLIOPOLIS,	8.49	"
" NIANTIC,	8.58	"
" SUMMIT,	9.07	"
Arrive at DECATUR,	9.24	"
Leave DECATUR,	9.29	"
" OAKLEY,	9.45	"
" CERRO GORDO,	9.54	"
" BEMENT,	10.13	"
" SADORUS,	19.40	"
Arrive at TOLONO,	10.50	"
Leave "	10.55	"
" PHILO,	11.07	"
" SIDNEY,	11.17	"
" HOMER,	11.30	"
" SALINA,	11.45	"
" CATLIN,	11.59	"
" BRYANT,	12.07 P. M.	
" DANVILLE,	12.12	"
Arrive at STATE LINE,	12.30 P. M.	

This train will be entitled to the road, *and all other trains must be kept out of the way.*

Trains to be passed and met must be on the side track at least 10 minutes before this train is due.

Agents at all stations between Springfield and State Line must be on duty when this train passes, and examine the switches and know *that all is right before it passes.*

Operators at Telegraph Stations between Springfield and State Line must remain on duty until this train passes, and immediately report its time to Chas. H. Speed, Springfield.

All Foremen and men under their direction must be on the track and know positively that the track is in order.

It is very important that this train should pass over the road in safety, and all employees are expected to render all assistance in their power.

Red is the signal for danger, but any signal apparently intended to indicate alarm or danger must be regarded, the train stopped, and the meaning of it ascertained.

Carefulness is particularly enjoined.

F. W. BOWEN,
Supt.

The Great Western Railroad issues this time card to its staff regarding the "Special Train" that would traverse the company's rails on the first day of Abraham Lincoln's inaugural journey from Springfield, Illinois, to Washington, D.C. The card includes the itinerary only up to the Indiana state line, at which point Lincoln's train will switch to another rail line, the Toledo & Wabash, for the second half of the day's journey.

enthusiasm and affection" shown by the "tall, stalwart Illinoisan" to the locals, and them to him. "Having spent his life in the very heart of the mighty West, having mingled with its people for a lifetime," Hay writes, "the sympathy between the constituent and the elect is as perfect as that between near kindred."

The farther Lincoln gets from Springfield, the larger the crowds grow. The trip's planners underestimated the enormous curiosity that had built up around this unusual-looking man who was to be the nation's leader. He's a person about whom many stories had been told, various myths circulated and shared, but who at this point is still an enigma.

But it's more than just curiosity. The country is now in crisis. The public's fear has steadily increased throughout the winter. With a half dozen Southern states now seceded—Louisiana became the sixth on January 19, and Texas is poised to follow suit—the future of the United States is entirely uncertain. More and more, there is talk of impending war. Outgoing President Buchanan has failed to provide leadership. Throughout the North and the border states, people now crave something, anything, to inspire confidence. Their untested new President, Abraham Lincoln, may be the nation's only hope.

At 10:50 a.m., the inaugural train pulls into the town of Tolono, Illinois, where a booming cannon and large crowd greet its arrival. Lincoln steps out to the platform to say a few spontaneous words to several thousand cheering spectators.

"I am leaving you on an errand of national importance, attended, as you are aware, with considerable difficulties," he says to the crowd. "Let us believe, as some poet has expressed it: Behind the cloud the sun is still shining. I bid you an affectionate farewell." However simple, these short remarks generate in the crowd "as wild an intensity of delight as if it had been a condensed embodiment of the substance of his inaugural."

Several towns and stops later, at precisely 12:30 p.m.—just as planned by William Wood's meticulous minute-by-minute schedule—the train approaches a crowd of thousands gathered at the Indiana border. Here, members of the Indiana legislature have organized a public reception to escort the President-elect into their state.

On a special decorated platform set up for the event, Lincoln receives the legislature's blessings. "I am under many obligations to you for your kind reception," he says in response, "and to Indiana for the aid she rendered our cause which is, I think, a just one."

Here at the state line, the inaugural train will transfer from the Grand Western Railroad line to a new one, the Toledo & Wabash. While the entourage lunches, brakemen link the passenger and baggage cars to a new locomotive designed for the specifications of the T&W tracks.

At reload time, several Indiana legislators board Lincoln's car to join him for the portion of the journey within their state—the first of many dizzying additions and subtractions to traveling personnel throughout the trip.

Passing through the rural counties of Indiana, Lincoln knows he's in a region that contains significant Democratic and pro-Southern sentiment. In the town of Lafayette, the train stops for yet another crowd, and Lincoln says a few more spontaneous words, trying to convey a message of unity: "While some of us may differ in political opinions, still we are all united in one feeling for the Union. We all believe in . . . every star and every stripe of the glorious flag, and permit me to express the sentiment that upon the union of the States, there shall be between us no difference."

These local stops, however brief, give the people a chance to get a sense of the President-elect, to gawk at his lanky frame and exceptional height, to catch a glimpse of his smile, to hear his unusual speaking rhythm.

When the train pulls into the depot in the small town of Thorntown, Indiana, the gathered crowd experiences a quintessential Lincoln moment. Standing on the train's rear platform, the President-elect says a few brief words and then, suddenly inspired, begins telling one of his long folksy jokes. He mistimes the delivery, however, and as a local newspaper reports it, "the train started before he got to the place where the laugh came in, and the people were left to wonder what the meaning might be."

Five minutes later, when the train pulls into the neighboring town of Lebanon, Lincoln is delighted to learn that "some of the Thorntown folks had followed the train on foot, and were panting outside to hear the conclusion of the story." He begins the long joke again, and this time reaches the conclusion to a round of applause.

By the late afternoon, Lincoln's train had passed through some two dozen towns across two states. Then, at 5:00 p.m., it pulls into the station at the first capital city along the route: Indianapolis, Indiana.

Indianapolis is still a relatively small metropolis at the time, with a population barely over eighteen thousand. Still, with visitors flowing from throughout the state into the city, a crowd of at least twenty thousand has turned out for this historic event. A thirty-four-gun salute greets the train's arrival in the station, and Lincoln's party is greeted by "deafening cheers" when they emerge from the station.

City officials transport Lincoln in an open barouche—a type of carriage—pulled by four white horses, and a local militia and marching band accompany the procession.

The small city, as it turns out, is unequipped to contain the crush of people that swarm the hotel where Lincoln and his entourage are staying. "All the streets in front, and the hallways and stairways of the house were so packed with an eager crowd that we could scarcely make our way through them," one of Lincoln's party complains. *The New York Herald*'s Henry Villard—now one of the reporters traveling with the entourage—describes the hotel as a "beehive" and writes that Lincoln was entirely "overwhelmed by the merciless throngs."

Amid this chaotic scene, Lincoln is compelled to give first one impromptu speech and then another, the second from the hotel's balcony in front of the sea of spectators. After this, he endures a long public reception in the hotel parlor where every hand must be shaken.

Late in the evening, the President-elect finally is able to sit down for a much-needed dinner in the still-busy hotel. This brief respite does not last long, however. At the start of the meal, Lincoln calls over his son Robert Todd and asks him for the "small black hand-bag" that he had given to Robert and asked him to keep in his possession every minute of the day. Protecting this bag was Robert's one and only responsibility on the trip.

Robert sheepishly responds that he gave the bag to a waiter earlier, and now the waiter seems to have disappeared.

What's in the bag? Papers containing all of Lincoln's prepared speeches for the duration of the trip. And also something else: the only typeset copies of Lincoln's inaugural address. Meaning, the speech he's been painstakingly working on for the past two months and that he is set to deliver in a few weeks with the entire country hanging on every word.

Yes, Robert Todd just lost the bag containing Lincoln's first inaugural address.

"My heart went up into my mouth," Lincoln later says about this moment. Not only might he have a lot of painful rewriting to do, but whatever stranger finds the bag could leak the inaugural to the press.

"A look of stupefaction passed over the countenance of Mr. Lincoln," John Nicolay reports, "and visions of that Inaugural in all the next morning's newspapers floated through his imagination." The President-elect jumps up from the dinner and races toward the corridor—jammed with people—that leads to the front lobby. With his aides following behind him, he pushes and jams his way through the crowd, eventually plunging in the direction of the hotel clerk's desk. Nicolay describes what happens next:

> With a single stride of his long legs, [Lincoln] swung himself across the clerk's counter, behind which a small mountain of carpetbags of all colors had accumulated. Then drawing a little key out of his pocket he began delving for the black ones, and opened one by one those that the key would unlock, to the great surprise and amusement of the clerk and bystanders, as their miscellaneous contents came to light.

Luckily, after several frantic minutes, "fortune favored the President-elect" and "after the first half dozen trials, he found his treasures."

After this anxious episode, the exhausted members of the inaugural party finally retire to their rooms. Day one of the long inaugural journey is behind them.

45

---•---

Warren County, Mississippi

February 11, 1861

Abraham Lincoln's departure from Springfield, Illinois, isn't the only journey that begins on the morning of Monday, February 11. By coincidence, on that very same day another politician also embarks on a multiday trip across several states. His destination, however, is very different.

Within hours of when Lincoln's train departs for the nation's capital, a tall, thin, well-dressed man in Warren County, Mississippi—more than six hundred miles south of Springfield—loads his belongings onto a small private boat. This boat will take him to catch a larger vessel, a steamboat, that will follow the Mississippi River to Vicksburg.

The small boat is leaving from a Mississippi plantation named Brierfield. The rowers on the boat are slaves. The tall, well-dressed man boarding with his belongings owns the plantation—and the slaves.

His name is Jefferson Davis, former Senator from Mississippi. He's one of several Senators from the seceded states who, after their states formally left the Union, stood up and ceremoniously walked out of the Senate chamber to resign from their positions in the federal government. Like Lincoln, Davis is traveling to his inaugural ceremony—to be sworn in as the provisional President of the Confederate States of America.

A week earlier, on February 4, a convention of delegates from the six seceded states had met in Montgomery, Alabama, to create this new unified body. The delegates had quickly drafted a provisional constitution, established a seat of government and capital building in Montgomery, and appointed Davis—who was not among them—as the acting President. Former Congressman Alexander Stephens of Georgia was appointed Vice President.

The next day, Davis received the news of his appointment while he was walking with his wife in a quiet garden on their plantation. Now, he's departing his hundred-plus acres and hundred-plus slaves to embark on the first day of a five-day journey to Montgomery to assume control of the fledgling government.

Like Lincoln, he will make several stops along the way—for receptions and to give speeches. In Davis's case, these appearances are meant to bolster support in the South for the new Confederacy.

Davis, a veteran of the Mexican-American War and former Secretary of War under President Franklin Pierce in the early 1850s, was for much of his political career considered a relative moderate among Southern lawmakers. But as the national fissure over slavery widened, he redefined his allegiances. After Lincoln's election, this Mississippian white supremacist slaveholder joined the secession march. "The time for compromise has now passed," he will declare in a speech at the conclusion of his own inaugural journey. "The South is determined to maintain her position, and make all who oppose her smell Southern powder and feel Southern steel."

These two men—Jefferson Davis and Abraham Lincoln—were born only about eight months apart and within roughly one hundred miles of each other in northern Kentucky. But their paths could not have been more different.

Davis grew up mostly in Mississippi to a moderately prosperous, slaveholding family. He attended fine schools, including West Point, and married the daughter of Southern plantation owners. Now he is devoting his life to splitting apart the United States in order to set up a government of slave states.

Lincoln grew up in Indiana and Illinois, in frontier poverty. He taught himself to read and write, rose to the Presidency in part based on opposition to the institution of slavery, and is now tasked as President of the United States to preserve the Union at all costs.

On February 11, 1861, both men begin their journeys, each set to assume control of their respective governments. Their successes—and their failures—will determine the fate and future of America.

46

Baltimore, Maryland

February 12, 1861

At the start of the workday, one of Allan Pinkerton's agents in Baltimore needs a pep talk. His name is Charles D. C. Williams, and he's one of the less experienced agents in the field.

Since arriving to bolster Pinkerton's team on the ground, Williams has operated undercover as a traveler from Mississippi, hanging out at bars where secessionists gather and striking up conversations with bartenders and patrons to learn more about their underground white supremacist networks. But as he describes in his morning briefing to Pinkerton, the previous night Williams struck up a conversation with a man who actually *was* from Mississippi and who wanted to talk to him about every town and city in the state.

Williams tells Pinkerton, "I was afraid I could not play my part, as I had come across a Mississippi man who knew every place." But Pinkerton persuades his agent to stick with it. As Williams writes in his report that day, "A.P. said there was no danger, and all I wanted was confidence." Apparently bolstered by his boss's encouragement, Williams keeps refining his Mississippi accent and heads back out into the field.

According to company policy, Pinkerton and each of his agents write up frequent reports detailing their observations and experiences throughout the investigation. Thankfully for posterity, many of these near-daily contemporaneous reports still exist, providing a chronicle of Pinkerton's team's progress. The rookie Williams dutifully described his worries and his boss's reassurances in one of these reports.

Williams is just one of several Pinkerton agents now spread around the city, each posing as a Southern extremist looking to connect with fellow secessionists and white supremacists in the social world and underground clubs of Baltimore.

As Pinkerton describes, "By assuming to be secessionists of the most ultra type," his agents were "to secure entrance into their secret societies and military organizations, and thus become possessed of their secret designs."

For example, agent Kate Warne's instruction is to "cultivat[e] the acquaintance of the wives and daughters of the conspirators." Drawing upon her experience in a previous case that took her undercover in Montgomery, Alabama, she now plays the role of an Alabama belle who is visiting the city and wants to enjoy the social life.

To blend in, she's adopted elaborate Southern manners and dress, including a specific symbol of cultural allegiance. As Pinkerton describes, "Mrs. Warne displayed upon her breast, as did many of the ladies of Baltimore, the black and white cockade, which had been temporarily adopted as the emblem of secession." These elaborate pinned brooches, sometimes including a palmetto symbol at their center, are instant indicators of allegiance to the pro-Southern, anti-Lincoln, white supremacist cause.

While Williams hits the bars and Warne embeds herself with wives and sisters of secessionists, another Pinkerton agent works a different angle—one that quickly bears fruit.

From the start of the investigation, Harry Davies's role was to infiltrate the privileged social world of Baltimore's young elites. Davies, the handsome former Jesuit student who had lived in the South, was well suited to emulate the look and style of the many young Southern aristocrats—the scions of wealthy slaveholding families—who mingle at the city's social clubs.

Upon their arrival in Baltimore, Pinkerton had instructed Davies to "obtain quarters at one of the first-class hotels" and to "assume the character of an extreme secessionist." Davies adopted the persona of a young aristocrat from New Orleans—a natural fit because he once lived in that city and could speak easily of places and people he knew there.

Under this guise of a Louisianan with fiery political views, he began seeking entry into the social clubs and secret societies of Baltimore. With politics the talk of the city, Davies sought out those who spoke with the greatest passion on the side of secession, and he expressed the same sentiments.

As Pinkerton described it, Davies "entered into their discussion, and by blatant expressions of the most rebellious nature, he was warmly welcomed by the coterie and instantly made one of their number." Once he'd established social contact, "his fine personal appearance, gentlemanly address and the fervor of his utterances soon won the favor of those with whom he associated."

One of those whose favor he wins is a young man by the name of Otis K. Hillard. Yes, the very same Otis K. Hillard who recently testified before the so-called Treason Committee of the House of Representatives regarding secret plots to prevent Lincoln's inauguration.

How did Davies first come in contact with Hillard? It's not clear whether Pinkerton and Davies somehow learned of Hillard's identity as a person of interest to the Treason Committee and specifically sought him out, or whether Davies simply met him in a social setting and sensed that he was a potential source.

Either way, Hillard perfectly fits the social class of those they hope to investigate: a young man from a wealthy Maryland family, possessed of strong pro-Southern political views, and well known in Baltimore. Once Davies befriends him, Hillard provides an entrée into the city's social elite. "This rebellious scion of Baltimore aristocracy," as Pinkerton later put it, "by reason of his high social position was able to introduce his friend [Davies] to the leading families and into the most aristocratic clubs and societies of which the city boasted."

Soon after making Hillard's acquaintance, Davies learns more about him. He's a member of a secret militia group called the Palmetto Guards, an organization whose very name honors the secessionists of South Carolina. Together with the Knights of the Golden

Circle, the National Volunteers, and the Constitutional Guards, that makes at least four secret societies or militia groups in Baltimore. Hillard is also, Davies learns, prone to drink and talk freely.

A perfect target for the investigation.

Davies quickly gains Hillard's confidence and encourages the Baltimorean to introduce him to the nightlife of the city. In Pinkerton's words, the two young men became "bosom friends and inseparable companions. They drank together, and visited theaters and places of amusement in each other's company."

Quickly, Davies gets the impression that Hillard knows something, some secret, that he wants to reveal. Indeed, when the talk turns to politics, Hillard begins to drop hints and suggestions of something important that he wishes he could share, but stops short.

On Tuesday, February 12—the second day of Lincoln's inaugural journey, and less than two weeks since Pinkerton's team has been in Baltimore—Davies and Hillard meet for drinks in the late afternoon. In his report of the day, Davies carefully chronicles their time together, so no detail will be forgotten.

After spending some time at the Fountain Hotel, the two men walk to Davies's hotel, known as Hall's, on Holliday Street. In the hotel's upscale lobby, Hillard introduces Davies to a friend named Hughes, and the three men talk politics. When Davies mentions to Hughes that he's from New Orleans, Hughes declares that New Orleans is "the Paradise of the United States" because "they are all secessionists there."

Then, unsolicited, Hughes mentions the state of affairs in Maryland. He says that he knows that the railroad companies have "men watching the railroad bridge between here and Philadelphia." The railroad company is "afraid that they will be destroyed—but I do not know if it will do any good."

Already, this little exchange provides Davies useful information. The secessionist crowd in Baltimore knows that the Philadelphia, Wilmington and Baltimore Railroad has people monitoring their track, for fear of sabotage. This is something that railroad head Samuel Felton will want to hear.

From Davies's hotel, the two men say goodbye to Hughes and

walk a few blocks to meet another friend of Hillard's, who joins them for a drink. After drinks, Davies and Hillard go to dinner at a popular restaurant called Mann's, and then go for more drinks at a club called Harry Hemling's Billiard Room. Here, they strike up a conversation with a man from South Carolina, who makes clear that he is "very much in favor of the Southern Confederacy."

This seems to be typical of Hillard's life in Baltimore—getting drinks, dining out, meeting friends, talking politics. But the night is just getting started. With several stiff drinks in him, Hillard decides that he and Davies should go to a concert saloon known as the Pagoda for music and even more drinking.

First, though, Hillard says, even before they go to the saloon, he wants to introduce Davies to someone. He leads Davies a few blocks down the bustling downtown Baltimore streets until they arrive at their next location: Barnum's City Hotel.

Davies already knows that Barnum's is a popular hangout for the secessionist crowd. He's likely on high alert.

But Hillard doesn't lead him into the hotel's lobby, lounge, or bar. The person he wants Davies to meet is downstairs, in the barbershop of all places.

His name, Hillard says, is "Captain Ferrandini."

47

Indianapolis, Indiana

February 12, 1861

Hope.

As Lincoln's inaugural train speeds its way eastward across the farm states, stopping frequently at small towns and cities along the way, and as throngs of people continue to swarm every station, every reception, and every speech—often doubling or tripling the populations of the towns and cities themselves—*hope* is what the President-elect can feel the people crave most.

For Lincoln, the second day of his inaugural journey—which also happens to be his birthday—began early in the city of Indianapolis, with a breakfast at the Governor's Mansion, followed by a ceremonial visit to the state capital to meet the state legislators.

After, he returned to the Bates Hotel to prepare for departure, during which time a crowd of thousands surged around the hotel, filling every street and sidewalk for several blocks, cheering and hoping to get a glimpse of the President-elect.

After an impromptu speech on the balcony, followed by a long round of handshaking on the front steps, Lincoln and his team finally escape through the back of the hotel, where they board a series of carriages headed to the train depot.

Lincoln feels a burst of good cheer when his wife and two younger children meet him just before departure time. Now, as the train speeds away from Indianapolis and through central Indiana, the whole Lincoln family is on board.

Traveling southeast toward the Ohio River, the inaugural train makes stops every several minutes at towns like Morris, Shelbyville, Greenburg, and Lawrenceburg. Even more than in Illinois, large crowds line the tracks, including between stops, waving flags and handkerchiefs, as if the train's journey was along "the crest of one continued wave of cheers," as John Hay describes it.

Lincoln, perhaps feeling more comfortable with his role at the center of attention than on the first day, adopts a relaxed demeanor with the festive crowds. When he gives small impromptu speeches at the train depots, he often starts with a self-deprecating joke regarding his now famously unhandsome appearance, remarking that "I have stepped out upon this platform so that I may see you and that you may see me, and in the arrangement I have the best of the bargain."

Along the route, the nonstop public and journalistic attention extends beyond Lincoln himself to the members of his family. Reporters soon give Robert Todd the nickname "Prince of Rails," a double pun that alludes to his role as the son of the "Rail Splitter," while also referencing a recent stateside visit from the Prince of Wales that garnered much publicity. Robert, not dwelling on his nearly catastrophic mishandling of his father's inaugural address, enjoys his role in the spotlight: He drinks too much wine in the boisterous passenger car, flirts with young women at the train depots, and—blessed with his mother's looks rather than his father's—becomes something of a heartthrob during the course of the journey.

When it comes to his younger sons, Willie and Tad, Lincoln mostly shields them from public view, but the reporters on the train write amusing anecdotes about the practical jokes the two boys play on various important dignitaries who join the train for different stretches. As usual, Lincoln indulges his boys and lets them run wild on the train, no doubt tormenting most of the adults.

Mary Todd also seems to enjoy herself, and keeps up "lively, spirited conversation" with other passengers. At first, she stays in the train during the various stops, but she soon gets over her shyness and,

Robert Todd Lincoln is an eighteen-year-old Harvard student when he joins his father's inaugural journey to Washington, D.C. On the trip, he drinks too much wine and earns the nickname "Prince of Rails."

yielding to the endless demand from journalists and the public to get a glimpse of her, begins accompanying her husband on the rear platform of the train for his short speeches. The crowds seem endlessly charmed and amused by the sight of the physically mismatched new First Couple, and Lincoln plays along by introducing himself and his wife to audiences as "the long and the short of it."

According to one reporter, Lincoln is the "merriest among the merry" on this afternoon, and with his good cheer and jovial banter keeps "those around him in a continual roar."

After roughly a dozen stops in eastern Indiana and western Ohio, the inaugural train slowly pulls into the city of Cincinnati at 3:00 p.m.

Here, for the first time, Lincoln and his entourage get a true sense of the seismic nature of his election.

At the time, Cincinnati is a powerful manufacturing hub and the seventh-largest city in the United States, with a population of over 160,000. Thus far, no other city they'd visited was anywhere close in size; the capital city of Indianapolis has fewer than 19,000 people.

Here, against the taller buildings and stately backdrop of a major city—and in a state where Lincoln enjoyed support in the election—the swarms of people are immense, larger than anyone present had seen before.

For the occasion, city officials had procured a grandiose open carriage pulled by six white horses. With the President-elect aboard, this stately vehicle leads a two-hour-long procession from the train station through the packed downtown city streets, amid the deafening cheers of the crowd.

"Every window was thronged, every balcony glittered with bright colors and fluttered with handkerchiefs," a dazzled John Hay reports. "The sidewalks were packed; even the ledges and cornices of the houses swarmed with intrepid lookers-on."

As the parade makes its way to the hotel, a vocal group from a local orphanage sings a choral arrangement, and at a prearranged moment, a thirty-four-gun salute blasts through the cold city.

Nothing, however, can compete with the sheer magnitude of the swarming crowds, and as the President-elect's carriage reaches his hotel and Lincoln himself steps out, the roar of applause and cheering is deafening. *The New York Herald's* Henry Villard, who has been following and reporting on Lincoln for some time and rarely indulges in hyperbole, is swept away.

A more magnificent ovation . . . was never witnessed west of the Alleghenies. It was not the military pageantry, not the stateliness of civil dignitaries nor any other formal display that made the occasion a perfect success, but the spontaneous turnout of at least a hundred thousand people, comprising all classes, from the rich merchant and manufacturer down to the humblest day laborer to do honor to the man that will be called upon to save the Union.

After a brief stop at the hotel, aides quickly escort Lincoln to another rally, this one sponsored by an organization of Ohio's German American workers. Lincoln had enjoyed widespread support among German Americans and other immigrant groups, and this occasion provided him a rare chance to speak warmly on a subject other than secession.

"I hold that while man exists, it is his duty to improve not only his own condition but to assist in ameliorating mankind," Lincoln declares. He adds, with some mirth in his voice: "In regard to Germans and foreigners, I esteem them no better than other people, nor any worse." This gets some laughs and applause. Then:

It is not my nature, when I see a people borne down by the weight of their shackles—the oppression of tyranny—to make their life more bitter by heaping upon them greater burdens; but rather would I do all in my power to raise the yoke . . . if there are any abroad who desire to make this the land of their adoption, it is not in my heart to throw aught in their way, to prevent them from coming to the United States.

For a group that had recently been the target of anti-immigrant rhetoric, including from some within Lincoln's party, these words carry massive weight.

After more applause, Lincoln's team again whisks him away, this time to rush to a large dinner and reception back at the Burnet House, where the Presidential party is staying.

But here, around the large hotel and in the lobby, the unrelenting throngs of people swarming around Lincoln and his handlers create a chaotic, nearly out-of-control scene.

Lincoln's bodyguards on duty—in this case, Major Hunter, Colonel Sumner, and the young militiaman Colonel Ellsworth—surround him and work mightily to protect the President-elect, but there's only so much they can do. The out-of-control crowds keep swarming Lincoln, "throwing their arms around him, patting him on the back, and almost wrenching his arm off."

Eventually Lincoln's handlers are able to get him and his family members safely to their rooms without further incident, but the experience of being mobbed weighs heavily on those entrusted to protect him.

The fact is, from the moment the group arrived in Cincinnati, Lincoln has been incredibly vulnerable. From the train station, he rode through the city in an open carriage, standing up and waving the entire way. At any moment, a would-be assassin with a firearm would've had an easy shot at him. And while surrounded by swarming crowds in confined spaces like the hotel, he's susceptible to any number of potential close-range attacks that his small security detail could scarcely prevent.

At this point, however, there's little that Lincoln or his team can do. For now, the exhausted members of the Presidential party gratefully retire to their rooms, hoping to catch a few hours of sleep before rising again for an early dawn departure.

Yet as Lincoln's aides and bodyguards go to bed, none of them realize the far more terrifying news that's about to be delivered. It comes from a mysterious stranger, one who's about to arrive in the dead of night.

48

***

Baltimore, Maryland

February 12, 1861

The barber isn't in.

When Otis Hillard asks for "Captain Ferrandini" at Barnum's City Hotel, he's told that Ferrandini has left for the evening.

This means Pinkerton's undercover agent Harry Davies, accompanying Hillard for a night on the town, will have to wait for another time to meet this mysterious man.

The two young men leave Barnum's. Davies, probably disappointed to miss out on a promising lead, follows Hillard to the Pagoda concert hall for music and more drinks. They stay there from approximately 8:00 p.m. to 10:00 p.m., at which point both men must be fully inebriated.

If Davies is hoping to get back to the hotel at a reasonable hour to write his daily field reports, he's mistaken. Hillard wants his new friend to accompany him for even more revelry, but this time at quite a different location. It's not a bar, or hotel lounge, or a social club. Instead, he gets a name and address: Annette Travis, No. 70 Davis Street.

Where is Hillard taking him now?

It's a house of prostitution, tucked away three or four blocks north of Barnum's Hotel, near the Calvert Street train station. Annette Travis is the madam.

Hillard, it becomes clear, is a regular—or at least, he regularly comes here to see a particular young woman named Anna Hughes. Anna is who he seeks tonight, dragging his new friend Davies with him into the brothel and up to Anna's room.

"Hillard and his woman seemed very much pleased at meeting, and hugged and kissed each other for about an hour," according to Davies's field report. Davies waits in the room awkwardly, and when the hour is up, tries to get Hillard to leave. But "Hillard's woman wished him to remain." Feeling uncomfortable, Davies heads for the door and "went out on to the sidewalk" until, several minutes later, Hillard finally joins him.

All evening, amid the drinking and revelry, Davies has been trying to steer the conversation to what counts: Lincoln's coming inauguration and any secret plots against the new President. Thus far, Hillard has given a few hints, but nothing substantial. Now, it's almost midnight. It'd be completely reasonable for Davies to give up.

Instead, he presses forward. Otis Hillard is thoroughly drunk. For Davies, it's an opportunity.

The two men return to Davies's hotel room, where, according to Davies, they "sat and talked until about 1 a.m." Here, Davies aggressively turns the conversation back to politics—and to the local resistance against Lincoln.

Sure enough, Hillard starts talking. He mentions that a group of National Volunteers was drilling earlier that night—more specifically, a "Company No. 4." Apparently, Hillard knows something about the organization and schedule of the group. He also says that his own company—the Palmetto Guards—will be drilling the next night. So are the Palmetto Guards directly affiliated with the National Volunteers? The answer's unclear.

Davies continues to pry for information, at which point, Hillard asks him a question.

"Have you seen a statement of Lincoln's route to Washington City?"

Davies answers that he has. While Lincoln's official itinerary has not been printed in eastern newspapers, it's widely speculated that for

the last leg of the inaugural journey, he will travel from either Philadelphia or Harrisburg to Baltimore and then to Washington, D.C.

"By the by," Hillard says, "that reminds me that I must go and see
a certain party in the morning the first thing."

"What about?" Davies asks, nonchalant.

"About Lincoln's route," Hillard replies. "I want to see about the
telegraph in Philadelphia and New York and have some arrangement
made about telegraphing."

Now it's getting interesting. Why is Hillard suddenly concerned
with telegraphing—especially along the cities of Lincoln's route? And
why would he have to go meet someone in the morning to discuss it?

"How do you mean?" Davies asks.

"Suppose that some of Lincoln's friends would arrange so that the
telegraph messages should be miscarried, we would have some signs
to telegraph by: for instance supposing, that we should telegraph to a
certain point 'all up at 7,' that would mean that Lincoln would be at
such a point at 7 o'clock."

Although Hillard's speech is a little jumbled, he seems to imply
that he and whatever group he's part of are devising a secret telegraph code that will help them track Lincoln's position during his
train route from the northeastern cities to Baltimore. Perhaps members of his gang are stationed in New York and Philadelphia and plan
to telegraph updates to Baltimore when Lincoln's train passes through
those cities. If so, they would want to send them using cipher, in case
authorities intercept them.

Naturally, this isn't something Hillard is doing alone. His plan
suggests a group—one that's secretly monitoring Lincoln's train
during its final passage to the capital. The question is, why would
they be monitoring the train's schedule and whereabouts? Are they
trying to sabotage the railroad tracks while Lincoln's en route—or is
their goal to hit Lincoln himself?

Whatever the answer, Hillard and his group are working hard to
keep it a secret from the authorities.

Davies quickly asks about the details of the telegraph code, though
Hillard only replies, "There is a plan."

"What is the plan?" Davies asks.

Hillard looks at him. "My friend, that is what I would like to tell you," he says, "but I dare not—I wish I could."

Davies, not for the first time, gets the feeling that this secret is weighing on Hillard—troubling him, even. But Hillard still won't reveal it.

Hillard tries to explain. "Anything almost I would be willing to do for you, but to tell you *that*," he says, "I dare not."

That's it. That's all he says.

Surely, Davies's mind is racing. Why do Otis Hillard and his cohorts need a telegraph cipher? Who is Hillard going to meet in the morning to discuss this plan? And perhaps most important, who is "Captain Ferrandini," whom they tried to visit earlier?

For Davies, there are no answers. His new Baltimore pal says goodbye for the night.

But Hillard, it turns out, doesn't plan to be by himself. At 1:00 a.m., just before he leaves, he tells Davies where he's going—back to the brothel at 70 Davis Street, to visit his "friend" Anna Hughes once more.

49

Cincinnati, Ohio

February 13, 1861

At approximately 2:00 a.m.—not long after Hillard and Davies say their goodbyes in Baltimore—a mysterious stranger arrives at the Burnet House hotel in Cincinnati, where Lincoln's entourage is staying.

The messenger demands to see a member of the Presidential party. *Right now,* he tells the concierge. Doesn't matter that it's the middle of the night—this is urgent.

Even more unsettling, he doesn't just want to see *anyone* from the party. No, he specifically wants to see Norman Judd—the bearded forty-five-year-old former member of the Illinois Senate who has known Lincoln personally and professionally for years.

Why Norman Judd? And why at this hour?

The concierge informs the visitor that "Judd had been in bed since about 11 o'clock" and that "they would not disturb him." The hotel is under strict orders to refuse any further demands on the party for the night—and to make sure no one is awakened.

But, the concierge says, you can find Judd first thing in the morning, before he departs the hotel at 9:00 a.m. Reluctantly, the visitor agrees to return in the morning.

The messenger's name, if he were willing to give it, is William

Scott. He's just come from Chicago. He works there—for Pinkerton's National Detective Agency.

Sure enough, at 7:00 a.m., Scott returns to the hotel lobby, once again in search of Norman Judd. Finally, at 8:00 a.m., he finds him.

Scott quickly pulls Judd into a private room. Here, the messenger hands Judd an urgent letter from his boss, Allan Pinkerton, currently in Baltimore. Given the circumstances, Scott explains to Judd, only a hand delivery could be trusted.

In front of the detective, Judd carefully reads the letter. Before he can speak, Scott tells him, "Pinkerton desire[s] this letter to him to be strictly confidential."

"That is true," Judd replies, "and I am very much obliged to you and Pinkerton for the information."

So what does the letter say?

To this day, the exact words are not known. The letter itself was not saved—in fact, Judd probably destroyed it immediately—and Scott, although he wrote in his field report that he delivered the letter to Judd, did not transcribe it.

Later, however, Pinkerton will explain the contents. He wrote the letter for Judd to receive "as the party reached Cincinnati, informing him that I had reason to believe that there was a plot on foot" that could put Abraham Lincoln's life in danger "on his passage through Baltimore."

Pinkerton doesn't provide Judd further details—indeed, he himself still doesn't know all the details—but he promises Judd to "advise him further as the party progressed eastward."

Basically, Pinkerton wants Judd to know what's coming—and establish ongoing contact with him. But why Norman Judd? Pinkerton knows him personally, through Chicago circles. He knows that Judd is trustworthy and responsible, making him the perfect confidential contact on Lincoln's team.

As Judd digests the unsettling news, Scott asks him if he wishes to telegraph a response to Pinkerton.

Judd thinks for a moment. "I think not," he says.

Guessing that Judd's response comes from the fear that a telegraph might be intercepted, Scott offers him one of Pinkerton's telegraph ciphers—to send an encrypted message.

Judd thinks on this, but again decides against it. For the time being, he'll wait to hear from Pinkerton again. From there, he provides Scott some details of the inaugural train's itinerary in the next few days, and when and where Judd can be reached if necessary.

Right now, Judd has a train to catch. Before they part, though, Judd speaks "very feelingly" of Pinkerton—he has a great deal of respect for the detective—and thanks them for their work.

As for the messenger, William Scott, he's already missed the morning train from Cincinnati back to Chicago. He'll have to wait for a later train that night. Having completed his duties, he heads to the station to watch the departure of Lincoln's inaugural train. Predictably, another cheering crowd has gathered to witness the departure.

Ten days. That's all they've got.

Ten days until Lincoln's train arrives in Baltimore.

50

---•---

Baltimore, Maryland

February 14, 1861

Lincoln is coming.

The fact that Lincoln's train is on the move—by the afternoon of Thursday, February 14, it's traversed from eastern Ohio into western Pennsylvania—has raised the already excited state of the Baltimoreans to a near fever pitch.

Every day, newspapers all over the country cover the details of Lincoln's journey, reporting on every stop, every parade, every speech, and every change in personnel on the journey. Because the route is entirely in Northern states, the supportive local press monopolizes the news coverage, and the wires are filled with admiring reports and endearing anecdotes of Lincoln and his family.

In the slave states, this fawning Northern news coverage only generates more rage.

As Allan Pinkerton reports from Baltimore, "As the daily papers, which chronicled the events which occurred upon the journey of Mr. Lincoln towards Washington . . . were perused by the people, or were read aloud in tavern or store[s], they would be greeted by alternate expressions of hate and malignity for the abolitionist and wild cheers for the rebellion."

The intensity of this "hate and malignity" is heightened by the fact that in a little over a week's time—on Saturday, February 23, according to the news reports—the inaugural caravan will travel directly into the city.

While Pinkerton's agent Harry Davies works on young socialite Otis Hillard, Pinkerton continues to target his office neighbor at 44 State Street, the stockbroker Thomas Luckett.

Pinkerton and his agents don't know it yet, but these two strands are about to converge.

Indeed, on Friday, February 15, Pinkerton and his team are still mostly in the dark. Feeling increasingly anxious, he stops into Luckett's office to make a little small talk. As always, the discussion quickly turns to politics.

Luckett brings up a subject of heated interest to all Marylanders: Governor Thomas Hicks's refusal to allow the state legislature to convene a special session to vote on whether to secede from the Union. As Lincoln's inauguration grows near, the secessionists in the state are increasingly enraged at the Governor for refusing to allow Maryland to follow in the path of its Southern allies. Yet without the Governor's consent, the state can never secede.

As Pinkerton describes in his field report, Luckett "damned Governor Hicks for the course he had taken." Pinkerton quickly and loudly agrees, which prompts Luckett to go even further.

"I tell you, my friend," he says to Pinkerton, "it will be a short time until you will find Governor Hicks will have to fly, or he will be hung—he is a traitor to his God and to his Country."

Luckett is convinced that despite Hicks's efforts, Maryland will soon secede, probably when neighboring Virginia does. And when that happens, he believes the first order of business should be a combined uprising to seize Washington, D.C., from the Union. "Let the consequences be what they may," he declares. "Those two States could concentrate a Hundred Thousand men around the Capital in a very short time."

In no time, Luckett is increasingly heated, and his new friend eggs him on. As Pinkerton describes it, he "fully endorsed" Mr. Luckett's views, "and took strong grounds for immediate secession, and the occupancy of the Capitol."

From there, the subject turns to the new President.

Like many in the South, Luckett views the coming Lincoln administration in apocalyptic terms. He declares, "I shall never, so help me God, acknowledge it as a Government—never, Mr. Hutcheson—never."

He believes forceful measures must be taken to prevent the calamity of Lincoln taking office. "The time has now come for us to act," he says, "and that action must be *soon*. Let them call it Treason," he adds, "but let us *act*."

What the moment requires, he explains, are men "who would not hesitate if necessary to peril their lives for the rights of Maryland and the Southern Confederacy."

Pinkerton agrees, loudly and adamantly. He can sense he's getting close to something. He just needs to keep pushing.

Sure enough, it works. Without warning, Luckett looks at him directly and says, in a clear, serious voice: We will "soon see a move made in the right direction," because there's "an organization here which [is] powerful enough to bid defiance to Lincoln and his Abolitionist Crew."

Luckett continues, "We are raising money and giving it to the organization to purchase arms, and getting arms, and ammunition on hand."

Right there, Pinkerton knows this is his chance—maybe his only chance—to get on the inside. Reaching into his pocket, he pulls out his wallet and looks Luckett in the eye.

"I am but a stranger to you," Pinkerton says, but "I ha[ve] no doubt but that money is necessary for the success of this patriotic cause."

As Pinkerton has learned over the years, when it comes to infiltrating a criminal enterprise, no tactic works better than a straight-up offer of cash.

He takes $25 in paper bills from his wallet—the equivalent of roughly $750 today—and hands it ceremoniously to Luckett. "I should be obliged," Pinkerton says, "if [you] would see that this was employed in the best manner possible for Southern rights." He adds that if more money is needed in the future, "I hoped he would call on me."

As an extra flourish, he asks Luckett to keep this donation secret. He is a man of discretion—and understands the risks of getting involved.

Luckett takes Pinkerton's money, and, sure enough, his demeanor changes. Adopting a more conspiratorial tone, he agrees that discretion is essential. He tells Pinkerton that the group of "Southern rights men" to which he refers is "exceedingly cautious as to who they talked with," because "some time ago they found that the Government had spies among them, and that since then they had been *very* careful." In fact, the members are "sworn to keep it a secret."

For Pinkerton, it's the jackpot. An organization sworn to secrecy, devoted to defying Lincoln, stockpiling guns and ammunition, and worried about government spies. It's all coming together. Pinkerton simply needs to learn more.

Slowly, carefully, Pinkerton begins to prod.

Luckett reveals that he himself is not a member of the organization, because, he says, "there are but very few who could be admitted." He merely helps fund it, and he "knows many" who are members.

Pinkerton continues to drill away. He knows he isn't getting anywhere until he gets names.

The "leading man," Luckett eventually says, is "Captain Ferrandini."

Finally. The name of the leader.

For Pinkerton, the pieces start coming together. According to his fellow detective Harry Davies, Captain Ferrandini was the person whom Otis Hillard tried to visit at Barnum's City Hotel—the same Otis Hillard who was drunkenly bragging about a secret telegraph cipher to communicate the whereabouts of Lincoln's train.

Pinkerton and his team are doing the one thing that the politicians on the so-called Treason Committee never could: tie these two men together.

If Otis Hillard is in the same secret group as Ferrandini . . . then the people working on the telegraph cipher are the same people who

Luckett just admitted were *also* buying and stockpiling weapons and ammunition.

It's a crucial moment for Pinkerton. Whatever's running through his head, he stays totally composed. He knows that if he shows emotion or lets on that he recognizes Captain Ferrandini's name, Luckett will know something's wrong.

The detective doesn't flinch. Instead, he calmly asks more about this so-called leader. And Luckett keeps talking.

Ferrandini, Luckett explains, is "a true friend to the South." A real Southern patriot "ready to lose his life for their cause." Most important, Ferrandini "had a plan fixed to prevent Lincoln from passing through Baltimore, and would certainly see that Lincoln never should go to Washington."

It's a bold threat—one that Luckett makes with utter confidence. Pinkerton has to know, though. How could anyone possibly guarantee that Lincoln won't get there?

"Every Southern Rights man had confidence in Ferrandini," Luckett explains, but only those in the inner circle really "knew his purpose." Apparently, Luckett himself isn't in the secret organization, but he is "a particular friend" of Ferrandini's—and it's Ferrandini to whom Luckett will donate Pinkerton's twenty-five dollars.

Pinkerton keeps digging. What's the so-called "purpose"? What's Ferrandini's "fixed plan" to prevent Lincoln's passage to Washington, D.C.?

These are the right questions. Luckett looks at Pinkerton and says, simply:

"Before Lincoln should pass through Baltimore, he would kill him."

There it is—the actual plot to assassinate Abraham Lincoln. Not in Washington, not at the inauguration, but right here. In Baltimore.

For America's first private detective, everything's led to this—all the hints, clues, rumors, and suggestions—these were the details he was searching for.

Before Pinkerton can even digest it, Luckett casually mentions that he's not going home that evening. Instead, he proposes a plan.

If Pinkerton will "meet him at Barr's Saloon on South Street," Luckett will introduce him to Ferrandini. In person.

Pinkerton calmly agrees. They'll meet at 7:00 p.m.—Barr's Saloon—just down the street from the office.

Pinkerton has only a few hours. Plenty of time to get ready.

51

———— · ————

Baltimore, Maryland

February 15, 1861

The stage is set.

Throughout his career, Pinkerton has gone undercover dozens of times. He's played many roles, worn many different disguises, and infiltrated all manner of criminal organizations.

Tonight, though, is different. The stakes are higher. He's just learned of a plan to assassinate the incoming President of the United States. As the only outsider who knows of it, he may be the only person alive who can stop it.

On top of that, he's going in alone. If his cover is blown, there's no backup.

Pinkerton knows what must be done. As every detective understands, success rests on learning the details. What's their exact plan? Who's behind it? Who is this mysterious Captain Ferrandini whom Pinkerton is supposedly about to meet? And is Ferrandini really the "leading man," as Luckett described him, or is there someone even bigger in charge?

At 7:00 p.m., Pinkerton—posing, of course, as Southern stockbroker John Hutcheson—enters Barr's Saloon on South Street.

Sure enough, Luckett is there with "several other gentlemen." When Luckett sees Pinkerton, he immediately invites him to join the group, introducing him to two of the men: a "Captain Turner" and, there he is, "Captain Ferrandini."

By way of introduction, Luckett describes Pinkerton as a "neighbor" and speaks highly of him to the others. He says that this was "the gentleman who had given the Twenty Five Dollars . . . to Ferrandini."

Pinkerton gets his first good look at this man Ferrandini. He is, as Pinkerton notes, "a fine looking, intelligent appearing person." He has a perfectly trimmed mustache—he is a barber, after all—and is well dressed and well mannered. He has bright eyes, according to Pinkerton, and a charming voice and manner.

As usual, the talk turns immediately to politics, and Ferrandini becomes "very excited" by the conversation. He argues passionately that the "South must rule," and believes Southerners have been "outraged in their rights by the election of Lincoln." As a result of this outrage, Ferrandini exclaims, Southern patriots are "freely justified resorting to any means to prevent Lincoln from taking his seat."

As Ferrandini holds forth, the others nod in agreement. He seems to exert a strange power over everyone listening. "As he spoke," Pinkerton notes, "his eyes fairly glared and glistened, and his whole frame quivered, but he was fully conscious of all he was doing." Ferrandini's rhetoric and delivery is theatrical, appealing to the emotions of the listener. "He is a man well calculated for controlling and directing the ardent minded."

Pinkerton also carefully observes the other man with him, Captain Turner. Turner agrees vehemently with everything Ferrandini says, but he seems to be a follower rather than a leader.

As Pinkerton describes him, "although very much of a gentleman and possessing warm Southern feelings, he is not by any means so dangerous a man as Ferrandini, as his ability for exciting others is less powerful." In fact, Turner seems to be "entirely under the control of Ferrandini."

Right there, Pinkerton sees how potentially dangerous Ferrandini is. "Even I myself felt the influence of this man's strange power," he observes, "and wrong though I knew him to be, I felt strangely unable to keep my mind balanced against him."

As the conversation continues, Ferrandini's rhetoric becomes increasingly violent. "Murder of any kind is justifiable and right to save the rights of the Southern people," he exclaims.

As the others nod in agreement, the barber continues, "Never, never shall Lincoln be President!" To prevent this, he says, his own life "is of no consequence—I am willing to give it for Lincoln's—I would sell it for that Abolitionist's."

Turning dramatically to Turner, Ferrandini adds, "We shall all die together, we shall show the North that we fear them not. Every Captain . . . will on that day prove himself a hero."

He seems to be reaching a crescendo. "The first shot fired, the main traitor Lincoln dead, and all Maryland will be with us, and the South shall be free, and the North must then be ours."

Finally, Ferrandini turns to Pinkerton and addresses him directly. "Mr. Hutcheson," he says, "if I alone must do it, I shall—Lincoln shall die in this city."

52

Westfield, New York

February 16, 1861

At roughly noon on a cold Saturday, Lincoln's inaugural train rolls into the small town of Westfield, New York, near the shore of Lake Erie in the far western corner of the state. The past few days have been a nonstop whirlwind: five states, a half dozen big cities, and scores of stops in smaller towns and villages. This morning alone, the train visited six towns in Ohio and three in western Pennsylvania before cutting northeast over the New York State line.

Both the crowds and the Presidential entourage have grown larger as the train has moved east, continuing on a route that will soon take them to the huge East Coast metropolises like New York City, Trenton, and Philadelphia. Those cities are still a few days away, however, and today the inaugural train has been traversing the flat, rural terrain of the southern Great Lakes region, visiting small villages and towns like this one.

Predictably, a crowd of thousands is gathered at Westfield's small train depot to cheer the Presidential train's arrival, and the familiar sight of flying banners and waving handkerchiefs greets the passengers.

At first, this seems to be a fairly typical small-town stop for the

Inaugural Express. But for the locals, Abraham Lincoln has a surprise in store.

A few days prior, Lincoln had recognized the town's name on the travel itinerary and quickly reached out to a local contact in the area. He asked if the contact could locate a family by the name of Bedell that lived in Westfield—and invite them to be at the station when Lincoln's train arrives.

Now, standing on the rear train platform before the crowd, Lincoln makes a special announcement.

"Some three months ago, I received a letter from a young lady here," he says. "It was a very pretty letter, and she advised me to let my whiskers grow, as it would improve my personal appearance." The crowd responds with cheerful applause. "Now, if she is here, I would like to see her." He calls out her name and scans the many faces before him.

According to a reporter at the station, a small boy who was standing on a post cried out, "There she is, Mr. Lincoln!" and pointed to a black-haired girl in the crowd.

Sure enough, it's eleven-year-old Grace Bedell, the little girl who told Lincoln to grow a beard. She's standing in the back of the crowd accompanied by her two sisters. In her hand, she clutches a bouquet of roses that she'd gathered in preparation for the moment.

While the President can now see Grace, little Grace can't see the President. As she would later recall, "The crowd was so large and I was so little that I could not see the President as he stood on the rear platform."

Lincoln quickly beckons her to come forward, and a family friend guides little Grace by the hand toward the train platform. The crowd parts and forms a lane to let her approach. When she nears the train, Lincoln steps down from the platform to the floor of the depot. He leans down to smile at her. "You see," he says, pointing at his beard, "I let these whiskers grow for you, Grace." He politely shakes her hand, then gently kisses her forehead.

According to a reporter, the little scene draws "yells of delight" from the crowd. Then, sticking to the tight travel schedule, Lincoln waves goodbye and hops back up on the platform. A moment later, he reenters the passenger car, and the train pulls away.

For the rest of her life, Grace Bedell would never forget what happened next.

"I was so surprised and embarrassed," she recalled, "that I ran home as fast as I could, dodging in and out between horses and buggies and once crawling under a wagon. Such was my confusion that I completely forgot the bouquet of roses that I was going to give the great man to whom I had offered such rare advice, and when I arrived home I had the stems, all that remained of the bouquet, still tightly clutched in my hand."

Bedell also remembers one other detail. "It seemed to me as the president stooped to kiss me that he looked very kind . . . and sad."

Lincoln never received his bouquet of roses. But this exchange with a young girl in Westfield, New York, would be one of the last carefree moments he'd ever know.

53

---•---

Montgomery, Alabama

February 16, 1861

Jefferson Davis has arrived.

He's here, in this capital city, to take over a brand-new self-styled government composed of the six currently seceded states. A seventh, Texas, is in the process of seceding and plans to join the Confederacy. In future weeks and months, Davis and his allies will exert continual pressure on other Southern and border states to support their cause. Eventually, four more states will join.

During his five-day journey from his Mississippi plantation, Davis was—much like Abraham Lincoln—often greeted by parades and rapturous crowds. Davis's arrival in Montgomery, at roughly 10:00 p.m. on Saturday, February 16, is the culmination. Cannons boom to greet him, and despite the late hour, many of the city's residents are out in the streets to cheer and pay their respects.

Montgomery will serve as the acting capital of the new Confederacy until a formal seat of government is formed.

Thirty-six hours after Davis's arrival, most of the city turns out again for Davis's official swearing in as President of the Confederate States. On the steps of the Alabama State Capitol, he swears his oath of office. Alexander Stephens of Georgia is his Vice President.

In the coming days, Davis and Stephens will oversee the ratification of a provisional constitution and the appointment of senior officials.

There is little mystery to the ideology of this new government. Each seceding state has declared the preservation of slavery a primary motive in their documents of secession, and the delegates of the new Confederate Congress appointed Jefferson Davis as someone known to be a "champion of a slave society" who embodies the "values of the planter class."

In six weeks, Vice President Stephens will deliver a speech that lays out the core beliefs of these new Confederate States. Of this new government, Stephens declares:

> Its foundations are laid, its cornerstone rests, upon the great truth that the negro is not equal to the white man; that slavery, subordination to the superior race, is his natural and normal condition. This, our new government, is the first, in the history of the world, based upon this great physical, philosophical, and moral truth.

Later known as the Cornerstone Speech, these words will soon become an iconic statement of the mission of the Confederate States of America.

Yet while the leaders abstractly philosophize about the nature of their ideal society, in the days following Davis's inauguration, they must also contend with some more immediate concerns.

Since South Carolina's formal secession roughly two months earlier, a key question has emerged. What will be the fate and status of federal properties—in particular U.S. military forts housing federal troops and weaponry—within seceded state lines?

South Carolina is home to several such forts, including Fort Moultrie and Fort Sumter, two Army installations in the Charleston Harbor. A garrison of U.S. Army regulars led by Maj. Robert Anderson had been stationed in Fort Moultrie for the past several months, maintaining a federal presence along the coast.

After South Carolina seceded, the state's Governor demanded the evacuation of all U.S. troops from forts within state lines. The federal government, however, had refused to formally honor South Carolina's secession—and therefore refused to remove the garrison from the state.

In fact, shortly after secession was declared, Major Anderson relocated his troops from Fort Moultrie to the stronger and more easily defended Fort Sumter as a precaution to keep his men safe. This move infuriated South Carolinians, and as other Southern states seceded, the remaining presence of federal troops at Fort Sumter increasingly became a flash point issue. The most aggressive leaders in the secessionist movement began to argue that the newly independent states needed to challenge the federal presence, with arms if necessary.

South Carolina's Governor has stationed local militias around Charleston Harbor to send a clear message to the isolated garrison. While some Southern leaders have urged negotiation to prevent a larger conflict, others are adamant that the federal troops must evacuate at once—or be forcibly removed.

In the North, the issue is similarly debated as a dilemma with the potential to become something much larger. Some Northern politicians have argued for simply removing the U.S. troops from South Carolina and other seceding states, so the more important political work of reconciliation can commence. Others have viewed any federal surrender or withdrawal as a dangerous capitulation to the seceded states.

Now, after Davis's inauguration, the matter of Fort Sumter takes on new urgency.

In Davis's inaugural address, he spoke of a hopeful peace between the new Confederate States and the United States of America. But in fact, the formal creation of the Confederacy has further emboldened the most fervent secessionists.

Outside Fort Sumter, local troops continue to surround the harbor that houses the fort. But now, they're not just there by the power of the state—they're backed by the Confederate States of America.

For two months now, it's been a stalemate, with no clear resolution in sight.

But as both the Confederacy and Abraham Lincoln's incoming government are about to learn, this standoff at Fort Sumter will soon take on brand-new significance.

54

Baltimore, Maryland

February 16, 1861

The investigation is now urgent.

A day earlier, Pinkerton stood face-to-face with a man who promised that Abraham Lincoln would not make it through the city of Baltimore alive.

Pinkerton has learned that this man, Ferrandini, is in charge of at least one militia company and belongs to a secret group that solicits money from wealthy Southern patrons to buy weapons. Ferrandini appears to be a true zealot—a secessionist and a political extremist—who exerts power and influence over those around him.

Most important, he has now clearly stated his goal and the goal of his men: to kill Abraham Lincoln.

Although Pinkerton didn't learn much more at the meeting with Ferrandini at Barr's Saloon that night, the experience left him no doubt that the conspiracy to assassinate Abraham Lincoln was very real.

While he and his agents continue to try to learn more about the plotters and their plan, Pinkerton must also begin to formulate a strategy for how to preserve Lincoln's safety. Based on both every rumor he's heard—and on common sense—the time of greatest vulnerability for Lincoln is during his party's transfer from one train station to another. Depending on the final train route, Lincoln and his team will arrive in Baltimore at either the President Street Station or the Calvert Street Station, and then cross the city by street in order to get to the Camden Street Station, where they will catch a final train to Washington, D.C.

For Pinkerton, this raises an essential question. What protection, if any, will the city provide for Abraham Lincoln and his inaugural party on February 23 when they cross through Baltimore on public streets in broad daylight?

The answer to that question rests almost entirely with George P. Kane, Baltimore's Marshal of Police. He's the one who will determine what sort of police escort the city will provide and is responsible for arranging and executing it.

However, from the very beginning of the investigation, Pinkerton has viewed Marshal of Police Kane with distrust.

Kane is widely known in Baltimore as a proslavery Democrat, a Southern extremist even, and through word of mouth, Pinkerton's agents soon come to suspect that Kane is part of the same social circle as the very people they're investigating. Naturally, most of the police officers follow in the mold of their leader.

As Pinkerton describes it, "The police force of the city was under the control of Marshal George P. Kane, and was almost entirely composed of men with disunion proclivities. Their leader was pronouncedly in favor of secession, and by his orders the broadest license was given to disorderly persons and to the dissemination of insurrectionary information."

In fact, back when railroad president Samuel Felton first began looking into the rumors that secessionists would sabotage his tracks—even before he hired Pinkerton—he, too, became wary of Marshal of Police Kane. When he'd sent an emissary from his company to meet with Kane and share their concerns, the Marshal of Police was entirely unresponsive, showed little or no respect for their fears, and failed to take any action. At the time, Felton determined that he would "have nothing more to do with Marshal Kane" and proceeded to hire Pinkerton.

Now, in Baltimore, the stakes surrounding Kane's conduct as Marshal of Police could not be higher. Pinkerton has heard firsthand from conspirators who plan to assassinate Lincoln during his passage through the city, and the presence of or *lack* of a police or military escort on that day is absolutely critical.

Whatever rumors Pinkerton and his agents have heard about Kane's political sympathies, Pinkerton must learn more specifically what Marshal of Police Kane will or will not do to protect Abraham Lincoln's safety.

On the evening of Saturday, February 16—the night after his meeting with Ferrandini—Pinkerton decides to secretly trail Marshal of Police Kane. Naturally, he does so under the guise of John H. Hutcheson, stockbroker.

Soon enough, Kane leads Pinkerton straight to Barnum's Hotel—the known secessionist hangout where Ferrandini himself works and holds court. On this night, however, Kane doesn't appear to be looking for Ferrandini. Instead, he meets several friends at the hotel bar. Quietly following Kane, Pinkerton finds a barstool several feet away from Kane's group so he can sit inconspicuously and listen to the conversation.

The problem is, the room is crowded. It's hard for Pinkerton to hear, though he manages to make out a few key words. After listening closely for several minutes, he's able to hear Kane state, quite clearly, the phrase "no police escort." Pinkerton continues listening and can hear Kane state it again: "no police escort."

This is all Pinkerton can discern before Kane departs with his friends.

Whether Kane was referring to Lincoln's arrival in the city when he used those words, Pinkerton can't know for sure. However, because Lincoln's arrival is one of the most-discussed subjects in the city, it certainly seems a very likely event for Kane to discuss at Barnum's Hotel.

What's more, Pinkerton does some quick research and learns that there is no other significant public event in the coming days that would warrant a police presence. No other famous persons or traveling dignitaries will be visiting the city. No parades or public gatherings. The only coming occasion that would warrant a police escort—or a police presence of any kind—is, in fact, Abraham Lincoln's passage through the city.

In the coming days, Pinkerton will become further convinced that Marshal of Police Kane is in fact directly coordinating with the

Baltimore conspirators. In Pinkerton's mind, Kane is aware of the assassination plot and is prepared to aid and abet the plot by making sure police are nowhere near the scene of the coming crime.

Pinkerton doesn't have proof of this theory, however, so it remains largely speculation on his part. Regardless, the most important discovery is this: Marshal of Police Kane apparently has no plan whatsoever to provide police protection to the President-elect during his passage through a hostile city. In the end, it doesn't really matter whether Kane is *intentionally* participating in the plot or simply being negligent. Either way, the lack of protection means that when Abraham Lincoln arrives, he'll be exposed and vulnerable.

55

---•---

Buffalo, New York

February 16, 1861

At almost the very same hour that Allan Pinkerton learns about the apparent lack of police protection during Lincoln's arrival in Baltimore, Lincoln's inaugural party learns how critical such protection can be.

After saying goodbye to Grace Bedell in Westfield, New York, Lincoln and his entourage continue their Saturday rail journey northeast along the icy shoreline of Lake Erie, stopping every hour or so at local towns and villages.

Now, as the train approaches the city of Buffalo, the exhausted members of the inaugural party are looking forward to a two-day stop in that city. Sunday will be a much-needed day of rest—most of all for Lincoln himself, whose exhaustion is evident and whose hoarse voice continues to suffer from the seemingly endless public remarks and speeches he is called on to make, often outside in the freezing winter air.

Shortly after 4:30 p.m., the train pulls into the Metropolitan Station on the south side of Buffalo, near the easternmost corner of Lake Erie. If the traveling party can just get through the next several hours of receptions and speeches without incident, everyone will be rewarded with a day of recuperation.

A gun salute greets the train as it approaches the station, as does a crowd of roughly ten thousand people, surging into and surrounding the building. Here, as usual, the inaugural party will disembark inside the depot and, guided by a local police and military escort, transfer to a series of carriages that will carry the members in a public procession to the designated downtown hotel.

Among those waiting in the train depot is former U.S. President Millard Fillmore, a Buffalonian, who is on hand to greet Lincoln and serve as his escort into the city.

Unlike in most other cities, however, the organizers of the reception had allowed public access to the actual train depot, probably assuming that the presence of both a police escort and an infantry company of the Seventy-Fourth Regiment would suffice for crowd control.

However, by the time the train pulls into the depot, a huge mass of people had pushed aggressively into the station and now threatens to overwhelm the police and soldiers. When the train finally stops in the depot, the passengers look out their windows to see a scene of emerging chaos.

At first, the military detail is able to create a space for Lincoln to step down on the platform near the door of the rear passenger car. According to plan, Lincoln's bodyguards are the first to emerge from the train's passenger door, followed by the President-elect himself. At that point, Fillmore steps forward to provide a ceremonial greeting.

Several reporters are present and witness what happens next.

"Mr. Fillmore had barely time to speak to Mr. Lincoln," writes one reporter, before "the swaying crowd" became "absolutely uncontrollable."

According to another reporter, "The crowd, in its crazed eagerness to get nearer to the distinguished visitor . . . became an ungovernable mob, making an irresistible rush towards him which swept the soldiers from their lines, and threw everything into the wildest confusion that we ever witnessed in our lives."

In no time, the security detail is overwhelmed, and the entire depot is a crush of bodies—with more trying to push their way in. A wave of panic sweeps through the crowd as the scene turns into one of "positive insanity." As people begin frantically trying to escape, even more get crushed by the push and pull of the crowd.

"Men were overcome with pressure to the point of fainting," one onlooker describes. "It was fearful . . . disorderly, terrible," another reporter puts it. "We never saw its like before, and never desire to see it again."

Lincoln himself, as well as Fillmore, have the benefit of a circle of armed soldiers around them, but even so, they're pressed tightly on all sides, with the crowd now grasping at Lincoln. From the center of this chaos, it took a "superhuman effort" for the soldiers to create enough room for Lincoln. Surrounded by bodyguards, the President-elect is shoved and squeezed through the crowd toward the depot door. Lincoln "did not escape uncrushed," one reporter wrote, "but he sustained no injuries." Fillmore also escapes without harm.

The same cannot be said for all of Lincoln's party. During the chaotic melee, Maj. David Hunter, one of the military officers serving as a Lincoln bodyguard, became separated from the others and was eventually pushed by the mass of people against a wall of the depot. There he was "ruthlessly crushed against the wall by the crowd" with such force that his shoulder is dislocated. He's soon rushed to receive medical attention, and doctors put a cast on his arm that remains for the rest of the inaugural journey.

The journalists on hand later reported that "there were many in the crowd injured." One older man had been "jammed in the doorway till he sank down exhausted" and, like Hunter, had to be rushed to receive emergency medical attention.

In the aftermath, the confusion was so overwhelming that the Presidential carriages left the station before every member of the party was able to board. As a result, some were left to walk in the cold from the station to the hotel.

Thankfully, once the Presidential procession reaches the hotel in Buffalo, the rest of the evening goes as planned, without disruption. Yet the chaos at the train station is a visceral reminder of Lincoln's vulnerability at every stage of the trip.

Among those in Lincoln's party who had to be most worried about the frightening incident at the Buffalo train station is Norman Judd. A few days earlier, Judd had received the ominous note from Allan Pinkerton about a dangerous plot afoot in Baltimore—a plot that put Lincoln's life in danger.

Here in Buffalo, the inaugural party had the benefit of a police escort, a military escort, and an overwhelmingly friendly crowd. The President-elect was nonetheless lucky to escape serious injury, and one of his bodyguards is now wearing a sling.

Judd knows as well as anyone that when the inaugural train arrives in Baltimore, the Presidential party will have to travel roughly a mile in carriages through the city streets in broad daylight. By then, their station and time of arrival will almost certainly have been published in newspapers, so the public will know exactly where they'll arrive and the likely procession route through the city.

Most important, for the first time on the journey, the huge crowds they'll face will not be friendly. Maryland is a slave state and, at a time of enormous political discord, Abraham Lincoln is the enemy.

Making matters worse, Judd is missing one key detail. He still has no idea what Pinkerton just learned on the ground in Baltimore. There will be "no police escort"—in fact, no protection whatsoever—for Abraham Lincoln as he makes his way through the city.

56

---·---

Baltimore, Maryland

February 18, 1861

The mission has changed.

For roughly two weeks, Pinkerton agent Kate Warne has been embedded with the society women of Baltimore, learning about the secret clubs and Southern extremist groups from a different angle than the male agents. Her goal was to meet and win the trust of women close to the organizations—the friends and relatives of members, for example—to gain more information about any secret whisperings or plots.

Posing as an Alabaman, complete with Southern accent and the cockade pinned to her Southern-style dress, she's been spending time in the most prominent gathering places in the city. In the previous two weeks, as Pinkerton puts it, "many hints were dropped in her presence which found their way to my ears, and were of great benefit to me."

It was some of these rumors and suggestions that initially encouraged Pinkerton to believe that a plot to assassinate Lincoln was a material threat and, since that time, Warne "had made remarkable progress in cultivating the acquaintance of the wives and daughters of the conspirators."

Now that Pinkerton and Davies have successfully infiltrated Ferrandini's inner circle, however, Pinkerton determines that Warne's efforts should be redirected. The time for investigating is largely over, and now the essential question is: How can they *save* Abraham Lincoln's life?

At roughly noon on Monday, February 18—now five days away from Lincoln's planned passage through Baltimore—Pinkerton calls an emergency meeting with Warne. For now, he tells her, she can lose the Alabama accent and the cockade. Instead, she'll be heading north for the next phase of the operation.

"Mr. P called and said I must get ready to go to New York on the 5:16 p.m. train. He also gave me my instructions and some letters for N.B. Judd, and E.S. Sanford," she writes in her daily log.

The latter name refers to Edward S. Sanford, the president of the American Telegraph Company. Pinkerton's National Detective Agency solved a major case for Sanford a few years earlier—the Maroney case, in which Warne figured prominently—and now Pinkerton plans to enlist Sanford's help to control telegraphic communications to and from Baltimore in the coming days.

The other name refers, of course, to Norman B. Judd, the Lincoln friend and handler whom Pinkerton's messenger recently met with in Cincinnati, Ohio. Warne must now try to reestablish contact with Judd to put a plan in place based on the latest information from Baltimore.

At 4:00 p.m., Warne settles her hotel bill in Baltimore and leaves for the train station. Pinkerton meets her there to discuss final arrangements for her mission in New York City. It's possibly here at this station that Pinkerton and Warne establish a brand-new rule for the investigation. From now on, everyone involved, especially the agents, must use code names in any written or verbal communication. For the protection of both themselves and the President-elect, they will never again refer to themselves verbally or in writing in any other way.

Pinkerton tells her that he'll be "Plums." Warne will be "Barley" or "Mrs. Barley."

With that settled, Mrs. Barley boards the 5:16 p.m. train from Baltimore to New York City.

If the schedule holds, she should arrive in New York City early the next morning—just in time to meet Lincoln's party as they visit the city.

57

————— · —————

New York, New York

February 19, 1861

Eleven hours.

That's roughly how long it takes Pinkerton agent Kate Warne—
now using the code name Mrs. Barley—to take a train from Baltimore to New York City.

Having boarded at 5:16 p.m. the previous night, she arrives in
New York City at roughly 4:00 a.m. the morning of Tuesday, February
19. According to Warne's daily report, she then takes a carriage from
the train station to the Astor House Hotel in lower Manhattan. The
Astor is where members of Abraham Lincoln's inaugural team are
scheduled to stay after they arrive in the city later that afternoon.

The early hour of Warne's arrival is fortunate because, after some
wrangling, she's able to secure a room at the Astor.

After Warne's all-night travel, there's no rest for the weary. "I got
a room, after much trouble," she writes in her report, "and went to
bed, but did not sleep."

Three hours later, after giving up on sleep altogether, she has a 7:30
a.m. breakfast at the hotel. As the morning begins, the hotel—and
the entire city—is preparing for the President-elect's long-anticipated
arrival.

If Warne happened to peruse a copy of *The New York Times* with her breakfast, she would've read breathless coverage of every phase of Lincoln's journey so far, an hour-by-hour breakdown of his visit to Albany the previous day, and a detailed account of New York City's preparations for the coming afternoon and evening. "The occasion will undoubtedly call forth immense throngs of people," the paper reports, "and special police arrangements have been made to preserve order."

Indeed, according to *The Times*, a total of 1,300 police officers have been enlisted for the day, with groups of officers stationed at every possible point from the moment Lincoln's train arrives in Manhattan. The newspapers report not only where the inaugural entourage will be staying—at the Astor House, where Warne now is—but the actual room numbers where everyone in Lincoln's party will sleep, including Lincoln himself and his family.

Warne's first order of business is to try to contact E. S. Sanford, president of the American Telegraph Company, so that she may hand-deliver Pinkerton's letter asking for his assistance in the days to come. She sends a note to Sanford's office requesting an urgent meeting, and after hearing no response, sends another. Finally, an emissary of Sanford—a young aide named George H. Burns—arrives at the Astor House and locates Warne. She gives him Pinkerton's letter to bring to Sanford, and they discuss arrangements for how and when Sanford can find her in person later that evening.

By this point, the entirety of downtown Manhattan is in a state of commotion as crowds begin to pour into the city in anticipation of Lincoln's arrival. By midday, most streets are barricaded.

The Astor House, at the corner of Broadway and Vesey, is to be the last stop on a grand procession that will transport Lincoln from the train station on West Thirty-First Street, through the midtown streets and down Broadway. Twenty police officers are assigned to the Astor House alone, with over a hundred more stationed in the surrounding blocks.

With regard to Warne's side of the investigation, her key question is this: Amid the commotion and with so much tight security, will she be able to establish contact with Norman Judd, or anyone else in the inaugural team, when the procession arrives at the hotel?

By 3:00 p.m.—the time of Lincoln's train's arrival on the west side—the din of the outside crowd becomes constant and can be heard in every corner of the hotel. Naturally, the noise grows steadily louder as the procession moves south down Broadway, getting closer to the Astor House.

When the procession finally approaches the hotel at 4:00 p.m., Kate Warne is one of those who catches a glimpse of the President-elect in his open carriage, waving to the throngs of people lining the streets. "Lincoln looked very pale, and fatigued," she reports. "He was standing in his carriage bowing when I first saw him."

Once the carriages arrive at the barricaded hotel steps, Lincoln steps out of his coach, and his handlers escort him to the top of the Astor's front steps. After a few waves to the mass of spectators surrounding the hotel in every direction, he enters the building. The crowds outside let out a deafening roar, hoping for some sort of speech or address. The roar continues for a several minutes. Then, as Warne reports, Lincoln "soon after appeared on the balcony, from where he made a short speech, but there was such a noise, it was impossible to hear what he said."

As it happens, Lincoln is all too aware of how impossible it is for anyone to hear him. If Warne were able to make out the words, she would've heard him say this to the crowd, "I could not be heard by any but a very small fraction of you at best; but what is worse than that is, I have nothing just now to say worth your hearing." With a smile, he offers a few more waves before reentering the building.

With the inaugural entourage in the hotel, Warne moves to her next order of business. "I then wrote a note to N.B. Judd, and asked him to come to my room so soon as convenient," she reports. "I gave the note to the bell-boy and told him to deliver it immediately."

For Pinkerton's team, this is the key moment. They have four days until Abraham Lincoln is set to be assassinated in Baltimore. To keep that from happening and to save the President-elect, the detectives must establish a secure and discreet channel of communication to Lincoln's party. If word of the plot falls into the wrong hands, or if its existence leaks to the press or public, Lincoln's potential killers would be tipped off. Not only that, but any news story regarding an assassination plot would undoubtedly create widespread panic and chaos.

Within a few minutes, the bellboy returns, still carrying Warne's note. He has bad news. Norman Judd is not at the hotel. In fact, he's not in New York City. That morning, Judd missed the inaugural train's departure from Albany, where the team stayed last night. The inaugural train simply continued on without him.

The good news is the bellboy thinks Judd caught the next train. If all goes well, he should be here sometime this evening.

It's a big *if.* Warne knows she's running out of time. Judd is the only person they trust—the dedicated contact person on Lincoln's team. If his train gets delayed—if they can't reach him—this may be the last chance to establish contact and make an actual plan.

Kate Warne stares at the young bellboy.

This train better not be late.

58

·

Baltimore, Maryland

February 19, 1861

Otis K. Hillard is about to break.

Harry Davies can sense it. Davies has now spent many days with the young, well-to-do Baltimore socialite. More and more, Hillard seems distracted and moody. He talks and acts as if he carries around a great weight—as if he's hiding a secret he longs to reveal. Increasingly, it's a secret that seems to make him unusually nervous.

Davies reports all of this to Pinkerton. The two detectives begin to suspect that Hillard, in fact, has mixed feelings about his involvement in what they now know is a violent conspiracy against Abraham Lincoln. The young man, it seems, is in over his head. This is a vulnerability—and one that skilled undercover agents know to exploit. As Pinkerton later describes it:

> Hillard soon proved a pliant tool in our hands. Being of a weak nature and having been reared in the lap of luxury, he had entered into this movement more from a temporary burst of enthusiasm and because it was fashionable, than from any other cause. Now that matters began to assume such a warlike attitude, he was inclined to hesitate before the affair had gone too far, but still he seemed to be enamored with the glory of the undertaking.

On February 19, Davies spends the afternoon with Hillard and continues to press him with questions about whatever secret group he belongs to. Davies frequently leads the conversation to Lincoln's pending passage through the city, trying to draw Hillard to reveal more about his plans for that day. Hillard speaks mostly in hypotheticals, but makes direct connections to a murderous plot.

"If our company would draw lots to see who would kill Lincoln, and the lot should fall on me, I would do it willingly," Hillard says to Davies. "If my Captain should tell me to do it I would do it."

But when Davies presses him for details, Hillard still declines to reveal more. "I have told you all I have a right to tell you," he says. "And I tell you all I dare without compromising myself, my friends, and my honor."

Later that afternoon, as the two men walk from Davies's hotel to a nearby restaurant called Mann's, Hillard mentions that after they dine, he will be visiting "the National Volunteers room."

Almost every day, Hillard has attended some sort of meeting with his militia group, either referring to the Palmetto Guards or the National Volunteers. It's hard to know if he always meets the same group of people, or whether different meetings involve different attendees.

Over the meal, Davies continues to ask questions. In response, Hillard nervously looks around the restaurant, saying that "government spies" might by trying to listen to their conversation. Davies obligingly speaks in hushed tones, but Hillard is still reluctant to say more. "We have taken a solemn oath, which is to obey the orders of our Captain, without asking any questions," Hillard says under his breath. "And in no case, or under any circumstances reveal any orders received by us, or entrusted to us, or anything that is confidential."

Whatever group Hillard belongs to, the members have taken official vows of secrecy.

Undeterred, Davies continues to press him. "What is the first object of the organization?" he asks.

"It was first organized to prevent the passage of Lincoln with the troops through Baltimore, but our plans are changed every day, as matters change," Hillard replies. "What its object will be from day to day, I do not know, nor can I tell. All we have to do is obey the orders of our Captain, and whatever he commands we are required to do."

Davies once again gets the feeling that Hillard wants to reveal more. But as before, the young man stops short. "What I can and dare tell you I am willing to and like to do it," Hillard says. But "I cannot come out and tell you all—I cannot compromise my honor."

The dinner ends, and the two men part. Presumably, Hillard is off to "the National Volunteers room" to attend another secret meeting.

Early the next morning, Davies shares everything he's learned with Pinkerton. Pinkerton, who has by now already been setting plans in motion and will himself soon need to leave the city to oversee them, impresses on Davies the urgency of penetrating Hillard's group. "I gave him such instructions as I deemed necessary under the circumstances," Pinkerton later explains. To find out the group's final plan, "he was to insist upon Hillard taking him to the meeting."

Pinkerton tells Davies that instead of just asking questions, he should offer his personal services and try to join Hillard's secret society.

Later that morning, according to Pinkerton's account, Davies "broached the matter to Hillard in a manner which convinced him of his earnestness." Just as Pinkerton hoped, Hillard "promised his utmost efforts to secure his admission."

By that afternoon, "Hillard joyfully informed his companion that his request had been granted, and that, upon his vouching for the fidelity of his friend, he had succeeded in obtaining permission for him to enter their society."

That night, Davies will join Hillard at the secret society's meeting. Finally, Pinkerton has a man on the inside.

59

New York, New York

February 19, 1861

Kate Warne is counting the minutes.

At 6:30 p.m., throngs of people pack the Astor House, desperately trying to get into a reception for Lincoln in one of the hotel's grand ballrooms.

Avoiding the crowd, Warne instead eats a quick dinner by herself. After the meal, she receives a message—the most important one of the day. Norman Judd has just arrived at the Astor House. He's received her note and wants to meet her as soon as possible.

Bring him to my room, she tells the bellboy, well aware of the need for privacy.

The bellboy finds Judd in the lobby, and then, as Judd recalls, "I followed the servant to one of the upper rooms of the hotel where, upon entering, I found a lady seated at a table with some papers before her. She arose as I entered."

Most likely, Judd is surprised that Pinkerton has sent a woman to discuss such urgent business, but there's no time to think much about it. Warne immediately explains that she has a letter from Allan Pinkerton, hand-delivered because Pinkerton "did not like to trust the mail in so important a matter." By now, Judd is used to this procedure.

Sitting down, and probably expecting the worst, Judd puts a cigar between his teeth and opens the letter.

Once again, the exact wording is not known, but Pinkerton would later summarize the letter's contents: yet more evidence has accumulated that a plot to kill Abraham Lincoln exists in Baltimore.

In the letter, he also lets Judd know that regarding Warne's role, "she had been delegated by me to arrange for a personal interview, at which all the proofs relating to the conspiracy could be submitted to him."

In other words, Judd and Warne need to work together and figure out how and when a secret meeting can be arranged with Judd, Pinkerton, and the railroad owner, Samuel Felton. In this meeting, Pinkerton promises to finally share all that he knows about the assassination plot in Baltimore and, most important, present a plan for how they may quietly evade it, without creating a public firestorm in an already dangerous political climate.

For Judd, another meeting is all well and good. But he wants—and demands—more details, right now. Sure, Judd understands the need for secrecy, but he has a President to protect. To plan accordingly, he absolutely must know more about this assassination plot.

Warne, however, refuses to reveal anything. "Mr. Judd asked me a great many questions, which I did not answer," she writes in her field report. "I told him that I could not talk on the business."

Judd presses her again, trying to convince her to provide more information. He also says he's eager to reveal the story to others. "He said he was much alarmed and would like to show the letter I had given him to some of the party, and also consult the New York police about it," she reports. But Warne, following Pinkerton policy, demands that he "do no such thing." For now, no one else can know.

Instead, Warne suggests that Judd write a letter to Pinkerton, which she'll hand-deliver to him back in Baltimore. In addition, she tells him that they need to pick a time and place for a confidential meeting along the inaugural train's route—somewhere before Baltimore—ideally Philadelphia, where Pinkerton will already be meeting with Felton—in the next two days.

For Judd, it's a moment of utter frustration. He's about to boil over. Yet before he erupts, a hotel messenger arrives.

According to the messenger, Edward S. Sanford—president of the American Telegraph Company—has just arrived at the hotel, asking to see Kate Warne.

For once, something seems to be going their way. A few moments later, Sanford enters the room.

Warne quickly introduces the two men, who have never met. The one thing they have in common? Both men have now received confidential letters from Allan Pinkerton regarding the assassination plot in Baltimore. And now, according to Warne, they need to work together to thwart it.

Sanford immediately tells Judd that "anything he can do for him he will do with pleasure." As the president of the largest telegraph company in the country, he can provide or shut down telegraphic communication as needed between any two locations, almost at will.

Judd is thankful for the offer of help and seems relieved that he's no longer the only person who knows of the plot. Eager to reconnect with the Lincoln party, he leaves the room, but promises to speak again to Warne before she leaves the next morning so they can finalize a plan.

With Judd gone, Sanford now subjects Warne to the same grilling that Judd did. He wants to know every detail of the plot and who's involved. Once again, following strict protocol, she refuses.

"There is no reason why I should tell you all I know, and I have no more to say," she insists.

Sanford stands there. He's not giving up. "Barley, there is something more," he persists, "and if you will only tell me how you are situated, and what you are doing in Baltimore I can better judge how to act."

Warne still won't budge.

It's a standoff—one that Sanford eventually realizes he won't win. "You are a strange woman," he finally says, admitting defeat.

For now, he'll just have to wait for more information as it comes and, like Judd, agree to an in-person meeting where Pinkerton will reveal everything he knows about the plot.

In the end, Sanford offers one final idea. He'd like to send his assistant, George H. Burns, to Baltimore to aid Pinkerton on the ground. According to Sanford, "it would be great assistance to Mr. Pinkerton" because Burns would have "full control of the telegraph wires from Baltimore to any point Pinkerton would wish."

Warne agrees to this.

For Sanford, it's a victory, even if it's a small one. Satisfied that he's done all he can for the time being, he finally relaxes and begins making small talk.

"He was very friendly and stayed until after 10 o'clock, when he bade me good night and left," Warne records.

At this point, Kate Warne has been awake and on the move for thirty-six hours straight and is no doubt exhausted. But just after Sanford leaves, a telegram arrives.

It's from Pinkerton himself and contains an important update to share with Judd. Immediately, she sends for Judd, and a few minutes later, he's back in her room.

She shows him the telegraph. It reads:

"Tell Judd I meant all I said, and that today they offer Ten for one, and Twenty for two."

Sounds like a code, but what the telegram actually means is this: "I meant all I said" verifies that everything Pinkerton has written to Judd thus far is absolutely serious. By "Ten for one" and "Twenty for two," he's referring to the current betting odds in Baltimore—the odds that Abraham Lincoln won't make it out of the city alive.

Judd is promptly sent into a panic.

Warne tries to calm him, assuring him that the Pinkerton Agency is working on a plan, but Judd remains agitated. He asks Warne if she can stay in New York City through the next day. Why? Because Vice President–elect Hannibal Hamlin is coming to town, and Judd wants them both to consult with him on the matter.

As Warne describes it, Judd "wanted to show [the telegraph] to Vice President Hamlin, and also that I should have an interview with Hamlin. I said that it would never do: that I could not say anything more to Hamlin than I had said to him, and that in the morning I should return to Baltimore."

It's an amazing moment. Kate Warne is so busy doing her job, she refuses to waste time meeting the next Vice President of the United

States. She also reinforces her most vital point. The only way Lincoln is going to survive is if they maintain absolute secrecy.

Before Judd leaves, he and Warne come to an agreement on the critical next step. Warne will pass along to Pinkerton a request from Judd to meet him in Philadelphia the evening of February 21, after the inaugural party's scheduled afternoon arrival in that city. There, Pinkerton can present everything he knows and share his plan to keep the President-elect safe—and Judd will be prepared to share all of this with Lincoln himself. At that point, it will be less than forty-eight hours before Lincoln's train is scheduled to arrive in Baltimore.

That'll give them less than two days to enact whatever plan Pinkerton comes up with.

By the time Judd finally leaves Kate Warne's room, it's 11:30 p.m.

In the past forty hours, she's been in two cities, switched aliases, witnessed Abraham Lincoln's arrival in New York City, conducted lengthy high-pressure conversations with both a Presidential advisor and a powerful tycoon regarding matters of national security, and turned down a meeting with the future Vice President of the United States. Forty hours—all without a minute of sleep.

But there's still one more thing she has to do.

"I then sent word to be wakened in time to take the early train to Baltimore in the morning," she writes in her daily logbook. Then, simply, "I went to bed tired."

60

———— • ————

Baltimore, Maryland

February 20, 1861

Finally, for Pinkerton agent Harry Davies, the night has come.

After weeks of carefully trying to gain the trust and friendship of young Baltimorean Otis K. Hillard, Davies has been invited to a key meeting of the secret group conspiring against President-elect Abraham Lincoln.

At least, that's how one account describes it. In fact, there is uncertainty about what transpires on this night. The only existing source for this meeting is Allan Pinkerton's memoir, written more than thirty years later. But unlike every other major detail of the investigation, the meeting is never referenced in the daily reports written by Pinkerton, Davies, or the other agents at the time. While the reports may simply have been lost, the events described nonetheless have as much quality of legend as they do verified detective work.

In any case, according to Pinkerton's account, on this night, Hillard leads Davies to an affluent home, on a quiet street not far from downtown. The front door opens to a large dimly lit drawing room, where the curtains are drawn to prevent any outsiders from seeing the activity within.

"As they entered the darkened chamber, they found many of the conspirators already assembled," Pinkerton later described. "The members were strangely silent, and an ominous awe seemed to pervade the entire assembly."

After being introduced to a few members, some of whom Davies recognized from Hillard's social group, he's led to the center of the room. The other members form a circle around him. In a special ceremony, they have him swear an oath of secrecy and loyalty to the group. Then, "having passed through the required formula, Davies was warmly taken by the hand by his associates, many of whom he had met in the polite circles of his society."

At this point, the group's leader, dressed all in black, stands before the small crowd. He is, of course, recognizable to everyone. The barber. As Pinkerton reports, "The President, who was none other than Captain Ferrandini, arose, and in a dramatic manner detailed the particulars of the plot."

Here, in detail, Ferrandini finally lays out what Pinkerton and his agents have been trying to uncover for so long: the plot to assassinate Abraham Lincoln.

It'll happen in less than three days, shortly after 1:00 p.m., on Saturday, February 23. That's the date and time when Lincoln's inaugural train was scheduled to arrive in Baltimore's Calvert Street Station via the Northern Central line from Harrisburg. According to the public itinerary, Lincoln and his entourage will then cross through the city by carriage to the Camden Street Station, where they'll board a connecting train to Washington, D.C.

The place to strike, Ferrandini explains, is right outside the first train station.

From what Davies can tell, "a vast crowd of secessionists were to assemble at that place to await the arrival of the train with Mr. Lincoln. They would appear early and fill the narrow streets and passages immediately surrounding it."

Rather than provide a proper law enforcement escort, Baltimore's Marshal of Police George Kane would make sure that only a few officers would be on hand. "Here it was arranged that but a small force of policemen should be stationed, and as the President arrived a disturbance would be created which would attract the attention of these guardians of the peace."

When the police rush away to "quell the disturbance," Lincoln and his party would be vulnerable, just as they passed through the station tunnel on foot and out to the crowded public streets. Here, Ferrandini's group would be waiting, mixed in with the gathered throngs.

"At this moment—the police being entirely withdrawn—Mr. Lincoln would find himself surrounded by a dense, excited and hostile crowd, all hustling and jamming against him, and then the fatal blow was to be struck."

To escape, the conspirators also arranged for a steamer to be stationed in Chesapeake Bay with a small boat waiting onshore. The steamer would be "ready to take the assassin on board as soon as the deed was done, and convey him to a Southern port, where he would be received with acclamations of joy and honored as a hero."

The main purpose of tonight's meeting, in fact, is to determine which among them would play this hallowed role.

With his members gathered, Ferrandini addresses the group. He's clear as can be, asking them, "Who should assume the task of liberating the nation of the foul presence of the abolitionist leader?"

After a pause, he adds that "tonight the important decision shall be reached."

Earlier, Ferrandini and the other leaders designed a system to select who would be entrusted with this sacred honor. As Pinkerton later describes, "It was finally determined that ballots should be prepared and placed in a box arranged for that purpose, and that the person who drew a red ballot should perform the duty of assassination."

There's another key rule the members must obey: No one will know which member among them has drawn the red ballot. This way, the assassin's identity would be concealed even to the other members. To enforce this rule, "the room was rendered darker, and everyone was pledged to secrecy as to the color of the ballot he drew."

One by one, the members approach the box, drawing a single ballot. In doing so, each man "believ[ed] that upon him, his courage, strength and devotion, depended the cause of the South—each supposing that he alone was charged with the execution of the deed."

This was a lie.

According to Pinkerton, there's more than one red ballot in the box. It's an insurance policy. If one potential assassin loses his nerve, they've got a few backups. As Pinkerton describes, "The leaders . . . had determined that their plans should not fail, and doubting the courage of some of their number, instead of placing but one *red ballot* in the box, they placed *eight*." For Ferrandini and his coconspirators, when it comes to the assassination of Abraham Lincoln, there's no room for error—and no one who can be trusted.

Once the ritual is done and they finish drawing ballots, Ferrandini again addresses the group. He "violently assailed the enemies of the South, and in glowing words pointed out the glory that awaited the man who would prove himself the hero upon this great occasion."

The solemn ceremony comes to an end.

It's no longer a hope. It's a plan.

61

——— • ———

Philadelphia, Pennsylvania

February 21, 1861

Allan Pinkerton has now learned everything he needs to know about the plot to kill Abraham Lincoln. Now, he must implement a plan to prevent it. To do so, he must share what he knows with the key players involved, convince them of the danger, and establish a clear program under highly complex circumstances.

He plans to do this today, in Philadelphia, where all the major players will converge.

For Pinkerton's plan to succeed, however, he must notify every party in precisely the right manner and in the right order. One failed communication, one misunderstanding, or one indiscreet moment could send the operation into chaos.

Yesterday, after Kate Warne's return from New York City, and while Harry Davies was infiltrating the inner circle of the conspirators, Pinkerton took a train from Baltimore to Philadelphia.

Now, his day here begins at seven in the morning.

His first stop is to meet with George H. Burns, who had been sent by Edward Sanford—the president of the American Telegraph Company, and a friend of Pinkerton's—as a result of Sanford's meeting with Warne at the Astor House in New York City. By Sanford's instructions, Burns will assist Pinkerton in any way that Pinkerton deems necessary, including the use of Sanford's telegraph wires.

Upon meeting with Burns, Pinkerton has an immediate request. He wants Burns to send a secure, confidential telegraph to Norman Judd, responding affirmatively to Judd's request—sent through Kate Warne—for a meeting that night.

The inaugural train is making stops at both Newark, New Jersey, and Trenton, New Jersey, that day, and Burns sends telegraphs to both locations. Upon any response, he'll notify Pinkerton instantly.

Pinkerton's next meeting is with Samuel Felton, president of the Philadelphia, Wilmington and Baltimore Railroad. Felton meets Pinkerton at a hotel called the La Pierre House, and the two men talk as they walk toward Felton's office at the PW&B depot in the city.

Felton, of course, is the person who hired Pinkerton's firm to investigate in Baltimore to begin with. Felton is the client and is paying for the investigation. For reasons ethical and otherwise, Pinkerton must fully brief Felton on the latest developments and get Felton's consent for the new direction the case is headed.

The problem is, Felton originally hired Pinkerton to protect his railroad tracks, not to investigate an assassination conspiracy. So for Pinkerton to succeed, he needs to convince Felton of the importance of this new, expanded mission.

While walking with Felton, Pinkerton makes his case. "I made a full report [to Felton] of what had come to my knowledge, in regard to an attempt being likely to be made upon the President-elect and his suite while passing through Baltimore." He further explains that "judging from the reports of my detectives . . . I had no doubt that there would be an attempt made to assassinate Mr. Lincoln."

How many conspirators were behind this plot? "Probably only fifteen or twenty men who would be reckless enough to attempt anything of the kind," Pinkerton explains. He then goes on to describe Otis K. Hillard as "a specimen of the recklessness of this class."

Furthermore, even if there are only a relatively small number of people willing to attack, all it takes is "a few determined men . . . taking advantage of the large crowd of people who would probably be turned out on the occasion of the passage of the President-elect," Pinkerton explains. "These determined persons could accomplish a great deal."

Finally, Pinkerton describes his concern that Baltimore's Marshal of Police, George P. Kane—the person supposedly in charge of protecting the President-elect—is in fact sympathetic to the secessionists. Pinkerton explains his suspicion that Kane will intentionally withhold a proper police escort for Lincoln's party during the critical period when they must travel the city streets in carriages—through what is sure to be a massive, hostile crowd—to transfer from one train station to another and continue the trip to Washington, D.C.

For Lincoln to survive, the detective explains to Felton, they need to properly inform the President-elect's team and divert Lincoln from harm's way.

If Pinkerton was worried that Felton might hesitate to endorse this ambitious undertaking, he needn't have been concerned. "Mr. Felton approved of what I had said and of the view I had taken of the case." More important, Felton "at once assented to my proposition and directed me to inform Mr. Lincoln of what had been discovered."

With this pledge of mutual support, the two men agree to meet later in the day.

From there, Pinkerton stops back at his hotel and consults briefly with Kate Warne, who had accompanied him to Philadelphia. Then, leaving Warne to coordinate communications with his agents in Baltimore, he proceeds again to meet Burns.

As instructed, Burns had telegraphed Lincoln team member Norman Judd in both Newark and Trenton—but has not yet heard a response. Pinkerton, concerned that Judd may've not received the telegraphs, sends Burns to the Kensington train depot to "await the arrival of the Presidential Party who was expected to arrive at 3 p.m." Burns is told to navigate through the crowd and "endeavor to see Mr. Judd, and arrange a meeting for myself and Mr. Felton at the earliest possible moment."

If they can't find Judd, there may be no other way to get word to Lincoln's inner circle.

While Burns heads to the station, Pinkerton rushes through the gathering crowds to La Pierre House, where he and railroad president Felton had agreed to meet for their follow-up planning session.

Here, Pinkerton puts all his cards on the table. To keep Lincoln alive, he plots, he plans, and he tells Felton that the only way they're going to be able to pull this off is if he's able to use Felton's railroad and personnel.

Thankfully, Felton accepts.

While the two men discuss arrangements, Pinkerton begins to hear music outside, an indication that the Presidential procession is under way. Rushing outside, Pinkerton starts pushing his way through the crowds. As he approaches the Kensington depot, he spots the procession of carriages on Walnut Street, heading in the direction of the Continental Hotel, where the Lincoln party will be staying.

As Pinkerton gets closer, he sees young Burns heading toward one of the carriages, pushing aggressively through the lines of police and spectators. As Pinkerton writes, "With superhuman strength I saw him go through the crowd like it was nothing, and bursting through the ranks of the police . . . reach the carriage."

At that moment, Burns reaches Norman Judd's carriage and sets up the meeting at the St. Louis Hotel that Pinkerton had asked for.

As Pinkerton is about to learn, it may be one of the most important meetings of his life.

62

———— • ————

Philadelphia, Pennsylvania

February 21, 1861

By 6:00 p.m., all is ready.

Allan Pinkerton is waiting at the St. Louis Hotel. Railroad owner Samuel Felton arrives soon after, and at roughly 6:45 p.m., they're joined by Norman Judd.

Needless to say, this wasn't an easy meeting to organize. But now, they're finally here, in the one place where Pinkerton, in a confidential face-to-face setting, can present everything he's learned to the one Lincoln advisor he truly trusts.

They start at the beginning. Felton—who goes first—explains his initial concern about the plot to sabotage his railroad, about how it led him to hire Pinkerton, and how that led Pinkerton to uncover the plot. In his report of the conversation, Pinkerton writes:

> Mr. Felton explained his cause for fearing that the track of the Philadelphia, Wilmington and Baltimore Rail Road was in danger, and consequently his employment of me, and how in my researches of this kind I had discovered the fact that some persons meditated the assassination of the President Elect.

Pinkerton then walks Judd though all the details his agents discovered and the undercover work that was done. Most vital, he shares his belief that Baltimore's Marshal of Police George P. Kane, a pro-Southern extremist, will fail to provide proper police protection on the day that Lincoln passes through the city. As a result, the President-elect will be exposed and vulnerable while traveling by carriage over a mile, straight through the crowded city, from one train station to another.

Pinkerton goes on to describe the Baltimoreans they encountered, like Otis K. Hillard, who were sworn members of the underground organization planning the attack:

> I communicated at some length on the character, standing, etc. of O. K. Hillard, and assumed that there was imminent danger from this class of men, whose patriotism was influenced, and who looked upon their Country as being entirely south of Mason and Dixon's Line, whose every sympathy was with the South and would deem it an honor to become martyrs in their cause.

And of course, he describes "Captain Ferrandini," the apparent leader of the group, and his plan for himself and a handful of conspirators to create a disturbance in the crowd, during which the armed assassins will rush Lincoln's carriage.

> I said to Mr. Judd that the danger was from a small number of men in the crowd acting in concert, and asked what would be the consequences where the Presidential Party was hemmed in [in] a crowd unable to move, and a few men bent on taking life—Armed, prepared and determined on doing so even if they had to give a life for a life—and argued that situated as the country was, this was no time to go into war, which would be the result if the President Elect was assassinated in Baltimore.

Listening carefully to each new piece of evidence, Judd is quickly convinced. He states clearly that "after what he had heard he believed there was great danger to Mr. Lincoln to attempt to pass through Baltimore" according to the scheduled program.

The only question now is: How do you keep the new President safe? Or to put it more succinctly: How can you possibly move Lincoln from Philadelphia to Washington, D.C., without traveling through Baltimore?

Right there, Pinkerton and Felton present their plan. They want to change Lincoln's schedule. Sneak him out tonight—a day and a half before the officially announced schedule—and put him on an overnight train that'll run through Baltimore before anyone knows he's there.

Judd thinks for a moment, trying to determine what to do. The President is booked solid the next day, in both Philadelphia and Harrisburg, Pennsylvania, with some of the most important public events of the entire trip. To change everything around—to cancel engagements that took weeks to plan—decisions like this were bigger than Judd.

To pull this off, they need to go to the top.

The very top.

Judd asks Pinkerton to "go with him to the Continental Hotel . . . and lay the subject before him."

Even back then, there was only one *him*.

With roughly thirty-six hours to go, it's time to talk to Abraham Lincoln.

63

———— · ————

Allan Pinkerton and Norman Judd are prepared to tell Abraham Lincoln that there's a plot to kill him—and it's only about thirty-six hours away.

First, however, Pinkerton and Judd must *get* to Lincoln, which is no easy matter.

The Continental Hotel, where the Lincoln party is staying, is only a few blocks from Pinkerton's room at the St. Louis. But the entire downtown Philadelphia neighborhood is completely packed with "immense crowds" that get increasingly dense near the Continental, where Lincoln is currently the guest of honor at a huge public reception.

Pinkerton and Judd try to push through the crowd, but they simply can't get near the Continental's front entrance. At this point, as Pinkerton reports, "I accordingly took Mr. Judd around to Samson Street where we obtained an entrance by the rear of the hotel."

Once inside, Judd heads toward his room, while Pinkerton tries to run to nearby Girard House to check in with Edward Sanford, head of the American Telegraph Company, who's waiting there for an update. For Pinkerton, though, it's "utterly impossible to get into that house owing to the denseness of the crowd."

Instead, he rushes back to the Continental and again enters

through the back door. His goal is to get to Judd's room, where the intended meeting with Abraham Lincoln is supposed to take place.

Pinkerton quickly finds out, however, that the inside of the Continental "was as densely crowded as was the outside," and the back stairs leading to Judd's room are entirely blocked by people.

Undeterred, the brawny former cooper presses through the crowded halls toward the front of the hotel, where the parlor is packed with people waiting in an unruly line to get upstairs for Lincoln's reception. As Pinkerton reports, "There was no way for me to get up but go into the jam and go up with the human tide, so I went in—but such a jam."

After some thirty minutes of wrangling in the hotel crowds, Pinkerton finally gets upstairs, breaks away from the crowd, and heads for Judd's room. Sure enough, Judd is there waiting. He explains that once Abraham Lincoln is finished with the long receiving line, Judd will seek him out.

Finally, at roughly 10:15 p.m., they get word that Lincoln has returned to his room. After a failed attempt by Pinkerton to deliver a note to Lincoln's room, Judd enlists Elmer Ellsworth, Lincoln's young bodyguard, to hand-deliver a note to Lincoln, from Judd, urging him to come to Judd's room on a matter of great importance.

The problem is, Lincoln is utterly exhausted after yet another brutally long and emotionally draining day. He has traveled to multiple towns and cities, given several speeches, led a welcoming parade, endured several reception ceremonies, attended a formal dinner, and stood at a packed receiving line for two hours shaking thousands of hands and greeting thousands of faces.

Now, just as he gets to his room—with the day finally over—he receives a cryptic but urgent message from one of his most loyal aides.

Later, Lincoln himself would recall what happened next, "Mr. Judd . . . sent for me to come to his room. I went, and found there Mr. Pinkerton, a skillful police detective, also from Chicago, who had been employed for some days in Baltimore, watching or searching for suspicious persons there."

The tired President-elect sits down, no doubt extremely curious as to why he's been summoned to meet with a private detective at such a late hour. Elmer Ellsworth, his young bodyguard, stands just outside the hotel room door to prevent anyone else from coming in. A din of crowd noise can still be heard in the hall, where various handlers and hangers-on are still up and about.

Judd begins the conversation.

As Pinkerton notes, "Mr. Judd briefly detailed to Mr. Lincoln the circumstances under which I had gone to Baltimore to operate . . . and that whilst so operating amongst the Secessionists I had discovered a determination amongst certain parties to attempt taking the life of him"—him being Abraham Lincoln—"whilst passing through Baltimore."

Judd goes on to describe the details that both Samuel Felton and Pinkerton relayed to him, and the accumulation of information related to the assassination plot. Judd tells Lincoln that "the evidence is such to convince all honest minds" and that he is "convinced there is danger."

Pinkerton carefully observes Lincoln during Judd's brief presentation, wondering how he'll react. "Whilst Mr. Judd was talking Mr. Lincoln listened very attentively, but did not say a word, nor did his countenance, which I had watched very closely, show any emotion. He appeared thoughtful and serious, but decidedly firm."

It's not Judd, however, who plays the biggest role in making the case. "When Mr. Judd had concluded," Pinkerton reports, "he requested me to detail the circumstances connected with Ferrandini, Hillard and others, and what my opinion was of the probable attempt."

At that moment, Pinkerton is all too aware that what he says in the next few minutes will probably determine whether Abraham Lincoln perceives the assassination plot as a serious threat—and whether he'll take any steps to avoid it.

Pinkerton is the detective. It's his job to make the case.

He begins by describing his recent eavesdropping of Baltimore's Marshal of Police, George P. Kane, whom heard say that there would be "no police escort," during "the passage of Mr. Lincoln through Baltimore."

Pinkerton goes on to describe the angry mood in the city, and the underground network of secessionists furiously plotting against the North. "I alluded to the expressions of Hillard and Ferrandini: that they were ready to give their lives for the welfare of their Country, as also that their country was South of Mason's and Dixon's line." Men like these, Pinkerton explains, "were ready and willing to die to rid their country of a tyrant as they considered Lincoln to be."

Pinkerton elaborates on the mind-set and ideology of the Southern extremists and white supremacists his team encountered. Using Hillard as an example, he explains: He is "a young man . . . thoroughly devoted to Southern rights, and who looked upon the North as being aggressors upon the rights of that section." Committed extremists such as Hillard view "every Northern man as an Abolitionist, and he"—Abraham Lincoln—"as the embodiment of all those evils, in whose death the South would be largely the gainers."

While Lincoln listens "with great attention," Pinkerton lays out what he believes is the essence of the conspirators' plan. Upon Lincoln's arrival at Baltimore's Calvert Street Station, a huge crowd is expected to be gathered, no different from every major city. This crowd, however, will be largely hostile, and the standard police escort will be inadequate or missing entirely.

More important, when Lincoln and his party attempt to cross the city in a procession of carriages to get to the Camden Street Station—a distance of just over a mile—Lincoln's group will be totally exposed to the public. Pinkerton alludes to the recent incident in Buffalo, where Lincoln and his party were put at risk:

[Lincoln] had had some experience of the danger in a large crowd from the accident which met Col. Hunter at Buffalo where the Police were loyal, but it would be infinitely worse in Baltimore . . . with "no police escort," or if there was an escort it would be by a disloyal police, and the slightest sign of discontent would be sufficient to raise all of the angry feeling of the masses, and that would be a favorable moment for the conspirators to operate.

In this environment, Pinkerton argues, "it would be an easy matter for any assassin to mix in with the crowd and in the confusion of the moment shoot Mr. Lincoln if he felt so disposed." Pinkerton's detectives had firsthand knowledge that this secret group of conspirators, led by Ferrandini, were planning to do just that.

Pinkerton concludes his remarks by telling the others, in summary, that "I felt satisfied in my own mind that if Mr. Lincoln adhered to the published program of his route to Washington that an assault of some kind would be made upon his person with a view to taking his life."

When Pinkerton finishes, Lincoln "remained quiet for a few moments apparently thinking."

Judd and Pinkerton can't help but wonder if Lincoln believed them. Did he find the case convincing?

Before the President-elect can answer either way, Judd presses forward and explains their plan for Lincoln to avoid the danger.

They'd have to move right now—this very night—and catch the late train from Philadelphia to Washington, D.C., a full day and a half ahead of the public schedule. Sure, they'd still have to travel into Baltimore and switch stations there, but if Lincoln's journey were kept secret, no one would notice his passage through the city in the middle of the night. Samuel Felton would provide the train, and Pinkerton would join him on the trip and make the arrangements.

By tomorrow morning, Abraham Lincoln would be safely in Washington, D.C.

Would you consent to leave on the train tonight? Judd asks the new President.

It's the only question that matters. But as Lincoln considers it, there's still one major problem with the plan.

As Judd noted earlier, Lincoln is booked solid the following day with public events in both Philadelphia and Harrisburg, Pennsylvania. These aren't just any events; first thing in the morning, Lincoln is scheduled to publicly commemorate George Washington's birthday in Philadelphia by personally raising an American flag over Independence Hall, where the Declaration of Independence was signed.

Washington is one of Lincoln's heroes. There's no way Lincoln can miss that. Then, by midday, he's scheduled to be in Harrisburg, the capital of Pennsylvania, to meet the Governor and local legislators in a state that was absolutely critical to his support. He's not missing that either.

Lincoln looks at the two men and says, simply, "No, I cannot consent to this. I shall hoist the flag at Independence Hall tomorrow morning, and go to Harrisburg tomorrow."

Lest there be any question, Lincoln also states that he would "meet those engagements under any and all circumstances, even if he met with death in doing so."

As Pinkerton explains, "The firmness of tone in which Lincoln spoke showed that there was no further use in arguing the proposition."

Right there, Pinkerton and Judd's carefully crafted plan to keep Lincoln safe evaporates.

Lincoln gives them one last thought to consider: while he is committed to the morning event in Philadelphia and the afternoon reception in Harrisburg, *after that* he's free and willing to change his plan as they see fit.

"Beyond that I have no engagements," Lincoln tells them. "Any plan that may be adopted that will enable me to fulfill those two promises I will carry out, and you can tell me what is concluded upon tomorrow."

With that, Lincoln leaves the room. He has no idea who's waiting for him.

64

---·---

As Abraham Lincoln walks back to his room, it's hard to imagine what's going through his head.

It's now after 11:00 p.m., and he's just had yet another sixteen-hour day comprising multiple cities, extensive travel, speeches, events, and endless unruly throngs of people. In addition to his exhaustion, he's just learned from one of his most trusted aides and one of the most respected lawmen in the country that a team of assassins currently lies in wait for him in the city of Baltimore, planning to murder him as he passes through two days from now.

What does he think of this incredible revelation? Does he believe the threat is real?

Lincoln later recalled that on the way back to his room, "I could not believe that there was a plot to murder me." Since his election, he hasn't given much credence to the many assassination threats he's received—and despite Pinkerton's credibility, he's not ready to start believing them now.

Then, just as Lincoln gets to his suite in the still-crowded hotel, his aides inform him that there's another unexpected visitor. He's waiting outside Lincoln's room—asking to speak to the President-elect about a matter of the utmost urgency.

This visitor is a young man, one with a familiar last name. He's Frederick Seward, currently serving as private secretary to his father, William H. Seward, Lincoln's soon-to-be Secretary of State. Down in the lobby, Frederick had explained that he was there on behalf of his father—and that he must absolutely see Lincoln tonight, under any circumstance.

Lincoln invites Frederick into his room, and the young man wastes no time. He explains to Lincoln that he's been sent "at the insistence of his father and General Scott"—that is, the two men who have taken the greatest responsibility for Lincoln's safety and security upon his arrival in the nation's capital. From there, Frederick hands Lincoln three letters.

Lincoln sits down at a table to read them. The first letter is from William Seward, urging Lincoln to speak to his son when he arrives—and to read the other two letters enclosed.

The second letter is from Gen. Winfield Scott to William Seward, insisting that Seward make contact with Lincoln as soon as possible because one of Scott's officers had "an important communication to make." This letter is what spurred the older Seward, who couldn't leave Washington himself, to send his son as a courier. Obviously, Seward trusted his son, but he also knew that Frederick could get an audience with Lincoln by stating his last name.

Which brings Lincoln to the third letter—the one with the "important communication." It's written by a military officer, Col. Charles P. Stone, informing his superior General Scott that he's just heard a report. In the city of Baltimore, "there is serious danger of violence to and the assassination of Mr. Lincoln in his passage through that city should the time of that passage be known." The assassination plot involves a band of "rowdies holding secret meetings" and "threats of mobbing and violence."

To Lincoln, it sounds nearly identical to what he's just heard down the hall only a few minutes earlier. So why's he hearing this same story again? Lincoln probably assumes Seward and General Scott must have somehow also learned of Pinkerton's investigation.

According to Frederick Seward, when Lincoln read the letters, he "made no exclamation" and there was "no sign of surprise on his face." When Lincoln does start asking questions, the foremost one is this:

"Did you hear any names mentioned . . . such a name as Pinkerton?"

No. As Frederick explains, the information has nothing to do with anyone named Pinkerton.

So where did it come from?

According to the younger Seward, General Scott and Senator Seward also heard early reports about the possibility of danger in Baltimore. Determined to ensure Lincoln's safe passage to the capital, they started their own investigation and made arrangements for two experienced New York City police detectives to go undercover in Baltimore.

Working entirely independently from Pinkerton—in fact, without having any idea that anyone else was also looking into it—these officers investigated some of the same places and organizations, learning much of the same information.

Remarkably, to keep Lincoln safe, the proposed solution offered by Colonel Stone in his letter—and now endorsed by General Scott and William Seward—is to institute "a change in the travelling arrangements which would bring Mr. Lincoln and a portion of his party through Baltimore by a night train without previous notice."

In other words, not only did this team of investigators learn about the same plot that Pinkerton did, but they've independently proposed the same solution to it.

For Lincoln, the news is altogether stunning. He explains to the younger Seward that he had just now heard from Allan Pinkerton in person, right here in the hotel, about a similar assassination plot.

"Surely, Mr. Lincoln, that is strong corroboration of the news I bring you," young Seward replies.

Lincoln, a trained lawyer, concedes readily that if "different persons, not knowing of each other's work," had found "separate clues that led to the same result," then the evidence is compelling indeed.

However, it's already midnight. At this late hour, Lincoln doesn't

286 Brad Meltzer and Josh Mensch

want to make a decision. Instead, he promises Frederick Seward he'll contemplate everything he's heard and decide in the morning.

Seward obliges and leaves the room.

Whatever skepticism the President-elect previously had, the evidence of an assassination plot now seems overwhelming. "I now believed such a plot to be in existence," as Lincoln later puts it.

Yet the question remains: What exactly should he do about it?

65

———— · ————

Philadelphia, Pennsylvania

February 22, 1861

It's just before dawn—barely six hours after the long meeting in Norman Judd's hotel room.

In Philadelphia, Abraham Lincoln rides in an open carriage along Chestnut Street. A marching band and small parade of veteran soldiers precede him, and several other carriages follow.

It's a cold but clear morning, and as Lincoln's carriage approaches the corner of Fifth Street, the first rays of sun land upon the redbrick walls of Independence Hall.

Here, eighty-five years earlier, delegates to the Second Continental Congress ratified the brand-new Declaration of Independence. At that moment, Gen. George Washington was in New York City with the Continental Army, preparing to defend the city against the British fleet and army in the first major battle of the Revolutionary War. Later, of course, George Washington would become the nation's first President.

Today is George Washington's birthday. If Abraham Lincoln lives, he will soon become the nation's sixteenth President and take the oath of office in the city named after Washington. He's here now to pay tribute to that lineage with a ceremonial flag-raising over this iconic building.

Lincoln will do so at a moment when the very future of the United States is in doubt—and not a person in the large crowd gathered for the event is unaware of it.

As has occasionally been the case during his long inaugural journey across the country, Lincoln arrives at the event to find that he is expected to give a full speech when he has none prepared. In this case, he's asked to speak inside Independence Hall to a roomful of Philadelphians just before the flag-raising outside is to commence.

As if to add to the pressure, the head of the Select Council of Philadelphia, chosen to announce the President-elect to the crowd, introduces Lincoln as the person "tasked to restore peace" to the nation.

Lincoln, gazing around the hallowed halls, draws on his own feelings to find the right words. "I am filled with deep emotion," he says, "at finding myself standing here in the place where were collected together the wisdom, the patriotism, the devotion to principle, from which sprang the institutions under which we live." He continues:

> You have kindly suggested to me that in my hands is the task of restoring peace to our distracted country. I can say in return, sir, that all the political sentiments I entertain have been drawn, so far as I have been able to draw them, from the sentiments which originated, and were given to the world from this hall in which we stand. I have never had a feeling politically that did not spring from the sentiments embodied in the Declaration of Independence. [great cheering]

For most of the inaugural journey, Lincoln has avoided talking directly about slavery, the great moral issue that has divided the country and that threatens its future. With the nation teetering on the verge of all-out conflict, he has exercised extreme caution to restrain his words until he assumes office and has the ability to act on them.

But here, in Independence Hall, he finds a way to address the great issue without saying the word.

"I have often inquired of myself," he says to the crowd, "what great principle or idea it was" that has so far kept the nation together. He continues:

> It was not the mere matter of the separation of the colonies from the mother land; but something in that Declaration giving liberty, not alone to the people of this country, but hope to the world for all future time. [applause] It was that which gave promise that in due time the weights should be lifted from the shoulders of all men, and that *all* should have an equal chance.

"*This,*" he says, "is the sentiment embodied in that Declaration of Independence."

Here in Philadelphia, where antislavery sentiment is strong and the Declaration of Independence is the sacred pride of the city, the gathered crowd is roused to enormous cheers.

What Lincoln says next, however, is even more extraordinary and unexpected. "My friends, can this country be saved upon that basis?" he asks. "If it can, I will consider myself one of the happiest men in the world if I can help to save it. If it can't be saved upon that principle, it will be truly awful. But, if this country cannot be saved without giving up that principle . . ." He trails off for a moment, as if thinking.

Then he continues, "I was about to say I would rather be assassinated on this spot than to surrender it."

It's almost impossible to imagine that when he says these words, Lincoln is not thinking about what he learned several hours earlier: that there is a very *real* plot to assassinate him, and his life is most certainly in danger.

Lincoln himself never commented on this connection. But Norman Judd, who is nearby watching and listening to his friend, has little doubt. The "reference to sacrificing himself for his country," Judd would write, "was induced by the incidents of the night preceding."

As if to confirm Judd's thought, Lincoln's remarks end this way. "My friends, this is a wholly unprepared speech . . . I may, therefore, have said something indiscreet."

"No, no!" people cry out.

"But I have said nothing but what I am willing to live by, and, in the pleasure of Almighty God, die by."

Whatever was running through Lincoln's mind as he delivered these unexpected words, there is little time for the spectators to guess, because Lincoln now joins a procession that starts from the inner chamber of the hall, out through the double front doors, and onto a large stage erected in the plaza just in front of Independence Hall.

Here, according to plan, Lincoln will personally hoist a huge new American flag set to fly above Independence Hall.

The crisp air and bright morning sun provide the perfect setting. On a crowded stage and in front of a large crowd gathered in the plaza, Lincoln says a few more words to the crowd, and then—"by the strength of my own feeble arm," as he later remarks—proceeds to pull the ropes that hoist the flag up above Independence Hall, where it flutters in the dazzling sun.

Shortly after dawn on February 22, 1861, President-elect Lincoln commemorates George Washington's birthday by raising a flag over Independence Hall in Philadelphia, Pennsylvania. Some onlookers climbed trees in the plaza to get a better view. The ceremony takes place only hours after Lincoln learned from Allan Pinkerton that an assassination plot put his life in danger.

As if this event were not already steeped in symbolism, the cloth Lincoln raises on this morning is no ordinary flag. It contains a brand-new star—the thirty-fourth—representing Kansas's admission into the Union one month earlier. The status of slavery in Kansas had been one of the most contentious and sometimes bloody disputes between North and South throughout the previous decade.

Because of the recent defection of Senators from the seceding states, Congress obtained a majority to admit Kansas to the Union as a free state.

That single star represents a victory for liberty. But it's a small victory against the scale of the massive conflict soon to come.

66

---•---

Among those in the crowd outside Independence Hall watching the flag-raising ceremony is Pinkerton agent Kate Warne—still using the alias Mrs. Barley.

Warne has been in Philadelphia for the past twenty-four hours, having come from Baltimore the day after her return from New York City. She's here to help in what has become an all-consuming operation: figuring out how to move Abraham Lincoln to Washington, D.C., both safely and in secret.

Immediately after the ceremony, Warne returns to the St. Louis Hotel, where both she and Pinkerton have set up offices in their rooms. At the end of her breakfast, a brief moment of relative peace is shattered by the frantic appearance of Allan Pinkerton, who has been up all night and is now in a mad scramble trying to make complicated arrangements.

In fact, this isn't the only time Warne has seen Pinkerton this early morning. He pounded on her door at 3:00 a.m., looking "sick, and tired out," to explain that their original plan—to have Lincoln catch last night's midnight train from Philadelphia—was rejected by Lincoln himself. It was time to recalibrate. Pinkerton raced away again just after 3:00 a.m., calling a carriage to take him somewhere else at that strange hour.

Now, at roughly 7:00 a.m., he's back—and able to more fully brief Warne on what happens next.

According to Lincoln's original travel itinerary—the one now published in newspapers—Lincoln is supposed to be traveling with his inaugural party from Harrisburg to Baltimore on the Northern Central Railroad the following morning, Saturday, February 23, departing at 9:00 a.m. Lincoln's party is scheduled to arrive in Baltimore at the Calvert Street Station at 1:00 p.m., transfer into carriages, cross through the city streets to the Camden Street Station, then board a 3:00 p.m. train to Washington, D.C.

That, of course, is precisely the plan they now want to avoid.

In the frantic late hours after Pinkerton and Judd met with Lincoln, they huddled and came up with a new idea—and most important, a new destination. The majority of Lincoln's party will still think the old schedule is in effect. Only a few—his true inner circle—will know the truth: that after Lincoln's afternoon obligations in Harrisburg, he'll secretly break away from the group and head back to Philadelphia. There, he'll board an 11:50 p.m. train to Baltimore operated by the Philadelphia, Wilmington and Baltimore Railroad—Felton's line—with a plan to arrive in Baltimore's President Street Station shortly after 3:00 a.m.

Not only is this in the middle of the night and ten hours before the public schedule, but it puts Lincoln's arrival at a different station from the one published in newspapers. So even if a rowdy overnight crowd were to gather at the station many hours in advance of Lincoln's arrival, they'll now be gathering at the wrong station. As long as they can keep Lincoln's trip entirely secret, he should be able to traverse the city unnoticed in the dark of night.

Of course, maintaining secrecy won't be easy.

Abraham Lincoln isn't a small man—or an easily overlooked one. Indeed, as the President-elect of the United States, he's the most recognizable and closely watched person in the country. Every hour of every day, dozens of reporters and thousands of supporters are following his every move. To make things even harder, at least part of the journey will be on trains that're open to the public—which means anyone can see him. They'll have to come up with strategies to keep him somehow concealed from view.

In the end, the ride will take him through four major cities, three separate railroad lines, six train stations, and several carriages—all without his being seen.

Pinkerton's agents know the consequences. One leak and the conspirators may learn Lincoln's whereabouts while he's traveling through a hostile slave state with only a few people with him for protection.

If he's recognized, it could all be over.

But if all goes well, by the time Ferrandini, Hillard, and the rest of the conspirators start their day in Baltimore, Lincoln will have already arrived in Washington, D.C.

For now, Pinkerton gives Kate Warne her directions: she'll be in charge of Lincoln's passage during the middle leg of the journey, from Philadelphia to Baltimore. In the coming hours, they'll work out minute-by-minute details of Lincoln's arrival, transfer, ticketing, and passage on the train.

They've got twelve hours to pull it off.

Oh, and since Abraham Lincoln is now officially part of the operation, he needs his own code name.

That code name, Pinkerton tells Warne, is *Nuts*.

67

—————·—————

Harrisburg, Pennsylvania

February 22, 1861

At 5:45 p.m., Abraham Lincoln feels a tap on his shoulder.

That's the signal.

He's currently wearing evening clothes at a lavish reception in Harrisburg, Pennsylvania, hosted by the state's Governor, Andrew G. Curtin. Earlier that day, Lincoln had visited the state legislature, given a speech, and attended various other ceremonial functions.

But now, with that tap on the shoulder, the real action begins.

Lincoln continues to make small talk with a few attendees, waiting for a good moment to make an exit. At a natural break in the conversation, Lincoln takes Governor Curtin by the arm, and the two casually walk out the back door of the hall, as if taking a short break to chat in private.

Lincoln, however, is not coming back. The event is supposed to continue for another hour or two, but the President-elect will not be there. The Governor knows this, because Norman Judd—probably the one who gave Lincoln the designated tap on the shoulder—enlisted the Governor's help to execute his boss's escape.

Pinkerton and Judd's elaborate plan is now officially in effect. Lincoln agreed to it, grudgingly, earlier that morning. He's secretly sneaking away from the rest of the inaugural party in Harrisburg and catching a train to Philadelphia.

The President-elect is, in fact, conflicted about it. Part of him still doesn't believe anyone would assassinate him, even the most rabid Southern secessionist. But at the end of the day, the evidence is too convincing. Norman Judd is his old friend and trusted advisor, and Pinkerton's skill and judgment are renowned. Gen. Winfield Scott and William H. Seward have now independently presented the same evidence via their own investigation of the facts. If all these credible people believe the Baltimore plot is real, Lincoln has almost no choice but to believe them.

Earlier in the day, Lincoln and Judd had confided in a few other trusted members of Lincoln's entourage to discuss the potential new plan. Some agreed with the change in route; others were against it. One strong argument against was the ridicule and condemnation that a changing of plans will likely generate in the press and public once it becomes known after the fact.

Col. "Bull Head" Sumner, the grizzled veteran soldier turned Lincoln bodyguard, was outraged, calling the idea "a damned piece of cowardice." His suggestion was to round up a big military company and march with them proudly through Baltimore, daring any conspirators to try their hand. This, of course, Lincoln would never do, knowing that mass violence could be the result.

Even Judd, who helped engineer the plan with Pinkerton, was fully aware that once the press learned of Lincoln's last-minute rerouting, he'd be exposed to the "scoffs and sneers of your enemies, and the disapproval of your friends." Still, Judd believed that Lincoln had no choice but to honor not just his own safety but the safety of the entire party.

Even putting aside Lincoln himself as a person, the political ramifications of a successful assassination attempt against the President-elect were terrifying, something that, in the nation's current state, could easily lead to greater violence if not war.

So, although Lincoln still had his doubts, he concluded at the meeting that "unless there are some reasons, besides fear of ridicule, I am disposed to carry out Judd's plan."

Governor Curtin, one of the very few in Harrisburg who were informed of Lincoln's change of plans, later remembered the President-elect's demeanor as they casually left the reception hall together. Lincoln "neither in his conversation or manner exhibited alarm or fear," Curtin recalled, but he "seemed pained and surprised that a design to take his life existed," and was "concerned for his personal safety as well as for the peace of his country."

In any case, the decision is made—now it's time to follow through.

Back in Philadelphia, Judd and Pinkerton agreed that only the bare minimum number of companions should join Lincoln on every stage of his secret journey. At most one or two, including one bodyguard.

Mary Todd Lincoln, the first person on Lincoln's team (after Judd) who learned about the plan, had already insisted on whom the bodyguard should be: Ward Hill Lamon, the two-hundred-sixty-pound barroom brawler, prolific whiskey drinker, and longtime friend of the Lincolns. Only with Lamon by Lincoln's side would she have any peace of mind. So, yes, Lamon it is.

Now, Lincoln, Lamon, Judd, and a superintendent of the Pennsylvania Railroad named G. C. Franciscus follow a prearranged plan and make their way to a carriage parked in a discreet spot in back of the hotel.

Before they board, however, Lincoln makes a few key adjustments. He throws on an atypical overcoat, puts a shawl around his neck, and—most dramatically—replaces his trademark stovepipe hat with a very different item on his head.

Based on varying reports from eyewitnesses, the exact nature of this replacement will remain in dispute for years to come. Most probably, it's a low, soft, wide-brimmed hat—essentially the opposite of the stovepipe—and it creates a marked change in Lincoln's appearance.

"I put on the soft hat and joined my friends," Lincoln would later recall, "without being recognized by strangers, for I was not the same man."

As Lincoln gets in the secret coach, he says goodbye to his friend Norman Judd, who will not be joining the trip to Philadelphia or to Baltimore. Nevertheless, Judd obviously played a key role in the evolution of the President-elect's plans, and it's entirely possible that without Judd, Lincoln would still be planning to take the inaugural train to Baltimore in the morning.

Without much fanfare, Lincoln leaves for the Harrisburg train station. He'll arrive just in time to catch a special chartered train to Philadelphia—arranged overnight by Pinkerton—that the Pennsylvania Railroad has agreed to make available for him.

Within an hour, Lincoln is traveling at top speed back to Philadelphia—and no one in the press or public has the slightest idea. By all official accounts, he's still in Harrisburg, preparing for his morning ride to Baltimore.

If only the rest of the trip went as smoothly.

68

Philadelphia, Pennsylvania

February 22, 1861

Allan Pinkerton is getting anxious.

It's almost 7:30 p.m., and he's just stopped at the telegraph and express office near his hotel to see if any telegrams have arrived in his name. Not his real name, that is, but in the name of John H. Hutcheson, the alias he's still using for all hotels, train tickets, and formal correspondence during this mission.

No telegrams, they tell him. It doesn't make sense.

Earlier that day, Pinkerton sent George H. Burns, Edward Sanford's assistant, on a train to Harrisburg with an essential instruction: Stay near Abraham Lincoln.

Once Burns can confirm that Lincoln is aboard the specially chartered 6:50 p.m. train from Harrisburg to Philadelphia—and also that the train departs on time—he's supposed to immediately telegraph Pinkerton. Only then can Pinkerton and Kate Warne finalize preparations for Lincoln's movements in Philadelphia.

It's now past 7:30 p.m. The train from Harrisburg should've left over forty minutes ago.

Why hasn't Burns notified him yet? Did Lincoln change his mind and refuse to get on board? Is there a problem or delay with the train? Because if there was a delay, the entire overnight schedule falls apart.

Pinkerton, in a "state of suspense," as he puts it, paces around his hotel, wondering what to do. By 8:30 p.m., when there's still no telegraph for him, he frantically sends one to Burns's attention in Harrisburg. It looks like this:

Geo. H. Burns

Harrisburg

Where is Nuts

J. H. Hutcheson

A half hour later, there's still no response. In Pinkerton's mind, the dominoes begin to topple—if Lincoln's first train is late, then maybe he should delay the next two trains that're supposed to transport Lincoln on the rest of the journey.

Finally, at 9:15 p.m., a telegram arrives. Pinkerton eagerly reads it:

J. H. Hutcheson

St. Louis Hotel Philadelphia

Nuts left at six—Everything as you directed—all is right.

Geo. H. Burns

Pinkerton can finally exhale; relief washes over him. It's not clear why Burns's simple message took so long to send or to arrive—perhaps it was just a delay on the part of the telegraph office—but in any case it's a question that Pinkerton doesn't have time to ponder.

Roughly thirty minutes later, he's in a carriage arriving at the West Philadelphia train station. He asks the carriage driver to wait for him, then quickly finds a quiet spot to stand alone near the station stairs.

Within minutes, Pinkerton hears the whistle of an incoming train. Just as planned, at 10:03 p.m., four men appear at the top of the stairs and walk down to meet him.

In the middle of the pack, shielded by the others, is the tall figure of Abraham Lincoln. Of course, he looks different. "Mr. Lincoln wore a brown Kossuth Hat, and an overcoat thrown loosely over his shoulders," Pinkerton notes.

Others who see Lincoln's disguise that night will slightly disagree with Pinkerton's specific description of the hat—a "Kossuth" is a banded and soft-brimmed military hat originating in eastern Europe, and Pinkerton is the only one who uses that term to describe it—but in any case, the modest disguise gives the President-elect a distinctly different appearance.

Two of the men with Lincoln are representatives of the Pennsylvania Railroad, whom Pinkerton had previously convinced to arrange the special train for Lincoln from Harrisburg to here. The two men quickly depart, and Lincoln and his massive bodyguard, Ward Hill Lamon, follow Pinkerton to the waiting carriage. Also now joining the group is a representative from the PW&B railroad named H. F. Kenney, whom Samuel Felton had dispatched to accompany Pinkerton. Kenney gets in the front seat with the driver, while Pinkerton, Lincoln, and Lamon step into the rear coach.

The carriage driver will take them across Philadelphia to the PW&B train depot, where, again according to plan, Lincoln will board the 11:50 p.m. southbound train.

Right now, though, as the carriage door closes and they're out of public sight, the three men take a breath, finally able to talk without fear of discovery.

Given the circumstances, Pinkerton is impressed at the President-elect's demeanor. "Mr. Lincoln was cool, calm . . . firm and determined in his bearing," he notes. "He evinced no sign of fear or distrust, and throughout the entire night was quite self-possessed."

Once the carriage is moving, Lincoln and Pinkerton discuss the extraordinary revelation of the previous night: that William Seward and General Scott had launched a parallel investigation in Baltimore, undertaken by New York City police detectives, that had uncovered a conspiracy similar to that which Pinkerton discovered.

As a result, "Mr. Seward had therefore sent a communication by his son Frederick to Mr. Lincoln to the effect that they had information of a plot to assassinate him in Baltimore, urging upon him to change his route."

Pinkerton is not learning of this for the first time—Norman Judd had filled him in on the development earlier that morning—but Lincoln now provides another detail that is additionally surprising.

According to the report Lincoln read in his hotel room, the detectives found evidence that not only was there a plan to assassinate the President-elect but also that "about fifteen thousand men were organized to prevent his passage through Baltimore." This huge number of people is well beyond what Pinkerton himself had uncovered, and if true speaks to an almost citywide effort to block Lincoln in Baltimore while the cabal of conspirators enacts their deadly plan.

As the carriage nears its destination, the men discuss the remaining arrangements for the night—including what happens when their train reaches Baltimore.

At this point in the conversation Lamon opens his jacket, revealing an array of weapons in various inside pockets. He offers Lincoln a loaded revolver and bowie knife for personal defense—just in case—especially as they get closer to Baltimore.

Pinkerton can't believe what he's seeing. "I at once protested, saying that I would not for the world have it said that Mr. Lincoln had to enter the National Capitol armed," he reports.

Lamon looks surprised. Pinkerton clarifies his point. "I anticipate no trouble," he tells them, "but if fighting had to be done, it must be done by others than Mr. Lincoln."

Both Lamon and Pinkerton turn to look at Lincoln, awaiting the final word.

"I want no arms," Lincoln says, refusing the weapons. "I have no fears and am satisfied that [the] plans will work right."

Lamon reluctantly agrees. He doesn't like leaving his good friend without any form of self-defense, but Lincoln's made himself clear.

In fact, this isn't the first time that Lamon has shown off the cache of weapons that he's been carrying since Springfield. One fellow traveler reported that during the trip Lamon had on him, at all times, "a brace of fine pistols, a huge bowie knife, a blackjack, and a pair of brass knuckles."

In any case, as the carriage carrying Lamon, Lincoln, and Pinkerton continues on its way to the PW&B train depot, one thing is abundantly clear: If Lincoln and his companions encounter any trouble in Baltimore, Ward Hill Lamon will be ready for a fight.

69

———— • ————

Philadelphia, Pennsylvania

February 22, 1861

At roughly the same moment Abraham Lincoln stepped off the train from Harrisburg and entered the West Philadelphia station, Kate Warne stepped out of a carriage across town and walked into Philadelphia's PW&B train depot.

As Lincoln, Pinkerton, and Lamon now travel across town in her direction, she's at this depot to make arrangements for one of the most unusual train rides this railroad line—or any railroad line, for that matter—has ever known.

According to plan, Warne meets in the station a young local messenger named George R. Dunn, whom Pinkerton recently hired to aid the mission. Dunn has just arrived by train from Baltimore, where Pinkerton had sent him to gather the daily briefings of every Pinkerton agent on the ground there.

Even while the focus is on getting Lincoln to Washington, D.C., as quickly and discreetly as possible, Pinkerton and Warne must stay on top of every development in Baltimore.

Dunn, who was given Warne's second pseudonym, "Mrs. Cherry," for the purposes of the mission, meets Warne in the ladies' lounge in the depot. There, he hands off the reports to her, to give to Pinkerton.

In addition, Warne and Dunn have a far more difficult task.

With Abraham Lincoln about to arrive at the depot with Lamon and Pinkerton, they need to figure out how to get Lincoln aboard a public passenger train without anyone recognizing him.

According to Warne's direction, Dunn goes to the ticket counter and purchases three berths in the rear sleeping car of the 10:50 p.m. Baltimore-bound train. The tickets are under three names: John H. Hutcheson, a Mrs. Cherry, and her unnamed "invalid brother."

Dunn then goes aboard the waiting train to scout the rear sleeper car and assess the level of privacy. When he walks on board, he spots trouble: "On the front platform and inside the front door of the Sleeping Car," he would later recall, "I noticed a small party of men, who from their quiet talk, vigilant appearance and watchfulness, seemed to be on the alert, for somebody or something—this feature was not at all satisfactory to me."

Paranoid, and rightly so, Dunn determines that it's better to avoid these men at the front of the sleeper car. Instead, they should make their entrance through the rear door—so that Lincoln can sneak in the back of the sleeper car without attracting any attention.

Dunn asks one of the railroad agents: Is it possible to enter through the rear door?

No, it's not.

Thinking on his feet, Dunn begs the agent for the key "for the accommodation of an invalid, who would arrive late, and did not desire to be carried through the narrow passageway of the crowded car." The pitch works. Dunn is given the key to the rear door.

Returning to find Warne, Dunn explains what he's done and escorts her into the rear sleeper car so she can determine the proper seating while Dunn stays on the lookout. Taking a quick look herself, she agrees that the rear door for boarding is "very correct." "So soon as the lady was comfortably fixed," Dunn recalls, "I slipped quietly out of the back door, locking it after me, and kept a good lookout."

Meanwhile, as Dunn waits outside on the platform, Warne identifies and tries to save the sleeping berths that will be the most discreet for entering and exiting. Unfortunately, since this is a public train, there's no way to reserve them, and the train begins to fill up.

"I found it almost impossible to save the berths together," she reports. "This sleeping car was conducted differently from any I ever saw before—they gave no tickets, and any person could take a Berth where they pleased."

Without discreet berths close together, the ride to Baltimore on an occupied train could present a number of problems. Scrambling, Warne quickly grabs a railroad attendant. "I gave the conductor half a dollar to keep my berths," she indicates, "and by standing right by myself we managed to keep them."

While Warne and Dunn are busy buying the tickets and securing the berths, a carriage pulls up to the rear of the depot and stops on Carpenter Street, a small side street, "so that its occupants might alight in the shadow of the yard fence there."

From the carriage, three men emerge and walk quickly along the shadowed fence to enter the depot as furtively as possible. When the three men enter, they quickly but quietly walk straight from the rear to the front of the building, moving directly toward the waiting train.

Anyone in the station paying attention would have noticed the distinct silhouettes of the three men. One is of medium-short height and compactly built, another has broad shoulders and an enormous belly, the third is tall and rail-thin with a wide-brimmed hat. The tall one seems to be "stooping considerably for the purpose of disguising his height," and clutches the arm of the shorter, stocky man as if limping or unwell.

Not a single person in the depot, neither passenger nor railroad staff, has any idea that this motley-looking crew includes the President-elect of the United States—the most closely scrutinized man in America—only ten days before he is set to take the oath of office and deliver his first inaugural address.

Young George Dunn, keeping lookout outside the rear of the car, quickly catches the eye of Allan Pinkerton—he's the stocky, medium-short one next to Lincoln and on whose arm Lincoln leans.

As the party approaches, Dunn immediately unlocks the back door of the rearmost sleeper car and, nodding thanks to the railroad attendant, escorts the three ticketed passengers, including the tall "invalid brother," in through the rear door. He locks it behind them and returns the key to the conductor.

Inside the sleeper car, Kate Warne is standing in the center aisle, waiting. When the men enter, she's suddenly standing face-to-face with the President-elect of the United States, who's wearing a ridiculous hat.

Of course, he must continue to play the role of the invalid—and Warne gently guides him to the privatest, rearmost sleeping berth. He slides in quietly, keeping the brim of his hat held low, and quickly assumes a horizontal position while Warne yanks the curtain shut. As usual on sleeper trains, his long legs don't fit along the sleeper seat, and he has to bend them slightly to stay inside the curtain.

Once their "invalid brother" is settled, the other two new passengers—Allan Pinkerton and Ward Hill Lamon—take their own berths, as does Kate Warne.

None of the passengers inside the train, or along the depot, notice when, just after the party of three enter the rear door, a fast-walking man carrying a sealed package crosses the depot and approaches the train's conductor.

After some brief words are exchanged, the conductor takes the package inside the train, and, a few seconds later, the train whistle blows, indicating the time of departure has come.

Inside the rear sleeping car, each of the four rearmost passengers breathes a quiet sigh of relief. Abraham Lincoln is safely aboard the train, and, at least for now, not a soul has recognized him.

"Everything went off well," Warne writes in her daily report. She also adds, "Mr. Lincoln is very homely, and so very tall that he cannot lay straight in his berth."

70

---•---

Maryland

February 23, 1861

It's roughly 12:45 a.m.

That's when the Philadelphia, Wilmington, and Baltimore train carrying Abraham Lincoln crosses the Delaware border and enters the state of Maryland.

To this day, no one knows what Lincoln was thinking at the time. The party is mostly silent. Kate Warne reports that although Lincoln is "very friendly," soon after, "we all went to bed early." Yet despite everyone's exhaustion, sleep does not come. "Mr. Pinkerton did not sleep, nor did Mr. Lincoln. The excitement seemed to keep us all awake."

During the trip, no other passengers or train personnel take any special notice of the unusually tall passenger behind the curtain in the rear berth. Not even the conductor catches a glimpse of him. As Pinkerton recalls, "When the Conductor came around for his tickets, I handed him the tickets for Mr. Lincoln. He didn't look in the berths at all—left and did not return again during the trip."

During his planning, Pinkerton had arranged for every imaginable precaution. At regular intervals, he peers outside into the darkness, looking for flashing lights ahead alongside the track. These are hand signals, sent by Felton's railroad men holding lanterns—men whom

Pinkerton ordered to scan each section of the track, and only give the signal if the track appears safe and stable.

For Pinkerton, it goes back to the Baltimore conspirators' potential sabotage of the railroad track that set the investigation in motion to begin with. He wanted to be sure that the train would encounter no such trouble while Lincoln was on board.

This is only one example of Pinkerton's extreme caution. There are plenty of others. Since dusk, citizens of both Harrisburg and Philadelphia suddenly find that they're unable to send telegrams to the city of Baltimore, and vice versa. Why? Pinkerton made unusual last-minute arrangements with Edward Sanford, the president of the American Telegraph Company.

To keep things safe, Sanford's men "cut the wires" between those cities to prevent any communication after dark. This way, if anyone in Harrisburg or Philadelphia spotted Lincoln, or happened to learn about the change in his itinerary, no one in Baltimore could possibly be notified about it.

And then there's the package.

Since the train's departure, a mysterious parcel has been on board, delivered by a stranger to the railroad staff back in the station at Philadelphia. According to a note affixed to the package, the contents are important official documents and the conductor must under no circumstances leave the station without the parcel on board, because "this package *must* go through to Washington on *tonight's train*."

In fact, only one person on board knows the true contents of the package, and that's Allan Pinkerton.

The delivery of the package was a plan devised by the detective along with Samuel Felton, the PW&B president, to ensure that the Philadelphia train did not depart without Lincoln on board. Earlier in the day, Felton sent a message to the staff at the Philadelphia depot to await an important parcel bearing his signature before the 10:50 p.m. train should depart the station. Then Felton instructed his emissary, H. F. Kenney, to meet Pinkerton at the West Philadelphia station, where Lincoln was arriving from Harrisburg, and accompany the group by carriage to the PW&B train depot.

Just before the carriage reached the depot, Kenney had disembarked by himself with the package. He entered the depot alone and found a spot with a clear view of the platform, where the 10:50 p.m. train to Baltimore was waiting on the track. Kenney carefully and surreptitiously observed as Lincoln, Pinkerton, and Lamon boarded the train, and only *after* they were safely on board did he personally deliver the package to the train's conductor.

This way, if the group had been running late and missed the original departure time, there was no possible way for the train to leave without Lincoln on board.

So what was actually in the package? Not the important documents that the conductor was told. As Felton later described, it was merely "a package of old railroad reports, done up with great care, with a great seal attached to it." It was all simply a means to ensure that Lincoln made it on the train *without* revealing to any member of the train staff that someone important was on board.

As the train now proceeds through Maryland, all of Pinkerton's precautions—the lantern signals, cutting the telegraph wires, the secret parcel—have so far ensured that his plan is running smoothly.

Of course, it's Baltimore that the detective is still most worried about. If somehow word leaked that Lincoln was on an overnight train arriving from Philadelphia, there's no telling what sort of trouble the conspirators could put in motion.

Right now, on the train, there are only three people protecting Lincoln—Pinkerton, Lamon, and Warne—and they're entering a city where tens of thousands view the President-elect as a mortal enemy.

By 3:00 a.m., some of the visual signs of the city come into view, looming in the darkness. By 3:15 a.m., the train is within city limits. Soon, the brakemen begin decelerating, and the train rolls into the President Street Station in the southeast corner of the city.

Here they are, finally, in Baltimore—the focus of so much concern and worry over the past several days.

But now, instead of encountering a huge throng of people clamoring and shouting at the President-elect in the brightness of day, Lincoln arrives in the dead of night. There's no crowd waiting—only darkness and silence.

Once they reach the station, passengers start getting out of the train. Among them is Kate Warne. Having done her duty from Philadelphia to Baltimore, she signs off. While Pinkerton and bodyguard Lamon stay with Lincoln for the rest of the journey, she stays in Baltimore to help monitor the various Pinkerton agents still at work here. As Warne exits, the other members of the group—Lincoln included—bid her a warm goodbye.

Now, they're down to three.

As is standard procedure for this particular railroad transfer, station workers detach the passenger car bound for Washington from the engine—with the remaining customers still inside—and affix it to horses that will pull it slowly through the city blocks from one train station to another.

From a strategic standpoint, it's an improvement over Lincoln's original route, where he would've been forced to disembark and ride in a standard passenger carriage.

However, it's still the moment of Lincoln's greatest vulnerability. As the horses begin their route, Lincoln, Pinkerton, and Lamon are essentially trapped in the single railroad car, being pulled slowly down a city street. If a hostile party began to attack, they'd have little means to defend themselves.

As the car is pulled downtown, it passes within about four blocks of Barnum's City Hotel, the hideout and regular meeting place where Southern extremists and secessionists—like the hotel barber Cypriano Ferrandini—have spent many days and nights loudly cursing the Northern abolitionists.

Now, though, it's sometime around three thirty in the morning. The hotel is quiet. So is most of the city. The horse-drawn train car heads toward its destination without incident.

Shortly before 4 a.m., it pulls into the Camden Street Station. Here, too, all is relatively quiet.

Train workers quickly detach the car from the team of horses and affix it to a waiting engine on the tracks of the B&O Railroad.

Soon, the engine will depart for Washington, D.C.

During the transition and waiting period, the passengers look out and find an unexpected amusement. Near the waiting train, a night watchman is trying repeatedly to wake up a ticket agent who's fallen asleep in a small wooden building near the tracks.

"Captain, it's four o'clock!" the watchman shouts, banging the side of the building with his club. It still doesn't wake the agent.

As Pinkerton records, "This he kept up for about twenty minutes without any change in the time, and many funny remarks were made by the passengers at the watchman's time always being the same."

Soon enough, Lincoln himself starts giggling from behind his curtain, and adds his own jokes to the mix. As Pinkerton reports, "Mr. Lincoln appeared to enjoy it very much and made several witty remarks."

Before they know it, at around 4:30 a.m., the engine's steam whistle blows and the wheels begin to turn. Abraham Lincoln is bound for his final destination—Washington, D.C.

In a few hours, Baltimoreans will wake up, ready to face this day that has put the city in a state of tension and excitement for weeks. When they awake, Ferrandini, Hillard, and other members of the National Volunteers and the Knights of the Golden Circle will be buzzing with anticipation, ready to make their grand violent gesture in the name of Southern rights and Southern honor. Today, they're ready to kill.

The problem is, they're already too late. Abraham Lincoln is long gone.

71

Washington, D.C.

February 23, 1861

Everyone's exhausted.

By the time the B&O's engine crosses the border from Maryland to the District of Columbia—shortly before the very first rays of sun appear over the Potomac River—Allan Pinkerton has not slept in close to forty-eight hours.

Abraham Lincoln, likewise, has had one brutally exhausting day after another, with rarely more than a few hours of sleep each night.

For these two, the sheer fatigue must add a surreal feeling as their train finally pulls into the station in Washington, D.C.

Naturally, Lincoln is still incognito at this point. For now, they need to conceal his identity. Pinkerton and Lamon are just two men. They're not enough to protect Lincoln from a large crowd or mob, which is exactly what would form if word suddenly got out that Abraham Lincoln is currently in the Washington train station.

In fact, as the three men sneak out of the train and head across the depot, Pinkerton isn't ready to breathe a sigh of relief. If anything, he's hit with a new wave of anxiety. Lincoln's entourage and handlers are all back in Harrisburg. Until the President-elect is 100 percent safe in this city, Pinkerton feels responsible for him.

As he's about to learn, he's right to be worried.

As the three men walk discreetly through the station, Pinkerton sees someone jump into his field of vision, a middle-aged man. He grabs at Abraham Lincoln, shouting the President-elect's name.

Instinctively, Pinkerton reacts. "I hit the gentleman a punch with my elbow," he says, "staggering him back." The man, undeterred, "again took hold of Mr. Lincoln," and again says his name.

Pinkerton panics, thinking "we were discovered . . . and that we might have to fight."

It wasn't supposed to be like this. Washington, D.C., is the place where Lincoln should be safe.

Pinkerton doesn't hesitate. Raising his fist, he lunges toward the stranger, ready to attack.

72

———•———

"Don't strike him!" Abraham Lincoln yells. "That is my friend!"

Allan Pinkerton is already on the move, fist raised, ready to fight the stranger who's grabbing the President-elect.

Pinkerton hears Lincoln's words just in time and quickly pulls his punch.

"That's my friend Washburne," Lincoln adds.

He means Elihu Washburne, Congressman from Illinois, and a good friend of Lincoln's. Washburne had learned of Lincoln's early arrival from Senator William H. Seward. Both men planned to come to greet Lincoln at the station, but Seward was delayed.

Pinkerton relaxes, quickly apologizing to the Congressman for nearly assaulting him. Smiling and clearly amused, Lincoln introduces the two men.

From there, Lincoln tells the group he's tired—he wants to go to bed. Before Lincoln's presence can attract any more attention, the group jumps into a carriage and proceeds to the Willard Hotel, where Lincoln will be staying the next several days.

Just after the group arrives, William H. Seward arrives to meet them. There, in the lobby of the Willard, the President-elect shakes hands with his soon-to-be Secretary of State.

Finally, Pinkerton can relax a little. Lincoln is among friends—people who will take care of him. For the first day in a long while, Abraham Lincoln's safety and well-being are no longer the responsibility of Pinkerton's National Detective Agency.

Pinkerton checks in to his own room at the hotel. As always, he has signed in under an alias—this time it's "E. J. Allen"—to avoid detection. He's still not quite ready to sleep, however. After stopping at his room, he goes to the nearest telegraph office and sends word of his and Lincoln's safe arrival to the key parties back in Philadelphia.

On this morning, in 1861, Abraham Lincoln has just made his historic first arrival in Washington, D.C. In ten days, he'll take the oath of office to become the sixteenth President of the United States. Yet one of the very first notices announcing his arrival is a cryptic little telegram that makes absolutely no sense, sent by a person who doesn't really exist. It reads, simply:

> Plum arrived here with Nuts this morning—all right.
> —E. J. Allen

"All right" is a good way to put it. The secret plot to kill Abraham Lincoln has been thwarted. The President-elect is once again safe.

In the days to come, there will be more to investigate—but for now, Allan Pinkerton has earned a little rest.

73

Washington, D.C.

February 23, 1861

By midday Saturday, the news spreads through the nation's capital. President-elect Abraham Lincoln arrived early in the city—on a secret train—almost ten hours before anyone expected. Furthermore, he did so for the most extraordinary reason: to avoid an assassination plot hatched against him in Baltimore, Maryland.

The political class and journalists in Washington, D.C., respond to the news in a manner exactly as one would expect. They completely lose their minds. Instantly, a swirl of rumors, misinformation, conjecture, accusations, and insults spreads through the city.

One of the first reporters to hit the wires with an actual news story about the assassination plot is Joseph Howard of *The New York Times,* who initially reports it with a lofty tone. "The country has been spared the lasting disgrace, which would have been fastened indelibly upon it had Mr. Lincoln been murdered upon his journey thither." His account of the overnight journey, however, which is gleaned from a mix of credible and dubious sources, gets several facts wrong. Most notably, this: that Lincoln, as part of his disguise, "wore a scotch plaid cap and a very long military cloak."

This description of Lincoln's wardrobe is later refuted by every person who saw it, including Lincoln himself—but it quickly becomes a rumor impossible to squelch. Political cartoonists have a field day, depicting Lincoln in a ridiculous plaid Scottish cap and long overcoat. To add to the humiliation, some even draw him in a kilt.

Aside from the embarrassment of his reported disguise, the news also opens up Lincoln to the more politically damaging attack—that his late-night evasion was a display of weakness and fear, unbefitting a President.

Naturally, the partisan Southern press hits him hard on this point. "Everybody here is disgusted at his cowardly and undignified entry," *The Charleston Mercury* declares, adding that the incident displays "the most wretched cowardice."

The Baltimore Sun, reporting from the city at the center of the storm, takes it a step further, denying that any assassination plot existed in the city and attacking the incoming President's lack of courage. "Had we any respect for Mr. Lincoln, official or personal, as a man, or as a President-elect of the United States . . . the final escapade by which he reached the capital would have utterly demolished it." The paper continues, "We do not believe the Presidency can ever be more degraded by any of his successors."

The Northern press is kinder, describing Lincoln's avoidance of the assassination plot as "judicious" and "wise." One Baltimore Republican—there are a few of them in the overwhelmingly Democratic city—writes to Lincoln that the plot to kill him was indeed "*meditated* and *determined*" and therefore "by your course you have saved *bloodshed* and a *mob.*"

Still, even some of Lincoln's Northern supporters are disappointed in the President's undignified arrival. *New-York Tribune* editor Horace Greeley, an influential voice in Northern Republican circles, opines that "Mr. Lincoln ought to have come through by daylight, if one-hundred guns had been pointed at him," and another Republican writer laments Lincoln's arrival in Washington as like a "thief in the night."

One of the most interesting and sympathetic responses comes from an unexpected source—abolitionist Frederick Douglass. Douglass grew up under slavery in the state of Maryland, including spending over a year in Baltimore. He understands the ferocity and zeal of the state's slaveholding class, and their hatred of those who dare challenge the institution.

While many white commentators write of the incident in satirical terms, Douglass finds nothing humorous about violent proslavery forces in Maryland plotting someone's murder. Indeed, Douglass's own escape from slavery was on the very same train line—the Philadelphia, Wilmington and Baltimore—and along the same route that Lincoln took under cover of darkness.

In an article in his newspaper responding to the event, Douglass draws a direct parallel between Lincoln's midnight journey and the plight of escaped slaves desperately trying to flee bondage. "Mr. Lincoln reached the Capital as the poor, hunted fugitive slave reaches the North, in disguise, seeking concealment, evading pursuers, by the Underground Railroad . . . crawling and dodging under the sable wing of night." Douglass adds that although Lincoln's act may at first appear "cowardly," in fact his evasion of "slave-holding assassins" showed "the merit of wisdom, forethought, and discretion."

As with so many events in this tumultuous era, opinions of Lincoln's secret overnight journey vary widely, usually reflecting the personal experiences or political orientation of whoever's judging it.

In any case, the furor over Lincoln's midnight journey would soon be overshadowed by other events—events that would change the nation forever.

74

Washington, D.C.

March 4, 1861

It's 5:00 a.m., and Abraham Lincoln is up. As much as he needs it, he can't sleep.

After an early breakfast with his family, he's back in his quarters. There are only a few hours left to prepare for the trial ahead.

Since his arrival in the nation's capital ten days ago, Lincoln's life has been a mad blur, not unlike the inaugural journey itself. Every day has been full of endless receptions, dinners, formal meetings, and obligatory socializing. He has met more public officials and shaken more hands than any of his aides can possibly keep track of.

But this morning, he needs to concentrate.

Since December, Lincoln has been working regularly on his inaugural speech. In the past few days, he has solicited feedback from several of his most trusted advisors, including, most recently, William Seward. Seward has become Lincoln's unofficial escort in Washington, D.C., and Seward's input on the speech is a marker of a political collaboration and a burgeoning friendship between the two former rivals.

Still, even with input from Seward and other advisors, Lincoln remains unsure of some of the language in the speech. He decides that he needs to hear the entire speech spoken aloud by another person to make last-minute adjustments. Ironically, for this task, he recruits Robert Todd Lincoln, who—as both father and son surely remember—nearly lost this very speech two weeks earlier in an Indianapolis hotel.

After listening to his words read aloud in an eighteen-year-old's voice, Lincoln makes a few final changes to the pages. That's it. There's no more time for revisions.

At noon, an open horse-drawn carriage pulls up in front of the Willard Hotel. Out of it steps current President James Buchanan, who will serve as Lincoln's escort to the Capitol several blocks away. When Lincoln emerges from the hotel, the two men shake hands and step up into the horse-drawn barouche.

The scene is witnessed by scores of advisors and reporters. The passage together of the current and future President is a symbol of the peaceful transfer of power—an ideal that both men want to reinforce in public during the current political moment.

Buchanan, aged sixty-nine, has had a beleaguered term in office. As a Northern Democrat, he was aligned with Southern slaveholders, but ultimately spoke out against secession—giving him no real base of support. He was often regarded as weak and ineffectual, and the press could be brutal to him. In the end, he seemed perpetually exhausted, as if he had simply given up. Nonetheless, on this day, he dutifully plays his role and welcomes his younger successor into the carriage.

As the carriage begins the journey to the Capitol, the two men sit next to each other and make small talk. At one point, according to a popular account, Buchanan says wearily to Lincoln that "if you are as happy, my dear sir, on entering the White House as I am in leaving it," then "you are the happiest man in the country."

Starting early that morning, crowds began coursing into the city, and now huge throngs of people line both sides of Pennsylvania Avenue and every nearby side street. As one observer describes, "Every available spot was black with human beings; boys and men clinging to rails and mounting on fences and climbing trees until they bent beneath the weight." All businesses are closed for the day, and flags hang from most homes and storefronts.

There's a dark undercurrent to the celebration, however. Even after Lincoln's successful evasion of the assassination plot in Baltimore, rumors persist of additional designs on Lincoln's life here in the capital. Indeed, many worry that the President-elect's secret overnight passage through Baltimore would further enrage extremists in Maryland and Virginia, who would redouble their violent efforts to prevent Lincoln's inauguration.

The previous day, *The New York Times* reported as much. "Strange to say," the story read, "heavy bets are pending on the question of [Lincoln's] safety through tomorrow's exercises, and great anxiety is felt at Headquarters concerning certain unpublished designs." The article also ominously warned of "a large body of men . . . arrived here from Baltimore and many from Virginia, part of whom are secessionists."

Because of these and other rumors, Gen. Winfield Scott, who had taken on the responsibility of protecting the capital city during the inauguration, had implemented an unprecedented range of security measures along the inaugural passage. Soldiers lined the route; sharpshooters were stationed on the roofs of most government buildings.

For onlookers, the effect was unsettling. "Files of cavalry, troops of infantry, riflemen, and a battery of artillery" are visible along the streets, noted a cousin of Mary Todd Lincoln's, "all betokening the feeling of unrest and possible danger."

Some observers, particularly Southerners, were critical of this show of force. "I have seen today such a sight as I could never have believed possible at the capital of my country," one Southern reporter wrote, "an inauguration of a President surrounded by armed soldiery, with loaded pieces and fixed bayonets." Another observer reported that the procession "seemed more like escorting a prisoner to his doom than a President to his inauguration."

General Scott, though, ignored these criticisms and concerns. His mission was simple: Protect the President's life. As Scott was later said to have put it, "I shall plant cannon at both ends of Pennsylvania Avenue, and if any of the Maryland or Virginia gentlemen who have become so threatening and troublesome of late show their heads . . . I shall blow them to Hell!"

All told, the lingering fear of violence—and the extensive military preparations—creates an unmistakable tension as the inaugural parade makes its way slowly down Pennsylvania Avenue toward the site of the swearing-in ceremony.

To some onlookers, the tense feeling persists even after Lincoln enters the Capitol itself. He arrives through the back and, still with Buchanan, finally emerges on the large platform erected at the east portico above the grand steps of the Capitol—the opposite side from our inaugurations today. Here, Lincoln looks out for the first time at the vast sea of spectators who have gathered in the Capitol plaza to witness this historic event.

At first, Lincoln takes a seat, flanked by rows of already seated family and aides on the crowded platform. Introductory remarks are given. A few minutes later, he knows.

It's time.

As Lincoln stands and walks to the lectern, he takes off his stovepipe hat—only to realize he's now not sure quite what to do with it. He can't hold it during his speech, nor does he want to put it on the ground. A very unlikely spectator, seated nearby on the platform, comes to his aid—none other than Senator Stephen Douglas, Lincoln's former debate rival in Illinois. Douglas had detected Lincoln's discomfort and now discreetly relieves Lincoln of the hat, holding it in his lap for the duration.

Slowly and deliberately, Lincoln situates himself at the podium, gathers his papers, and begins to speak.

"Fellow citizens of the United States," he begins.

Onlookers are surprised by Lincoln's uncanny ability to project his slightly nasal voice. That voice "rang out over the acres of people before him with surprising distinctness, and was heard in the remotest parts of his audience," one journalist writes. The crowd before him is probably somewhere over twenty thousand people, and one onlooker guesses that Lincoln's words are heard by "at least ten thousand persons before him."

Lincoln may not have known it, but scattered throughout the vast audience are plainclothes police officers and soldiers, planted

On March 4, 1861, Abraham Lincoln delivers his first inaugural address before a public crowd of tens of thousands. On this day, there is more security and military protection in Washington, D.C., than for any other public gathering in the city's history at the time.

by General Scott to "strike down any hand which might raise a weapon."

Newspaper editor Horace Greeley, seated on the speaking platform, would later recall this feeling of danger as Lincoln begins the speech. "I sat just behind him as he read it, expecting to hear its delivery arrested by the crack of a rifle aimed at his heart."

But there is no crack of a rifle—not on this day.

The inaugural speech itself is for the most part careful, cautious, and analytical. Lincoln's original draft had utilized stronger, more forceful language. After receiving feedback from several advisors, he softened the tone to cause less offense to Southerners and to those in the border states, while still maintaining his core principles. Lincoln's goal, and the goal of Seward and others who advised him, is to maintain the path to peace negotiations.

For the seceding states, he makes clear that he will execute his role as the chief executive of the United States with firmness. In other words, he will enforce all federal laws—but he otherwise intends them no harm. If there is to be violence, it will not begin on the Union side.

> In your hands, my dissatisfied fellow countrymen, and not in mine, is the momentous issue of civil war. The government will not assail you. You can have no conflict, without being yourselves the aggressor. You have no oath registered in Heaven to destroy the government, while I have the most solemn one to "preserve, protect, and defend it."

Compared to some of Lincoln's later Presidential speeches, this first inaugural doesn't have the heightened moral poetry that illuminates his greatest words. Here, he's crafting a careful, almost legalistic argument, designed primarily to make sure he doesn't offend any faction in the current splintered political environment.

The speech ends, however, with a genuinely heartfelt plea for reconciliation that contains some of his most memorable phrasing. Looking out upon the vast sea of faces before him—people from the North, the South, and in between—he reads these words carefully and distinctly:

> We are not enemies, but friends. We must not be enemies. Though passion may have strained, it must not break our bonds of affection. The mystic chords of memory, stretching from every battlefield, and patriot grave, to every living heart and hearthstone, all over this broad land, will yet swell the chorus of the Union, when again touched, as surely they will be, by the better angels of our nature.

It's a pure expression of generosity, of patriotism, and, perhaps most important, of hope.

Having said these words, however, Lincoln shows signs that he himself understands the true depths of the struggle that lies just ahead. After speaking these final phrases, according to one onlooker's later recollection, Lincoln "bowed his head as if in silent prayer." Then, he "sighed wearily as if he knew that he had failed to touch the Southern heart."

After the speech, at just past 1:00 p.m., aging Supreme Court Chief Justice Roger B. Taney—author of the infamous *Dred Scott* decision of 1857, which so adamantly defended the rights of slaveholders— stands up and shuffles to the podium to administer the oath of office. Without question, he's no fan of Lincoln.

For the Presidential oath, Lincoln's personal family Bible was still on its way from Springfield at the time, so William Thomas Carroll, the Clerk of the Supreme Court, acquired a new one that was bound in burgundy velvet with a gold-washed metal rim around the edges.

Lincoln puts his left hand on this new Bible, raises his right, and carefully repeats the Presidential oath as Chief Justice Taney reads it.

Ten days earlier, Abraham Lincoln narrowly avoided an assassination plot that threatened his life. Today, with a solemn vow, as thousands erupt into applause, he becomes the sixteenth President of the United States.

Now comes the hard part.

PART IV

Aftermath

75

When Abraham Lincoln first won the Presidency in 1860, only three days had passed before South Carolina took its first steps toward seceding from the Union. It was a decision that plunged the nation into an unprecedented crisis, changing the course of Lincoln's coming term.

Four months later, when Lincoln is sworn in to office, it won't even be three days before his Presidency is faced with an emergency that will thrust the country into even greater turmoil.

The very next morning after his inaugural ceremony—literally on his first day in office—Lincoln receives an urgent report, delivered by Gen. Winfield Scott.

Maj. Robert Anderson, still garrisoned at Fort Sumter, believes he and his men have only enough provisions to last another six weeks. South Carolinian militias, eager to wrest the fort from federal hands, had recently blocked all supply lines to it. To resupply and secure the fort, Anderson estimates an expeditionary force of some twenty thousand soldiers will be necessary. It's the only way to prevent a surrender.

It immediately puts Lincoln in a terrible bind.

At the very start of his Presidency, voluntarily surrendering a federal fort to the new Confederate States would be an embarrassing show of weakness. Many in the North would be disappointed—indeed, furious—at such a capitulation. But any military incursion into Confederate territories—and a resupply force of twenty thousand is certainly a military incursion—would provoke fury throughout the South. More states may be drawn to secede, including the critical border states.

The previous day, in Lincoln's inaugural speech, he'd made several pledges with regard to federal properties in the seceded states. He pledged, for one, that he would "hold, occupy, and possess the property, and places belonging to the government"—that is, he'll never surrender the South Carolina forts. But secondly, he pledged that in the interest of preserving peace, he would undertake no "armed invasion" into the Confederate States.

Now, whatever he chooses, he's breaking one of those promises. Either he's surrendering federal property . . . or embarking on an armed mission to save that property. The former is a political disaster; the latter could provoke a civil war.

At this point, not a single member of Lincoln's cabinet has yet been approved or confirmed. He has no staff to speak of beyond his two young secretaries, Nicolay and Hay. He hasn't moved into the White House, much less organized his papers and files. He barely knows the layout of his new office or living space. He's still exhausted from the most relentlessly busy few weeks of his life. And he still hasn't learned even the most basic rules and procedures of the job. After only half a day to get his bearings, he now faces an impossible choice with no good options and the highest imaginable stakes.

As word of the dilemma gets out, opinions pour in from all sides. Everyone claims that one choice or the other will be a catastrophe, but the voices are split on which is the better course. Lincoln's own cabinet, once finally formed, is bitterly divided—and some members threaten to resign depending on whichever decision he makes.

The quandary sends Lincoln into deep distress. He soon confides to a friend that "all the troubles and anxieties of his life had not equaled" those which befell him in the weeks following his inauguration. According to Mary Todd, he was under so much stress that on some occasions he physically collapsed—he "keeled over," she said—from exhaustion and the pain in his head.

The press, meanwhile, begins to heap scorn on the new President. WANTED—A POLICY, one headline shouts, part of an endless chorus condemning Lincoln's seeming indecision. Word spreads around the capital that the Rail Splitter is, at best, out of his depth.

With each day, the dilemma gets further mired in logistical and political complications, but Lincoln finally makes his decision. Against the counsel of Seward, he adopts a plan to resupply the fort via a naval route into Charleston Harbor. On April 9, 1861, a large navy steamer loaded with soldiers, and two tugboats containing supplies, sail south out of New York City.

Critically, Lincoln sends a State Department official in advance to deliver a message to the South Carolina Governor, Francis W. Pickens, notifying him of the coming resupply and establishing these terms: "An attempt will be made to supply Fort-Sumter with provisions only; and that, if such attempt be not resisted, no effort to throw in men, arms, or ammunition, will be made."

While this advance notice makes the mission less likely to succeed—it takes away the element of surprise—it creates a clear record of Lincoln's peaceful intentions. If there is to be violence, it will be initiated by the Confederacy.

Pickens notifies Jefferson Davis of Lincoln's message. Sure enough, the Confederate leaders quickly determine that this coming resupply is a direct sovereign threat.

At noon on April 11, they send a demand to Major Anderson to surrender and evacuate. He refuses.

Less than twenty-four hours later, at 4:30 a.m. on April 12, 1861, a Confederate battery opens fire on Fort Sumter.

They are the first shots fired in the Civil War.

Abraham Lincoln has been in office for thirty-nine days.

Militarily, for the Union, the mission is a bust. The naval resupply gets caught in a storm and never makes it into the harbor. After thirty-three hours of continual shelling from Confederate batteries, Major Anderson raises a white flag over the fort. He and his troops safely evacuate, and on the afternoon of April 13, the South Carolinian soldiers take Fort Sumter.

Neither side suffers casualties, minus one accidental death during a ceremonial gun salute. And truthfully, there's not much strategic significance to the loss of a single federal fort. But as Lincoln, Jefferson Davis, and everyone else knows, the political significance of the episode is massive.

Lincoln took a stand to protect federal property, and in response, the Confederates turned their hostile fire on soldiers defending the United States of America.

On both sides, the momentum toward military escalation is now impossible to stop.

On April 15, two days after Anderson's forced surrender, Lincoln issues a public proclamation calling for seventy-five thousand troops from the Union states. Suddenly, for the North, the ambiguity is gone. Here is the stunning clarity of war. Rallies are held in every major city. Northern newspapers explode with headlines supporting the cause, and the states begin immediately raising troops to send to the capital, at the service of their Commander in Chief.

Abraham Lincoln is now more than just a new and inexperienced President. He's a new and inexperienced President *at war*.

And this is no ordinary war. In the history of the United States, no conflict will compare to the magnitude of what's ahead. There is no precedent, no model, for what a conflict between the states, fought entirely on American soil, might bring. The only thing that reigns is uncertainty.

Lincoln, who has no real military experience and who has always advocated policies based on peace, now finds himself at the helm of what will become the bloodiest and most momentous war in American history, with the very future of the nation on the line.

76

Back on the morning of February 23, when Allan Pinkerton sent his telegrams announcing the arrival of "Nuts" into Washington, D.C., he was eager to return to Baltimore.

For Pinkerton, the investigation still wasn't over. His agents were still undercover in Maryland, and the danger remained that the conspirators might destroy the railways or make another attempt to sabotage Lincoln's inauguration.

After packing his bags at the Willard Hotel, Pinkerton sent a card to Lincoln's room—of course, he signed it "E. J. Allen"—requesting to see the President-elect quickly.

Lincoln was in the midst of hosting a reception for members of Congress in his suite, but he urged Pinkerton to stop by. When Pinkerton arrived, the two men entered a side room and spoke privately.

According to Pinkerton, "Mr. Lincoln . . . thanked me very kindly for the services I had rendered him, saying that he fully appreciated them . . . and requesting me to call upon him every time I came to Washington, and let him know when he could be of any service to me." Pinkerton offered the same sentiment in return.

The two Illinoisans shook hands and said goodbye.

By late that afternoon, Pinkerton pulled into the Camden Street Station back in Baltimore—and arrived to a city in a state of chaos.

As expected, throngs of people had taken to the streets in anticipation of Lincoln's arrival earlier in the day. When Lincoln's train arrived—without him on it—the gathered crowds were thrown into a state of confusion and disbelief.

Upon Pinkerton's arrival in the city later that afternoon, one of the first persons he encountered was none other than James Luckett, the stockbroker who introduced him to Ferrandini in the first place. Luckett pulled Pinkerton aside—addressing him as Hutcheson, of course—and launched into a diatribe that confirms much of what Pinkerton suspected.

Fuming from frustration at the "damned spies" who must've tipped off Lincoln, Luckett described to Pinkerton his understanding of what would've transpired had the President-elect arrived as originally planned. As Pinkerton reported:

> [Luckett] said . . . that the men were all ready to have done the job, and were in their places, and would have murdered the d___d abolitionist had it not been that they were cheated. He said that Captain Ferrandini had about twenty picked men with good revolvers and knives: that their calculation was to get up a row in the crowd with rotten eggs, and brick-bats, and that while the Police (some of whom understood the game) would be attending to this, that Captain Ferrandini and his men should attack the carriage with Lincoln and shoot everyone in it.

As Luckett was saying this, he didn't realize, of course, that the man in front of him was one of the "damned spies" who tipped off Lincoln to the plot.

At the time that Lincoln was supposed to originally arrive, Pinkerton's Baltimore agents did not track Cypriano Ferrandini's movements. But undercover agent Harry Davies did spend most of the day with conspirator Otis K. Hillard. Before noon, the two men had pushed through the crowded downtown streets—teeming with ten or fifteen thousand people, according to Davies's report—so that Hillard could be in the area of Calvert Street Station in advance of Lincoln's planned arrival.

Yet before they arrived at the station, the shocking news was already spreading through the crowd. Abraham Lincoln was not on the train. He'd already snuck through the city in the middle of the night.

Hillard, like everyone else, was in a state of disbelief. Only in the chaotic aftermath, as the two young men navigated the streets and the confused crowds, did Davies lay eyes on a large, organized gathering of men who had taken planned positions along the carriage route that Lincoln would have traveled. According to Davies, "The street on each side of the hill from the top down was crowded with men, standing close, side by side, probably two thousand or more."

Later that day, as the confusion died down, Hillard explained to Davies the meaning of this assembled group. As Davies recounted:

> Hillard afterwards told me that all those men standing there were National Volunteers, and that they stood in that position on the side of the hill so as that when the carriage containing Lincoln should come up the hill they could rush en masse upon it, and around it, when Lincoln was to be slain—the reasoning that with such a dense crowd around the carriage, it would be impossible for any outsider to tell who did the deed.

Hillard's vivid description of the plan suggests that even if the number of potential assassins was relatively small—fifteen or twenty, according to Pinkerton's earlier guess—a much larger group, possibly the entirety of the National Volunteers organization, was also in on the plot, planning to swarm Lincoln's carriage and provide cover to the assassins.

Before the day was done, Hillard made one more remarkable statement to Davies regarding the failed plot. He revealed that according to the instructions given to him, and based upon where he originally planned to situate himself near Calvert Street Station for Lincoln's arrival, "from his position he would have had the first shot."

It may be that Hillard was just boasting to his friend—anyone could make such a claim after the plan had been called off. But it also could be that Hillard was indeed one of the selected assassins that day.

If so, a young, debauched Baltimore socialite might have been the one to pull the trigger and end the life of Abraham Lincoln before his inauguration—and in doing so, forever change the course of history.

Once the dust settled in Baltimore, Pinkerton and his agents stayed in the city for another ten days. They continued following the conspirators and tracking rumors of further plots and plans. Only after Lincoln's inauguration on March 4 did Pinkerton finally wrap the investigation.

In the end, though, Pinkerton's overnight journey with Abraham Lincoln, on February 23, 1861, wouldn't be their last adventure together.

After Pinkerton returned to Chicago, he closely followed news reports chronicling the early days and weeks of the new administration. Early April brought the standoff in South Carolina. With the attack on Fort Sumter and Lincoln's proclamation calling for troops, Pinkerton—like most Northerners—was galvanized.

"The effect of this proclamation upon the people of the North was almost electrical," Pinkerton wrote, "and the heart of the whole nation throbbed with its patriotic emotions as that of a single individual."

The very day after Lincoln's call for troops, Pinkerton wrote a letter to the President from his Chicago office.

> Dear Sir,
> When I saw you last I said that if the time should ever come that I could be of service to you I was ready—If that time has come I am on hand—
> I have in my Force some sixteen to eighteen persons on whose courage, skill & devotion to their country I can rely. If they with myself at the head can be of service in the way of obtaining information of the movements of the traitors, or safely conveying your letters or dispatches . . . I am at your command.
>
> > Respectfully yours,
> > Allan Pinkerton

Since Confederate sympathizers were now sabotaging the railways in Maryland, Pinkerton doesn't trust the mail service to deliver the letter to President Lincoln. Instead, he and Kate Warne sew the letter into the clothing of Pinkerton agent Timothy Webster—he's the broad-shouldered athletic former police officer, originally from England—with instructions to hand-deliver it to Lincoln in Washington, D.C.

Several days later, Webster returns to Chicago. Hidden in a small compartment in his walking stick is a handwritten note from Abraham Lincoln to Pinkerton. The message is simple: Come see me in Washington immediately—and bring your best agents.

War is here, and Lincoln wants help.

At the time, Pinkerton's National Detective Agency was busy and successful. Nevertheless, Pinkerton responds to the President's call. "I soon found my services were needed," he later wrote, "and putting aside all considerations of a private or business nature . . . I rendered every assistance that lay in my power to further the cause of the union, and to serve the country of my adoption."

This would begin yet another dramatic chapter in Allan Pinkerton's career. Within weeks, Pinkerton will serve alongside a rising officer in the fledgling Union Army named George McClellan, whom Pinkerton knew personally through railroad connections, and who at that time holds command of the Department of the Ohio—encompassing all federal troops stationed in Ohio, Indiana, and Illinois—in the growing war effort.

By the middle of May, Pinkerton and McClellan have organized "McClellan's Secret Service," headed by Pinkerton, which will become a pioneering military intelligence operation during the war.

When the unit is formed, Pinkerton's agents in Chicago, formerly trained to solve bank robberies and catch counterfeiters, will join Pinkerton on the front lines of the Civil War as full-blown military spies. The group includes Kate Warne, Timothy Webster, Hattie Lawton, and several others.

As before, the essence of Pinkerton's service is undercover work. His agents create Southern aliases, adopt Southern accents, wear Confederate uniforms, and embed with the enemy army to gather intelligence for Northern Generals.

When Lincoln gives McClellan the momentous command of the Army of the Potomac in July 1861, including with it the responsibility to defend the nation's capital from the Confederate States Army, the General brings Pinkerton with him. Acting under the official title of "Major E. J. Allen"—he always uses aliases, of course—the detective is given rein to create and oversee an elaborate military intelligence operation.

Pinkerton devises novel methods to gain confidential information about Southern troop strength and vulnerabilities. At one point, Pinkerton sends his own fifteen-year-old son, William, in a hot air balloon over enemy territory to observe troop movements—one of the first-ever aerial reconnaissance missions in U.S. Army history.

Pinkerton himself sometimes goes on undercover missions, but more often, he confers with McClellan and other top Union officers, strategizing and providing intelligence reports. When Abraham Lincoln visits the Union camps in Virginia to meet with his Generals, Pinkerton is often in those meetings.

During his wartime years as a military intelligence officer, Pinkerton's service will remain most closely associated with General McClellan. McClellan's reputation will diminish during the war, however, and many will blame the General's excessive caution for allowing the Confederate States Army a series of early strategic victories. Pinkerton himself does not escape blame for McClellan's decision-making, and some have argued that the detective's overestimation of enemy troop numbers contributed to McClellan's famous reluctance to attack.

Today, historians still debate whether this criticism of Pinkerton's intelligence gathering is warranted. In any case, it's hard to deny the ambition and innovation of Pinkerton's wartime operation, or the daring of his agents. His military "Secret Service" organization, sometimes called the Union Intelligence Service, is at least in part the forerunner to the U.S. Secret Service as we know it today.

Pinkerton's war service also includes a terrible tragedy. His long-time operative Timothy Webster—always one of Pinkerton's favorite and most loyal agents—spends many months deep undercover in the Confederate capital of Richmond, Virginia, secretly sending ciphered intelligence reports back to Pinkerton. When Webster falls ill and ceases communicating, Pinkerton grows alarmed and sends two other

Allan Pinkerton *(left)* poses with President Lincoln and Maj. Gen. John McClernand at a Union encampment in Sharpsburg, Maryland, on October 3, 1862. In Pinkerton's role as head of the Union Intelligence Service, he operates under the alias "Major E. J. Allen"—the same name he'd used during his overnight journey through Baltimore with Lincoln.

agents to rescue him. Sadly, the new agents' arrival blows Webster's cover, and all three are captured as Union spies.

The two secondary agents are imprisoned and eventually released, but Webster himself is convicted of espionage and sentenced to death.

No amount of intervention can save him. On April 29, 1862, Timothy Webster is hanged in Richmond, his body denied a proper burial.

Webster's death devastates Pinkerton, and by some accounts, he never fully recovers from the trauma. After the war, he arranges to have Webster's remains transported to Chicago, to be given a proper burial in Pinkerton's family lot.

Years earlier, back during the Baltimore investigation, Timothy Webster's role was not particularly significant. He'd gone undercover with militias north of the city who were suspected of plotting to sabotage the railroad tracks. But given Pinkerton's grief, it's understandable why he embellishes his fallen soldier's role in the inscription that appears on Timothy Webster's memorial:

ON THE NIGHT OF FEBR. 22, 1861,

ALLAN PINKERTON,

TIMOTHY WEBSTER

and KATE WARNE

SAFELY ESCORTED

ABRAHAM LINCOLN,

A CONSPIRACY HAVING BEEN DISCOVERED

FOR HIS ASSASSINATION, FROM

PHILADELPHIA TO WASHINGTON,

WHERE HE WAS INAUGURATED

PRESIDENT OF THE U.S.

on

MARCH 4TH, 1861

Kate Warne, also mentioned on the memorial, will continue to work for Pinkerton's agency both during and after the war. Again, though, when it comes to his family of agents, tragedy strikes.

Warne dies of an uncertain illness in 1868, at the age of thirty-five. Pinkerton reportedly sat at her bedside until she passed and arranged her burial in the same family lot that held Webster's body.

Warne receives little fanfare in death—same as her life. Only now, over a century later, is her genuinely groundbreaking role as America's first woman detective receiving greater recognition.

After the Civil War, Pinkerton's National Detective Agency continues to thrive in private practice. Among other major cases, the Pinkertons are contracted to track and capture legendary train robber Jesse James. The agency never does catch the famous outlaw, but they do successfully investigate several other high-profile train robberies.

Later in life, Pinkerton writes several memoirs describing his most famous cases. Some of these are later published posthumously; others are probably ghostwritten. The books are full of fascinating stories and details, but some of them contain passages that are embellished or of dubious veracity.

Allan Pinkerton dies in 1884 at the age of sixty-four. His former partners and sons continue to run the agency without him. Sadly, the Pinkerton legacy will be tarnished in the late nineteenth and early twentieth centuries when the company contracts itself repeatedly as a "union-busting" security force on behalf of railroads and other large corporations.

Several headline-grabbing incidents make the company name almost synonymous with anti-labor violence during that era. Ironically, of course, Pinkerton began his own career in Scotland as a fiery young union organizer, always prepared to fight for the poor laboring classes.

Today, Pinkerton's National Detective Agency still exists as a high-tech consulting and investigations firm. Allan Pinkerton is a member of the Military Intelligence Hall of Fame, and his many innovations had an undoubted impact in many fields of law enforcement.

Still, arguably no case in his long career will ever be more important than his firm's investigation into the plot to kill Abraham Lincoln.

77

With the beginning of the Civil War, Abraham Lincoln, Allan Pinkerton, and others involved in thwarting the 1861 Baltimore assassination plot began devoting all their energies to the pressing matters of war.

But what became of the individual most responsible for planning the plot itself? What became of the barber Cypriano Ferrandini?

As the war broke out in April 1861, Ferrandini at first seemed to continue his role on the front lines of Maryland's secessionist movement. On April 25, twelve days after the surrender of Fort Sumter, local newspapers report several new local militia companies in Baltimore. Among these are a group called the Winan's Guards, described by *The Baltimore Sun* as "a company of young men, formed for the present emergency." The Captain and presiding officer, according to *The Baltimore Sun,* is "C. Ferrandini."

Little is known about the group, but the political affiliation isn't hard to deduce. The name *Winan* was likely an homage to a prominent Baltimore citizen—an inventor and state legislator named Ross Winans—who was an outspoken secessionist and who would soon be arrested by federal authorities.

The Winan's Guards are also included among a handful of local militias who are organizing under a single corps under the larger umbrella of the National Volunteers.

The Baltimore Sun reports that "at a meeting . . . held on Wednesday evening at their headquarters, Calvert Station, it was resolved to name the corps the 'Byrne's Guards,' out of compliment to the president of the National Volunteers."

In fact, William Byrne, the founder and president of the National Volunteers, was a fellow member with Ferrandini in the Baltimore chapter of the Knights of the Golden Circle before—and the two probably knew each other. In any case, based on these associations, the pro-Southern political orientation of Ferrandini's new company is clear.

After the group's founding, the Winan's Guards receive no further mention in newspapers or city records. Perhaps Ferrandini's new company simply fizzles, or perhaps the changing state of affairs in Maryland makes it impossible to maintain a pro-Southern militia.

Despite the widespread Southern sympathy throughout the state, Maryland remains in the Union throughout the war. With an increasing presence of federal troops stationed in the state to protect Union supply lines, and after the arrest of a number of public officials known to have Confederate sympathies, the secessionist crowd in Baltimore can no longer be so brazen.

Still, later in the war, Ferrandini's political sympathies again get him in trouble. In May 1863, *The Baltimore Sun* runs the following local news item:

Took the Oath—On Saturday evening Col. Fish released C. Ferrandini from custody after he had taken the oath of allegiance. Mr. F[errandini] addressed a letter to Col. Fish, expressing regret for the language he had used, and promised to do so no more.

Apparently, a Union officer had arrested Ferrandini for expressing Confederate sympathies in public. To obtain his release, Ferrandini was forced to swear a "loyalty oath" to the United States of America. Such cases were common throughout the war, for both public officials and ordinary citizens. The same news story describes another Baltimore civilian who was "arrested on the charge of cheering for Jeff. Davis, took the oath, and was released on parole."

Throughout this time, Ferrandini never leaves his post as the barber at Barnum's City Hotel. He continues to occasionally post help wanted ads for assistant hairdressers—always white, of course. And apart from the one incident mentioned in *The Baltimore Sun,* Ferrandini keeps a low profile for the rest of the war.

In fact, given that this man once conspired to assassinate a President-elect in broad daylight, what may be most remarkable about the rest of Ferrandini's life is how utterly ordinary it is.

After the war, the Barnum's barber more or less resumes the same role he'd occupied back in the 1850s: as a well-liked citizen active in local affairs. He joins a building association, serves on the jury for local trials, becomes the director of a French Benevolent Society, and joins a social organization called the Crescent Club. He even dabbles in local politics, sometimes attending fund-raisers for Democratic mayoral or gubernatorial candidates.

His life also includes some major difficulties. In 1870, his wife dies in a house fire, and in 1889, after the barber gets remarried, his eight-year-old son, Raphael, dies in a terrible sewer accident. The story briefly becomes a national news item, with Ferrandini successfully suing the city for damages. Then, in 1895, he and his second wife lose their seven-week-old twins to illness.

Eventually, on December 20, 1910, Cypriano Ferrandini dies from natural causes at the age of eighty-eight. The initial death notice contains the headline WAS BARBER AT OLD BARNUM'S and includes this paragraph: "Born in Corsica Mr. Ferrandini came to New York when a young man and later settled in Baltimore. While at the Barnum Hotel, he became acquainted with the best citizens in town and enjoyed waiting on them."

The next day, *The Baltimore Sun* runs a longer, more elaborate obituary. The headline reads, ADORNED CITY'S FINEST, and goes on to recount Ferrandini's "Active Life in Famous Hostelry." According to the obit, "He was a man of genial disposition and pleasant manner and won many friends."

The obituary also includes this previously unknown story about Ferrandini from the 1860s. "During the Civil War, when his home on Baltimore street, near Bond street, was about to be visited by Union soldiers, he took up portions of the flooring, and by hiding such firearms, flags and valuables as were in the house and replacing the flooring and carpets, fooled the enemy."

Clearly, throughout the war and probably beyond, Ferrandini's loyalty to the South never wavered.

At the time of his death, the only two known photographs of Cypriano Ferrandini emerge. The photos show that even later in life, he wore the same carefully manicured mustache that Allan Pinkerton noticed so many years earlier.

Cypriano Ferrandini, the longtime barber at Barnum's City Hotel in Baltimore, Maryland, as photographed on an unknown date shortly before his death in December 1910.

78

⸻ · ⸻

They started calling it "the Baltimore Plot." But to this day, like Cypriano Ferrandini himself, some aspects remain steeped in mystery.

One interesting question that still remains unanswered is which of the various secret societies, militias, and white supremacist organizations operating in Baltimore was truly responsible for the plot to assassinate Abraham Lincoln.

Ferrandini, of course, was a member of the Knights of the Golden Circle. Fellow Baltimore conspirator Otis K. Hillard was probably also a member. Given the political orientation of the KGC and its prominence in Baltimore secessionist circles, it's very possible that other participants in the assassination conspiracy were associated with the group.

There is no evidence, however, that the KGC national leadership helped plan or support it—or indeed that they had any working knowledge of it. Regardless of how many sworn Knights were involved, or how much inspiration they took from the secret society, the Baltimore conspirators almost certainly acted independently of the formal organization.

As for the rest of the Knights of the Golden Circle, the organization continued to operate in the United States in the early 1860s.

Yet their activities were almost entirely subsumed by the secession movement and then the war. Many of the eager KGC recruits from the 1850s—those who originally signed up for a proposed military mission to spread slavery into Mexico and South America—were instead urged by the group's leadership to enlist in the Confederate States Army and serve the South. To that end, throughout the Civil War, the Knights turned their efforts to recruiting soldiers for the Confederacy, and a number of Confederate officers were known to be active KGC members or were recruited by them.

The impact of the group goes beyond just counting the rebel officers who were card-carrying members, however. The organization's proslavery, pro-white, pro-Southern ideology was interwoven with the politics of the time, and was part of the texture of the extremist secessionist movement. Politicians, prominent citizens, and tens of thousands of ordinary people were associated with the group and worked to spread its message.

In fact, one of those prominent citizens known to be a member at the KGC's peak was a famous stage actor who enthusiastically adopted the group's tenets and beliefs.

His name was John Wilkes Booth—and soon he would find his own violent means of implementing an extremist pro-Southern philosophy.

Whatever the KGC's impact, by late 1863, the organization's leadership fell into disarray and the group tried to reconfigure under different names. It is possible that the KGC continued to operate underground for decades after the war—some have speculated that outlaw Jesse James was a member—but regardless, the secret society eventually disappeared.

Perhaps the Knights of the Golden Circle can now best be viewed as the forerunner and early inspiration for another more overtly violent secret society that would emerge soon after the Civil War: the Ku Klux Klan. In addition to their shared usage of complex rituals, titles, and codes, the two groups utilized similar organizational structures. And the lineage of white supremacy and vigilante violence from one group to the other is clear to see.

Still, back in Baltimore in early 1861, there was another militant political organization on the ground that both Ferrandini and Hillard were connected to: the National Volunteers. Based on what Pinkerton and his detectives learned about the plot, it was this group—not the KGC—that was either officially or unofficially behind the conspiracy. In fact, further events soon provided more evidence that the plot was deadly serious—and that the National Volunteers were the key players supporting it.

On April 19, 1861, six days after the fall of Fort Sumter and four days after Lincoln's proclamation calling for 75,000 Union troops, a trainload of Union soldiers—the Massachusetts Sixth Regiment—travels from Massachusetts toward Washington, D.C. Their mission is to fortify the nation's capital.

These are some of the first Union soldiers to be called into official duty. To get from Massachusetts to Washington by rail, they must, of course, travel through Baltimore.

It's the same passage Lincoln took during his overnight journey—and like Lincoln, to get from one train depot to another, these troops will cross through the Baltimore city streets in detached train cars pulled by teams of horses.

Unlike Lincoln's secret midnight passage, however, these troops travel through Baltimore in the middle of the day. As a result, once word gets out who's coming, throngs of angry Southern sympathizers greet the traveling soldiers to protest their passage through the city.

The day before, the National Volunteers had held a rally denouncing any passage of Union troops through the city—and promised armed resistance. And now, these National Volunteers are among the angry crowd surrounding the train cars and preventing their passage through the streets.

With no other choice, the Massachusetts troops bravely exit the train cars and attempt to march by foot through the city. The mob soon attacks, and a melee ensues. By the end of it, ten Union troops are killed and a few dozen are wounded.

These are the first Union soldiers to die in the Civil War.

To give it context, their deaths occur less than two months after the planned assassination plot—partly instigated by the same group—and only a few blocks from where Lincoln himself was to be murdered. Although there's no way to be sure, it's possible that Cypriano Ferrandini and Otis K. Hillard were among the National Volunteers in the mob that day.

In the immediate aftermath of the bloody event, Baltimore secessionists run rampant in the city. One group of pro-Southern city leaders leads a band of arsonists to burn railroad bridges and destroy telegraph lines north of the city, to prevent additional Northern troops from entering the city. One of those leading these vandals is none other than Baltimore's Police Marshal George P. Kane—the same police marshal whom Pinkerton suspected was in league with the conspirators.

Clearly, Pinkerton and Felton were right to distrust this man. In fact, two months later, in June 1861, federal authorities will arrest and imprison Kane for continuing to work with Southern sympathizers to block Northern troops from traveling through Baltimore.

After these events, and as the Civil War envelops the nation, the Baltimore Plot largely fades from public consciousness. The rush of events is so fast, and the death and devastation of the war so vast, a failed assassination plot becomes mostly a forgotten footnote.

After the war is over, however, as stories of the era begin to be told and retold, historians and participants alike begin to reexamine the strange events of late February 1861. This reexamination is amplified by an unexpected development: a feud between two of the key players at Lincoln's side during his fateful overnight journey.

From the outset, Allan Pinkerton didn't get along with Lincoln's friend and bodyguard Ward Hill Lamon. Perhaps it began that night in Philadelphia, when Lamon tried to offer Lincoln weapons and Pinkerton sternly rebuked him. If so, their antipathy increased even more in the days after the group safely arrived in Washington, D.C.

Lamon very quickly sought out reporters to tell the story. Pinkerton had instructed the opposite, telling everyone on the team to maintain absolute secrecy. The detective had worked hard to disguise his own involvement, and he started to suspect that Lamon was leaking his name to the press. Lamon is a "brainless, egotistical fool," Pinkerton wrote in his field notes at the time.

These words, although written in confidential private documents, will eventually backfire on Pinkerton. Several years after the war, Lamon undertakes to write a personal biography of Abraham Lincoln. To do so, Lamon acquires a trove of research papers that include many of Pinkerton's field notes from the plot—including the unflattering note about Lamon.

Furious to find Pinkerton's insult, Lamon writes disparagingly of Pinkerton—and in fact claims that there was no Baltimore plot to kill Lincoln. According to Lamon, Pinkerton pushed for the risky change of travel plans that fateful night not because the evidence in Baltimore warranted it, but because he wanted to draw attention and acclaim to his firm once the story was in the newspapers.

To defend himself from this and other accusations, Pinkerton collects and publishes signed testimonials from others who played a role in thwarting the plot. They all back up the detective's side of the story. Yet for everyone involved, the waters are now muddied, and both historians and the public no longer know what to make of the matter.

Later in life, Pinkerton does himself no favors when he publishes a collection of memoirs of his most famous cases, including the Baltimore Plot. They're written with an eye toward the mass market and occasionally contain embellishments and some inconsistencies with the factual record.

It begs the question: Is it possible that Pinkerton exaggerated the Baltimore threat from the outset—and that he pushed Lincoln to take drastic measures that night solely to draw attention to himself?

Today, researchers continue to debate some details of the plot—but after all these decades, the evidence largely weighs in Pinkerton's favor.

While it's impossible to truly know what would've happened had Lincoln kept to his original Baltimore itinerary, Pinkerton's contemporaneous field notes and the field notes of his agents paint a thorough and convincing story.

Perhaps most important, it's not just a Pinkerton story. This was a conspiracy so serious, many other credible participants—including Samuel Felton, Norman Judd, and Edward Sanford—all believed the President's life to be in danger.

For Pinkerton to have exaggerated the scenario at the time, he would've had to have fabricated his contemporaneous notes and instructed his agents to do the same—at a time when he had no intention of the notes being published.

Moreover, in the midst of all this lying, he'd be asking the President-elect of the United States to undertake a profoundly risky plan that easily could've placed Lincoln in unnecessary harm's way—completely destroying Pinkerton's own reputation and the firm he'd built over the previous decade.

Lamon's suggestion that Pinkerton's motive was to seek personal acclaim also doesn't square with the historical record. At the time, Pinkerton went to great lengths to ensure that neither he personally nor any of his agents could ever be identified, and he was angry when he thought Lamon had mentioned his name to the press.

Furthermore, Pinkerton kept all his files locked away specifically so his role would not be discovered. Essentially, Pinkerton did everything possible to *avoid* his name ever being connected to the Baltimore Plot—and it was years before he even publicly admitted his involvement. If his goal was to win acclaim for himself or his firm, none of this behavior makes sense.

Finally, there's the evidence that ultimately convinced Abraham Lincoln himself that the plot was real: A team of credible police detectives, backed by William H. Seward and Gen. Winfield Scott and working entirely separately from Pinkerton—in fact with no knowledge of Pinkerton's efforts—independently came to essentially the same conclusion. These detectives also determined that a conspiracy to assassinate Abraham Lincoln existed in Baltimore—and believed that the danger was so great that Lincoln should change his itinerary to save his own life.

A century and a half later, whatever criticism Lincoln and his team may have taken for their decision that fateful night, the fact remains: If the President-elect kept to his original plan, he very well may've never made it to his inauguration ceremony—and if so, would not have been President of the United States during the most tumultuous four years of the nation's history.

79

---•---

Boston, Massachusetts

January 1, 1863

The crowd is ready. It's January 1—the first night of 1863—and everyone's packed into Tremont Temple, a Baptist church in Boston, Massachusetts.

For more than eighteen months, the Civil War has raged, causing destruction and loss of life of a magnitude the country has never before seen. The Union Army, despite its superior size, has suffered waning morale and flagging enlistment. There is no clear end in sight.

Tremont Temple is a frequent meeting spot for abolitionists, and tonight it is abolitionists who crowd the space. Most of the faces are not white. They're dark-skinned. Among them is perhaps the most recognized abolitionist of all, Frederick Douglass.

On this night, Douglass and several others have prepared to give speeches, but it's not the speeches that the crowd has gathered for. They've been waiting, for hours now, for news that has been expected all day but has still not come.

Since Lincoln's inauguration in March 1861—now almost two years ago—Douglass has closely followed every development of the Lincoln administration and of the war. He's written many essays and given many speeches, analyzing and critiquing each decision President Lincoln has made and the positions he has taken. Douglass has spoken personally with Northern Senators and other elected officials, trying to influence the direction of events, always with one transcendent goal in mind—the abolition of slavery.

At many points over the past two years, Douglass has been one of Lincoln's harshest critics. After supporting Lincoln in the Presidential election, he's been frequently disappointed by Lincoln's caution and hesitance on the issue of slavery. It began with Lincoln's inaugural speech, where Douglass was furious that Lincoln, a supposed antislavery candidate, didn't forcefully condemn slavery before the nation.

Once the war began, Douglass was similarly angry when Lincoln resisted the call to allow blacks to enlist and serve in the Union Army.

But in the war's second year—as Union enlistment and morale sagged, and as the Confederate States Army continued to hold or gain ground in bloody battle after bloody battle—the President began to see the war in a new way. In the fall of 1862, he issued a preliminary executive order stating that he, as Commander in Chief, has the authority to free all slaves in Confederate States as an act of war. If the Confederate States do not cease fighting by January 1, 1863, he will issue a proclamation declaring all of these enslaved persons—that's over three million people—to be forever free.

For abolitionists, it appears too good to be true. If, on New Year's Day, the Confederate States haven't laid down their arms—and they haven't—this final "Emancipation Proclamation" will be enacted.

Today is supposed to be that day. And yet, still nothing. It's getting late, and the news still hasn't come. Maybe the motion was delayed or abandoned. Perhaps, as had happened on other issues, the Lincoln administration capitulated in the face of proslavery opposition from the border states.

As Douglass later described that night, "We were now met together to receive and celebrate the first utterance of the long-hoped-for proclamation, *if* it came . . . for in view of the past, it was by no means certain that it would come. The occasion, therefore, was one of both hope and fear."

Douglass, of course, had experienced the horrors of slavery firsthand. Since his escape as a young man, he's spent every day of his life pushing to end it. He and many others have fought ceaselessly—facing every imaginable resistance—for the cause of freedom, hoping to end the moral scourge that has caused incalculable human suffering and torn the nation apart. Every day of the struggle, those like Douglass who have escaped from bondage are conscious of the millions who have not—the men, women, and children now living in a state of anguish.

In and around this church tonight, the gathered crowd has dared to feel a glimmer of hope for the many who now suffer in bondage. As Douglass would later describe:

> We were waiting and listening as for a bolt from the sky, which should rend the fetters of four millions of slaves; we were watch-ing, as it were, by the dim light of the stars, for the dawn of a new day: we were longing for the answer to the agonizing prayers of centuries. Remembering those in bonds as bound with them, we wanted to join in the shout for freedom, and in the anthem of the redeemed.

And yet, after hours of waiting and hoping, the news hasn't ar-rived.

To make sure there was no delay, the church organizers had even set up a line of messengers between the telegraph offices and the church. Time passes. Still no word.

By 10:00 p.m., after hours of waiting, "patience was well-nigh exhausted, and suspense was becoming agony."

Suddenly, a man advances through the crowd and, "with a face illuminated by the news he bore, exclaimed in tones that thrilled all hearts, 'It is coming!'"

The crowd erupts in cheers. "The effect of this announcement was startling beyond description," Douglass would write. "Joy and gladness exhausted all forms of expression from shouts of praise, to sobs and tears."

Just like that, literally overnight and by the stroke of Abraham Lincoln's pen, more than three million enslaved persons are, at least on paper, now declared free. It is, by many estimations then and now, the most radical and far-reaching political document since the Declaration of Independence.

At the time, the liberty granted by the Emancipation Proclamation is incomplete; as an executive order, it has the built-in limitation that a future President could overturn it. It also does not apply to the border slave states that remain within the Union.

Still, it is a momentous achievement that directly paves the way for the full abolition of slavery soon to follow.

The Proclamation also does something else. It formally opens the Union Army to black soldiers. This, Lincoln hopes, will be precisely the jolt of energy that the Northern war effort desperately needs.

80

---·---

Washington, D.C.

August 1863

Frederick Douglass is at the White House. It's seven months later, and the war is still raging. It doesn't slow Douglass down. He's here, today, on a mission.

Shortly after the Emancipation Proclamation was signed, Union recruiters in the Northeast had reached out to Douglass, enlisting his help recruiting black soldiers. Douglass made an arrangement with the War Department and threw himself into this recruitment task. Utilizing his influence and his platform as a newspaper editor, he published essays, wrote flyers, and gave speeches encouraging blacks to join.

Soon thereafter, in March 1863, when Massachusetts raised the North's first all-black military unit—the legendary Massachusetts Fifty-Fourth Regiment—Douglass's sons Charles and Lewis were among the very first to sign up.

Now, a few months later, Douglass comes to the White House to register a complaint. He's here personally to plead for equal pay and medical services for the more than one hundred thousand black soldiers who're now serving. His argument is clear: The all-black regiments have thus far fought with valor and skill, suffering enormous loss of life. Yet they're paid less and, due to inferior medical care, die of sickness and disease in far greater numbers than white soldiers. The Massachusetts recruiters hope that a personal plea from Douglass will spur the White House to take action.

As he waits in a White House hallway with scores of others—a black man among many whites—Douglass has a moment to consider his position. "I was an ex-slave, identified with a despised race, and yet I was to meet the most exalted person in this great republic . . . I could not know, what kind of a reception would be accorded me. I might be told to go home and mind my business . . . or I might be refused an interview altogether."

Soon, he's called in to the busy room where President Abraham Lincoln is at work. It's a moment he'll never forget.

"He was seated when I entered, in a low arm chair," Douglass later recalled. "The room bore the marks of business, and the persons in it, the President included, appeared to be much over-worked and tired." He goes on to describe Lincoln's features. "Long lines of care were already deeply written on Mr. Lincoln's brow, and his strong face, full of earnestness, lighted up as soon as my name was mentioned."

As Douglass approached and was introduced to the President, Lincoln rose and extended his hand to welcome him.

"I at once felt myself in the presence of an honest man," Douglass later wrote, "one whom I could love, honor, and trust without reserve or doubt."

It didn't take long for Douglass to make his case. "Mr. Lincoln listened with patience and silence to all I had to say . . . He impressed me with the solid gravity of his character, by his silent listening not less than by his earnest reply to my words."

Throughout the rest of the war, Lincoln and Douglass remain in contact. Douglass still sometimes publicly criticizes Lincoln when he believes the President is moving too slowly in the fight against slavery, but over time, the two men develop a mutual respect. Lincoln will invite Douglass back to the White House on two more occasions.

In fact, a year and a half after their first meeting, as the war nears its close, Douglass is in the front of the crowd when Lincoln delivers his second inaugural address. In his speech, Lincoln hits slavery head-on, speaking in moral and spiritual terms:

> Fondly do we hope—fervently do we pray—that this mighty scourge of war may speedily pass away. Yet, if God wills that it continue . . . until every drop of blood drawn with the lash, shall be paid by another drawn with the sword . . . so still it must be said, "the judgments of the Lord, are true and righteous altogether."

This sort of language—a biblical condemnation of slavery—is what abolitionists have used in their rallies and meetings. Now, it's being spoken by the President of the United States at the U.S. Capitol, for the entire nation to hear.

After the speech, at Lincoln's invitation, Frederick Douglass attends the inaugural reception at the White House. According to Douglass's recollection, when Lincoln spots him in the receiving line several feet away, the President loudly calls out, so that everyone around him hears it, "Here comes my friend Douglass."

"I am glad to see you," Lincoln continues, now shaking his hand. "I saw you in the crowd today, listening to my inaugural address; how did you like it?"

"Mr. Lincoln," Douglass replies, "I must not detain you with my poor opinion, when there are thousands waiting to shake hands with you."

"No, no," Lincoln says, "there is no man in the country whose opinion I value more than yours. I want to know what you think of it."

Douglass pauses for a moment, then: "Mr. Lincoln, that was a sacred effort."

81

———— • ————

All his life, Abraham Lincoln was haunted by tragedy and death. Loss and grief were with him constantly: as a child, as a young man, and as a father.

During his Presidency, death will haunt him still—more so than it has any Commander in Chief before or since.

Throughout the long four years of the Civil War, more Americans will die than in any other war in the nation's history—in fact, more Americans will die in the Civil War than in every other war *combined* from the American Revolution through the Korean War, including both World Wars. On average, nearly 3,500 lives are lost every week during the Civil War, meaning that on a typical day, Abraham Lincoln feels the burden of 500 dead.

From Virginia to Georgia, from Tennessee to Pennsylvania, bloody battles ravage the countryside, leaving fields full of dead bodies and scattered limbs. Individual battles have casualties as high as ten thousand, twenty thousand, thirty thousand, and, in the case of Gettysburg, over fifty thousand. Violence and loss destroy families, destroy communities, destroy cities.

Everywhere he goes, Lincoln is surrounded by it. He visits battlefields full of corpses, sits in hospitals with the mortally wounded, stands solemnly in graveyards, and commemorates fallen troops in memorial services and letters to grieving families.

All of this changes Abraham Lincoln.

Without question, he's not the same person who, just over four years ago, said farewell to Springfield, Illinois, and boarded that inaugural train. And how could he be? The kindness is still there in his eyes, but the twinkle and humor have faded. As one friend describes, he began to look "weary, care-worn, and troubled," with "a cadence of deep sadness in his voice." There had always been a sadness to him, but now it's different, amplified with the loss—over six hundred thousand of them—of every young man who's buried.

In February 1862, less than a year into his Presidency, death strikes Lincoln's own family again. This time, it's the terrible, unexpected loss to illness of Lincoln's son, eleven-year-old William Lincoln. Willie was sweet-natured and studious—the one who most resembled his father and whom his father famously doted on. The loss is utterly devastating, casting a pall of grief over every moment of family life.

Still, Lincoln must work—not for himself, for the nation. With criticism coming from all sides and with the war's terrible cost on his conscience, he makes one impossible decision after another, always struggling, always weary, but never yielding to hopelessness even when no other feeling seems possible.

Back on that night he was first elected President, Abraham Lincoln looked in the mirror and saw a double image, a premonition of his own death.

The early death that he foresaw may well have claimed him before he became President. We even know the date it could've come—February 23, 1861—when a band of assassins lay in wait for him in Baltimore, Maryland, planning to murder him during his passage to the nation's capital. Thankfully, with help from Allan Pinkerton, Kate Warne, Norman Judd, Samuel Felton, and others, Lincoln's life was spared that day.

Of course, this raises the question: How would history have changed if the plot against Lincoln had not been foiled? How would *America* be different?

When this lanky, little-known Illinoisan with no formal education was first elected President, no one could have imagined the true scope of the trials he'd face.

If Lincoln had been killed on that train, would Vice President Hannibal Hamlin of Maine—or some other Commander in Chief—have made the same decisions and achieved the same results? Would they have managed to keep the critical border states in the Union, maintaining an advantage for the North? What about mobilizing the vast Union Army, overseeing the logistics of the war, or making all the painful decisions that it took to win? And with that win, could anyone else have expressed such empathy for those who suffered the greatest losses? Could anyone else have found the words to inspire the righteous and comfort the fallen?

Maybe. If Lincoln had died, whoever took over might have done just as well.

But there's a reason Abraham Lincoln is, to this day, perhaps our most revered President—and it has to do with more than just his skill as a political strategist and Commander in Chief.

Back when Lincoln was a teenager, he'd lie in the grass with his legs up on a tree stump. There, teaching himself to read, he found in the language of his most revered document, the Declaration of Independence, the words of a promise. It was a promise that even someone like him—a kid born into poverty, who taught himself to write with a stick in the dirt—was entitled to the same opportunities and rights as any other person.

Lincoln's life and personal struggle would embody that promise, from his most humble beginnings, to holding the highest position in the land.

As a politician, he strove to ensure that the promise would be kept for others like him.

But as President, with the war raging around him and the very future of the nation on the line, he saw that the promise wasn't enough. He had to win the war and preserve the Union not just for those *like him* but for those who *weren't* like him. He had to extend that promise to *everyone,* black and white, in the North and in the South.

Before the war, Abraham Lincoln believed that slavery was wrong, and he often said so. Yet as a politician, he at first allowed himself to tolerate that wrongness. As a politician, when it came to slavery, he exercised caution, prudence, and restraint.

However.

At the exact right moment, Lincoln overcame that caution, knowing this was the issue that mattered more than any other. Amid the dark chaos of wartime, he saw a rare chance to reach for the brightest light. In that precious moment, he reached for something transcendent, something greater than the war, something greater than himself.

For two and a half centuries, the horror of slavery was a scourge upon the nation, a moral travesty and an unforgivable sin. After decades of struggle, those who had fought so long, so hard, and so bravely to end this suffering would eventually find, in this skinny man from Illinois, their unlikely ally. As Frederick Douglass put it, "The hour and the man of our redemption had somehow met in the person of Abraham Lincoln."

The Emancipation Proclamation was the first great step. But it was two years later, near war's end, that Lincoln would throw his support behind the monumental Thirteenth Amendment, formally declaring the practice of slavery illegal, forever, throughout the United States.

For Lincoln—and for the country—there will be many struggles still ahead in the pursuit of true equality in America. Yet these are, without question, two of the greatest pillars erected for human liberty in the nation's history.

Of course, back on that day in February 1861, Lincoln eluded his assassins in Baltimore—but his premonition of death would soon catch up to him. Whether by fate or chance, Lincoln's prediction on the night of his first election—that he would live through his first term in office and perish during his second—would soon be proven true.

Just months after his triumphant reelection, just weeks after the passage through the House of Representatives of what would become the Thirteenth Amendment, and just days after Robert E. Lee surrendered his rebel army at the Appomattox Court House in Virginia, President and Mrs. Lincoln make plans to attend the play *Our American Cousin* at Ford's Theatre.

On that Friday night—Good Friday, actually—a different assassin claims Abraham Lincoln's life. Different, yes, but driven by the same forces that drove Cypriano Ferrandini, Otis K. Hillard, and the others in Baltimore: bigotry, hatred, grievance, and rage.

Those are the forces that successfully take Lincoln's life—in the form of a bullet fired from white supremacist John Wilkes Booth's gun into the back of Lincoln's head on April 14, 1865.

The next morning, some of Abraham Lincoln's closest advisors, together with distraught family members, gather around the mortally wounded President's bed for the final moments of his life. For those there, the shock and pain are too much to bear. Some of these men, his colleagues, had at first looked down on Lincoln, doubted him, even belittled him. Eventually, they came to revere and love him. Now, along with the family and friends who know him best, they openly weep.

At 7:22 a.m., the President of the United States draws his final breath.

Abraham Lincoln is dead. But he's never truly gone.

During his famous speech at Gettysburg, Lincoln told the crowd that no one would remember what he said that day. He was wrong.

As he proved there and throughout his life, sometimes the hardest fights don't reveal a winner—but they do reveal character.

In those hardest moments, when darkness descends, we must reach for the light. As Lincoln himself said, "Stand with anybody that stands right. Stand with him while he is right and part with him when he goes wrong."

It is one of the foundational pillars of Abraham Lincoln—and of America itself. We're not simply a country of ideas; we're a country of ideals. What makes America exceptional is not our weapons or our might. It's our principles and our continuing fight to live up to them. Faced with darkness, we must reach for the light.

It was true a century and half ago at Gettysburg, but it's just as true today:

When you speak your mind—and speak for those who need help—there's no more powerful way to be heard.

Postscript

Whatever happened to the conspirators?

One of the hardest parts of telling stories from history is making various decisions about what to leave out. There's always more to add: more details, more context, more side stories, and more explanations about why events may have unfolded the way they did. But to keep a story manageable, we as authors have to make tough decisions about what *not* to include.

It's only after readers get their eyes on a book that we learn which parts of the story still leave unanswered questions—and where it is that readers are eager to learn more.

With that in mind, we'd like to take this opportunity to answer one of the most-asked questions we've received about *The Lincoln Conspiracy*: Why didn't authorities arrest or kill the conspirators who plotted to kill Abraham Lincoln on February 23, 1861?

We've asked ourselves that same question. Once Lincoln was safely in Washington, D.C., law enforcement would have had more than enough information to round up suspects and begin interrogations. Allan Pinkerton and his agents had gathered names, workplaces, and home addresses for many of the key conspirators, including alleged ringleader Cypriano Ferrandini. With even a cursory investigation, authorities could have verified this information and sought to learn more.

More important, Abraham Lincoln himself, once he took the oath of office, could have pushed for an investigation and prosecution of those who planned to murder him. So why didn't he? Why didn't the government seek to punish these men?

The answers to these questions are speculative, because in truth, there is no clear record of whether Lincoln, his advisors, or any authorities in Washington, D.C., or the state of Maryland considered pursuing justice against the plotters—or why they chose not to. Despite the public attention paid to the story, the few people who actually knew what happened—Pinkerton, Kate Warne, Norman Judd, Ward Hill Lamon, and a few others—remained secretive about it for several years. If there were ever high-level conversations about whether or how to prosecute the plotters, they were not documented.

Still, by studying the circumstances, it's possible to speculate and make educated guesses as to why the government chose not to act.

For one thing, at the time, there was no federal law enforcement mechanism set up to pursue such a case. Today, if investigators learned of a credible threat to assassinate a President-elect, we can all imagine the black helicopters descending to surround the suspects' homes or meeting places—and a team of high-level government prosecutors ready to issue criminal indictments.

But in 1861, there was no Federal Bureau of Investigation with field agents ready to trail suspects and make arrests. The FBI wasn't created until 1935, and its precursor, the Bureau of Investigation, was not formed until 1908. In the nineteenth century, the closest equivalent was the U.S. Marshals Service, but the Marshals had limited power and resources and were not set up to run complicated investigations into criminal activity.

Likewise, when Lincoln took office, there was no Department of Justice or anything like it. The DOJ was not created until 1870, in the post–Civil War era following Lincoln's death. Although the position of Attorney General had existed since the Founding era, for a long time it was considered a part-time job. It wasn't until 1818 that Congress authorized the A.G. to hire even a single clerk. Before the creation of the DOJ, the government usually had to outsource most prosecutions to private law firms, a cumbersome process.

Still, these limitations do not entirely explain the lack of action against the Baltimore conspirators. Had their murderous plot succeeded, the damage to the country could have been immense. Why wasn't there at least some effort to bring the criminals to justice?

According to one plausible theory, the failure to pursue justice against the Baltimore plotters was not about logistics, but politics.

On April 17, 1861, roughly six weeks after Lincoln's inauguration and just as the war was beginning, the commonwealth of Virginia seceded from the Union and joined the newly formed Confederate States of America. This momentous event meant that Washington, D.C., was now just across the Potomac River from the enemy. Virginia's secession also meant that Maryland was the capital's only geographic connection to the north. If Maryland were to also secede, Washington, D.C., would be completely surrounded by Confederate territory.

In other words, for the Lincoln administration, it was absolutely essential to keep Maryland in the Union.

As our story of the Baltimore Plot illustrates, Maryland was a state full of Southern sympathizers. Many state and local officials were eager to secede, and the public was largely behind them. Only the Governor, Thomas H. Hicks, was able to prevent Maryland from taking that step. But Hicks was hanging by a thread, and in early 1861 many worried the state would fall. As the war began, tensions in Maryland were at a breaking point.

For that reason, the last thing Lincoln would've wanted was a lengthy and complicated prosecution of Baltimore citizens, culminating in a high-profile trial. At best, it would be a distraction; at worst, a provocation to push Maryland to leave the Union and join the Confederacy.

It's worth noting that Lincoln wasn't afraid to use a heavy hand against suspected secessionists in Maryland. Later in 1861 Lincoln and his Secretary of State, William H. Seward, pushed executive power to the limit to quash southern sympathizers in the state. At various points Lincoln declared martial law, suspended habeas corpus, and sent soldiers to arrest scores of Marylanders for advocating secession, including state legislators and prominent newspaper editors. These would be some of the most controversial acts of Lincoln's Presidency.

But these tactics were, as the Lincoln administration saw it, necessary wartime measures using the President's authority as Commander in Chief. They were a swift response to an immediate national threat. On the other hand, a long, drawn-out prosecution and trial of Baltimore citizens for an alleged crime that took place *before* the war had started would have been an entirely optional undertaking without any military rationale. Given Maryland's precarious position as a Confederate-sympathizing state that Lincoln desperately needed to stay in the Union, pursuing justice for the Baltimore plotters would've been bad politics.

Finally, in addition to the above, we can speculate on Lincoln's personal motives for declining to pursue and punish those who sought to murder him.

The fact is, the entire business of the Baltimore Plot was something Lincoln had every reason to put behind him. The story of his secret overnight train ride was a source of political embarrassment, and the press coverage of it was full of sensationalism and gossip. As a new President about to lead the nation at a time of peril, Lincoln needed to project dignity and strength. Wild rumors and speculation about the assassins who plotted to kill him were likely the last thing he wanted the public to focus on. Pushing for a prosecution of the Baltimore plotters would be a guaranteed way to keep the story in the press, rather than make it go away.

During his inaugural journey, we know that Lincoln repeatedly stressed that the Presidency was not about him personally, but about the higher duty of the office. For him to spend valuable government resources pursuing a vengeful prosecution against the men who planned to kill him could have appeared vindictive and driven by personal anger. From the moment he assumed the Presidency, Lincoln needed to show that every action he took was for the benefit of the nation, and not for the benefit of himself.

In the end, we may never know with certainty why the Baltimore plotters were never arrested or put on trial. But the fact is, after Abraham Lincoln took the oath of office, he had to move forward and not look back. He had a war to win—and the future of the nation was at stake.

Acknowledgments

From Brad

This book was an adventure. So before anything else, I want to thank my fellow adventurer, Josh Mensch. Without question, Josh is a painstaking researcher, thoughtful analyst, and an exceedingly brilliant writer. But throughout this book, what I admired most was his dedication to making sure that we saw an Abraham Lincoln who was always . . . human. It's easy to put your heroes up on pedestals and pretend they're perfect. Instead, in these pages, you'll find a Lincoln who is self-assured and utterly overwhelmed, one who's committed to his principles, but also a shrewd compromiser. Depending on the moment, you'll see Lincoln as brave, terrified, soaring, devastated, heroic, and gutted. But as we were working on this book, I realized that the greatest attribute of our sixteenth President is that—even when the Civil War hits and the country is divided, even when it'd be easy to make a choice based on self-interest—Abraham Lincoln continually reaches for the light and chooses to help others. Now, I realize I'm already in the land of hyperbole, but let me explain why that reminds me of Josh. Put aside Josh's research and writing abilities. At the end of the day, Josh always reaches for the light and tries to do what's right. He is a fine human being and I'm honored to work with him. Thank you for your friendship, pal. This book wouldn't exist without you.

I also owe thank-yous to the following: My first lady, Cori, who forever pushes me to the better angels of my nature. Jonas, Lila, and Theo are my life. If they learn nothing else, I hope they'll always use their voices to speak up—especially when someone else needs help. Jill

Kneerim, my friend and agent, is with me since Chapter 1. Friend and agent Jennifer Rudolph Walsh at WME built this entire dream—and I love that she is now pursuing her own. Special thanks to Hope Denekamp, Lucy Cleland, Ike Williams, and all our friends at the Kneerim & Williams Agency.

I want to also thank my sister, Bari, who understands me at a molecular level. Also to Bobby, Ami, Adam, Gilda, and Will, for always supporting us.

My Pinkerton Agency is full of cleverness and guile: Noah Kuttler, Ethan Kline, Dale Flam, Matt Kuttler, Chris Weiss, and Judd Winick protect my life. They're never afraid to tell me when I'm wrong—and every page is the better for it. Additional love goes to Chris Eliopoulos, Katy Greene, Marie Grunbeck, Nick Marell, Staci Schecter, Liz Sobel, Nicole Delma, Jason Sherry, Jim Day, Denise Jaeger, Katriela Knight, and Maria Venusio.

For research and historical support, we could've never managed the minutiae of Civil War history—as well as all the Abraham Lincoln details—without Walter Stahr. His expertise and experience is interwoven throughout. Thank you, Walter, for keeping us on the right path.

Special thanks to James Swanson, for always being my Lincoln shaman; our family on *Lost History*, and at HISTORY and Left/Right, for bringing this band together: Nancy Dubuc, Paul Cabana, Mike Stiller, Ken Druckerman, Mike Mezaros, Mary Robertson, and Lee White; and to Rob Weisbach, for being the very first.

I also want to thank everyone at Flatiron and Macmillan: our leader and friend Don Weisberg, Cristina Gilbert, Marlena Bittner, Nancy Trypuc, Amy Einhorn, the production team of Rafal Gibek, Lena Shekhter, Emily Walters, Donna Noetzel, and Keith Hayes, as well as Astra Berzinskas, Jeff Capshew, Malati Chavali, Hank Cochrane, Cristina Cushing, Leigh George, Jenn Gonzalez, Jonathan Hollingsworth, Matt Johnson, Don O'Connor, Laura Pennock, Brad Wood, Jeanette Zwart, and the entire sales force who do all the real magic. I can't say it enough: They're the true reason this book is in your hands.

I want to add a special thank-you to our tireless editors, Jasmine

Faustino and Lauren Bittrich, who moved true mountains, pitched in at absurd levels, and saved us on a nearly daily basis. Especially at the end. Thank you for that! Finally, I need to thank our true Commander in Chief Bob Miller. He was the one who believed. His constant friendship and endless enthusiasm conjured this book. I owe him forever for opening this chapter of my life. Thank you, Bob, for your faith.

From Josh

First of all, thank you once again to Brad for inviting me on this creative journey. Studying and writing about history is a privilege, and Brad is a great partner with whom to share it. As anyone who knows Brad can attest, his energy and optimism are an inspiration—in books and in life. He is a generous collaborator and a generous friend. Thanks, Brad, and much love from me and my family to you and yours.

On this project I owe a warm and sincere debt of gratitude to Walter Stahr, our historical consultant. His thoughtful insights, patient feedback, and deep knowledge of the era have enriched the work immeasurably. Stahr's book *Seward: Lincoln's Indispensable Man* is a definitive modern biography of William Henry Seward, and essential reading for anyone interested in Abraham Lincoln or the Civil War era.

Once again, I'd like to extend the greatest possible thanks to Bob Miller at Flatiron for making our work possible. His enthusiasm and generous support bolstered us from beginning to end. Thanks also to Jasmine Faustino for her work on this book and the last, and to our editor Lauren Bittrich, whose great effort and guidance always kept us on track. Thanks to my agent, Lisa Grubka, for her advice and consultation throughout the project. Thanks to Laura Hanafin for her work on images and visuals, and thanks to so many others at Flatiron, in every department, who have worked so hard on this book and will continue to do so. It's an incredible team.

As always, Brad and I owe a debt of gratitude to the many great institutions that make our research possible. On this project the staff and resources of the New York Public Library, the National Archives and Records Administration, and the Library of Congress were especially valuable. More broadly we'd like to thank the unsung heroes at historical societies and local libraries all over the country who work so hard to preserve and help us better understand the past.

My greatest thanks are for family and loved ones who offered such support through the past year. Thank you to my mother, Elizabeth Mensch, for so much encouragement and feedback. Thanks to my father, Steven Mensch, and to Greg Patnaude, for always being there. Thanks to my five brothers: Jonathan Mensch, Jacob Mensch, Joseph Mensch, James Freeman, and Jeremy Freeman. Thank you to Pamela Mensch for her advice and consultation. Thank you to my beautiful nieces Libby Mensch and Claire Mensch. Thank you to Mary Ellen Smith for helping us so much. Thank you to the Acunto family: John, Anna, John Andrew, Kara, London, Mila, and August. Thank you to Lynn James, Daeon James, and Denae James for being in our lives.

Above all, thank you to my wife, Mary Robertson, and our children, Malcolm and Maxine. My love is infinite.

Credits

Page 145   Alabama secession headline. Copyright © Alabama Department of Archives and History.

Page 157   Postcard of Barnum's Hotel. Copyright © Barnum's City Hotel. Lithograph by E. Sachse & Co. circa 1850. Hambleton Print Collection. Special Collections Department, Maryland Historical Society.

Page 163   Lincoln's route to Washington from Harrisburg, Pennsylvania, through Philadelphia to Baltimore and finally arriving in Washington, D.C. Route illustration copyright © LHInc. Detail based on G. W. & C. B. Colton & Co and Norfolk, Wilmington and Charleston Railroad. Library of Congress, Geography and Map Division.

Page 202   Great Western Railroad time card for a special train, Monday, February 11, 1861. Copyright © Brady-Handy photograph collection, Library of Congress, Prints and Photographs Division.

Page 217   Robert Todd Lincoln circa 1860. Copyright © Brady-Handy photograph collection, Library of Congress, Prints and Photographs Division.

Page 290   President-elect Abraham Lincoln raising a flag at Independence Hall, Philadelphia. Copyright © F. De B. Richards, Library of Congress, Prints and Photographs Division.

Page 323   Inauguration of Mr. Lincoln, March 4, 1861. Copyright © Library of Congress, Prints and Photographs Division.

Page 339   Antietam, Maryland. Allan Pinkerton, President Lincoln, and Maj. Gen. John A. McClernand; another view. October 3, 1862, photograph from the main eastern theater of the war, Battle of Antietam, September–October 1862 © Alexander Gardner, 1821–1882, photographer. Civil War photographs, 1861–1865, Library of Congress, Prints and Photographs Division.

Page 345   Cypriano Ferrandini. Copyright © *The Baltimore Sun* archive photograph/Tribune News Service via Getty Images.

Notes

Abbreviations Used

AL   Abraham Lincoln

ALPLC   *Abraham Lincoln Papers.* Library of Congress, Manuscript Division. Series 1. General Correspondence, 1833–1916. Washington, D.C.: American Memory Project, 2000.

CWAL   Roy P. Basler, et al., eds., *The Collected Works of Abraham Lincoln.* 9 vols. (New Brunswick: Rutgers University Press, 1953).

LBP   Norma Cuthbert, ed., *Lincoln and the Baltimore Plot, 1861: From Pinkerton Records and Related Papers.* (San Marino: The Huntington Library, 1949).

Epigraph

x   *"If they kill me, I shall never die another death":* Hannah Armstrong, 1846, recollection of conversation with AL in February 1861. As compiled in Don E. Fehrenbacher and Virginia Fehrenbacher, eds., *Recollected Words of Abraham Lincoln* (Stanford: Stanford University Press, 1996), 17.

Prologue

1   *In the northeastern . . . darkness:* Based on the train's departure time of 11:00 p.m. from Philadelphia, the train would be crossing northeastern Maryland at approximately 1:00 a.m., well after dark.

1   *By appearances . . . brother:* In some accounts, the fourth passenger is an "invalid friend" rather than "invalid brother." The description of the passenger as "invalid brother" is from Allan Pinkerton, *The Spy of the Rebellion: Being a True History of the Spy System of the United States Army During the Late Rebellion* (New York: G. W. Carleton & Co., 1886), 93. The description as "invalid friend" is in George R. Dunn to Allan Pinkerton, November 7, 1867, in Pinkerton, *History and Evidence of the Passage of Abraham Lincoln from Harrisburg, Pa. to Washington, D.C. on the 22d and 23d of February, 1861* (privately printed, 1868), 35–36.

1   *Before its departure . . . strict secrecy:* The box was sent on board by Samuel Felton, president of the Philadelphia, Wilmington and Baltimore Railroad.

His full account is in William Schouler, *A History of Massachusetts in the Civil War* (Boston: E. P. Dutton & Co., 1868), 1:63–64.

2 *One of the men . . . bowie knives:* The man carrying weapons is Ward Hill Lamon. Evidence of his weaponry is described in Allan Pinkerton, report on February 22, 1861, *LBP,* 79.

2 *The name on her ticket . . . secret mission:* Pinkerton agent Kate Warne's multiple aliases are described in *LBP,* 21.

2 *his low felt hat . . . could see it:* Description of wardrobe from *LBP,* xv–xvi.

2 *he cannot stretch out his legs:* Kate Warne report, February 22, 1861, *LBP*, 81.

4 *From this moment . . . matter of hours:* The plot is set to trigger at roughly 12:15 p.m. on February 23, 1861, shortly after Lincoln's planned arrival in Baltimore's Calvert Street Station. This would be approximately twelve hours from the moment on the train depicted in this chapter.

Chapter 1

7 *In an isolated . . . cold:* For a full description of geography and topography of the Little Pigeon Creek region in southwest Indiana, see Michael Burlingame, *Abraham Lincoln: A Life* (unedited manuscript), 1:80–83, https://www.knox.edu/about-knox/lincoln-studies-center/burlingame -abraham-lincoln-a-life. All subsequent references to this title are to this unedited manuscript edition.

7 *Although only eighteen . . . tall frame:* David Herbert Donald, *Lincoln* (New York: Simon & Schuster, 1995), 33. If Lincoln was six foot two and 160 pounds at age sixteen, he would presumably be slightly taller and heavier at age eighteen.

7 *His long arms . . . a long swinging ax:* Lincoln would later write in an autobiographical sketch that as a youth he "had an axe put into his hands at once; and that from that till within his twenty-third year, he was almost constantly handling that most useful instrument." *CWAL,* 4:62.

8 *Nine years earlier . . . a disease:* Lincoln's mother, Nancy Lincoln, died of the "milk sickness" on October 5, 1818. Burlingame, *Abraham Lincoln,* 1:88–89.

8 *When their father . . . "ragged & dirty":* Dennis Hanks, interview with William Henry Herndon, June 13, 1865. Compiled in Douglas L. Wilson and Rodney O. Davis, eds., *Herndon's Informants: Letters, Interviews, and Statements About Abraham Lincoln* (Chicago: University of Illinois Press, 1998), 41.

8 *It was only after . . . "looked more human":* Ibid.

8 *A relative would later recall . . . "his mother":* Sarah Lincoln's brother-in-law Raymond Grigsby, as quoted in Burlingame, *The Inner World of Abraham Lincoln* (Urbana: University of Chicago Press, 1994), 95.

8 *"They were close companions and were a great deal alike":* John W. Lamar, quoted in Jonathan T. Hobson, ed., *Footprints of Abraham Lincoln: Presenting Facts, Reminiscences, and Illustrations Never Before Published* (Dayton, OH: Otterbein Press, 1909), 24.

8 *"kind, tender, and good natured" young woman:* John Hanks interviews with William Henry Herndon, 1865–66. Wilson and Davis, *Herndon's Informants,* 456.

8 *"sat down on a log . . . fingers":* Redmond Grigsby in the *Evansville Journal-News,* October 1, 1902. Quoted in Burlingame, *Lincoln,* 1:159.

9 *"from then on he was alone in the world you might say":* John W. Lamar quoted in Hobson, *Footprints,* 24.

9 *"those present turned away in pity and left him to his grief":* Grigsby, *Evansville Journal-News.* Quoted in Burlingame, *Lincoln,* 1:159.

Chapter 2

10 *The speech . . . public distribution:* Sumner's speech would be published in book form as *The Crime Against Kansas: Speech of Hon. Charles Sumner in the Senate of the United States* (Boston: John P. Jewett & Co., 1856).

11 *He intended his speech . . . "Against Kansas":* Ibid.

11 *"Can't you manage to get her out?":* Quoted in Joanne Freeman, *The Field of Blood: Violence in Congress and the Road to Civil War* (New York: Farrar, Straus and Giroux, 2018), 220.

12 *"Mr. Sumner . . . punish you for it":* Ibid., 220–21. Brooks's statement is quoted according to his own memory. Sumner has a slightly different recollection of Brooks's statement, although the meaning is essentially the same. For discussion of the differences see Donald, *Charles Sumner,* 363, n33.

12 *Sumner . . . head and face:* These and other physical details of the incident from Freeman, *The Field of Blood,* 220–21; Donald, *Charles Sumner,* 246–48; and Manisha Sinha, "The Caning of Charles Sumner: Slavery Race, and Ideology in the Age of the Civil War," *Journal of the Early Republic* 21 (2003).

12 *"Don't kill him!":* United States Congress, *Congressional Globe,* June 11, 1856 (Washington: Blair & Rives, 1834–73).

12 *Finally . . . even thirty blows:* Brooks later said that he delivered to Sumner "about 30 first rate stripes." Donald, *Charles Sumner,* 247.

Chapter 3

13 *In fact . . . knives or guns:* For a thorough survey of the history of violence in the halls of Congress in the decades prior to the Civil War, see Freeman, *Field of Blood.*

13 *There were close to . . . the population:* The first United States Census was not conducted until 1790, and population estimates during the colonial period were inexact. The figures indicated are extrapolated from prominent pre-1790 population studies here cited by the U.S. Census Bureau: https://www2.census.gov/prod2/decennial/documents/00165897ch01.pdf, 8.

14 *By the mid-1850s . . . the United States:* This figure is extrapolated from U.S. Census numbers indicating approximately 3.2 million slaves in 1850

and applying a metric of population increase consistent with the contemporaneous rate: https://www2.census.gov/library/publications/decennial/1850/1850a/1850a-02.pdf?#.

14 *"persuaded by arguments . . . two billion dollars?":* Quoted in Douglas R. Egerton, *Year of Meteors: Stephen Douglas, Abraham Lincoln, and the Election that Brought on the Civil War* (New York: Bloomsbury Press, 2010), 37.

15 *"that domestic institution of the South . . . and State policy":* Senator Clement C. Clay Jr., quoted in *American Annual Cyclopedia and Register of Important Events of the Year 1861* (New York: D. Appleton, 1930), 2:306.

15 *The negro . . . religion and civilization:* T. W. MacMahon, *Cause and Contrast: An Essay on the American Crisis* (Richmond, VA: West & Johnston, 1862), ix–x.

15 *"Never before . . . morally and intellectually":* Senator John C. Calhoun, speech to the United States Senate, February 6, 1837. *The Works of John C. Calhoun,* 2 vols. (New York: D. Appleton & Co., 1883), 2:630.

16 *Some Northern whites . . . goods:* See, for example, Anne Farrow, Joel Lang, and Jenifer Frank, *Complicity: How the North Promoted, Prolonged, and Profited from Slavery* (New York: Ballantine Books, 2005), xxv–xxvii.

16 *"there is not a . . . slavery":* Ohio Representative Edward Wade speech before House of Representatives, August 2, 1856. Quoted in Hinton Rowan Helper, *Compendium of the Impending Crisis of the South* (New York: A. B. Burdick, 1860), 147.

16 *"monstrous wrong":* Theodore Parker, quoted in Frances Power Cobbe, ed., *The Collected Works of Theodore Parker,* vol. 5, *Discourses on Slavery* (London: Trubner & Co., 1863), 80.

16 *"a great evil":* Ibid., 5:18.

17 *"an irrepressible conflict . . . nation":* William H. Seward, "Irrepressible Conflict" (speech, Rochester, NY, October 25, 1858) in George E. Baker, ed., *The Works of William H. Seward* (New York: Redfield, 1853–84), 4:292–93.

17 *In 1856 there were thirty-one . . . slave:* For map and population figures of free and slave states, see Rogers, Henry D. *General Map of the United States, Showing the Area and Extent of the Free & Slave-Holding States, and the Territories of the Union: Also the Boundary of the Seceding States.* (London: E. Stanford; Edinburgh: W. & A.K. Johnston, 1857), https://www.loc.gov/item/97682063/.

17 *The spread of slavery . . . colleague:* Sumner, *Crime Against Kansas.*

18 *Many argued that the attack was "barbarous":* "The Sumner Case," *The Living Age,* 2nd series, vol. 14 (1856), 376.

18 *"an outrage":* Ibid.

18 *"the hellish malignity of the spirit which sustains slavery":* Quoted in Sinha, "The Caning," *Journal of the Early Republic* 21 (2003), 246.

18 *A glorious deed! . . . a stick: Richmond Whig* (1856), n.d. Quoted in *The Suppressed Book About Slavery* (New York: Carleton, 1864), 368.

18 *"are begged for as sacred relics":* Preston Brooks, "Statement of Preston Brooks," May 28, 1856. Preston Smith Brooks Papers.

18 *A House committee . . . guilty of the assault:* See U.S. House of Representatives Report 182, 34th Congress, 1st Session: Select Committee Report, Alleged Assault upon Senator Sumner (Washington, D.C.: Government Printing Office, 1855–56), 1–5.

18 *A few months later, he ran . . . and won easily:* Freeman, *The Field of Blood*, 230–31.

19 *"So far as I know . . . bowie knife":* Senator Hammond to Francis Lieber, April 19, 1860, in Thomas Perry, ed., *The Life and Letters of Francis Lieber* (Boston: James R. Osgood & Co., 1882), 310.

Chapter 4

21 *"the most interesting political battleground in the Union":* "Senator Douglas at Chicago," *The New York Times,* July 13, 1858.

21 *Close to ten thousand out-of-town visitors:* Donald, *Lincoln,* 215.

21 *Indeed, in a demographic sense . . . Philadelphia:* To give a sense of party demographics at the time, in the 1856 Presidential election, the Republican candidate, John C. Fremont, won eleven states entirely in New England and the upper Midwest; the southernmost state Fremont carried was Ohio. The Democratic candidate, James Buchanan, won the Presidency by sweeping the South and every slave-owning border state. Source: https://www.270towin.com/1856_Election/.

21 *The party arose as a fusion . . . territories:* The formation and rise of the Republican Party in the 1850s is of course a much more complex subject beyond the scope of our story. Many books have been written on this; one recent treatment of the subject is included in Heather Cox Richardson, *To Make Men Free: A History of the Republican Party* (New York: Basic Books, 2014).

22 *"the town resembled a vast smokehouse":* *Chicago Press and Tribune,* August 23, 1858.

22 *"rough and tumble skirmish":* Reporter Horace White, quoted in William Herndon and Jesse Weik, *Abraham Lincoln: The True Story of a Great Life,* 2 vols. (New York: D. Appleton & Co., 1888), 2:105.

22 *"constant roar":* *Daily Illinois State Register,* August 24, 1856.

22 *When the candidates' entourages . . . collapses:* Donald, *Lincoln,* 216.

22 *"He had a lean, lank, indescribably gawky figure":* Henry Villard, *Memoirs of Henry Villard: Journalist and Financier, 1835–1900* (Boston: Houghton, Mifflin, and Co., 1904), 1:93.

22 *"ungainly body":* Carl Schurz, *The Reminiscences of Carl Schurz,* 3 vols. (New York: McClure, 1907–08), 2:90–91. Schurz's comments here and below were made in relation to Lincoln's appearance at a later debate in the schedule. Because the comments reflect the writer's first impressions of Lincoln in a nearly identical setting only a few weeks later, we include them here.

22 *"odd-featured, wrinkled, inexpressive, and altogether uncomely face":* Villard, *Memoirs,* 1:93.

23 *"a rusty black coat with sleeves that should have been longer"*: Schurz, *Reminiscences*, 2:91.

23 *"permitted a very full view of his large feet"*: Ibid.

23 *"several public men . . . grotesque, as Lincoln's"*: Ibid.

23 *"more liquor than all the boys of the town together"*: AL, first debate with Stephen A. Douglas at Ottawa, Illinois, August 21, 1858. *CWAL*, 3:6.

23 *Although false . . . relentless attack*: Charles W. Marsh, *Recollections, 1837–1910* (Chicago: Farm Implement News Co., 1910), 74.

23 *"springing panther"*: Congressman William Cullen, undated statement, Ida M. Tarbell Papers, Allegheny College, Meadville, PA.

23 *"raved like a mad bull"*: *Ottawa Republican*, August 28, 1858.

23 *"he ranted, he bellowed . . . domineered"*: *Chicago Press and Tribune*, August 26, 1858.

24 *"I believe it was made . . . inferior races"*: *CWAL*, 3:9.

24 *"I do not question . . ." [cheers]*: Ibid., 3:10.

25 *"roused the existing . . . to the highest pitch"*: Gustave Koerner, *Memoirs of Gustave Koerner*, 2 vols. (Cedar Rapids, IA: Torch Press, 1909), 2:63.

25 *"If you desire negro citizenship . . . Republicans!"*: *CWAL*, 3:10.

25 *"His gestures were . . . in a very ungraceful manner"*: Charles Schurz, quoted in Ronald C. White Jr., *A. Lincoln: A Biography* (New York: Random House, 2009), 282. See notes above regarding the date of Schurz's observations.

25 *"He used singularly awkward, almost absurd . . . his arguments"*: Henry Villard, quoted in White, *A. Lincoln*, 266.

25 *"so clear and distinct that every word . . . pleasant to listen to"*: *New-York Tribune* (semiweekly ed.), October 26, 1858. This comment refers to Lincoln's performance in the seventh debate in the series, on October 15, 1858, in Alton, Illinois.

25 *"When a man hears himself misrepresented . . . it is more apt to amuse him"*: *CWAL*, 3:13.

25 *"a specious and fantastic arrangement of words . . . chestnut horse"*: Ibid., 3:16.

26 *"This . . . zeal for the spread of slavery . . . injustice of slavery itself"*: Ibid., 3:14.

26 *"I hate it because it deprives our . . . civil liberty"*: Ibid.

26 *"rang out in clearness and . . . inspiring eloquence and argument"*: Jeriah Bonham, "Recollections of Abraham Lincoln," *Chicago Tribune*, May 12, 1895.

26 *"I hold that . . . entitled to these as the white man"*: *CWAL*, 3:16.

26 *"in the right to eat the bread . . . equal of every living man"*: Ibid.

26 *"go back to the era of our Independence . . . annual joyous return"*: Ibid., 3:29. Here Lincoln loosely quotes one of his idols, the late Kentucky Senator Henry Clay Sr.

26 *"blow out the moral lights . . . perpetuate slavery in this country!"*: Ibid.

27 *"Don't, boys! Let me down!"*: Ida M. Tarbell, *The Life of Abraham Lincoln* (New York: S. S. McClure Co., 1895), 1:312.

27 *"I'll get even with you, you rascal!"*: Richard Hughes, undated statement, Tarbell Papers.

27 *"magnetized the big crowd by his audacity and supreme self-confidence"*: Koerner, *Memoirs*, 2:63.

27 *"impressed his audiences by . . . his appeals to their higher nature"*: Ibid.

27 *"I must confess that long Abe's . . . magnetic influence"*: *New York Evening Post*, August 27, 1858.

27 *"All Men Are Created Equal . . . No Nigger Equality"*: Language of banners from White, *A. Lincoln*, 269.

27 *Before the campaign ends, both men will log:* During the campaign, Douglas traveled a total of 5,227 miles and Lincoln a total of 4,350 miles. See Donald, *Lincoln*, 214.

Chapter 5

29 *The man is of medium height . . . with a close-trimmed beard:* See photograph on page 30 for the standard version of Pinkerton's beard. On some occasions he wore the beard without mustache, perhaps as a means of disguise.

29 *For the past few years . . . America's first private detective:* Some may argue that other persons or entities in the country preceded Pinkerton in offering private policing or security services. However, there is no record of these other entities engaging in the investigative "detective"-like work that Pinkerton pioneered, and certainly not at the level at which he practiced. At best, the matter may be debated as one of semantics. In any case, no other practitioner in the era comes anywhere remotely close to Pinkerton in success achieved or notoriety received. For more on this question of whether Pinkerton was truly the first, see John Mackay, *Allan Pinkerton: The First Private Eye* (New York: John Wiley & Sons, 1997), 71–72.

31 *In fact, recently he's been working one of his biggest . . . now on the run:* The forger's name is Jules Imbert. Pinkerton will later chronicle the details of the case in a perhaps exaggerated fashion under the title "The Frenchman: or, the Bills of Exchange" in his book *Claude Melnotte as a Detective, and Other Stories* (Chicago, W. B. Keen, Cooke & Co., 1875), 235–82.

31 *Pinkerton looks up from his files:* The details and general depiction of Pinkerton meeting Warne are as later described by Pinkerton in Allan Pinkerton, *The Expressman and the Detective* (Chicago: W. B. Keen, Cooke & Co., 1874), 94–95.

31 *"It was not the custom to employ woman detectives":* Quoted in Chris Enss, *The Pinks: The First Women Detectives, Operatives, and Spies with the Pinkerton Detective Agency* (Guilford, CT: TwoDot, 2017), 38.

31 *It will be another thirty-five years . . . woman investigator or police officer:* The first woman police officer was probably Marie Owens, hired by the Chicago Police Department in 1891. See, for example, Colleen Mastony, "Was Chicago Home to the Country's First Female Cop?" *Chicago Tribune*, September 1, 2010.

31 *She says her name is Kate Warne. Twenty-six years old:* Warne was born in 1830, according to the March 21, 1868, edition of the *Philadelphia Press*.

31 *"Women," she explains, "could be most . . . gain access":* Pinkerton, *Express-man,* 95.

32 *"men become braggarts . . . women . . . and are excellent observers":* As quoted in the Pinkerton Government Services website: https://web.archive.org /web/20061015194719/http://www.pinkertons.com/webster.htm.

32 *"graceful in movement . . . select her as a confidante":* Pinkerton, *Express-man,* 94.

32 *"she had evidently given . . . of service":* Ibid, 95.

32 *She agrees, saying she'll return the next day to hear his answer:* Ibid.

Chapter 6

33 *Today, over a century and a half later, it's still difficult to tell what exactly transpired . . . something like this:* The description and details of this scene are from Allan Pinkerton's account of it twenty-five years later in Pinkerton, *The Spy of the Rebellion,* 76–79. Pinkerton's memoir is the only source for this meeting. Presumably, Pinkerton's account is based upon undercover agent Harry Davies's firsthand description of it to him. However, Harry Davies makes no mention of the event in his field reports at the time. The lack of supporting evidence makes the veracity of the scene, as Pinkerton describes it, difficult to verify. See endnotes for chapter 60 for a more detailed discussion of the credibility of Pinkerton's account.

33 *Tonight, heavy curtains . . . moonlight:* Pinkerton, *The Spy of the Rebellion,* 76.

33 *Earlier in the night, one . . . a special ceremony:* Ibid., 77.

34 *"Southern ideals":* This language is Ferrandini's as heard by Pinkerton four days earlier. From Allan Pinkerton, report on February 15, 1861, in *LBP,* 37.

34 *"enemies of the South":* Pinkerton, *The Spy of the Rebellion,* 79.

34 *"the glory that awaited . . . great occasion":* Ibid.

34 *"Everyone was pledged to . . . the ballot he drew":* Ibid., 78.

34 *He is a President of the North—an abolitionist, they believe:* Ibid. According to Pinkerton's description, at one point in the meeting Ferrandini specifically refers to Abraham Lincoln as an "abolitionist leader."

34 *Each of them will carry a firearm . . . honor of pulling the trigger:* Ibid., 77. As will be described in later chapters, the leaders of the group actually placed as many as eight red ballots in the box, as insurance should the chosen assassin lose courage. The members drawing ballots do not know this at the time, however. See ibid., 78–79.

Chapter 7

36 *Allan Pinkerton was born in Glasgow . . . 1819:* Mackay, *Allan Pinkerton,* 20.

36 *He grew up poor in a poor country . . . most notorious slums:* The neighborhood is called the Gorbals. For a description, see ibid., 15–17.

36 *At age twelve, he talked his way . . . commonly called a* cooper: Ibid., 28.

36 *"searching, cool blue-gray eyes . . . intense drive that animated him":* Quoted

in James D. Horan, *The Pinkertons: The Detective Dynasty That Made History* (New York: Crown Publishers, 1967), 6.

36 *At the age of eighteen, Pinkerton joined the coopers' union:* Mackay, 28.

36 *Inspired by the union, he also joined . . . the Chartists:* The "Chartist" movement derived its name from the so-called People's Charter, a platform devised by leaders of the organized labor movement in the 1830s. See "The Chartists," National Archives of the United Kingdom, https://www.nationalarchives.gov.uk/education/politics/g7/.

37 *"I had become an outlaw with a price on my head":* Allan Pinkerton to William Pinkerton, 1879 (exact date unknown).

37 *They settled in a small town in western . . . his own barrel-making shop:* Allan Pinkerton, *Professional Thieves and the Detective* (New York: G. W. Carleton & Co., 1880), 19.

37 *While scanning the banks . . . of a strange campsite:* Ibid., 24.

37 *A few nights later . . . arrested the strangers:* Ibid., 25.

38 *His renown had an . . . counterfeiting-related matter:* Ibid., 24.

38 *The proprietors believed . . . spreading fake bills in the area:* Ibid., 25.

38 *they wondered if Pinkerton . . . man's arrest:* Ibid., 52.

38 *"The country being new . . . detective skill":* Ibid., 54.

39 *Their new name? The North-Western Police Agency:* Mackay, *Allan Pinkerton,* 70.

39 *America's first private detective was born:* See note beginning *"For the past few years"* on page 377, regarding whether Pinkerton was truly the first private detective in the country.

39 *One night in 1853 while . . . point-blank range:* Shooting as reported in *The Daily Democratic Press,* September 1853.

Chapter 8

41 *Indeed, today's packed crowd . . . makeshift tent:* Some visual details of the convention are from White, *A. Lincoln,* 21.

42 *"I am informed that a distinguished citizen . . . seat on the stand":* Oglesby's announcement and description of his delivery from Ward Hill Lamon, *The Life of Abraham Lincoln: From His Birth to His Inauguration as President* (Boston: James R. Osgood & Co., 1872), 444.

42 *Then, finally, he makes the introduction: "Abraham Lincoln!":* Ibid.

42 *In the last two years, the issue of . . . speeches of his career:* Less than three months earlier, on February 27, 1860, Lincoln delivered his famous "Cooper Union Speech" at the Cooper Institute in New York, New York. AL Address at Cooper Institute, New York City, *CWAL,* 3:522–50.

43 *"kicking, scrambling—crawling—upon the sea of heads":* Wilson and Davis, eds., *Herndon's Informants,* 463.

43 *Once on the stage, he "rose bowing and blushing":* Ibid.

43 *In big printed letters, the banner reads:* New-York Tribune, May 22, 1860. Different sources contain variations of the exact wording on the banner, but the essential meaning is the same.

44 *"Identify your work!"*: Recollection of Richard Price Morgan, collected in *Abraham Lincoln, By Some Men Who Knew Him* (Bloomington, IN: Pantagraph Printing & Stationery Co., 1910), 90.

45 *"Where did you get the rails?"*: Ibid., 91. Other accounts vary on the exact language used here and in the following exchange between Lincoln and Hanks, but the basic content and meaning is similar across sources.

45 *"At the farm . . . black walnut"*: Ibid.

45 *"I can only say I have split . . . better-looking ones"*: Ibid., 92.

45 *"three more for 'Honest Abraham . . . next President'"*: Ibid.

45 *"in a moment there was a rush of delegates . . . sawed off for souvenirs"*: Ibid.

45 *"I think the Illinois delegation will . . . is preferred to me"*: AL to Richard M. Corwine, May 2, 1860, *CWAL*, 4:47.

46 *"Resolutions were unanimously . . . Illinois for the Presidency"*: "Illinois Republican Convention," *The New York Times*, May 11, 1860.

Chapter 9

47 *"short and simple annals of the poor"*: Lincoln used this phrase to describe his upbringing in a brief autobiographical essay he provided to the journalist John L. Scripps in 1860. As Lincoln indicated, he drew the phrase from the poem "Elegy Written in a Country Churchyard" (1750) by Thomas Gray.

47 *by some accounts would strike . . . if he didn't obey:* Several accounts of Thomas Lincoln hitting or beating his son are collected in Burlingame, *The Inner World of Abraham Lincoln*, 38–39.

47 *"He never did more . . . bunglingly sign his own name"*: AL, *Autobiography* written for John L. Scripps, June 1860, *CWAL*, 4:61.

48 *"Owing to my father . . . so little of our family history"*: AL to Solomon Lincoln, March 8, 1848, *CWAL*, 1:456.

48 *"angel Mother"*: Josiah G. Holland, *The Life of Abraham Lincoln* (Springfield, MA: Gurdon Bill, 1866), 23.

48 *"kind disposition"*: White, *A. Lincoln*, 18.

48 *During several weeks of clearing . . . every day and night:* Burlingame, *Abraham Lincoln*, 1:79–80.

49 *At one point during this chore . . . knocked him unconscious:* White, *A. Lincoln*, 28–29.

49 *He watched her fall ill . . . for the young boy:* Nancy Lincoln died from the "milk sickness" on October 5, 1818. Details from Burlingame, *Abraham Lincoln*, 1:88–89.

49 *It is with deep grief . . . make you some less miserable now:* AL to Fanny McCullough, December 23, 1862, *CWAL*, 6:16–17.

49 *"How he could chop! His ax . . . and down it would come"*: Quoted in Burlingame, *Abraham Lincoln*, 1:116–17.

50 *That moment, he vowed to never hunt large game again:* Details of hunting incident from White, *A. Lincoln*, 21.

50 *On another occasion . . . the defenseless animal:* Wayne Whipple, *The Heart of Abraham Lincoln* (Philadelphia: Biddle Press, 1909), 17.

50 *"No, it enjoys living just the same as we do!":* Charleston, Illinois, *Plaindealer,* February 1892, Abraham Lincoln Association reference files, Lincoln Presidential Library, Springfield, IL.

50 *"There now, my last hope is gone":* Story and quote from Wilson and Davis, eds., *Herndon's Informants,* 262.

50 *"Gentlemen, you may laugh . . . have rung in my ears":* Joshua Speed, *Reminiscences of Abraham Lincoln and Notes of a Visit to California* (Louisville: John P. Morton & Co., 1884), 26.

51 *"the aggregate of all his schooling did not amount to one year":* AL quoted in Doris Kearns Goodwin, *Team of Rivals: The Political Genius of Abraham Lincoln* (New York: Simon & Schuster, 2005), 51.

51 *"to write words . . . improved his capacity for writing":* Quoted in Burlingame, *Abraham Lincoln,* 1:122.

51 *"We had a broad wooden shovel . . . again and again":* Wilson and Davis, *Herndon's Informants,* 126.

51 *"When he worked for us he read . . . fire—read by it":* Ibid.

51 *"While other boys . . . thinking and reflecting":* Ibid.

52 *"on that account we used to think . . . that counted":* Quoted in Alonzo Hilton Davis, "Lincoln's Goose Nest Home," *Century Magazine,* September 1892, 798–99.

52 *He had read the Bible . . . poetry of Robert Burns:* Donald, *Lincoln,* 30–31.

52 *One of his favorites as a teenager was . . .* Life of George Washington*:* Burlingame, *Abraham Lincoln,* 1:125.

52 *He also studied . . .* History of the United States*:* Ibid.

53 *Then he said goodbye and struck out on his own:* Donald, *Lincoln,* 36–37.

Chapter 10

54 *That's how the poet Walt Whitman . . . United States of America:* The poem is "Year of Meteors," in Walt Whitman, *Leaves of Grass* (Boston: James R. Osgood & Co., 1881), 190–91.

54 *Back in the 1856 Presidential election . . . won comfortably:* Election map from 1856, https://www.270towin.com/1856_Election/.

54 *In 1857, the Court's infamous Dred Scott . . . "the United States":* Scott v. Sandford, 60 U.S. 393, at 404–05 (1857).

55 *In the 1858 midterms, the Democrats . . . upstart Republican Party:* See United States Senate, "The 1858 Midterm Elections," https://www.senate.gov/artandhistory/history/minute/The_1858_Midterm_Election.htm.

55 *This waffling infuriated hard-line . . . 1860 Presidential election drew near:* A thorough account of the split within the Democratic Party in 1860 is provided in Egerton, *Year of Meteors.*

55 *"The Democratic party is a proslavery party . . . leprosy of Abolitionism":* Quoted in Egerton, *Year of Meteors,* 42.

55 *The hostility extended beyond the floor . . . other across the room:* Ibid., 69.

56 *The second fight could be stopped only . . . for a duel:* Ibid.

56 *Soon, most of the delegates from Louisiana, . . . joined the walkout:* Ibid., 77.

56 *But compromise proved impossible, and . . . no agreed-upon nominee:* Egerton, *Year of Meteors,* 80–81.

Chapter 11

57 *"time and space would fail me . . . circulated through the cars":* The New York Times, May 18, 1860.

58 *"he was almost too much of a candidate to . . . stay home":* Leonard Swett, May 1860 recollection of conversation with Lincoln. Quoted in Fehrenbacher and Fehrenbacher, eds., *Recollected Words,* 440.

59 *Seizing an opportunity, Lincoln's campaign . . . duplicate tickets:* Goodwin, *Team of Rivals,* 247.

60 *"would be the most corrupt":* Senator James Dixon of Connecticut, quoted in Walter Stahr, *Seward: Lincoln's Indispensable Man* (New York: Simon & Schuster, 2012), 186.

61 *"something in his nature . . . simplicity of the rural populations":* Quoted in Egerton, *Year of Meteors,* 129.

61 *"I suppose I am not the first choice . . . first love":* AL to Samuel Galloway, March 24, 1860, CWAL, 4:34.

61 *A journalist covering the event . . . "resounded far and wide":* Quoted in Goodwin, *Team of Rivals,* 247.

Chapter 12

64 *"His long arms and long legs served . . . from every angle":* Quoted in Harold Holzer, *Lincoln and the Power of the Press: The War for Public Opinion* (New York: Simon & Schuster, 2014), 203.

64 *"Mr. Lincoln was not a good player . . . was too old":* Quote attributed to William Donnely, the caretaker of the makeshift court on which Lincoln and the others played. David Levinson and Karen Christenson, eds., *Encyclopedia of World Sport* (Oxford, UK: Oxford University Press, 1999), 164.

64 *"leaps, and strides to strike . . . in the extreme":* Rufus Rockwell Wilson, *Intimate Memories of Lincoln* (Elmira, NY: Primavera Press, 1945), 141.

64 *"as vigorously engaged in the sport . . . until nearly exhausted":* T. W. S. Kidd, "How Abraham Lincoln Received the News of his Nomination for President," *Journal of the Illinois State Historical Society* 15, no. 1–2 (1922): 508.

65 *When he first came to Springfield . . . glumly wrote to one of his friends:* AL to Mary Owens, May 7, 1837, CWAL, 1:78.

65 *During this time, he could . . . a law book with the other:* Donald, *Lincoln,* 159.

65 *"These children would take down . . . to wring their little necks," he groused:* William Herndon quoted in ibid., 160.

66 *"It is my pleasure that my children . . . a child to its parents":* Mary Todd

Lincoln, interview with William Herndon, September 1866. Wilson and Davis, eds., *Herndon's Informants*, 357.

66 *Then, just before noon, the editor . . . telegram from Chicago:* White, *A. Lincoln*, 326.

Chapter 13

68 *"We did it—Glory to God":* The telegram is from Nathan Knapp. White, *A. Lincoln*, 329.

68 *"Illinois, Indiana, and Ohio . . . acted like madmen":* The New York Times, May 21, 1860.

68 *"a peal of human voices, a grand chorus . . . shouted for joy":* John A. Andrews, speech on May 25, 1860, in Boston's Faneuil Hall. As reported in *Chicago Press and Tribune*, May 30, 1860.

68 *"Well, gentlemen, there is a little woman . . . dispatch than I am":* AL quoted in Donald, *Lincoln*, 251.

68 *"The hearty western populace . . . in the high west wind":* John Hay, as quoted in Goodwin, *Team of Rivals*, 253.

69 *"did not suppose the honor . . . representation of a great party":* AL on May 18, 1860, *CWAL*, 4:50.

69 *"The youngster who, with ragged trousers . . . the National Republican Party":* Joseph Howard, special dispatch to *The New York Times*, May 18, 1860.

Chapter 14

70 *There is a single, distinct knock . . . called an* 11: "Identification Rules for Knights of the Golden Circle," c.1854–63, Records of the Office of the Judge Advocate General (Army), 1792–2010, Record Group 153, National Archives at College Park, College Park, MD (online version available through the Archival Research Catalog [ARC Identifier 595496] at www.archives.gov).

70 *This is a 9:* Ibid.

70 *This is a 15:* Ibid.

71 *In Texas alone, there are . . . thirty castles:* See, for example, Randolph B. Campbell, "Knights of the Golden Circle," Texas State Historical Association, https://tshaonline.org/handbook/online/articles/vbk01, accessed January 2, 2020.

71 *many of them local residents from "respectable families":* Daily Ohio Statesman, March 30, 1860, quoting a report from "a Baltimore paper."

71 *At least one castle is known to exist:* David C. Keehn, *Knights of the Golden Circle: Secret Empire, Southern Secession, Civil War* (Baton Rouge: Louisiana State University Press, 2013), 28.

71 *Once an initiate becomes a Knight . . . a hierarchy of "Degrees":* A more detailed description of the KGC's "Orders" and "Degrees" is in Ibid., 10–11, 38–42.

71 *Recently . . . has surged:* KGC leader Virginius Groner boasted to Mississippi Governor John Pettus that by the fall of 1860 the group "now

numbered 120,000 members who are fully organized." Groner to Pettus, December 6, 1860, Mississippi Department of Archives and History. While this number is impossible to verify and is probably exaggerated, the statement suggests the swell of excitement and confidence within the KGC's ranks.

Chapter 15

73 *"The nomination of Mr. Lincoln . . . the Country by surprise":* Frederick Douglass, "The Nomination in Chicago," *Douglass' Monthly,* June 1860.

73 *Douglass was born into slavery . . . east of the Chesapeake Bay:* Details of Douglass's early life from Frederick Douglass, *Narrative of the Life of Frederick Douglass, an American Slave* (Boston: Anti-Slavery Office, 1849), 1–3.

74 *She died when he was seven . . . illness, death, or burial:* Ibid., 3.

75 *I have often been awakened at the dawn . . . blood-clotted cowskin:* Ibid., 6.

75 *"the blood-stained gate, the entrance . . . I was about to pass":* Ibid.

75 *"A nigger should know nothing . . . spoil the best nigger in the world":* Ibid., 33.

75 *"I distinctly remember being, even then . . . silence or extinguish":* Frederick Douglass, *My Bondage and My Freedom* (New York: Miller, Orton & Mulligan, 1855), 91.

76 *"I often found myself . . . should have been killed":* Douglass, *Narrative,* 41.

76 *"Many persons in the audience . . . utterly at a loss to devise":* From Garrison's *The Liberator,* quoted in Philip S. Foner, ed., *The Life and Writings of Frederick Douglass,* vol. 1 (New York: International Publishers, 1950), 59.

77 *"it enabled me to participate in . . . witnessed in the United States":* Frederick Douglass, *Life and Times of Frederick Douglass* (Hartford, CT: Park Publishing Co., 1881), 254.

77 *"Mr. Lincoln is a man of unblemished . . . in political life":* Douglass, "The Nomination in Chicago," *Douglass' Monthly,* June 1860.

77 *"The language is, 'We the People' . . . was ordained and established":* Frederick Douglass, "The Constitution, the Union, and Slavery," *The Liberator,* June 8, 1849.

78 *"forever forbid the two races living together":* AL, fourth debate with Stephen Douglas, September 18, 1858. *CWAL,* 3:145–146.

78 *"slow process of a cautious siege" rather . . . "a storming party":* Douglass, "The Nomination in Chicago."

78 *"it is to be regretted that they . . . million slaves at a single blow":* Ibid.

78 *No recent American President has made this declaration:* At the time, the most recent American President to hold antislavery views was John Quincy Adams, who served the office from 1825 to 1829. The issue of slavery did not play a major role in his Presidency, but in his later career in Congress he was a strong antislavery advocate. Adams's congressional rival Henry A. Wise once referred to him as "the acutest, the astutest, the archest enemy of southern slavery that ever existed." Gary V. Wood, *Heir to the Fathers: John Quincy Adams and the Spirit of Constitutional Government* (Lanham, MD: Lexington Books, 2004), 159.

Chapter 16

79 *"Lincoln is the leanest, lankest . . . ugly," one Democratic paper writes:* Goodwin, *Team of Rivals,* 258.

79 *"without a respectable education . . . conduct of a gentleman":* T. W. MacMahon, *Cause and Contrast: An Essay on the American Crisis* (Richmond, VA: West & Johnston, 1862), 127–28.

79 *Democratic newspaper describes him as a "third-rate Western lawyer":* Manchester Union Democrat, n.d., 1860.

79 *"fourth-rate lecturer":* The New York Herald, May 19, 1860.

79 *"shed bitter tears":* Quoted in Egerton, *Year of Meteors,* 14.

80 *"a great portion of the East . . . dissatisfied at his nomination":* Leonard Swett, quoted in Herndon and Weik, *Abraham Lincoln,* 240.

80 *When the door opens, the men are further irritated . . . by two scruffy "ragamuffins":* Roland W. Diller's recollections, in Paul Hull, "Lincoln in Springfield," *New York Mail and Express,* February 8, 1896, 15.

80 *"Mr. Lincoln received us in the parlor . . . bare-looking room":* Schurz, *Reminiscences,* 187–88.

80 *"There he stood . . . in his haggard face":* Ibid., 188.

80 *"dignified little speech" in which . . . "doubts of his own abilities":* Ibid.

80 *"Most of the members of the Committee . . . picture it in their imagination":* Ibid.

81 *"I beat you. I am six feet four without my high-heeled boots":* C. C. Coffin, in Allen Thorndike Rice, ed., *Reminiscences of Abraham Lincoln by Distinguished Men of His Time* (New York: North American Review, 1888), 169–70.

81 *"I am glad that we have found a candidate . . . we can look up to":* Ibid.

81 *"Then followed some informal talk . . . Lincoln's nature shone out":* Schurz, *Reminiscences,* 2:188.

81 *"An undertone of resignation and . . . contact with the great world":* Ibid., 188–89.

82 *"You fellows knew at Chicago . . . given us a rail splitter":* Statement is from an unnamed Republican supporter, as later recalled by Addison G. Proctor in *Lincoln and the Convention of 1860* (Chicago: Chicago Historical Society, 1918), 16.

Chapter 17

83 *With a population of more than two hundred thousand . . . south of Pennsylvania:* U.S. Bureau of the Census, "Population of the 100 Largest Urban Places: 1860," https://www.census.gov/population/www/documentation/twps0027/tab09.txt.

83 *A city directory from the era . . . "Silversmiths" and "soap":* From Scott Shane, "The Secret History of City Slave Trade . . . 1880," *The Baltimore Sun,* June 20, 1999.

84 *This barber, in his late thirties . . . Cypriano Ferrandini:* The spelling of Cypriano Ferrandini's name sometimes varies in contemporaneous sources. His first name is occasionally spelled "Cipriani," and his last name as

"Ferrandina." When quoting different sources, we always standardize to the correct spelling "Cypriano Ferrandini."

84 *After immigrating to the United States . . . two decades in Maryland:* According to Ferrandini's later testimony before a special committee of the House of Representatives, he had lived in the city of Baltimore for sixteen years. *Report of the Select Committee of Five,* 36th Congress, 2d Session, Report No. 79 (Washington, D.C.: Government Printing Office, 1861), 132.

84 *He has been the barber . . . a dozen years:* Ferrandini posted an August 5, 1848, help wanted ad in *The Baltimore Sun,* seeking a hairdresser to assist him at Barnum's City Hotel. It is unknown for how long he was employed at the hotel barbershop before posting this ad.

85 *He's a member of the Knights of the Golden Circle:* Ferrandini's membership in the Knights of the Golden Circle is explored at some length in David C. Keehn, *Knights,* starting page 29.

85 *The Knights of the Golden Circle was . . . named George Bickley:* Keehn, *Knights,* 15.

86 *Drawing inspiration from earlier movements . . . other southern territories:* Keehn, *Knights,* 9–11.

86 *According to newspaper estimates . . . forty thousand:* The New Orleans *Courier* on March 6, 1860, estimates the KGC's membership at over 30,000. In a public address in May of the same year, KGC leader George Bickley claims the number is 48,000. See "KGC . . . The Following Pages Are Addressed to the Citizens of the Southern States by Order of the Convention of KGC Held at Raleigh, N.C., May 7–11th, 1860," Library of Congress, https://www.loc.gov/item/rbpe.1350100a/.

86 *Ferrandini joined the KGC in the summer of 1859:* Keehn, *Knights,* 262 n4.

86 *Not much is known about his specific role . . . into that country:* Ferrandini refers to his trip to Mexico in *Report of the Select Committee,* 132.

Chapter 18

88 *"The institution of human bondage . . . spared in behalf of the slave":* Pinkerton, *The Spy of the Rebellion,* 25–26.

89 *In no time . . . the Underground Railroad:* As described in Lloyd Lewis, "Lincoln and Pinkerton," *Journal of the Illinois State Historical Society* 41, no. 4 (December 1948), 374–75.

89 *"I have assisted in security and freedom . . . act was to be performed":* Ibid., 26.

89 *He opened it to find the legendary radical . . . through three states:* Incident as described in Mackay, *Allan Pinkerton,* 83–84.

90 *"was my bosom friend . . . striving for his liberty":* Pinkerton, *The Spy of the Rebellion,* 26.

90 *"While Pinkerton's right hand caught lawbreakers, his left hand broke the law":* Lewis, *Lincoln and Pinkerton,* 376.

90 *"I have not a single regret for the course I then pursued":* Pinkerton, *The Spy of the Rebellion,* 26.

90 *A year earlier, in 1859 . . . railroad-based delivery service:* Pinkerton provides a full chronicle of the case, as described below, in Pinkerton, *The Expressman.*

92 *"succeeded far beyond my utmost expectations":* Ibid., 95.

92 *Naturally, he put Kate Warne in charge of it:* Mackay, *Allan Pinkerton,* 74.

Chapter 19

94 *His small law office is immediately . . . a few blocks away:* Donald, *Lincoln,* 252.

95 *"good-looking whether the original would justify it or not":* Nicolay to Therena Bates, Springfield, August 26, 1860. Michael Burlingame, ed., *With Lincoln in the White House: Letters, Memoranda, and Other Writings of John G. Nicolay* (Carbondale: Southern Illinois University Press, 2000), 5.

95 *"a very fair representation of my homely face":* Donald, *Lincoln,* 252.

95 *"so much good sense, such intuitive . . . favorably with his fitness":* Barnes, *Life of Thurlow Weed, Volume I: Autobiography of Thurlow Weed* (New York: Da Capo Press, 1970), 603.

95 *"commenced talking about political affairs . . . Oneida County than I [was]":* Goodwin, *Team of Rivals,* 264.

95 *When the candidate makes a rare . . . horse to make his escape:* Donald, *Lincoln,* 254.

96 *He is "coarse, vulgar, and uneducated":* New Bern (North Carolina) *Weekly Progress,* May 29, 1860.

96 *"weak and unfit man for so high a place":* The *New York Herald,* May 19, 1860.

96 *"an illiterate partisan . . . predilections for negro equality":* Richmond *Enquirer,* May 22, 1860.

96 *"extreme abolitionist of the revolutionary type":* Chicago *Herald,* May 21, 1860.

96 *"to sink the proud Anglo-Saxon . . . lowest races of mankind":* Richmond *Enquirer,* August 17, 1860.

96 *"we shall have the nigger . . . in the legislature":* Illinois *State Register,* August 22, 1860.

96 *"ate nigger—they drank nigger . . . they saw a nigger in the fence":* John Cochrane, speech in New York, October 8, The *New York Times,* October 8, 1860.

97 *"As soon as Lincoln is installed . . . torch and steel":* Corsicana (Texas) *Navarro Express,* June 2, 1860.

97 *"Let the North . . . we must not submit":* Montgomery *Weekly Mail,* October 26, 1860.

Chapter 20

98 *"whatever sluggish spirits there might be among the populace":* Quoted in Goodwin, *Team of Rivals,* 276.

98 *"was chatting with three or four friends . . . started on a picnic":* Samuel R. Weed, "Hearing the Returns with Mr. Lincoln," The *New York Times Magazine,* February 14, 1932.

99 *"welcomed him with immense . . . up stairs into the Court room":* Quoted in Goodwin, *Team of Rivals,* 276.

99   *"one would have concluded that the District Attorneyship . . . than the Presidency"*: Weed, *The New York Times Magazine*, February 14, 1932.

100   *"Uncle Abe, you're the next President, and I know it"*: Lyman Trumbull, quoted in Goodwin, *Team of Rivals*, 277.

100   *"The excitement . . . was upon me"*: Gideon Welles to Isaac N. Arnold, November 27, 1872. Quoted in Goodwin, *Team of Rivals*, 279.

100   *"Looking in that glass," . . . "from the tip of the other"*: Lincoln, conversation with Noah Brooks, as later recollected by Brooks. Brooks's recollection is as quoted in Tarbell, *The Life*, 1:199.

100   *"one of the faces was a little paler . . . than the other"*: Ibid.

100   *"the illusion vanished"*: Ibid.

100   *but when he lies on the lounge . . . "mocking its healthy and hopeful fellow"*: Ward Hill Lamon, *Recollections of Abraham Lincoln, 1847–1865*, ed. Dorothy Lamon (Chicago: A. C. McClurg and Co., 1895), 111–13.

101   *But sometimes, especially in darker hours . . . superstitions of his youth*: Burlingame, *Lincoln* 1:84.

101   *Here, tonight, this strange, pale double . . . "premonition of impending doom"*: Lamon, *Recollections*, 113.

101   *"the mystery had its meaning," and that "the illusion . . . close of the second"*: Ibid., 112.

101   *There, in the mirror, . . . not by natural causes*: Apart from the accounts of Brooks and Lamon as cited above, there is another version of the story of Lincoln seeing the double image, as later recounted by artist F. B. Carpenter, who says Lincoln spoke of it to him in 1864. Unlike the others, Carpenter places the incident just after the Chicago convention rather than on election night, and denies that Lincoln attached supernatural significance to the double image. However, the two other accounts are from those who were close to Lincoln near the time it occurred, and both persons independently placed it on the night of the general election. These factors seem to favor the Lamon and Brooks versions. For the Carpenter account, see *The Magazine of History with Notes and Queries*, 9, no. 33–36 (New York: William Abbat, 1915), 145–46.

101   *The ghostly image signifies that he "would . . . fall by a murderous hand"*: Lamon, 112.

Chapter 21

105   *In the first few days after his election, his office . . . seventy per day*: Harold Holzer, *Lincoln, President-elect: Abraham Lincoln and the Great Secession Winter, 1860–1861* (New York: Simon & Schuster, 2008), 64.

106   *He had become smitten . . . Lincoln's "ardent personal follower"*: Quoted in Burlingame, ed., *With Lincoln*, xiv.

106   *after the Chicago convention, Nicolay . . . Lincoln's official biographer*: For Nicolay's own account of his hiring, see ibid., xvi.

106   *Lincoln didn't need an official biographer . . . Nicolay accepted*: Ibid.

106 *Smith wanted to share that his son . . . the first "Young Abe"*: Holzer, *Lincoln, President-elect*, 65.

106 *Along with this flattery, Smith attached . . . purchase a policy*: Ibid.

107 *"His mail was infested with brutal . . . zealous and nervous friends"*: John G. Nicolay, *A Short Life of Abraham Lincoln* (New York: Century Co., 1902), 533.

107 *"There were threats of hanging him . . . flogging him"*: Henry C. Whitney, *Life on the Circuit with Lincoln* (Boston: Estes & Lauriat, 1892), 492.

107 *Old Abe Lincoln . . . eternal god damnation*: Pete Muggins to AL, November 25, 1860. Quoted in Harold Holzer, ed., *Dear Mr. Lincoln: Letters to the President* (Carbondale: Southern Illinois University Press, 1993), 340.

107 *"God damned Old Abolitionist son of a bitch"*: Ibid.

107 *"Sir: You will be shot on the 4th of March 1861 . . . our aim is true"*: Ibid., 342.

108 *One promises . . . to "put a spider" . . . resign immediately*: A. G. Frick to AL, February 14, 1861. Ibid., 341.

108 *Along with the threats are various warnings . . . "administer Poison to you"*: R. C. Carter to AL, November 12, 1860. Abraham Lincoln Papers at the Library of Congress: Series 1, General Correspondence, 1833–1916, manuscript/mixed material.

108 *A chemistry professor in Iowa . . . a knife or a bullet*: Holzer, *Lincoln, President-elect*, 285.

108 *"a number of young men in Virginia . . . should you be elected"*: David Hunter to AL, October 20, 1860, *ALPLC*.

108 *"[Lincoln] had . . . a heart so kindly . . . to lead to murder"*: Nicolay, *A Short Life*, 533.

Chapter 22

109 *"The existence of slavery is at stake" . . . secede from the Union*: *The Charleston Mercury*, November 3, 1860.

109 *"We can never submit to Lincoln's inauguration . . . Union of the South"*: William C. Davis, *Look Away! A History of the Confederate States of America* (New York: Free Press, 2002), 26.

110 *not a single person voted for Abraham Lincoln in Alabama, Arkansas . . . or Texas*: The list of states does not include South Carolina, which at the time still used a delegate system rather than a popular vote for the Presidency. Had the state administered a popular vote, Lincoln surely would also not have been on the ballot there. A breakdown of state-by-state election returns, including for states where no ballot was distributed for Lincoln, can be seen at Dave Leip's Atlas of U.S. President Elections, "1860 General Election Results," https://uselectionatlas.org/RESULTS/national.php?year=1860.

110 *But in the popular vote, he won . . . the total vote*: Ibid.

110 *"A party founded on the single sentiment . . . controlling power"*: *Richmond Enquirer*, November 7, 1860.

111　*"The Northern people in electing Mr. Lincoln . . . slaveholding states":* Eric Foner, *The Fiery Trial: Abraham Lincoln and American Slavery* (New York: W. W. Norton & Co., 2010), 144.

111　*"Lincoln intends to use every means . . . females among the negroes":* George M. Brinkerhoff to Edward McPherson, Springfield, January 30, 1861. Burlingame, *Lincoln,* 1:1886.

111　*They'll vote on a hastily crafted . . . interests of the slaveholding states:* "Resolution to Call the Election of Abraham Lincoln as U.S. President a Hostile Act and to Communicate to Other Southern States South Carolina's Desire to Secede from the Union," November 9, 1860, *Resolutions of the General Assembly, 1779–1879,* S165018, South Carolina Department of Archives and History, Columbia, SC.

111　*"said election . . . slaveholding states":* Ibid.

111　*"South Carolina is now ready to dissolve . . . of the United States":* Ibid.

Chapter 23

112　*"the old game of scaring and bullying . . . Southern demands":* As printed in *The New York Herald,* October 18, 1860.

113　*Hon. A. B. Lincoln . . . Grace Bedell:* Grace Bedell to AL, October 15, 1860, *ALPLC.*

114　*Miss Grace Bedell . . . A. Lincoln:* AL to Grace Bedell, October 19, 1860, *CWAL,* 4:129.

115　*Similarly, the portrait artist Jesse Atwood . . . the wrong shape:* Holzer, *President-Elect,* 88.

Chapter 24

116　*The room they stand in is on the second floor . . . in Baltimore, Maryland:* Details of the room and the men drilling are from Cypriano Ferrandini's February 5, 1861, testimony before a select committee of the House of Representatives. *Report of the Select Committee of Five,* (Washington, D.C.: Government Printing Office, 1861), 132–34.

117　*the organization of armed volunteer militias:* See, for example, William G. Merkel and H. Richard Uviller, *The Militia and the Right to Arms, or, How the Second Amendment Fell Silent* (Durham, NC: Duke University Press, 2002), 125–26.

117　*In 1852, he was a founding officer of . . . the Lafayette Guards:* As announced in *The Baltimore Sun,* July 10, 1852. In the announcement, the group was introduced as the "Baltimore Lafayette Guards," but in subsequent notices is listed as the "Lafayette Guards" or occasionally as the "Guarde Lafayette."

117　*Ferrandini soon became the captain of the company:* Ferrandini's promotion to Captain is announced in *The Baltimore Sun,* February 1, 1855.

117　*His name was mentioned in Baltimore . . . leadership of the group:* In *The Baltimore Sun,* Ferrandini's name appears in public announcements connected with the Lafayette Guards on June 24, 1853; June 29, 1853; July

12, 1853; October 20, 1853; December 13, 1853; July 1, 1854; February 1, 1855; February 23, 1855; May 22, 1855; October 20, 1855; October 31, 1855; December 17, 1855; June 18, 1856; November 25, 1856; October 19, 1859; and on several other occasions. Many of these announcements also receive a notice in the competing *The Baltimore Daily Exchange,* for example on October 19, 1859.

117 *By early 1858, Ferrandini resigned from the Lafayette Guards:* In the spring of 1858, *The Sun* reports that the "Lafayette Guards . . . were handsomely entertained by their ex-commander, Mr. Ferrandini, at his residence on East Baltimore Street," *The Baltimore Sun,* May 4, 1858.

117 *still maintaining an honorary title . . . Knights of the Golden Circle:* Keehn, *Knights,* 263 n4.

117 *He will later testify that he traveled . . . "army of Juárez":* Cypriano Ferrandini testimony before the House Select Committee, February 5, 1861. *Report of the Select Committee,* 132.

117 *After the election in 1860, Ferrandini is . . . Constitutional Guards:* Ibid., 133.

117 *"political in nature":* Ibid.

118 *But it is a very small one . . . Abraham Lincoln:* William J. Evitts, *A Matter of Allegiances: Maryland from 1850 to 1861* (Baltimore: Johns Hopkins University Press, 1974), 150.

118 *Statewide, the percentage is even smaller . . . he received zero:* Ibid.

118 *Ferrandini's small militia group will soon be . . . the National Volunteers:* Cypriano Ferrandini to House Select Committee, February 5, 1861. *Report of the Select Committee,* 133.

Chapter 25

119 *referred to as the "Team of Rivals":* The phrase "Team of Rivals" has often been applied to Abraham Lincoln's cabinet since the publication of Doris Kearns Goodwin's, *Team of Rivals: The Political Genius of Abraham Lincoln* (New York: Simon & Schuster, 2005).

120 *Seward nobly campaigned all over . . . its leader:* Seward's campaigning on behalf of Lincoln is documented in Stahr, *Seward,* 201–07.

121 *On December 8, he writes two letters . . . Secretary of State:* AL to William Seward, December 8, 1860, "Nomination of Seward for Secretary of State," *ALPLC.*

121 *I beg you to be assured that I have said nothing . . . be made:* AL to William Seward, December 8, 1860, "Seward's Appointment as Secretary of State," *ALPLC.*

122 *"a little time to consider whether I possess . . . the public service":* Seward to AL, December 13, 1860, *ALPLC.*

Chapter 26

123 *"People of the South have too much good sense . . . government":* AL to John B. Fry, August 15, 1860, *CWAL,* 4:95.

123 *"a sort of political game of bluff, gotten up . . . the North":* AL's view as summarized by Donn Piatt in Rice, ed., *Reminiscences,* 480.

124 *"There is nothing in all the dark caves of human . . . for the Yankees":* Quoted in James M. McPherson, *The Battle Cry of Freedom: The Civil War Era* (New York: Oxford University Press, 1988), 234.

124 *At the start of 1860, South Carolina contains a higher . . . 57 percent:* U.S. Census Bureau, *Population of the United States in 1860: Compiled From the Original Returns of the 8th Census* (Washington, D.C.: Government Printing Office, 1864), 452.

124 *"the loss of liberty, property, home . . . life worth having":* McPherson, *Battle Cry,* 241.

124 *"If you are tame enough to submit [to Lincoln] . . . black husbands":* South Carolina Baptist clergyman James Furman, quoted in ibid., 243.

124 *The following day, a special committee . . . "hereby dissolved":* South Carolina Constitutional Convention, *Declaration of the Immediate Causes Which Induce and Justify the Secession of South Carolina from the Federal Union; and the Ordinance of Secession,* S 131055, December 24, 1860 (Charleston, SC: Evans & Cogswell, 1860), 11.

124 *"Declaration of the Immediate Causes . . . from the Federal Union":* Ibid., 3–10.

125 *"an increasing hostility on the part . . . Slavery":* Ibid., 7.

125 *Furthermore, the Northern states have "denounced . . . citizens":* Ibid., 9–10.

125 *"united in the election of a man . . . hostile to slavery":* Ibid., 9.

125 *"war must be waged against slavery . . . the United States":* Ibid., 10.

125 *The American flag that had flown above . . . palmetto tree:* The South Carolina legislature officially adopted a flag bearing the palmetto tree on January 26, 1861. "Flag of South Carolina," *Encyclopedia Britannica,* https://www.britannica.com/topic/flag-of-South-Carolina.

127 *The main actor stops mid-performance to . . . into cheers:* Reported, for example, in the *Richmond Enquirer,* December 25, 1860.

Chapter 27

128 *Many reports are circulated . . . speak it:* C. Dupont Bird to AL, November 8, 1860, *ALPLC.*

129 *"I could say nothing which I have . . . inspection of all":* AL to Truman Smith, November 10, 1860, *ALPLC.*

129 *"ultimate extinction":* Lincoln had frequently used the phrase "ultimate extinction" to refer to the hoped-for demise of slavery should it be confined to the Southern states. Perhaps most notably, he used the phrase in his famous "A House Divided" speech in 1858. See AL, "A House Divided": Speech at Springfiled, Illinois, June 16, 1858, *CWAL,* 2:461.

130 *"The North would despise such an act, and by . . . the South":* H. Wigand to AL, November 9, 1860, *ALPLC.*

130 *"On reaching Washington I found great numbers . . . secessionists":* George F. Fogg to AL, December 17, 1860, *ALPLC.*

131 *"Let there be no compromise on the question . . . Stand firm":* AL to Lyman Trumbull, December 10, 1860, *CWAL,* 4:149–50.

131 *"There is no possible compromise. . . . a chain of steel":* AL to Elihu B. Washburne, December 13, 1860, *CWAL,* 4: 151.

131 *"On the territorial question, I am inflexible . . . be restricted":* AL to John A. Gilmer, December 15, 1860, *CWAL,* 4: 152.

131 *"[Lincoln] will live up to the principles on which he . . . of ages":* Francis Blair to Montgomery Blair, February 14, 1861. Blair Family Papers, Library of Congress. Quoted in Burlingame, *Lincoln* 1:1956.

132 *"Lincoln stands firm," Sumner says. "I know it":* Sumner to Joseph R. Hawley, January 31, 1861. Ibid.

Chapter 28

133 *"was in a condition . . . Government":* Henry Adams, "The Great Secession Winter, 1860–1861," in George Hochfield, ed., *The Great Secession Winter of 1860–61 and Other Essays* (New York: Sagamore Press, 1958), 3. Henry Adams is the son of Congressman Charles Francis Adams, the grandson of President John Quincy Adams, and the great-grandson of President John Adams. Due to his deep connections in Washington, D.C., Adams had inside access to the halls of Congress during this winter. He wrote the cited essay for the *Atlantic* magazine in the spring of 1861—immediately following the events covered—but the essay was shelved and not published until 1910. For more, see Ernest Samuels, *Henry Adams* (Cambridge, MA: Harvard University Press, 1989), 43.

133 *"The most flagrant . . . proclaimed":* Ibid., 7.

134 *"Crowds came up to the . . . and always increasing":* Ibid., 4–5.

134 *"panic had already risen . . . month":* Ibid., 7.

134 *"no doubt in my mind of the complicity . . . secessionists":* Ulysses Doubleday to John G. Nicolay, November 18, 1860, *ALPLC.*

134 *"The greatest apprehensions . . . a traitor to it":* Worthington G. Snethen to AL, December 8, 1860, *ALPLC.*

134 *"It was well known that three of the Cabinet . . . their sight":* Adams, "The Great Secession Winter," 5.

135 *"Secretary Floyd is a traitor and deserves" . . . Congressman wrote:* Joseph Medill to AL, December 18, 1860, *ALPLC.*

135 *"Clerks in the Government Departments . . . Lincoln":* Adams, "The Great Secession Winter," 9.

135 *"men drilling at midnight in the environs of the city . . . Capitol":* Ibid., 7.

135 *"The evidences of my ears and eyes are . . . view":* Joseph Medill to AL, December 26, 1860, *ALPLC.*

136 *"sworn armed men, and branches or . . . the bayonet":* Ibid.

136 *"There is a feverish excitement here . . . ten days earlier":* William Seward to AL, December 28, 1860, *ALPLC.*

136 *"A plot is forming . . . without announcement":* Seward to AL, December 29, 1860, *ALPLC.*

Chapter 29

139 *"had an important communication to make"*: From Samuel Felton's account of his meeting with Dorothea Dix, compiled in Schouler, *History*, 1:59.

139 *She insists it must be in private:* Ibid.

139 *"brought her in contact with the prominent . . . political machinery"*: Ibid.

139 *"There was a deep-laid conspiracy . . . in the capital of the country."*: Ibid.

139 *"if this plot did not succeed, then to murder him . . . revolution"*: Ibid.

139 *"extensive and organized . . . hands of insurgents."*: Ibid.

139 *"Mr. Lincoln's inauguration was thus to be prevented . . . inauguration"*: Ibid.

140 *"tangible and reliable shape"*: Ibid.

140 *After securing meetings with top officials in Washington:* Samuel Felton's associate N. P. Trist meets personally with Gen. Winfield Scott, whom Lincoln recently put in charge of protecting Washington, D.C., against threats of violence or assassination plots up to and including the date of Lincoln's inaugural address.

140 *"a party" . . . protect the capital:* Schouler, *History*, 1:60.

141 *"had combustible materials to pour over the bridges . . . way"*: Ibid.

141 *Kane, rather than expressing alarm . . . Baltimore:* Ibid., 61.

141 *"investigate the matter in his own way"*: Ibid.

141 *"celebrated detective" . . . "resources"*: Ibid.

Chapter 30

142 *That's the name soon given:* There is no precise record of who first coined the phrase "Great Secession Winter" to refer to the winter of 1860–61, or of when, precisely, he or she coined it. However, in early 1861, the journalist Henry Adams used the phrase in the title of his previously cited essay "The Great Secession Winter of 1860–61." Adams originally wrote this essay in the spring of 1861 for the *Atlantic* magazine but then withdrew it, and the essay remained unpublished until 1910. Because there are no known earlier uses of it, Adams probably originated the phrase. The essay is compiled in Adams, *The Great Secession Winter of 1860–61 and Other Essays*, ed. George Hochfield (New York: Sagamore Press, 1958).

143 *"Violence, murder, poisons . . . brethren"*: *The Charleston Mercury*, n.d., quoted in Avery O. Craven, "The Fatal Predicament," in Norman A. Graebner, ed., *Politics and the Crisis of 1860* (Urbana: University of Illinois Press, 1961), 132.

143 *"the designs of the abolitionists are . . . embrace of buck negroes for wives"*: Quoted in McPherson, *Battle Cry*, 229.

143 *"Our young girls—Daughters—from 12 to 15 . . . 'amalgamation'"*: Quoted in William Barney, *The Road to Secession: A New Perspective on the Old South* (New York: Praeger, 1972), 199.

143 *"Among us the poor white laborer . . . white men"*: Quoted in McPherson, *Battle Cry*, 243.

143 *The vigilantes round up and terrify . . . trial or jury:* Keehn, *Knights,* 78–81. For more on these incidents, see Donald E. Reynolds, *Texas Terror: The Slave Insurrection Panic of 1860 and the Secession of the Lower South* (Baton Rouge: Louisiana State University Press, 2007).

144 *"It can no more be checked . . . watering pot":* Judah P. Benjamin to Samuel L. M. Barlow, December 9, 1860. Barlow Papers, Henry E. Huntington Library.

144 *"dissolve the union . . . 'United States of America'":* An Address Setting Forth the Declaration of Immediate Causes Which Induce and Justify the Secession of Mississippi From the Federal Union, and the Ordinance of Secession (Jackson: Mississippi Book and Job Printing Office, 1861), 6.

144 *"The State of Florida hereby . . . America":* Florida Convention of the People, 1860–61, "Ordinance of Secession," January 10, 1861. State Libraries and Archives of Florida.

144 *"Our position is thoroughly . . . civilization":* Declaration of Immediate Causes Which Induce and Justify the Secession of Mississippi, 3.

144 *"the election of Abraham Lincoln . . . security":* "An Ordinance to Dissolve the Union Between the State of Alabama and other States," in *Ordinances and Constitution of the State of Alabama, with the Constitution of the Provisional Government and of the Confederate States of America* (Montgomery: Barrett, Wimbish, & Co., 1861), 3.

145 *"The Union is already dissolved . . . Lincoln":* Montgomery Weekly Advertiser, January 9, 1861.

146 *"the thorny crown of horrors you will be compelled to wear":* James E. Harvey to AL, November 29, 1860, *ALPLC.*

Chapter 31

147 *"I entertained no serious . . . crushed":* Pinkerton, *The Spy of the Rebellion*, 46.

147 *"Special efforts had been made to render . . . abhorrence":* Ibid., 43–44. In the original text Pinkerton uses the anachronistic word "Especial" to begin the paragraph. We have changed the word to "Special" for modern readers.

148 *"At this time I received a letter . . . importance":* Ibid., 46.

148 *"It appeared that rumors . . . was the president":* Ibid.

148 *"It was feared that their designs . . . River":* Ibid., 46–47.

149 *"This letter at once aroused me to . . . power":* Ibid., 47.

149 *Within forty-eight hours . . . Philadelphia:* In Pinkerton's memoir *The Spy of the Rebellion,* he states on page 47 that he brought "four members of my force" with him to Philadelphia. This appears not to be the case. He will, however, bring four or more members of his force with him on a train ride to Philadelphia in the near future, en route to Baltimore. Perhaps Pinkerton misremembered or was consolidating the multiple train trips for purposes of simplifying the story.

149 *"Upon arriving in that city . . . secessionists":* Pinkerton, *The Spy of the Rebellion,* 47.

Chapter 32

150 *Dating back to George Washington . . . office:* Holzer, *Lincoln, President-elect,* 271.

151 *As a resident of the westernmost . . . record:* Ibid., 273.

151 *"I think Mr. Lincoln's preferences . . . safety":* Henry Villard, *The New York Herald,* January 25, 1861.

152 *"He knew that incitements to murder . . . safety":* Nicolay, *A Short Life,* 533.

152 *"Your life . . . force":* Horace Greeley to AL, December 22, 1860, *ALPLC.*

152 *"He knows . . . gratify this":* *The New York Herald,* January 25, 1861.

152 *Wood first appeared in Springfield . . . trip:* Holzer, *Lincoln, President-elect,* 277.

152 *To piece together a . . . regulations:* For the long list of different railroad companies included in the final itinerary, see *LBP,* 137 n38.

153 *"His life was therefore in . . . it":* Nicolay, *A Short Life,* 533.

154 *Among the bigger cities . . . capital:* A version of Lincoln's inaugural itinerary as released to the public is compiled in *LBP,* 136–137, n. 38.

Chapter 33

155 *Cypriano Ferrandini starts his . . . Baltimore:* *The Baltimore Sun* describes Cypriano Ferrandini as a "resident on East Baltimore Street, near Broadway," May 4, 1858.

155 *"WANTED—a good white . . . street":* *The Baltimore Sun,* August 5, 1848.

156 *"New infantry company.— . . . Lieut.":* *The Baltimore Sun,* July 10, 1852.

156 *Around six months after the formation . . . Hotel:* *The Baltimore Sun,* February 24, 1853.

157 *That year, the Baltimore Lafayette Guards . . . city:* *The Baltimore Sun,* July 12, 1853.

157 *In 1855, Ferrandini was promoted . . . "Captain Ferrandini":* *The Baltimore Sun,* February 1, 1855.

157 *"The spirited corps of the LaFayette Guards . . . corps":* *The Baltimore Sun,* February 23, 1855.

158 *At one point, he hosts a ceremony with the Lafayette . . . "epaulettes":* *The Baltimore Sun,* November 25, 1856.

158 *"At an early hour yesterday morning . . . war":* *The Baltimore Daily Exchange,* October 19, 1859.

158 *"it was deemed unnecessary to call their services into action":* Ibid.

159 *But the KGC had . . . year:* Keehn, *Knights,* 28.

159 *During his time there, Bickley edited and . . . Civilization:* Ibid., 29.

159 *The convention included somewhere . . . guests:* Ibid., 34.

159 *The conference was billed as a means . . . "more permanent":* Ibid., 35.

159 *A reporter who gained entrance . . . "was expressed":* "The K. G. C. in Action," *Arkansas True Democrat,* September 7, 1859. The reporter who attended and originally filed the story was possibly from the *New-York Tribune.* See Keehn, *Knights,* 264 n24.

159 *"most dangerous man" who . . . "Southern people":* Ibid.

160 *Byrne was a local businessman who, like . . . President:* Keehn, *Knights,* 112–13.

160 *In the summer of 1860, shortly before . . . Volunteers:* Ibid., 112.

160 *After Breckinridge's defeat by Lincoln . . . militant mission:* Ibid., 113.

160 *According to their postelection . . . "Black Republican party":* As reported in the *Richmond Times,* January 18, 1860.

160 *The incoming administration is, in their words . . . "emphatic rebuke":* Ibid.

160 *As these new plans take shape . . . National Volunteers:* Cypriano Ferrandini to House Select Committee, February 5, 1861. *Report of the Select Committee,* 133.

Chapter 34

162 *"This road was the great . . . North":* Pinkerton, *The Spy of the Rebellion,* 47.

164 *He met extensively with Felton's associate . . . the railroad lines:* Ibid.

164 *Dear Sir . . . allude to:* Allan Pinkerton to Samuel Felton, January 27, 1861. Compiled in *LBP,* 23.

165 *Pinkerton and these "four to six operatives" . . . "join the same":* Ibid.

165 *"As soon as we learn positively . . . moment":* Ibid.

165 *"I could be able to learn their secrets . . . you":* Ibid.

165 *"Secrecy is the lever of any success . . . same":* Ibid., 24.

166 *Pinkerton sends the letter via express . . . few days later:* Felton's letter responding to Pinkerton is lost, but Pinkerton soon embarks on the investigation in precisely the manner laid out in his letter to Felton, indicating that Felton quickly agreed to Pinkerton's requests.

Chapter 35

167 *This special "Committee of Five" . . . January 9:* Date as stated in *Report of the Select Committee,* 1.

167 *"Select Committee of Five" to examine "Alleged" . . . Treason Committee:* The "Committee of Five" is referred to as "the Treason Committee" in *Harper's Magazine,* January 19, 1861, and in *The Philadelphia Inquirer,* February 2, 1861. *The New York Times* on August 26, 1861, will also employ the term for a later iteration of the committee.

168 *"Resolved, That the select committee . . . thereof":* Report of the Select Committee, 1.

168 *"The extraordinary excitement . . . elsewhere":* Ibid., 1–2.

169 *"slightest ground" that . . . "Washington":* James G. Berret testimony before Select Committee of the House of Representatives, January 29, 1861. *Report of the Select Committee,* 3.

169 *"I do not believe there is a solitary . . . Lincoln":* Ibid.

169 *"I know them to be not only respectable . . . city":* Ibid., 4.

169 *"a secret organization called the 'K. G. C.' . . . here?":* Ibid., 5.

169 *"I have never heard of any such . . . was":* Ibid.

169 *"There was a general rumor about . . . it":* George R. Wilson testimony before Select Committee, January 30, 1861. *Report of the Select Committee,* 28.

170   *"I have had a vast number of intimations . . . Lincoln"*: Charles P. Stone testimony before Select Committee, January 31, 1861. *Report of the Select Committee*, 89.

170   *"I have been informed that . . . city"*: Ibid., 91.

170   *"innumerable letters" from . . . "seven a day"*: Gen. Winfield Scott testimony before Select Committee, January 31, 1861. *Report of the Select Committee*, 52.

170   *"seizure of the Capitol" and "other public . . . Vice President"*: Ibid., 53.

170   *"so much precision" and detail . . . "to exist"*: Ibid., 56.

170   *"vast numbers of men . . . "put to death"*: Ibid., 53.

171   *"You can hardly be fully acquainted with the . . . office"*: Ibid., 57.

171   *"if the attempt be made to inaugurate Mr. Lincoln . . . you are aware"*: Ibid.

171   *"some sort of conspiracy undoubtedly exists"*: Ibid., 53.

Chapter 36

172   *He travels there not with his aides . . . Illinois:* In addition to Hanks, Lincoln is accompanied by State Senator Thomas A. Marshall, Judge John Petit, and Henry Clay Whitney. Holzer, *Lincoln, President-elect*, 247.

173   *At one point, they have to step out in . . . Kickapoo Creek:* Journey with Dennis Hanks as described in ibid., 249.

173   *He and his father were never close . . . time:* Ibid.

173   *"the best boy I ever saw." She . . . "same channel"*: Sarah Bush Lincoln, interview with William Herndon, September 8, 1865. Wilson and Davis, eds., *Herndon's Informants*, 108.

173   *By one account, Lincoln wraps his long . . . "cried over him"*: Holzer, *Lincoln, President-elect*, 249.

174   *"she had been his best Friend in this . . . her"*: Francis Fisher Browne, *The Every-Day Life of Abraham Lincoln: A Biography of the Great American President* (New York: Thompson Publishing Co., 1887), 376.

174   *"He seemed to enjoy it so much . . . smile"*: Holzer, *Lincoln, President-elect*, 250.

174   *"she would never be permitted to see" . . . "assassinate" him:* Ibid., 251.

174   *"They will not do that: trust in the Lord . . . again"*: Wilson and Davis, eds., *Herndon's Informants*, 137.

174   *"I did not want Abe to run for President . . . more"*: Ibid., 108.

Chapter 37

176   *"He was a man of great physical strength . . . shot"*: Pinkerton, *The Spy of the Rebellion*, 59.

176   *"No danger was too great, no trust too responsible . . . attempt"*: Ibid., 33.

176   *Another member of the team is . . . "personal appearance"*: Ibid., 60.

176   *by the name of Harry Davies:* Throughout his memoir *The Spy of the Rebellion*, Pinkerton uses Harry Davies's alias "Joseph Howard" rather than his real name. Pinkerton was probably trying to protect Davies's identity.

When quoting from *The Spy of the Rebellion,* we change the original wording of the text to accurately reflect Davies's name.

176 *"had a thorough knowledge of the South . . . men":* Pinkerton, *The Spy of the Rebellion,* 55.

176 *"She appeared careless and entirely at ease . . . accomplished":* Ibid., 402.

176 *Some researchers today speculate that Lawton was of mixed race:* Enss, *The Pinks,* 38.

177 *"In my service, you will serve your . . . down":* Ibid., xi.

177 *"Of rather a commanding person" . . . "favorable impression":* Pinkerton, *The Spy of the Rebellion,* 75.

Chapter 38

178 *He was born and raised in the city, but has . . . "for pleasure":* Otis K. Hillard testimony before Select Committee, February 6, 1861. *Report of the Select Committee,* 155.

178 *"I have some knowledge of such an institution" . . . the Knights:* Ibid., 145.

179 *"It numbers six thousand men," he says:* Ibid., 146.

179 *"You know what Baltimore city is; it is a wild place . . . be":* Ibid., 150.

179 *to prevent "any armed body of men, from coming . . . be":* Ibid., 145–46.

179 *"I reside in Baltimore. My place of business is under Barnum's Hotel":* Cypriano Ferrandini testimony before Select Committee, February 5, 1861. *Report of the Select Committee,* 132.

Chapter 39

180 *At the hotel, Lincoln also set up a local . . . businessman:* Lincoln advertises his home furniture sale in the *Illinois Daily Journal* on January 30, 1861.

180 *At the local Springfield bank, he took out . . . account:* Holzer, *Lincoln, President-elect,* 288.

181 *Abraham Lincoln . . . President of the United States:* There are several possible metrics for determining the relative wealth of U.S. Presidents, but by almost every measure Lincoln was poorer than all of his predecessors. One ranking with Lincoln below all who came before him can be found at *24/7 Wall Street,* "American's 9 Poorest Presidents," https://247wallst.com/special-report/2019/02/05/americas-9-poorest-presidents-2/3/.

181 *Two more states, Louisiana and Texas, have recently seceded:* Louisiana seceded on January 26, 1861, and Texas on February 1, 1861. In Texas's case, the state still awaits a public referendum to ratify the state legislature's ordinance, but this step is correctly thought to be a foregone conclusion.

181 *"No, indeed we have not":* Conversation as recalled by Herndon in William Herndon and Jesse Weik, *Abraham Lincoln: The True Story of a Great Life,* 3 vols. (New York: D. Appleton & Co., 1888), 3:483.

182 *"swung on its rusty hinges . . . "nothing ever happened":* Quotes and details here and above from ibid., 483–84.

182 *"I am sick of office-holding already . . . still ahead":* Ibid., 484.

Chapter 40

183 *"I was at one time commanding the Lafayette Guards . . . Maryland"*: Cypriano Ferrandini testimony before Select Committee, January 31, 1861. *Report of the Select Committee*, 132.

184 *"[We] have adjourned now to the headquarters . . . there"*: This and above series of questions and answers from ibid., 132–33.

184 *"a political association" but that . . . "military volunteer corps"*: Ibid., 133.

184 *"to prevent northern volunteer companies . . . Maryland"*: Ibid., 134.

184 *"A northern invasion; that is about the whole of it"*: This and above series of questions and answers from ibid, 134.

Chapter 41

186 *"Men indulged in fierce arguments, in which both . . . yet"*: Pinkerton, *The Spy of the Rebellion*, 48.

187 *"serious damage might be done to the company" . . . "bitter"*: Ibid.

187 *"I therefore left one man at this place, with instructions . . . intentions"*: Ibid., 48–49.

187 *"the feeling was considerably more intense . . . 'alive'"*: Ibid., 49.

187 *"I have always found it a truism that 'a barking dog never bites' . . . possible"*: Ibid.

188 *"carefully note everything that transpired . . . measures"*: Ibid.

188 *"the opposition to the government . . . resistence and force"*: Ibid.

188 *another agent, John Seaford*: Ibid., 49–50.

188 *"The opposition to Mr. Lincoln's inauguration . . . apprehended"*: This and above quote from Ibid., 50.

Chapter 42

190 *"A. Lincoln, White House, Washington, D.C."*: Donald, *Lincoln*, 273.

190 *"gloom and depression . . . almost of solemnity"*: John G. Nicolay and John Hay, *Abraham Lincoln: A History*, 10 vols. (New York: Century Co., 1890), 3:290.

191 *"almost all of whom I could recognize"*: Later described by Lincoln in speech at Lafayette, Indiana, February 11, 1861, *CWAL*, 4:192.

191 *"his face was pale, and quivered with emotion . . . word"*: *The New York Herald*, February 12, 1861.

191 *My friends . . . farewell*: AL, Farewell Address at Springfield, Illinois, February 11, 1861, *CWAL*, 4:190. There are a few conflicting transcriptions of this extemporaneous speech, remembered or recorded differently by the reporters and members of Lincoln's team who were present. The version used here is that which Lincoln quickly wrote out himself once he was inside the train. While the exact wording varies among the different transcriptions on record, the substance and sentiment is largely consistent.

191 *"left hardly a dry eye in the assemblage"*: *New-York World*, February 11, 1861.

191 *"Many eyes were filled to overflowing as Mr. Lincoln . . . commence":* Quoted in Donald, *Lincoln,* 273.

Chapter 43

195 *That's the name on the door of a suite of . . . district:* For more details on street address and location of building, see Michael J. Kline, *The Baltimore Plot: The First Conspiracy to Assassinate Abraham Lincoln* (Yardley, PA: Westholme Publishing, 2008), 67.

196 *"in a position where I could receive . . . metropolis":* Pinkerton, *The Spy of the Rebellion,* 50–51.

196 *"so constructed that entrance . . . streets":* Ibid., 51.

196 *"I could not fail to notice an increase . . . Confederacy":* Ibid., 58.

196 *"the state of feeling in Baltimore" is so "embittered" . . . "the Union":* Allan Pinkerton to William Herndon, August 23, 1866, compiled in *LBP,* 5.

196 *The chief opposition seemed to be to the inauguration . . . place:* Pinkerton, *The Spy of the Rebellion,* 51.

198 *maintaining his alias "John Hutcheson":* In some isolated cases, Pinkerton and others spell the alias name as "Hutchinson." For consistency sake, we've adjusted these instances so the spelling of the name is always "Hutcheson."

198 *"Head Quarters of Secessionists from all parts of the country":* Pinkerton to William Herndon, August 23, 1866, *LBP,* 5.

198 *"The visitors from all portions of the South . . . interests":* Pinkerton, *The Spy of the Rebellion,* 59.

198 *"There every night I mingled among them I could . . . men":* Pinkerton to William Herndon, August 23, 1866, *LBP,* 7.

Chapter 44

199 *There's another fresh-faced young acolyte, John Hay . . . aides:* For a more comprehensive list of Lincoln's colleagues, aides, and friends aboard the train, see Holzer, *Lincoln, President-elect,* 279–81 and 297–98.

201 *Finally, a handful of reporters from newspapers . . . cities:* The array of journalists on board includes reporters from, among other publications, *The New York Times, The New-York World,* the *Chicago Tribune,* the *Cincinnati Gazette, The Philadelphia Inquirer,* and at least five correspondents from the Associated Press. Holzer, *Lincoln, President-elect,* 298.

201 *"I never knew where all the people came from . . . country":* John W. Starr Jr., *Lincoln and the Railroads: A Biographical Study* (New York: Dodd, Mead, 1927), 180.

201 *"all enthusiastic, vociferous and fluttering with handkerchiefs and flags":* John Hay as compiled in Michael Burlingame, ed., *Lincoln's Journalist: John Hay's Anonymous Writings for the Press, 1860–1864* (Carbondale: Southern Illinois University Press, 1998), 25.

201 *"moves rapidly through the crowd at the depot, shaking hands left and right":* *Illinois State Journal,* February 13, 1861.

201 *"frank, hearty display . . . near kindred":* John Hay as compiled in Burlingame, *Lincoln's Journalist,* 25.

203 *"I am leaving you on an errand of national importance . . . farewell":* AL remarks at Tolono, Illinois, February 11, 1861, *CWAL,* 4:190.

203 *"as wild an intensity of delight as if it had been a . . . inaugural":* Burlingame, *Lincoln's Journalist,* 25.

204 *"I am under many obligations to you for your kind . . . one":* AL remarks at Indiana state line, February 11, 1861, *CWAL,* 4:192.

204 *"While some of us may differ in political opinions . . . difference":* AL speech at Lafayette, Indiana, February 11, 1861, *CWAL,* 4:192.

204 *"the train started before he got to the place . . . be":* AL remarks at Thorntown and Lebanon, Indiana, February 11, 1861, *CWAL,* 4: 192–93. Reporting of the incident is from the *Indianapolis Daily Sentinel,* February 12, 1861.

204 *"some of the Thorntown folks . . . of the story":* Ibid.

205 *"deafening cheers" when they emerge from the station:* Details of arrival and crowd in Indianapolis from Holzer, *Lincoln, President-elect,* 307–08.

205 *"All the streets in front, and the hallways" . . . party complains:* Orville Browning, *The Diary of Orville Hickman Browning, Vol. 1: 1850–1864* (Springfield: Illinois State Historical Library, 1925), 454.

205 *"beehive" and writes that Lincoln . . . "the merciless throngs":* Henry Villard, *The New York Herald,* February 12, 1861.

205 *Robert sheepishly responds . . . disappeared:* Account of exchange with Robert Todd from Holzer, *Lincoln, President-elect,* 311.

206 *"My heart went up into my mouth":* Rice, ed., *Reminiscences,* 224.

206 *"A look of stupefaction passed over . . . imagination":* Michael Burlingame, ed., *An Oral History of Abraham Lincoln: John G. Nicolay's Interviews and Essays* (Carbondale: Southern Illinois University Press, 1996), 109.

206 *With a single stride of his long legs . . . light:* Ibid., 110.

206 *"fortune favored the President-elect" and . . . "his treasures":* Ibid.

Chapter 45

207 *This boat will take him to catch a larger vessel . . . Vicksburg:* White, *A. Lincoln,* 369.

208 *A week earlier, on February 4, a convention . . . states:* Texas's state legislature has also voted to secede—making it the seventh—but the state's secession is still waiting for ratification via a public referendum, scheduled for February 23, 1861.

208 *The next day, Davis received . . . plantation:* Davis's whereabouts on this occasion is taken from Shelby Foote, *The Civil War: A Narrative* (New York: Vintage Books, 1986), 1:17. The date of Davis receiving notice of his appointment is from *The Civil War, A Visual History* (New York: DK Publishing, 2015), 44.

208 *"The time for compromise has now passed . . . steel":* Jefferson Davis, speech on February 16, 1861. *The American Annual Cyclopedia and Register of Important Events of the Year 1861* (New York: D. Appleton & Co., 1866), 127.

Chapter 46

210 *"A.P. said there was no danger, and all I wanted was confidence"*: Charles D.C. Williams, report on February 12, 1861, *LBP,* 26.

211 *The rookie Williams . . . one of these reports:* As cited in the previous note, the report in question is Charles D.C. Williams, report on February 12, 1861, *LBP,* 26.

211 *"By assuming to be secessionists of the most ultra type . . . secret designs"*: Pinkerton, *The Spy of the Rebellion,* 55.

211 *"cultivat[e] the acquaintance of the wives and daughters of the conspirators"*: Ibid., 75.

211 *"Mrs. Warne displayed upon her breast . . . secession"*: Ibid.

211 *"obtain quarters at one of the first-class hotels . . . secessionist"*: Ibid., 56.

212 *"entered into their discussion . . . associated"*: Ibid., 60.

212 *"This rebellious scion of Baltimore aristocracy . . . boasted"*: Ibid., 67.

213 *"bosom friends and inseparable companions . . . company"*: Ibid.

213 *"the Paradise of the United States" because "they are all secessionists there"*: Harry C. Davies, report on February 12, 1861, *LBP,* 28.

213 *"men watching the railroad bridge between . . . good"*: Ibid.

214 *"very much in favor of the Southern Confederacy"*: Quote and locations from ibid., 28–29.

214 *His name, Hillard says, is "Captain Ferrandini"*: Ibid., 29. In his notes, Davies incorrectly spells Ferrandini's name as "Farridina."

Chapter 47

215 *Governor's Mansion . . . of the President-elect:* Details of the morning in Indianapolis from Holzer, *Lincoln, President-elect,* 312.

216 *"the crest of one continued wave of cheers"*: Burlingame, ed., *Lincoln's Journalist,* 29.

216 *"I have stepped out upon this platform"*: See, for example, AL on February 16, 1861, *CWAL,* 4:218.

216 *"Prince of Rails"*: John S. Goff, *Robert Todd Lincoln: A Man in His Own Right* (Norman: University of Oklahoma Press, 1968), 37.

217 *"the long and the short of it"*: Larry D. Mansch, *Abraham Lincoln, President-Elect: The Four Critical Months From Election to Inauguration* (Jefferson, NC: McFarland & Co., 2005), 178.

217 *"merriest among . . . continual roar"*: *The New York Herald,* February 13, 1861.

218 *seventh-largest . . . over 160,000:* U.S. Bureau of the Census, "Population of the 100 Largest Urban Places," 1860, https://www.census.gov/population/www/documentation/twps0027/tab09.txt.

218 *"Every window was thronged"*: Quoted in Burlingame, ed., *Lincoln's Journalist,* 29.

218 *"A more magnificent ovation"*: Quoted in Holzer, *Lincoln, President-elect,* 317.

219 *"I hold that while man . . . nor any worse.":* AL, speech to Germans at Cincinnati, Ohio, February 12, 1861, *CWAL*, 4: 202–03.

219 *"It is not my nature":* Ibid.

220 *"throwing their arms around him":* Holzer, *Lincoln, President-elect,* 318.

Chapter 48

221 *a name and address:* Harry Davies, report on February 12, 1861, *LBP,* 29.

222 *a particular young woman named Anna Hughes:* Ibid.

222 *"Hillard and his woman" . . . joins him:* Ibid.

222 *"Have you seen a statement":* This and conversation below from ibid.

224 *"My friend, that is what . . . I wish I could":* Ibid., 30.

224 *"I dare not":* This and remaining details of conversation from ibid.

Chapter 49

225 *"Judd had been in bed":* Conversation and general account of the messenger visit is from William H. Scott, report on February 13, 1861, *LBP,* 31.

226 *"Pinkerton desire[s]" . . . "for the information":* Ibid.

226 *"as the party reached . . . through Baltimore":* Pinkerton, *The Spy of the Rebellion,* 74.

226 *Scott asks him . . . an encrypted message:* All details and quoted conversation are from Scott, report on February 13, 1861, *LBP,* 31.

227 *"very feelingly":* Ibid.

Chapter 50

228 *"As the daily papers":* Pinkerton, *The Spy of the Rebellion,* 58.

229 *"damned Governor Hicks . . . to his Country":* Allan Pinkerton, report on February 15, 1861, *LBP,* 32–34.

229 *"Let the consequences . . . around the Capital in a very short time":* This and subsequent conversation from ibid.

230 *"who would not hesitate if necessary":* Ibid.

230 *"I should be obliged":* Conversation and details of the money exchange are from ibid., 34–35.

231 *"Southern rights men . . . keep it a secret":* Ibid., 35.

231 *The "leading man" . . . is "Captain Ferrandini":* Ibid. In this report and elsewhere, Pinkerton incorrectly spells Ferrandini's last name as "Ferrandina." The name is corrected in our text.

232 *"a true friend to the South . . . go to Washington":* Ibid., 35–36.

232 *"Before Lincoln should pass through Baltimore":* Ibid.

233 *"meet him at Barr's Saloon":* Ibid., 36.

Chapter 51

234 *"several other gentlemen . . . Captain Ferrandini":* Allan Pinkerton, report on February 15, 1861, *LBP,* 36.

235 *"a fine looking, intelligent appearing person":* Ibid., 36.

235 *"South must rule . . . taking his seat":* Ibid., 36–37.

235 *"As he spoke . . . the ardent minded":* Ibid., 37.

235 *"Even I myself felt the influence":* This and all remaining details and conversation from ibid., 37–38.

236 *"Mr. Hutcheson," he says, "if I alone must do it":* Ibid., 37. In Pinkerton's report he spells the alias name "Hutchins" here, perhaps imitating Ferrandini's mispronunciation of the name.

Chapter 52

238 *"Some three months ago, I received a letter":* AL remarks at Westfield, New York, February 16, 1861, *CWAL*, 4:219.

238 *"There she is, Mr. Lincoln!":* The boy and his declaration are as described in *The Philadelphia Inquirer,* February 20, 1861.

238 *"The crowd was so large":* Reminiscence of Mrs. Grace Bedell Billings, as compiled in *Lincoln's Beard: Reproduction of Correspondence Between Abraham Lincoln and Grace Bedell* (Fort Wayne, IN: Lincolniana Publishers, 1935), 14.

238 *"You see," he says, pointing at his beard, "I let these whiskers grow":* Ibid., 15.

238 *"yells of delight":* The Philadelphia Inquirer, February 20, 1861.

239 *"I was so surprised . . . in my hand ":* Grace Bedell Billings in *Lincoln's Beard,* 15.

239 *"It seemed to me . . . and sad":* Ibid.

Chapter 53

240 *swears his oath of office:* Jefferson Davis's inaugural address, delivered on February 18, 1861, can be read here: https://jeffersondavis.rice.edu/archives/documents/jefferson-davis-first-inaugural-address.

241 *"champion of a" . . . "planter class":* Joan E. Cashin, *First Lady of the Confederacy: Varina Davis's Civil War* (Cambridge, MA: Belknap Press, 2006), 4.

241 *"Its foundations are laid":* Alexander Stephens, speech on March 21, 1861. Collected in Henry Cleveland, *Alexander H. Stephens in Public and Private: With Letters and Speeches, Before, During, and After the War* (Philadelphia: National Publishing Co., 1886), 717–29.

Chapter 54

244 *"The police force of the city":* Pinkerton, *The Spy of the Rebellion,* 50.

244 *"have nothing more to do with Marshal Kane":* Samuel Felton as quoted in Schouler, *History,* 1:59–62.

245 *After listening closely for several minutes, he's able to hear Kane:* Allan Pinkerton, report on February 21, 1861, *LBP,* 53. In this report from the following week, Pinkerton recalls overhearing Kane make this comment on "Saturday last," which would put it on the evening of Saturday, February 16, as indicated.

Chapter 55

248 *"Mr. Fillmore had barely time"*: *Buffalo Daily Republic,* January 18, 1861.
248 *"The crowd, in its crazed eagerness"*: *Buffalo Morning Express,* January 18, 1861.
249 *"positive insanity"*: Ibid.
249 *"Men were overcome with pressure"*: Ibid.
249 *"It was fearful . . . see it again"*: *Buffalo Daily Republic,* January 18, 1861.
249 *"did not escape uncrushed"*: Ibid.
249 *"ruthlessly crushed against the wall by the crowd"*: Ibid.
249 *"there were many in the crowd injured" . . . medical attention*: Ibid.

Chapter 56

251 *"many hints were dropped in her presence"*: Pinkerton, *The Spy of the Rebellion,* 75.
251 *"had made remarkable progress in cultivating"*: Ibid.
252 *"Mr. P called"*: Kate Warne, report on February 18, 1861, *LBP,* 40.
252 *Pinkerton meets her there to discuss final arrangements*: Ibid.
252 *he'll be "Plums." Warne will be "Barley" or "Mrs. Barley"*: For examples of how "Plums" is used to refer to Pinkerton, see *LBP,* 74–75, 84. For explanation of Kate Warne as "Mrs. Barley," see ibid., 21. Sanford refers directly to Warne as "Barley" in Warne's report of February 19, 1861, ibid., 43.

Chapter 57

254 *from the train station to the Astor House Hotel*: Kate Warne, report on February 19, 1861, *LBP,* 41.
254 *"I got a room, after much trouble"*: Ibid.
255 *"The occasion will undoubtedly call forth"*: *The New York Times,* February 19, 1861.
255 *1,300 police officers have been enlisted . . . Lincoln himself and his family*: Ibid.
256 *"Lincoln looked very pale"*: Warne, report on February 19, 1861, *LBP,* 41.
256 *"soon after appeared on the balcony"*: Ibid.
256 *"I could not be heard by any but a very small fraction"*: AL, remarks upon arriving at the Astor House, New York City, February 19, 1861, *CWAL,* 4:230.
256 *"I then wrote a note to N.B. Judd"*: Warne, report on February 19, 1861, *LBP,* 41.
257 *Judd caught the next train*: Ibid.

Chapter 58

258 *"Hillard soon proved"*: Pinkerton, *The Spy of the Rebellion,* 67. Here and in other places, Pinkerton refers to Hillard as "Hill." We've corrected this error for our text.
259 *"I have told you all I have a right to tell you"*: Harry Davies, report on February 19, 1861, *LBP,* 46–47.

259   *"We have taken a solemn oath"*: This and remaining conversation between Davies and Hillard is from Davies, report on February 19, 1861, *LBP,* 47–48.

260   *"I gave him such instructions as I deemed necessary"*: Pinkerton, *The Spy of the Rebellion,* 76.

260   *"broached the matter . . . enter their society"*: Ibid.

Chapter 59

261   *"I followed the servant to one of the upper rooms"*: Norman Judd to Allan Pinkerton, November 3, 1867. Pinkerton, *History and Evidence,* 17.

261   *"did not like to trust the mail in so important a matter"*: Ibid.

262   *"she had been delegated by me"*: Pinkerton, *The Spy of the Rebellion,* 79.

262   *"Mr. Judd asked me a great many questions"*: This and all subsequent conversation is from Kate Warne, report on February 19, 1861, *LBP,* 42–44.

263   *"anything he can do . . . with pleasure"*: Ibid.

263   *"There is no reason . . . more to say"*: This and remainder of conversation from ibid., 43–44.

264   *"Tell Judd I meant all I said"*: Ibid., 44.

264   *"wanted to show [the telegraph]"*: Ibid.

Chapter 60

266   *Finally . . . the night has come:* The date for the alleged event described here is not certain, and some researchers have suggested different dates. Author Michael Kline, for example, suggests February 18. Based on our analysis of the timeline, however, we've concluded that February 20—a day after rather than before Harry Davies's field report of February 19—is more likely. For Kline's version see Kline, *The Baltimore Plot,* 255–56.

266   *The front door opens to a large dimly lit drawing room:* The scene portrayed in this chapter is drawn from Allan Pinkerton's later account of it in his memoir, *The Spy of the Rebellion.* The depiction of the scene is presumably based on Davies's verbal account of it to him. However, unlike almost all other aspects of the investigation, this particular scene is not reported in any of Pinkerton's or his agents' contemporaneous reports, including those of Davies himself. While it's possible the original reports are simply lost, it's also possible Pinkerton embellished this scene for the purposes of the memoir and based the description of the scene on what he thought such a meeting would entail. Because it's impossible to prove or disprove either way, we've chosen to include it but provide this caveat. In every other instance where Pinkerton's memoir deviates from his or his agents' contemporaneous field reports, we've adhered only to the reports.

266   *"As they entered the darkened chamber . . . assembly"*: Pinkerton, *The Spy of the Rebellion,* 76.

267   *"having passed through the required formula"*: This and other details and conversation from the room are from ibid., 77–78.

267 *"a vast crowd of secessionists":* Ibid., 78.
267 *"Here it was arranged that but a small force":* Ibid., 68.
268 *"At this moment—the police being entirely withdrawn":* Ibid., 78.
268 *"Who should assume the task . . . reached":* Ibid.
268 *"It was finally determined that ballots should be prepared":* Ibid.
269 *"The leaders . . . they placed* eight*":* Ibid., 78–79. Pinkerton never explains how he or his agents may have learned that multiple red ballots were drawn instead of one.
269 *"violently assailed the enemies of the South":* Ibid., 79.

Chapter 61

270 *his day here begins at seven in the morning:* Description of the events of the morning are from Pinkerton's report, February 21, 1861, *LBP,* 52–54.
271 *"I made a full report . . . assassinate Mr. Lincoln":* This and all conversation between Pinkerton and Felton is from ibid.
271 *"Probably only fifteen or twenty men":* Ibid. Pinkerton never explains how he arrived at "fifteen or twenty" for the estimated number of conspirators.
272 *"Mr. Felton approved . . . had been discovered":* Ibid., 53.
272 *"await the arrival of the Presidential Party . . . earliest possible moment":* Ibid., 55.
273 *"With superhuman strength I saw him go":* Ibid., 58.
273 *the St. Louis Hotel:* The name of the hotel is referred to in ibid., 56 and 58.

Chapter 62

274 *Mr. Felton explained his cause for fearing:* This and all conversation and details from the meeting is based on Allan Pinkerton's report from February 21, 1861, *LBP,* 58–62.
275 *"I communicated . . . in their cause":* Ibid., 59.
275 *"I said to Mr. Judd . . . Baltimore":* Ibid., 60.
276 *"go with him to the Continental Hotel":* Ibid., 62.

Chapter 63

277 *"immense crowds":* Allan Pinkerton report, February 21, 1861, *LBP,* 62–66.
277 *"I accordingly took Mr. Judd":* This quote and other details of the evening's events are from ibid.
277 *"utterly impossible . . . denseness of the crowd":* Ibid.
278 *"was as densely crowded . . . such a jam":* Ibid.
278 *"Mr. Judd . . . persons there":* Benson J. Lossing, recollection of 1864 conversation with Lincoln. Compiled in Benson J. Lossing, *Pictorial Field Book of the Civil War* (Philadelphia: G.W. Childs, 1866–68), 1:279–80.
279 *"Mr. Judd briefly detailed to Mr. Lincoln":* Pinkerton, report on February 21, 1861, *LBP,* 62–66.

279 *"the evidence is such to convince all honest minds"*: Ibid.

279 *"Whilst Mr. Judd was talking . . . the probable attempt"*: This and subsequent conversation from ibid., 64–68.

280 *"I alluded to the expressions . . . considered Lincoln to be"*: Ibid., 65.

280 *"had some experience . . . conspirators to operate"*: Ibid., 65–66.

281 *"I felt satisfied . . . taking his life"*: Ibid., 66.

282 *"No, I cannot consent . . . death in doing so"*: Lincoln's words as reported by Pinkerton in ibid.

282 *"The firmness of tone . . . the proposition"*: Ibid., 67.

282 *"Beyond that I have no engagements"*: Norman Judd to Allan Pinkerton, November 3, 1867. Pinkerton, *History and Evidence*, 17.

Chapter 64

283 *"I could not believe that there was a plot"*: Benson J. Lossing, recollection of 1864 conversation with Lincoln. Compiled in Lossing, *Pictorial Field Book,* 1:279–280.

284 *"at the insistence of his father"*: Ibid.

284 *"an important communication to make"*: Gen. Winfield Scott to William H. Seward, February 21, 1861, *ALPLC.*

284 *"there is serious danger . . . threats of mobbing and violence"*: Memorandum from Charles P. Stone, February 21, 1861, *ALPLC.*

284 *"made no exclamation"*: Frederick Seward, "How Lincoln Was Warned of the Baltimore Assassination Plot," in William Hayes Ward, ed., *Abraham Lincoln: Tributes from His Associates* (New York: Thomas Y. Crowell, 1895), 60–63.

285 *"a change in the travelling arrangements"*: Memorandum from Stone, February 21, 1861, *ALPLC.*

285 *"Surely, Mr. Lincoln, that is strong corroboration"*: Seward, "How Lincoln," 61–63.

285 *"different persons, not knowing of each other's work"*: Benson J. Lossing, recollection of 1864 conversation with Lincoln. Compiled in Lossing, *Pictorial Field Book, 1:279–280.*

286 *"I now believed such a plot to be in existence"*: Ibid.

Chapter 65

288 *"tasked to restore peace"*: The president of the Select Committee of Philadelphia—the person who introduces Lincoln to the room—is Theodore L. Cuyler. After Cuyler's introduction, Lincoln alludes to Cuyler's words in his own speech: "You have kindly suggested to me that in my hands is the task of restoring peace to our distracted country." AL, speech in Independence Hall, Philadelphia, Pennsylvania, February 22, 1861, *CWAL,* 4:240.

288 *"I am filled with deep emotion"*: Ibid., 240–41.

288 *"You have kindly suggested"*: Ibid.

289 *"It was not the mere matter of the separation"*: Ibid.
289 *"My friends, can this country . . . to surrender it."*: Ibid.
289 *"I was about to say I would rather be assassinated"*: Ibid.
289 *"reference to sacrificing himself for his country"*: Norman Judd to Pinkerton, November 3, 1867. Allan Pinkerton, *History and Evidence*, 20.
289 *"My friends, this is a wholly unprepared speech"*: CWAL, 4:240–41.
290 *"But I have said nothing . . . die by."*: Ibid.
290 *"by the strength of my own feeble arm"*: AL to the Pennsylvania General Assembly at Harrisburg, February 22, 1861. *CWAL*, 4: 244–45.

Chapter 66

292 *the frantic appearance of Allan Pinkerton*: Kate Warne, report on February 22, 1861, *LBP*, 80.
293 *According to Lincoln's . . . departing at 9:00 a.m.*: See, for example, *The Baltimore Sun*, February 18, 1861.
294 *That code name . . . is Nuts*: Ibid.

Chapter 67

296 *"damned piece of cowardice"*: Quoted in Holzer, *Lincoln, President-elect*, 391.
296 *"scoffs and sneers of your enemies"*: Judd to Pinkerton, November 3, 1867. Pinkerton, *History and Evidence*, 20.
296 *"unless there are some reasons . . . Judd's plan"*: Lincoln's words as later recalled by Ward Hill Lamon in Lamon, *Recollections*, 42.
297 *"neither in his conversation or manner"*: Andrew G. Curtin to Pinkerton, December 8, 1867. Pinkerton, *History and Evidence*, 37.
297 *Mary Todd Lincoln . . . Ward Hill Lamon*: Kline, *The Baltimore Plot*, 193.
297 *"I put on the soft hat"*: Benson J. Lossing, recollection of 1864 conversation with Lincoln. Compiled in Lossing, *Pictorial Field Book*, 1:279–80.

Chapter 68

299 *It's almost 7:30 p.m.*: Account of evening is drawn from Allan Pinkerton, report on February 22, 1861, *LBP*, 76–79.
300 *Geo. H Burns . . . J.H. Hutcheson*: Ibid., 76.
300 *J.H. Hutcheson . . . Geo. H. Burns*: Ibid., 77.
300 *"Mr. Lincoln wore a brown Kossuth Hat"*: This and remaining details and conversation are from ibid., 77–79.
301 *"Mr. Seward had therefore sent"*: Pinkerton to Herndon, Aug 23, 1866, *LBP*, 13–14.
302 *"about fifteen thousand men"*: Pinkerton report, February 22, 1861, *LBP*, 78–79.
302 *"I at once protested"*: This and additional quotes and details in the carriage from ibid.
302 *"I want no arms . . . will work right"*: Ibid, 79. Lincoln's statement is here

transposed to the first person from Pinkerton's original report. In the report Pinkerton writes it this way: "Mr. Lincoln said that he wanted no arms; that he had no fears and that he felt satisfied that all my plans would work right."

302 *"a brace of fine pistols"*: Holzer, *Lincoln, President-elect*, 391.

Chapter 69

303 *he hands off the reports:* This and subsequent details are from Kate Warne, report on February 22, 1861, *LBP,* 80–81.

304 *"invalid brother":* The detail of the "invalid brother" is as later recollected by Pinkerton in *The Spy of the Rebellion*, 93. In a minor difference, George R. Dunn later recollects that the ticket was purchased for an "invalid friend." George R. Dunn to Allan Pinkerton, November 7, 1867, in Pinkerton, *History and Evidence*, 35–36.

304 *"On the front platform and inside the front door":* George R. Dunn to Pinkerton, November 7, 1867 in Pinkerton, *History and Evidence*, 35–36.

304 *"for the accommodation of an invalid":* Ibid.

304 *"So soon as the lady was comfortably fixed":* Ibid.

304 *"I found it almost impossible to save the berths together":* Warne, report on February 22, 1861, *LBP,* 80–81.

305 *"I gave the conductor half a dollar":* Ibid.

305 *"so that its occupants might alight":* H. F. Kenney to Pinkerton, December 23, 1867. Compiled in Pinkerton, *History and Evidence*, 28.

305 *"stooping considerably for the purpose of disguising his height":* Warne, report on February 22, 1861, *LBP,* 80–81.

306 *"Everything went off well":* Ibid.

Chapter 70

307 *"very friendly . . . keep us all awake":* Kate Warne, report on February 22, 1861, *LBP,* 80–81.

307 *"When the Conductor came around":* Pinkerton, report on February 22, 1861, *LBP,* 79.

307 *These are hand signals:* Pinkerton, *The Spy of the Rebellion*, 96. For more on the lantern signals see also Kline, *The Baltimore Plot*, 258.

308 *Sanford's men "cut the wires":* Kline, *The Baltimore Plot*, 234–35. Sanford's employee who personally climbed the telegraph to cut the wires is Andrew Wynn. Wynn's recollection of his assignment is in Andrew Wynn to Pinkerton, November 3, 1867. Pinkerton, *History and Evidence*, 41.

308 *"this package must go through":* Pinkerton report, February 22, 1861. *LBP,* 75-76.

308 *Felton instructed his emissary, H. F. Kenney:* As described by Samuel Felton in Schouler, *History* 1:63.

309 *only* after *they were safely on board:* Ibid.

309 *"a package of old railroad reports":* Ibid.

311 *"Captain, It's four o'clock!"*: Allan Pinkerton, report on February 23, 1861, *LBP,* 81–83.

311 *"This he kept up for about twenty minutes"*: Ibid.

311 *"Mr. Lincoln appeared to enjoy it very much"*: Ibid.

Chapter 71

313 *"I hit the gentleman a punch with my elbow"*: Allan Pinkerton, report on February 23, 1861, *LBP,* 81–83.

313 *"we were discovered . . . and that we might have to fight"*: Ibid.

Chapter 72

314 *"Don't strike him, Allan! . . . my friend Washburne"*: Allan Pinkerton, report on February 23, 1861, *LBP,* 81–83.

314 *Both men . . . Seward was delayed:* Sources conflict on whether Seward was at the station to greet Lincoln that morning, but the balance of evidence suggests he was not. Neither Pinkerton nor Lamon report seeing him there. For more on this question see Stahr, *Seward,* 238.

314 *the President-elect shakes hands:* See preceding note regarding whether Seward first greeted Lincoln at the train station or at Willard's Hotel.

315 *"Plum arrived here with Nuts"*: Pinkerton, report on February 23, 1861, *LBP,* 84.

Chapter 73

316 *"The country has been spared . . . long military cloak"*: The New York Times, February 24, 1861.

317 *"Everybody here is disgusted"*: The Charleston Mercury, February 26, 1861.

317 *"Had we any respect . . . of his successors"*: The Baltimore Sun, February 25, 1861.

317 *"meditated and determined"*: William Louis Schley to AL, February 23, 1861, *ALPLC.*

317 *"Mr. Lincoln ought to have come through by daylight"*: New-York Tribune, February 26, 1861.

317 *like a "thief in the night"*: Quoted in Holzer, *Lincoln, President-elect,* 398.

318 *"Mr. Lincoln reached the Capital as the poor"*: Douglass' Monthly, April 1861.

Chapter 74

320 *he recruits Robert Todd Lincoln:* Holzer, *Lincoln, President-elect,* 446.

320 *"if you are as happy . . . in the country"*: James Buchanan, quoted in Goodwin, *Team of Rivals,* 329.

320 *"Every available spot was black"*: The Boston Post, March 4, 1861.

321 *"Strange to say . . . secessionists"*: The New York Times, March 4, 1861.

321 *sharpshooters were stationed:* Donald, *Lincoln,* 283.

321 *"Files of cavalry"*: Elizabeth Todd Grimsley, "Six Months in the White House," *Journal of the Illinois State Historical Society* 19 (October 1926–January 1927), 44–45.

321 *"I have seen today such a sight"*: *The Charleston Mercury,* March 7, 1861.

321 *"seemed more like escorting a prisoner"*: Rufus Rockwell Wilson, *Lincoln Among His Friends* (Caldwell, ID: Caxton Printers, 1942), 308.

321 *"I shall plant cannon"*: Gen. Winfield Scott, quoted by Jesse W. Weik in *Century Illustrated Monthly Magazine* 81 (November 1910–April 1911), 594.

322 *Douglas had detected Lincoln's discomfort . . . relieves Lincoln of the hat:* Donald, *Lincoln,* 283.

322 *"Fellow citizens of the United States"*: AL, First Inaugural Address, March 4, 1861, *CWAL,* 4:262–63.

322 *"rang out over the acres"*: Quoted in Donald, *Lincoln,* 283.

322 *"at least ten thousand persons"*: *Washington National Intelligencer,* March 5, 1861.

323 *"strike down any hand"*: Stone, "Washington on the Eve of War," 466.

323 *"I just sat behind him as he read it"*: Quoted in Daniel Stashower, *The Hour of Peril: The Secret Plot to Murder Lincoln Before the Civil war* (New York: St. Martin's Press, 2013), 16.

324 *"In your hands, my dissatisfied fellow countrymen"*: *CWAL,* 4:262–63.

324 *"We are not enemies, but friends"*: Ibid.

325 *"bowed his head as if in silent prayer"*: Recollection of Stephen Fiske, as described over three decades later in Stephen Fiske, "When Lincoln Was First Inaugurated," *Ladies Home Journal,* 14, no. 4 (March 1897), 8.

325 *For the Presidential oath . . . around the edges:* Details on the Bible are from, for example, Katharine Q. Seelye, "Obama to Take Oath on Same Bible as Lincoln," *The New York Times,* December 23, 2008. Both President Barack Obama and President Donald Trump used this Bible in their own inaugural ceremonies. See Eric McCann, "The Two Bibles Donald Trump Used at the Inauguration," *The New York Times,* January 18, 2017.

Chapter 75

329 *expeditionary force of twenty some thousand:* Donald, *Lincoln,* 285.

330 *"hold, occupy, and possess"*: AL, First Inaugural Address, March 4, 1861, *CWAL,* 4:262–63.

330 *not a single member of Lincoln's cabinet:* Donald, *Lincoln,* 285.

330 *"all the troubles and anxieties of his life"*: Orville Browning, diary entry, July 3, 1861, recollecting Browning's conversation with Lincoln. Quoted in Allen C. Guelzo, *Abraham Lincoln as a Man of Ideas* (Carbondale: Southern Illinois University Press, 2009), 203.

331 *"keeled over"*: Mary Todd Lincoln, quoted in Donald, *Lincoln,* 289.

331 *"WANTED—A POLICY"*: *The New York Times,* April 3, 1861.

331 *"An attempt will be made to supply Fort-Sumter"*: AL to Robert S. Chew, April 6, 1861, *CWAL,* 4:323–24.

332 *Lincoln issues a public proclamation:* AL, Proclamation Calling Militia and Convening Congress, April 15, 1861, *CWAL*, 4:331–32.

Chapter 76

333 *Pinkerton sent a card:* Allan Pinkerton, report on February 23, 1861, *LBP,* 88.

333 *"Mr. Lincoln . . . thanked me very kindly":* Ibid.

334 *"the men were all ready . . . shoot everyone in it":* Ibid., 89.

334 *Before noon . . . planned arrival:* Description of Hillard's movements and of the crowd size are from Harry Davies, report on February 23, 1861, *LBP,* 90–92.

335 *"The street on each side":* Ibid., 91–92.

335 *"Hillard afterwards told me . . . did the deed":* Ibid., 92.

335 *"from his position . . . the first shot":* Ibid., 92.

336 *"The effect of this proclamation":* Pinkerton, *The Spy of the Rebellion*, 107.

336 *"Dear Sir, When I saw you last":* Pinkerton to AL, April 21, 1861, *ALPLC.*

337 *Hidden in a small compartment:* Mackay, *Allan Pinkerton*, 108.

337 *"I soon found my services were needed":* Pinkerton, *The Spy of the Rebellion*, 104–05.

338 *"Major E. J. Allen":* Mackay, *Allan Pinkerton*, 119.

338 *Pinkerton sends his own fifteen-year-old son:* Stashower, *Hour of Peril*, 314.

338 *Pinkerton himself . . . McClellan's famous reluctance to attack:* See, for example, Stephen W. Sears, *George B. McClellan: The Young Napoleon* (New York: Ticknor & Fields, 1988), 107.

338 *forerunner to the U.S. Secret Service:* Gary J. Byrne and Grant M. Schmidt, *Secrets of the Secret Service: The History and Uncertain Future of the U.S. Secret Service* (New York: Hachette Book Group, Inc., 2017), chapter 3.

340 *On April 29, 1862, Timothy Webster is hanged:* Kline, *The Baltimore Plot*, 394. For more details on Webster's death, see Corey Recko, *A Spy for the Union: The Life and Execution of Timothy Webster* (Jefferson, NC: McFarland & Company, Inc., 2013), 122–31.

340 *ON THE NIGHT OF FEBR. 22, 1861:* Webster's gravestone and memorial are in Graceland Cemetery, Chicago, Illinois. Section C, the Pinkerton Lot, Memorial ID 10747.

341 *"some of them contain passages . . . dubious veracity":* Regarding Pinkerton's later memoirs, author S. Paul O'Hara refers to Pinkerton as "far from a reliable narrator." S. Paul O'Hara, *Inventing the Pinkertons, or Spies, Sleuths, Mercenaries, and Thugs* (Baltimore: John Hopkins University Press, 2016), 6. More to the point, Pinkerton's 1887 memoir of the plot to assassinate Lincoln does not always align with his own contemporaneous field notes during the investigation. For example, in the memoir he describes that he was with agent Harry Davies when he first met Cypriano Ferrandini at a restaurant called Guy's, and only after Davies's introduction to him (Pinkerton, *The Spy of the Rebellion*, 64–65). Pinkerton's original field notes, however, show that he met Ferrandini on his own at Barr's Saloon, and based on an introduction from James Luckett (*LBP*, 35–38). As stated

in a previous note, we've deferred to the field notes and not the memoir regarding the factual matters of the case.

341 *Pinkerton's National Detective Agency still exists:* The current company's website is pinkerton.com. The agency offers its services as a "global leading provider of comprehensive risk management solutions."

Chapter 77

342 *"a company of young men":* The Baltimore Sun, April 25, 1861.

342 *The name* Winan: Ross Winans's obituary in *The New York Times* refers to his pro-secessionist activities and his arrest by federal authorities, *The New York Times,* April 12, 1877. For more on Winans's pro-Southern activities in early 1861 that may have inspired the use of his name, also see Kline, *The Baltimore Plot,* 348.

343 *"at a meeting . . . held on Wednesday":* The Baltimore Sun, April 26, 1861.

343 Took the Oath: *The Baltimore Sun,* May 4, 1863.

344 *"arrested on the charge of cheering":* Ibid.

344 *his wife dies in a house fire: Richmond Dispatch,* December 26, 1870.

344 *becomes a national news item:* See, for example, the *Chambersburg Public Weekly Opinion,* June 21, 1889; the *Alexandria Gazette,* June 15, 1889; the *Frederick News,* July 12, 1889. The story is also covered in many other places.

344 *Ferrandini successfully suing: Alexandria Gazette,* February 27, 1890.

344 *he and his second wife:* The Baltimore Sun, July 18, 1895.

344 *Eventually, on December 20 . . . eighty-eight:* The age of eighty-eight is as reported by *The Baltimore Sun* obituary on December 21, 1910. Some other sources cite Ferrandini's birth date in 1823, which would make him eighty-seven at the time of his death.

344 *"Born in Corsica":* The Baltimore Sun, December 21, 1910.

344 ADORNED CITY'S FINEST . . . *"many friends":* The Baltimore Sun, December 22, 1910.

345 *"During the Civil War":* Ibid.

Chapter 78

346 *Otis K. Hillard was probably also a member:* Keehn, *Knights,* 112.

347 *the Knights turned their efforts . . . recruited by them:* For an overview of KGC recruiting efforts for the Confederacy, see ibid, 199–206.

347 *Jesse James was a member:* Michael Benson, *Inside Secret Societies* (Kensington Publishing Corp., 2005), 86.

348 *protest their passage through the city:* For a more detailed description of these events, see Kline, *The Baltimore Plot,* 349–50.

348 *The day before . . . armed resistance:* Keehn, *Knights,* 196. See also Horace Greeley, *The American Conflict: A History of the Great Rebellion in the United States of America, 1860–1865,* vol. 1 (Hartford, CT: O.D. Case & Co., 1865), 462.

348 *ten Union troops are killed:* Kline, 350.

348 *a few dozen are wounded:* McPherson, *Battle Cry*, 285.

348 *These are the first Union soldiers to die:* Ibid.

349 *started to suspect Lamon was leaking:* Pinkerton recounts in depth his frustrations with Lamon talking to reporters in his field notes immediately following their arrival in Washington, D.C. See Allan Pinkerton, report on February 23, 1861, *LBP,* 85–88.

349 *"brainless, egotistical fool":* Ibid., 86.

350 *Pinkerton collects and publishes:* Pinkerton compiles and publishes these letters together as *History and Evidence of the Passage of Abraham Lincoln from Harrisburg, Pa. to Washington, D.C. on the 22d and 23d of February, 1861.*

351 *he was angry when he thought Lamon:* Following Lincoln's arrival in Washington, D.C., Pinkerton was absolutely adamant that his own name and that of his firm not be in any way revealed or leaked in connection with the plot. See Pinkerton, report on February 23, 1861, *LBP,* 85.

Chapter 79

353 *"We were now met together to receive":* Douglass, *Life and Times,* 275.

354 *"We were waiting and listening":* Ibid., 276.

354 *"patience was well-nigh exhausted":* Ibid.

354 *"The effect of this announcement":* Ibid.

354 *more than three million enslaved persons:* Foner, *The Fiery Trial,* 241–42.

Chapter 80

356 *Douglass's sons:* David W. Blight, *Frederick Douglass: Prophet of Freedom* (New York: Simon & Schuster, 2018), 392.

357 *"I was an ex-slave":* Douglass, *Life and Times,* 271.

357 *"He was seated when I entered":* This and all conversation from Douglass's meeting with Lincoln are as recounted by Douglass in ibid., 271–72.

358 *"Fondly do we hope":* AL, Second Inaugural Address, March 4, 1865, *CWAL,* 8:333.

358 *"Here comes my friend Douglass":* Douglass's interactions and conversations with Lincoln at the reception are as recounted in Douglass, *Life and Times,* 286–87.

358 *"Mr. Lincoln, that was a sacred effort":* Ibid.

Chapter 81

359 *more Americans will die:* As asserted, for example, in McPherson, *Battle Cry.* 854. For the numbers behind this assertion and for more on Civil War casualty numbers in relation to other American wars, see the American Battlefield Trust: www.battlefields.org/learn/articles/civil-war-casualties.

359 *3,500 lives are lost:* Estimates of total casualties from the Civil War are

subject to debate. The figure of 504 casualties per day—or the equivalent of 3,528 per week—is cited from "The Civil War by the Numbers," *American Experience: Death and the Civil War* companion website, www.pbs.org /wgbh/americanexperience/features/death-numbers/.

359   *over fifty thousand:* Casualties in major Civil War battles are compiled here: www.battlefields.org/learn/articles/civil-war-casualties.

360   *"weary, care-worn, and troubled":* Quoted in Goodwin, *Team of Rivals,* 461.

360   *The loss is utterly devastating:* For an account of Willie's death and its immediate impact on Lincoln and his wife, see, for example, Goodwin, *Team of Rivals,* 415–23.

362   *"The hour and the man of our redemption":* Frederick Douglass, "The Freedman's Monument" speech, April 14, 1876, in C. M. Whitman, ed., *American Orators and Oratory* (San Francisco: Occidental Publishing Co., 1884), 598.

362   *President and Mrs. Lincoln made plans to attend:* The performance of *Our American Cousin* was on Friday night, April 14, 1865. White, *A. Lincoln,* 672.

363   *they openly weep:* Goodwin, *Team of Rivals,* 742. Even Edwin Stanton, the famously stern Secretary of War, sheds tears in front of the group.

363   *At 7:22 a.m, the President:* Ibid., 743.

363   *Lincoln told the crowd that no one would remember:* AL, Address Delivered at the Dedication of the Cemetery at Gettysburg, *CWAL,* 7:17–18.

363   *"Stand with anybody that stands right":* AL, Speech at Peoria, Illinois, October 16, 1854, *CWAL,* 2:273

Afterword

366   *Despite the public attention:* In 1868 *Harper's* published an essay entitled "The Baltimore Plot to Assassinate Abraham Lincoln" that contained access to Pinkerton's field records from the Baltimore investigation. This essay, seven years after the plot, may have been the first time Pinkerton shared his knowledge of events with the public. See Isaac Newton Arnold, "The Baltimore Plot to Assassinate Abraham Lincoln," *Harper's New Monthly Magazine,* vol. XXXVII (New York, Harper & Brothers, Publishers, June-November 1868).

366   *The FBI wasn't created until 1935:* See, e.g., https://www.fbi.gov/history /brief-history.

366   *In the nineteenth century, the closest equivalent was the U.S. Marshals Service:* For a brief history of the U.S. Marshals Service, see https://www .usmarshals.gov/history/broad_range.htm.

366   *The DOJ was not created until 1970:* Jim Martin, "The Creation of the Department of Justice," The Library of Congress, December 4, 2017, https:// blogs.loc.gov/law/2017/12/the-creation-of-the-department-of-justice/.

366   *It wasn't until 1918:* Ibid.

367   *On April 17, 1861:* Delegates at the Virginia Convention of 1861 voted to approve the Virginia Ordinance of Secession on April 17, 1861, and

a statewide referendum confirmed secession on May 23. For the text of the ordinance, see: Ordinance of Secession, 1861. Virginia. Convention (1861). Records, 1861–1961. Accession 40586. State Government Records Collection, The Library of Virginia, Richmond, Va.

367 *At various points Lincoln declared martial law*: See, e.g., Michael Burlingame, *Abraham Lincoln: A life* (unedited manuscript), II:2456-2458, https://www.knox.edu/about-knox/lincoln-studies-center/burlingame-abraham-lincoln-a-life.

Selected Bibliography

Books, Papers and Articles

Abraham Lincoln Papers. Library of Congress, Manuscript Division. Series 1. General Correspondence, 1833–1916. Washington, D.C.: American Memory Project, 2000.

Adams, Henry. "The Great Secession Winter, 1860–1861." *The Great Secession Winter of 1860–61 and Other Essays*, edited by George Hochfield. New York: Sagamore Press, 1958.

Barney, William. *The Road to Secession: A New Perspective on the Old South*. New York: Praeger, 1972.

Basler, Roy P., et al., eds. *The Collected Works of Abraham Lincoln*. 9 vols. New Brunswick, NJ: Rutgers University Press, 1953.

Blight, David. *Frederick Douglass, Prophet of Freedom*. New York: Simon & Schuster, 2018.

Browne, Francis Fisher. *The Every-Day Life of Abraham Lincoln: A Biography of the Great American President*. New York: N. D. Thompson Publishing Co., 1887.

Burlingame, Michael. *Abraham Lincoln: A Life*. 2 vols. Baltimore: Johns Hopkins University Press, 2008.

———. *Abraham Lincoln: A Life*. 2 vols. (unedited manuscript) https://www.knox.edu/about-knox/lincoln-studies-center/burlingame-abraham-lincoln-a-life.

———. *The Inner World of Abraham Lincoln*. Urbana, IL: University of Chicago Press, 1994.

———, ed. *Lincoln's Journalist: John Hay's Anonymous Writings for the Press, 1860–1864*. Carbondale: Southern Illinois University Press, 1998.

———, ed. *With Lincoln in the White House: Letters, Memoranda, and Other Writings of John G. Nicolay*. Carbondale: Southern Illinois University Press, 2000.

Chittenden, Lucius Eugene. *Recollections of President Lincoln and His Administration*. New York: Harper & Brothers, 1891.

Cleveland, Henry. *Alexander H. Stephens in Public and Private: With Letters and Speeches, Before, During, and After the War*. Philadelphia: National Publishing Co., 1886.

Cooper, William J. *We Have the War Upon Us: The Onset of the Civil War, November 1860–April 1861*. New York: Alfred A. Knopf, 2012.

Currie, Stephen. *The Quest for Freedom: The Abolitionist Movement*. Farmington Hills, MI: Lucent Books, 2006.

Cuthbert, Norma, ed. *Lincoln and the Baltimore Plot, 1861: From Pinkerton Records and Related Papers*. San Marino, CA: Henry E. Huntington Library Publications, 1949.

Davis, William C. *Look Away! A History of the Confederate States of America*. New York: Free Press, 2002.

Donald, David Herbert. *Charles Sumner and the Coming of the Civil War*. Naperville, IL: Sourcebooks, 2009.

———. *Lincoln*. 1961. Reprint, New York: Simon & Schuster, 1995.

Douglass, Frederick. *Life and Times of Frederick Douglass*. Hartford, CT: Park Publishing Co., 1881.

———. *My Bondage and My Freedom*. New York: Miller, Orton & Mulligan, 1855.

———. *Narrative of the Life of Frederick Douglass, an American Slave*. Boston: Anti-Slavery Office, 1849.

Egerton, Douglas R. *Year of Meteors: Stephen Douglas, Abraham Lincoln, and the Election That Brought on the Civil War*. New York: Bloomsbury Press, 2010.

Elster, Jean Alicia, ed. *The Outbreak of the Civil War*. Farmington Hills, MI: Greenhaven Press, 2003.

Enss, Chris. *The Pinks: The First Women Detectives, Operatives, and Spies with the Pinkerton Detective Agency*. Guilford, CT: TwoDot, 2017.

Evans, George W. "The Militia of the District of Columbia." *Records of the Columbia Historical Society, Washington, D.C.* 28 (1926): 95–105. http://www.jstor.org/stable/40067276.

Evitts, William J. *A Matter of Allegiances: Maryland from 1850 to 1861*. Baltimore: Johns Hopkins University Press, 1974.

Fehrenbacher, Don, and Virginia Fehrenbacher, eds. *Recollected Words of Abraham Lincoln*. Stanford, CA: Stanford University Press, 1996.

Fitzhugh, George. *Sociology for the South, or the Failure of Free Society*. Richmond, VA: A. Morris, 1854.

Foner, Eric. *The Fiery Trial: Abraham Lincoln and American Slavery*. New York: W. W. Norton & Co., 2010.

Foote, Shelby. *The Civil War: A Narrative*. 3 vols. New York: Vintage Books, 1986.

Freeman, Joanne B. *The Field of Blood: Violence in Congress and the Road to Civil War*. New York: Farrar, Straus and Giroux, 2018.

Goodwin, Doris Kearns. *Team of Rivals: The Political Genius of Abraham Lincoln*. New York: Simon & Schuster, 2005.

Graebner, Norman A., ed., *Politics and the Crisis of 1860*. Urbana: University of Illinois Press, 1961.

Helper, Hinton Rowan. *Compendium of the Impending Crisis of the South*. New York: A. B. Burdick, 1860.

Herndon, William H., and Jesse W. Weik. *Abraham Lincoln: The True Story of a Great Life*, 2 vols. (New York: D. Appleton & Co., 1888).

———. *Herndon's Lincoln: The History and Personal Recollections of Abraham Lincoln*. 3 vols. Springfield, IL: Herndon's Lincoln Publishing Co., 1886.

Hobson, J. T., ed. *Footprints of Abraham Lincoln: Presenting Many Interesting Facts, Reminiscences and Illustrations Never Before Published*. Dayton, OH: Otterbein Press, 1909.

Holzer, Harold, ed. *Dear Mr. Lincoln: Letters to the President*. Carbondale: Southern Illinois University Press, 1993.

———. *Lincoln and the Power of the Press: The War for Public Opinion*. New York: Simon & Schuster, 2014.

———. *Lincoln, President-Elect: Abraham Lincoln and the Great Secession Winter, 1860–1861*. New York: Simon & Schuster, 2008.

Horan, James D. *The Pinkertons: The Detective Dynasty That Made History*. New York: Crown Publishers, 1967.

Keehn, David C. *Knights of the Golden Circle: Secret Empire, Southern Secession, Civil War*. Baton Rouge: Louisiana State University Press, 2013.

Kendi, Ibram X. *Stamped from the Beginning: The Definitive History of Racist Ideas in America*. New York: Nation Books, 2016.

Kline, Michael J. "The Baltimore Plot—Fact or Fiction?" In *Exploring Lincoln: Great Historians Reappraise Our Greatest President*, edited by Harold Holzer, Craig L. Symonds, and Frank J. Williams pg. 18–35. New York: Fordham University Press, 2015.

———. *The Baltimore Plot: The First Conspiracy to Assassinate Abraham Lincoln*. Yardley, PA: Westholme Publishing, 2008.

Koerner, Gustave. *Memoirs of Gustave Koerner*. 2 vols. Cedar Rapids, IA: Torch Press, 1909.

Lamon, Ward Hill. *The Life of Abraham Lincoln: From His Birth to His Inauguration as President*. Boston: James R. Osgood & Co., 1872.

———. *Recollections of Abraham Lincoln, 1847–1865*. Edited by Dorothy Lamon. Chicago: A. C. McClure and Co., 1895.

Lewis, Lloyd. "Lincoln and Pinkerton." *Journal of the Illinois State Historical Society* 41, no. 4 (December 1948).

Lincoln's Beard: Reproduction of Correspondence Between Abraham Lincoln and Grace Bedell. Fort Wayne, IN: Lincolniana Publishers, 1935.

Lossing, Benson J. *Pictorial History of the Civil War in the United States of America*. 3 vols. Philadelphia: G.W. Childs, 1866–68.

Mackay, James. *Allan Pinkerton: The First Private Eye*. New York: John Wiley & Sons, 1997.

MacMahon, T. W. *Cause and Contrast: An Essay on the American Crisis*. Richmond, VA: West & Johnson, 1862.

Mansch, Larry D. *Abraham Lincoln, President-Elect: The Four Critical Months From Election to Inauguration*. Jefferson, NC: McFarland & Co., 2005.

McPherson, James. *Battle Cry of Freedom: The Civil War Era*. Oxford, UK: Oxford University Press, 1988.

Moffet, Cleveland. "How Allan Pinkerton Thwarted the First Plot to Assassinate Lincoln." *McClure's Magazine*, vol 3. no. 6, November 1894.

Newton, Joseph Fort. *Lincoln and Herndon*. Cedar Rapids, IA: Torch Press, 1910.

Nicolay, John G. *A Short Life of Abraham Lincoln: Condensed from Nicolay and Hay's Abraham Lincoln: A History*. New York: Century Co., 1902.

O'Hara, S. Paul. *Inventing the Pinkertons, or Spies, Sleuths, Mercenaries, and Thugs*. Baltimore: Johns Hopkins University Press, 2016.

Pinkerton, Allan. *The Expressman and the Detective*. Chicago: W. B. Keen, Cooke & Co., 1874.

———. *History and Evidence of the Passage of Abraham Lincoln from Harrisburg, Pa. to Washington, D.C. on the 22d and 23d of February, 1861*. (Privately printed, 1868.)

———. *Professional Thieves and the Detective, Containing Numerous Sketches from the Private Records*. New York: G. W. Carleton & Co., 1883.

———. *The Spy of the Rebellion; Being a True History of the Spy System of the United States Army During the Late Rebellion*. New York: G. W. Carleton & Co., 1886.

———. *Thirty Years a Detective: A Thorough and Comprehensive Exposé of Criminal Practices of all Grades and Classes*. New York: G. W. Dillingham Co., 1900.

Rice, Allen Thorndike. *Reminiscences of Abraham Lincoln by Distinguished Men of His Time*. New York: The North American Review, 1888.

Schouler, William. *A History of Massachusetts in the Civil War*. Vol 1. Boston: E. P. Dutton & Co., 1868.

Schurz, Carl. *The Reminiscences of Carl Schurz*. 3 vols. New York: McClure, 1907–08.

Seward, Frederick W. "How Lincoln Was Warned of the Baltimore Assassination Plot." In *Reminiscences of Soldiers, Statesmen and Citizens*, edited by William Hayes Ward. New York: T. Y. Crowell & Company, 1895.

Sinha, Manisha. "The Caning of Charles Sumner: Slavery, Race, and Ideology in the Age of the Civil War," *Journal of the Early Republic* 21 (2003).

Stahr, Walter. *Seward: Lincoln's Indispensable Man*. New York: Simon & Schuster, 2012.

Stashower, Daniel. *The Hour of Peril: The Secret Plot to Murder Lincoln Before the Civil War*. New York: St. Martin's Press, 2013.

Steers, Edward. *Blood on the Moon: The Assassination of Abraham Lincoln*. Lexington: University Press of Kentucky, 2001.

Stringfellow, Thornton. *Scriptural and Statistical Views in Favor of Slavery*. Richmond, VA: J. W. Randolph, 1856.

Tarbell, Ida M. *The Life of Abraham Lincoln*. New York: S. S. McClure Co., 1895.

Tilton, Clint Clay. "First Plot Against Lincoln." *National Republic*, February 1936.

Villard, Henry. *Memoirs of Henry Villard: Journalist and Financier, 1835–1900*. 2 vols. Boston: Houghton, Mifflin, and Co., 1904.

Warren, Ebenezer W. *Southern Slavery and the Bible: A Scriptural Refutation of the Principal Arguments upon which the Abolitionists Rely; A Vindication of Southern Slavery from the Old and New Testaments.* Macon, GA: Burke, Boykin & Company, 1864.

Washington, John E. *They Knew Lincoln.* New York: E. P. Dutton & Co., 1942.

White, Ronald C., Jr. *A. Lincoln: A Biography.* New York: Random House, 2009.

Wilson, Douglas L., and Rodney O. Davis, eds. *Herndon's Informants: Letters, Interviews, and Statements About Abraham Lincoln.* Urbana: University of Illinois Press, 1998.

Government Documents

An Address Setting Forth the Declaration of Immediate Causes Which Induce and Justify the Secession of Mississippi From the Federal Union; and the Ordinance of Secession. Jackson: Mississippi Book and Job Printing Office, 1861.

Declaration of the Immediate Causes Which Induce and Justify the Secession of South Carolina from the Federal Union. Carolina Constitutional Convention (1860–62). S 131055. Columbia, SC: South Carolina Department of Archives and History, December 24, 1860.

Ordinances and Constitution of the State of Alabama, with the Constitution of the Provisional Government and of the Confederate States of America. Montgomery: Barrett, Wimbish, & Co., 1861.

Report of the Select Committee of Five, 36th Congress, 2d Session, Report No. 79. Washington, D.C.: Government Printing Office, 1861.

"Resolution to Call the Election of Abraham Lincoln as U.S. President a Hostile Act and to Communicate to Other Southern States South Carolina's Desire to Secede from the Union," November 9, 1860. *Resolutions of the General Assembly, 1779–1879,* S165018. South Carolina Department of Archives and History, Columbia, SC.

Newspapers and Journals Frequently Cited

The Baltimore Daily Exchange
The Baltimore Sun
Buffalo Daily Republic
Buffalo Morning Express
The Charleston Mercury
The Chicago Daily Tribune
The Chicago Press & Tribune
The Daily Exchange
Douglass' Monthly
The Liberator
Montgomery Weekly Advertiser
The National Intelligencer (Washington, D.C.)
The New York Herald

The New York Times
New-York Tribune
The New York World
The Philadelphia Inquirer
The Richmond Weekly Examiner
The State Journal Register (Illinois)

Index

BRAD MELTZER is the #1 *New York Times* bestselling author of *The Escape Artist*, *The Inner Circle*, and ten other bestselling thrillers, as well as the Ordinary People Change the World series. He is also the host of the History Channel TV shows *Brad Meltzer's Decoded* and *Brad Meltzer's Lost History*, which he used to help find the missing 9/11 flag that the firefighters raised at Ground Zero. Find more about him at BradMeltzer.com.

JOSH MENSCH is a *New York Times* bestselling author and documentary television producer with a focus on American history and culture. He is the co-author with Brad Meltzer of *The First Conspiracy: The Secret Plot to Kill George Washington*. For television he has written, directed, and been a showrunner on nonfiction series for PBS, the History Channel, National Geographic, and many other networks. He lives in Brooklyn, New York, with his wife and children. Find out more about him at joshmensch.com.